11-13-75

# RESOURCE ECONOMICS

*Selected Works of Orris C. Herfindahl*

*Orris C. Herfindahl*

# RESOURCE ECONOMICS

*Selected Works of*
*ORRIS C. HERFINDAHL*

*Edited by DAVID B. BROOKS*

*Published by Resources for the Future, Inc.*

*Distributed by The Johns Hopkins University Press*
*Baltimore and London*

Resources for the Future is a nonprofit corporation for research and education in the development, conservation, and use of natural resources and the improvement of the quality of the environment. It was established in 1952 with the cooperation of the Ford Foundation. Part of the work of Resources for the Future is carried out by its resident staff; part is supported by grants to universities and other nonprofit organizations. Unless otherwise stated, interpretations and conclusions in RFF publications are those of the authors; the organization takes responsibility for the selection of significant subjects for study, the competence of the researchers, and their freedom of inquiry.

Orris C. Herfindahl was research associate and later senior research associate in RFF's energy and minerals program from 1957 until his death in 1972. David B. Brooks is research director of the Office of Energy Conservation, Department of Energy, Mines and Resources, Government of Canada. The charts were drawn by Clare Ford. The book was edited by Marget Ingram. The jacket design is by Clare Ford. Terry Pagos prepared the index.

*RFF editors:* Mark Reinsberg, Joan R. Tron, Ruth B. Haas, Margaret Ingram

Distributed by The Johns Hopkins University Press, Baltimore, Maryland 21218

Library of Congress Catalog Card Number 74–6814
ISBN 0–8018–1645–9

# CONTENTS

Foreword    ix

Introduction    xi

## PART ONE
### The Nature and Scope of Resource Economics

1. Is Resource Economics Unorthodox?    3

2. Identification and Study of Policy Problems in the Minerals Industries    7

3. Time for Stock-Taking (with Allen V. Kneese)    15

## PART TWO
### Natural Resource Supply and Conservation

4. Some Fundamentals of Mineral Economics    35

5. What Is Conservation?    47

6. Goals and Standards of Performance for the Conservation of Minerals    58

7. Depletion and Economic Theory    64

## PART THREE
### Application of Economics to the Minerals Industry

8. The Process of Investment in the Mineral Industries    93

9. Changes in the Size of Copper Mining Companies    113

10. Deterioration, Output, and the Price of Copper    119

11. Review of *Capital and Output Trends in Mining Industries, 1870–1948*    133

12. Development of the Major Metal Mining Industries in the United States, 1839–1909    139

## PART FOUR
### *The Supply of Natural Resource Information*

13. Some Guidelines for Organization and Administration of Information Activities    171

14. The Question of Exploration Strategy    218

15. Economic Considerations in Assessing the Role of Remote Sensing in Country Development    225

16. The Value of Mineral Surveys to Economic Development    236

## PART FIVE
### *The Quality of the Natural Environment*

17. Effects of Resource Depletion and Economic Growth on the Quality of Life    255

18. Can Increasing Demands on Resources Be Met?    274

19. "Natural" Areas (with Allen V. Kneese)    284

## APPENDIXES

A. Assignments and Activities    291

B. Backpacking Checklist    293

C. Across the Barrens by Canoe    297

Bibliography    305

Index    311

# FOREWORD

Only a few economists have dealt much with mineral economics. Among these few, Orris C. Herfindahl has probably probed the most deeply. He was, moreover, one of the first fully competent economists to enter the new field of environment and pollution, which he did with his customary insight and thoroughness. We offer this volume in the conviction that Herfindahl's work in the several related areas contributes significantly to the field of resource economics and should be made readily accessible to students and resource specialists. We hope that readers will be enlightened by this selection of economic writings. Taken along with other pieces not reprinted here, they provide the broadest, most penetrating treatment of the subjects mentioned that we know of.

For those of us who were Orris Herfindahl's colleagues at Resources for the Future, this volume is very special. In gathering this collection of his writings together, we pay our respects to the most exacting economic analyst among us. His judgment was keen and his standards high, whether his own work or that of others was under scrutiny. We always figured that if anything one of us drafted could get past Orris Herfindahl, it would be found acceptable by the profession at large. But Herfindahl commanded more than our respect for his analytical competence: his closest colleagues valued his friendship highly and held him in great affection.

Our special thanks go to David Brooks for the skill and care with which he has selected the items for inclusion here, and for his introductory essay.

January 1974

*Joseph L. Fisher*
*Resources for the Future, Inc.*

ix

# INTRODUCTION

## DAVID B. BROOKS *

One of Orris Herfindahl's favorite quotations was written by Vilhjalmur Stefansson: "My favorite thesis is that an adventure is a sign of incompetence. . . . If everything is well managed, if there are no miscalculations or mistakes, then the things that happen are only the things you expected to happen, and for which you are ready and with which you can therefore deal." Orris Herfindahl not only liked that quotation, he also lived by it. I was fortunate to have known him in three capacities: as a teacher, as a colleague, and as a camping companion. He approached each task with the same caution and the same insistence that careful analysis would usually demonstrate that surprises could be avoided, that future developments would be an extension of past knowledge, and that analysis could help to indicate the linkages. It is characteristic of Herf, as most of us called him, that he never used words like *breakthrough* or *revolution* and equally characteristic that (at least to my knowledge) he never tipped over in a canoe, despite passing through some very rough water.

### BIOGRAPHY

Orris Clemens Herfindahl was born at Parshall, North Dakota, on June 15, 1918. He spent most of his early life around Stanton, Iowa, a Swedish farming community where he early developed a keen awareness of nature and skill at using his hands. These two interests remained with him throughout his life; they were well known to his colleagues and even reflected in some of his work. What is less well

* Research Director, Office of Energy Conservation, Department of Energy, Mines and Resources, Government of Canada.

known to those who knew him only as an economist is that his original love was music. His ability with the clarinet earned him a scholarship to Interlochen Music Camp in Traverse City, Michigan, and he entered the University of Minnesota with the intention of majoring in music. Although he changed his major, first to school administration and then to business administration, he kept an interest in music throughout his life and passed it on to his children. Moreover, it was as a member of the University of Minnesota band that, in his sophomore year, clarinet-player Orris Herfindahl met trombone-player Anna Marie Rogers. Orris Herfindahl always had a sense of humor and was something of a tease, so the story may well be true that Orris would not lend Anna Marie some scores she needed unless she went to the band formal with him. In any case, they were married on August 25, 1940.

Herfindahl's career at the University of Minnesota was a distinguished one, and he was recognized both for his music and for his academic accomplishments. He worked closely with Professor Frederick B. Garver and graduated in 1939 with high honors and a Phi Beta Kappa key. Although his degree was in business administration, Herfindahl had taken a number of courses in economics, and, after a year of graduate study at the University of Minnesota, he accepted a position teaching economics at St. Olaf College in Northfield, Minnesota.

In 1942 Orris and Anna Marie Herfindahl moved to Washington, D.C., where he had taken a job with the National Income Unit of the U.S. Department of Commerce. The war had attracted many extremely able people to Washington, and friendships that would last throughout his life began at this time. Herfindahl next spent three years in the U.S. Navy. His duties there included neither the study nor the practice of economics, but he did teach himself both calculus and German.

After his discharge from the Navy in 1945, he returned to the National Income Unit for several months, and then began the studies that would eventually lead to a doctorate in economics at Columbia University. He spent about two and a half years at Columbia, from September 1945 until the summer of 1948. His thesis advisor was George Stigler, whose exacting neoclassical standards accorded well with Herfindahl's own approach. However, his dissertation was not complete when, along with about twenty other economists, he went to the University of Illinois as an assistant professor under Howard Bowen. The dissertation, "Concentration in the Steel Industry" [27] [1] was finished in 1950, and in 1951 Columbia University awarded Orris C. Herfindahl the degree of Ph.D. in economics.

---

[1] A full bibliography is provided.

The academic year 1950–1951 at the University of Illinois was highlighted by a struggle between Howard Bowen and his "young turks" arrayed against a coalition of conservative faculty members and political forces in the state. The motivations for the attack on Bowen and his associates were complex and confused. However, late in 1950 after a hearing before the Board of Trustees, Bowen was fired, to the intense and lasting shock of many of his colleagues. Their loyalty to Bowen and their outrage at the tactics used to "get him" were such that within one year more than fifteen faculty members (Orris Herfindahl among them) had resigned—though many of the group continued to meet periodically at informal "Bowen alumni" reunion dinners.

Thus, in 1951 the Herfindahls moved back to Washington, D.C., which was to be their home for the rest of his life. He joined the staff of the Bureau of Mines, U.S. Department of the Interior, which at that time had put together an economics team it has never since equalled. He directed a small policy analysis group that turned out a number of thoughtful internal memoranda on mineral taxation and other such issues.

Apparently those two years with the Bureau of Mines reinforced Herfindahl's earlier interest in the economics of minerals. He had had no particular bent toward the minerals industry when he chose his dissertation topic, but that study of competition in the steel industry began an association with the industry that continued for most of his life. Characteristically, even for his dissertation he had probed more deeply than was required for the immediate question, inquiring into the absolute level of steel and iron ore prices, so that he very quickly became involved in theoretical questions about the long-run supply of minerals. His first published paper [9]—prepared while he was at the Bureau of Mines—dealt with this subject (the paper is reprinted here as selection 4).

In 1953 Herfindahl temporarily left the field of natural resources as such to spend several years in the Washington office of the Committee for Economic Development, where he reviewed, with generally favorable words, fiscal and monetary policies for countercyclical purposes. Several early papers were published that express his views on these matters [10], [12].

In 1957 Orris Herfindahl joined Resources for the Future in Washington, D.C., as a research associate (later senior research associate), and he was to stay with the organization until his death. For the next fifteen years he could usually be found in his office thinking or writing, yet always ready to help a colleague, to criticize a manuscript—or to talk about wilderness camping.

Of these activities, Herf unquestionably found writing to be the most difficult. He used to remark that writing was the hardest work he did, and he labored over each paragraph, sentence, and even word to ensure that it said exactly what he wanted. He was a stickler for correct use of grammar and syntax. His approach to writing, in fact no different from his approach to economic theory, served him well; the results are both clear and direct. He developed the facility, particularly in his later writing, of adjusting his style to the audience. One cannot mistake the tone of writing in *Copper Costs and Prices,* aimed at other economists, for that in *Quality of the Environment,* aimed at the public. Perhaps he felt a little more comfortable with the works aimed at his colleagues, for the characteristic dry humor, which those of us who knew him well came to look for and enjoy, turns up more frequently in his earlier works.

During the early portion of Herfindahl's tenure with RFF, he continued to emphasize the two subjects to which his doctoral dissertation and his work at the Bureau of Mines had introduced him: mineral resource supply and competition in the minerals industry. He recognized that both, along with the subject of conservation itself, had been neglected by economists and that this neglect was leading to some poorly conceived policies. For the most part his works during this period were fairly technical and aimed at his professional colleagues.

In 1963 he spent several months in India, the first of two significant assignments outside Washington.[2] The trip to India, at the request of the Indian Government, to work on mineral-related aspects of the Fourth Plan [30] was something of a turning point. For one thing, Herfindahl began to consider the general problems of providing natural resource information. For another, from this point on more of his work appeared in the form of reports and oral presentations than in books and economics journals. The invitation also showed that his reputation in the field of mineral economics had spread beyond the circle of his professional colleagues.

In 1966 and 1967 he was Resources for the Future's representative in the office of the Latin American Institute for Economic and Social Planning at Santiago, Chile. Out of this experience he wrote his book on natural resource information [5] (excerpts are reprinted here as selections 13 and 14). Characteristically disdaining a tourist's approach to this assignment, he became fluent enough to converse and later write in Spanish [32], [4], [6], [24], simply by insisting upon living and working in the language once he had acquired a basic classroom knowledge of it.

---

[2] Appendix A provides a chronological list of Herfindahl's special assignments and consultancies.

In addition to his work abroad, he held several teaching assignments, although his only full-time teaching position after receiving the doctorate came during the summer of 1960 at the University of Colorado. That summer provided me with my first contact with Orris Herfindahl; the impression was a strong one, if a little slow to develop.

He had come to the university to teach a course in mineral economics, and, along with other doctoral candidates interested in natural resources, I was quick to enroll. Earlier courses of the same sort had proved to be pretty descriptive, and I settled back for a relatively easy time. I was mildly surprised when Herfindahl started off by reviewing supply and demand curves, and several days later I woke up to the fact that we were moving headlong into capital theory. Needless to say, it was no snap course. However, the effort at catching up was well worth my while, for a year later it was arranged informally that I could go to Resources for the Future to write my doctoral dissertation; I therefore had the unique opportunity of being Orris Herfindahl's only Ph.D. student.

Throughout the 1960s Orris Herfindahl had also maintained an interest in natural resources other than minerals. Whenever possible, as with his work on conservation, he emphasized resources in general rather than minerals alone. Moreover, he began to take an active interest in water resources and published, in collaboration with his close friend Irving Fox, an article on the efficiency of water resource development [17].

The interest in other natural resources gradually broadened until it encompassed the whole question of the quality of the environment. An initial overview of the problems, *Quality of the Environment: An Economic Approach to Some Problems in Using Land, Water, and Air,* appeared in 1965 and was the first of several studies in this subject area that Herfindahl coauthored with Allen Kneese [3], [25], [7]. Just as with the material on natural resource information, a great deal of this work was aimed at the general public or at government agencies and either remains unpublished or has been incorporated in books and reports.

The last few years of his life were taken up to a significant degree by his collaboration with Allen Kneese on their advanced text in the economics of natural resources [7]; Herfindahl wrote many of the theoretical portions of this work, including some very technical sections on capital theory (the concluding chapter is reprinted here as selection 3). Thus, in this last work he returned in a sense to the starting point of his career, emphasizing the economics of natural resource supply and conservation. His working career had progressed from this topic through applications of economic theory to the minerals industry, to natural resource information and to the quality of natural environment, and finally back to the theory of resource supply once again. The text also marks a return to writing largely for his colleagues rater than for the public. Perhaps this book will prove to be a companion volume to that text, albeit at a less advanced level, for many of the ideas developed at length in the text can be found in their original form in the selections published here.

No one who knew Orris Herfindahl at all well could fail to be impressed by two special characteristics: his interest in philosophy and his love of the out-of-doors. He was a sincerely religious man and coupled this to his lifelong interest in both philosophy and economic theory. He was always searching for explanatory systems on a universal scale, and this is what is common to his interest in religion, in philosophy, and in economic theory. He loved to argue ethics, with points strongly stated, in order to see where they led. In fact, one of his great strengths was that he never forgot the ethical basis of economics, and he re-emphasized this wherever he could (see, for example, selections 3, 5, 6, and 17). For the most part he found that neoclassical economic theory, which he knew thoroughly, measured up quite well in terms of his ethical-religious precepts, but as a good economist he tried to make these values explicit and periodically asked himself whether they still made sense.

Politically, the same precepts were reflected in a strong, almost Burkeian conservatism and respect for traditional values. Herfindahl preferred to use the word *liberal* in its original nineteenth-century sense to emphasize his reliance on individualism and on free market forces. Thus, in today's world he was innately a conservative, but he was in no sense a reactionary. He combined at every stage a deep honesty about and a sensitivity for social problems. Although these could not always be reconciled with his market economics, he was always aware of their importance.

Perhaps not so different from this philosophical-religious bent was his feeling toward nature. It was as if he found God in the wonder of nature. It was a rare weekend that he and his family were not on a river or in the mountains on a trip lasting from a few hours to several weeks. He and Anna Marie led a Girl Scout program in canoeing for many years. He taught many people, myself included, to begin to handle a canoe in white water with some skill, though few of us ever reached his level. In my mind I can still picture Herf in the fifteen-foot, keelless fiberglass canoe that he made himself, looking over a stretch of white water, unerringly picking the best course, and then effecting the descent without so much as grazing a rock.

In a canoe or on foot, Herf accepted nature on its own terms; he used motors only for initial access, and firearms not at all. He and Anna Marie designed and made much of their own equipment, including tents and sleeping bags. Parents of a devoted family, they took backtrips of a week or longer with the four children—Anne (Mrs. William Sare), Henry, Cynthia, and Erika—that others would have hesitated to take with adults. Together they hiked in the Wind River Mountains of Wyoming, in Teton National Park, in Dinosaur National Monument, South Yellowstone, and other places. He also led a four-week, 500-mile canoe trip down the Hanbury and Thelon rivers in the Northwest Territories of Canada, a trip on which his son Henry, Irving Fox, and I accompanied him. It is accurate to say that, for the most part, Herf both conceived and planned these trips and that their success—their lack of "adventures"— was in no small measure the result of his planning. One of the basic elements in this planning was a list that I still use in preference to the dozens of others that have come my way since (see appendix B). Just as important, Herfindahl was exacting about his own physical conditioning and swam, ran, and exercised regularly throughout the year. In preparation for a trip he would read everything he could get on the history of the region and on previous trips. And he would review maps and photographs in great detail, committing much to memory and the rest to notes. This attitude toward operating in remote areas, together with his feeling for countryside, is well expressed in his article on our canoe trip, reprinted as appendix C.

In November 1972, Orris and Anna Marie Herfindahl left for a hiking trip in the foothills of Mt. Everest in eastern Nepal, a trip that had been a long-time ambition for both. Flying in from lower elevations, they joined an organized trip already in progress at 10,000 feet. Moving fairly quickly on foot to elevations of 17,000 feet, Herf, despite his fine physical condition, developed a severe case of high-altitude pulmonary edema. The attack built up slowly, and, in the absence of medical advice, its seriousness was not recognized early enough. Even cutting the length of the hike and beginning to move downhill was insufficient. He died on December 16, 1972, before medical help could be obtained. As Herf wrote in the article on our canoe trip: "The final cause of disaster often cannot be traced clearly to any specific lack. Instead a whole series of little inadequacies seem often to exert more and more pressure until . . ." He was fifty-four years old at the time of his death. All of us who knew him feel the loss of his thoughts, his honesty, and his combination of penetrating criticism and subtle humor.

Orris Herfindahl's work can be divided into five major topic areas; each constitutes one section of this volume. In order of presentation, these areas are:

(1) the nature and scope of resource economics;
(2) natural resource supply and conservation;
(3) the application of economics to the minerals industry;
(4) the supply of natural resource information;
(5) the quality of the natural environment.

The five topic areas, and the selections within each, are reviewed briefly below. First, however, the general criteria for selection should be indicated. Within the overriding criterion of providing students and specialists with a compilation of Herfindahl's main ideas, some emphasis was given to lesser known or unpublished materials. An effort has been made not only to achieve balance among the five topic areas, but also to reflect the several audiences for which Herfindahl wrote—his colleagues, government, and the public—and to include the main themes he emphasized throughout his career: the conviction that natural resources can and should be studied by conventional economic methods; investment as a process (mineral exploration, information); the use of measurement in economic analysis (concentration of industry, data on the environment); and pure theory-cum-philosophy (long-run price of minerals, ore deposits as capital). These themes will be reviewed very briefly in the final section of the introduction. Finally, none of the work that was originally presented in Spanish has been included. To do them justice, such works should appear in the original; the same ideas and approaches can be found in his English works.

*The Nature and Scope of Resource Economics*

Always a penetrating critic, Orris Herfindahl reserved his sharpest sallies for those who contended that resource economics was a special discipline, distinct from traditional economics. Of course, he recognized that study of the economics of natural resources required an extensive knowledge of industrial activity and technology, as well as of physical-biological relationships. But these were differences of application, not of principle. This point of view is brought out unmistakably in the first selection in the volume, "Is Resource Economics Unorthodox?" The final sentence, in which Herfindahl advises people studying natural resources "not to abandon conventional economic principles but rather to learn enough about the problem at hand to apply them usefully," is characteristic of his whole approach. The article was written in 1969, but it would have been little different had he written it at the very start or the very end of his career.

Herfindahl was almost equally sharp in his criticism of those people who pointed to the normal working out of supply and demand as "problems." Rising or falling prices for some commodity may indeed create problems, but the fact of changing prices does not in itself constitute a problem. He expressed this view orally in many contexts, but, to my knowledge, only wrote it expressly in an unpublished work prepared for a House of Representatives Republican Task Force on Earth Resources and Population, from which the second selection is excerpted.

Finally, although I have in general avoided taking excerpts from the Herfindahl-Kneese text in resource economics, an exception was made for the final chapter of the text, entitled "Time for Stock-Taking," which, according to Allen Kneese, was largely Herfindahl's work. This is a rather philosophical view of what economic theory has been able to do, and of what it has not been able to do, in the way of analyzing the economics of natural resources. It was one of the last things that Orris Herfindahl wrote and is as suggestive of paths for the future as it is reflective of the road already traveled.

*Natural Resource Supply and Conservation*

The material in this area may well be regarded as the most important of Herfindahl's career. It is significant both for its advances in thinking about certain aspects of resource supply and also for its exposition of several subjects that others often left analytically empty and thus useless for policy purposes. However, it forms a relatively small part of his written work, which is a tribute to the careful thought process and tight writing style that are always present, but particularly noticeable when he turned to theory.

Throughout most of this work, Herfindahl is interested in industry output rather than the output of a single mine, a point sometimes neglected by critics. Therefore, when Herfindahl concludes that the quantities available for commercial exploitation are very large in relation to consumption, he is referring to very broad geographic areas, not to a single country, much less to a single mine. Furthermore, in most of this work he abstracts from noncompetitive influences on price, largely because he did not believe that, over the long term, they were dominant. Finally, he also neglected such complicating factors as recycling of metals, in this case not because he felt that they were unimportant, but because they were unnecessary complications which, if pursued, would only reinforce his theoretical and empirical conclusions.

The first selection is his first published article, which, although little known except to specialists, is a clear primer of the principles of resource supply for a firm or an industry producing an exhaustible resource. The article provides references to and a brief discussion of the literature on the economics of exhaustible resources.

The second selection is a remarkable piece of writing entitled "What Is Conservation?" delivered as a lecture at the Colorado School of Mines, first printed in *Three Studies in Minerals Economics* [2] in 1961, and reprinted many times since. In this paper Herfindahl, following Ciriacy-Wantrup's lead,[3] gives economic content to the idea of conservation and shows that the same term had been used in the past to mean different and even conflicting things. It is characteristic of Herfindahl for several reasons. For one thing, after the case had been made, it all sounds very simple; one tends to forget the long period of thought that preceded the writing. For another, the work combines philosophical and practical content. It is soundly based in economic theory, with a touch of general philosophy as well. Moreover, although there are no mathematical symbols in the paper, one can feel them just below the surface. Finally, the article is straightforward and direct with sentences whose meaning cannot be mistaken; one might disagree with Orris Herfindahl, but one was seldom confused by him. Thus, in discussing one of the most popular definitions of conservation (see selection 5), he writes:

When this definition is read off rapidly—conservation is the use of natural resources for the greatest good of the greatest number for the longest time— the three superlatives have a delightful ring. If this is conservation, how could anyone be opposed to it? No one could be, of course, unless he stops to ask himself how three variables can be maximized at the same time. Imagine a father trying to distribute a bag of candy to his children so as to maximize the amount of candy received by each child who gets candy *and* the number of children receiving candy *and* the length of time the candy will be visible.

The third selection is a portion of a paper entitled "Goals and Standards of Performance for the Conservation of Minerals," in which Herfindahl spends considerable time destroying, on both practical and ethical grounds, the notion that capital in general ought to be accumulated for the future. Only the shorter portion relating specifically to conserving minerals is presented here. Whereas the general proposition on saving capital never had much practical content, ideas about saving minerals for the future are very much alive today. In fact, the excerpt is reprinted partly because it helps to clarify ideas that have

[3] S. V. Ciriacy-Wantrup, *Resource Conservation* (Berkeley: University of California Press, 1952).

recently reappeared, notably in the limits-to-growth debate, and partly because it can be compared with Herfindahl's later works on the quality of the natural environment (see especially selection 18), to show the changing nature of his concern for the future.

The final selection for this area is "Depletion and Economic Theory," a paper contributed to the book, *Extractive Resources and Taxation*. This paper presents most of the important aspects of the economics of supplying minerals over the long term, and includes material published in earlier similar studies (for example, "The Long-Run Cost of Minerals," in *Three Studies in Minerals Economics*). While maintaining that the "basic and definitive treatment" was given to the same subject by Hotelling in 1931,[4] Herfindahl reinterprets the material in a more modern context and makes it more accessible to the average reader. Moreover, by use of comparative statics he is able to indicate the likely effects of the sorts of change that will be important in a modern world, as with new technology or growing demand. Finally, and again characteristically, Herfindahl does not stop with the theory, but goes on to ask whether the facts of mineral prices accord with the theory. Needless to say, he finds that they do; had they not, he would have immediately gone back and reevaluated the theory. The theory of mineral supply has been refined a little since this article was published,[5] but its heart can be found here.

*Application of Economics to the Minerals Industry*

This topic area includes the largest single block of Herfindahl's writing and is no doubt the area for which he is most widely known. Certainly it is the work that first brought him to the attention of policy makers in government. One of his major contributions was simply recognizing that, although the minerals industry had been largely neglected by economists since the turn of the century, economic theory could usefully be applied to it. Of course, there had been many books on minerals and on topics that could be called mineral economics, but only a few had substantially involved the use of economic theory for explanatory purposes. Most tended to be descriptive surveys reporting what had happened and suggesting what might happen, but seldom asking "why" or "so what."

---

[4] Harold Hotelling, "The Economics of Exhaustible Resources," *Journal of Political Economy*, Vol. 39 (April 1931), pp. 137–175.

[5] Richard L. Gordon, "Conservation and the Theory of Exhaustible Resources," *Canadian Journal of Economics*, Vol. 32 (August 1966), pp. 319–326; Paul G. Bradley, "Increasing Scarcity: The Case of Energy Resource," *American Economic Review*, Vol. 63 (May 1973), pp. 119–125.

The selections in this section all emphasize the more theoretical portions of this body of work, including applications of concepts from structure of industry and capital theory. To some extent, this means that Herfindahl's policy prescriptions have been slighted. However, in the end he was far more interested in his analysis, which is not time-bound, than he was in policy prescriptions specific to a particular date or a particular administration. Moreover, the policy prescriptions themselves were not unique. Many can be put forward after institutional analysis, or for less well-founded reasons, so that in most cases others were advocating the same things.

Two other characteristics emerge in these selections. First, Herfindahl's facility for dealing with numbers comes to the fore here, where he had to demonstrate the applicability of his conclusions, something that was less immediate in abstract questions about resource supply. Second, in reading these works, one cannot but be aware that Herfindahl knew very well the industries with which he was dealing. He followed his own statement that one of the few reasons for distinguishing resource economics, apart from a small amount of particularly applicable theory, seemed to be the need to know more about the industries under study than was necessary for manufacturing or service sectors.

The first three selections all come from Herfindahl's first major work, *Copper Costs and Prices: 1870–1957,* published in 1959. The first selection is chapter 3 of that book, which provides the most succinct statement of Herfindahl's view of investment in minerals as a systematic process. Supporting the now widely accepted view that an ore deposit is better treated as a form of capital than as "land," Herfindahl pointed out that the capital good is produced by exploration and development of the mineral deposit. (In the minerals industry, the word *exploration* refers to the search for new deposits, whereas the word *development* refers to the preparation of known deposits for production.) Thus, the production of ore deposits is a part of the output of the industry at the same time that other ore deposits are typically serving as inputs to a production process that results in metal.

While no one denies that the process of developing ore deposits is systematically based on expectations of profit, it was and is maintained that exploration is not a systematic process, but rather a matter of chance discoveries or politically determined decisions. Even today such views are common, reinforced by the industry's emphasis on the high risks it faces in exploration. Herfindahl did not deny that exploration might be risky, though he noted many ways in which this risk could be moderated, but he did attack the ideas that the volume of exploration was independent of profit expectations and that the volume of discovery (that is, the value of capital produced) was independent of the volume of exploration. The distinctions are important. If discovery is accidental, the supply of mineral resources available for exploitation at any one time is a random variable. If, however, exploration is systematic, we can expect that discovery will be responsive to long-run trends in supply and demand, and, with appropriate qualifications, we can undertake economic analysis on the minerals industry, using prices (which are generally known) as proxies for costs (which are generally unknown). It also means that over time about as much will be spent in finding ore deposits as the ore deposits are worth, though of course the value of individual discoveries need not have the same direct correspondence with their cost.

The second selection from *Copper Costs and Prices* is a brief discussion of concentration in the copper industry, something that is at the heart of the book and described most clearly in these several pages. In this section Herfindahl uses a concentration coefficient he developed for his Ph.D. dissertation, which combines in one measure the number of firms in an industry as well as their relative sizes.

The final excerpt from *Copper Costs and Prices* is taken from the conclusions. It could almost as well appear with his work on resource supply, for it tells us what can be learned about copper resources from price and cost trends. He emphasizes that conclusions about the deterioration (a word he preferred to depletion) of copper resources cannot be very useful unless one carefully defines deterioration and incorporates notions about economic as well as physical availability. By showing that the systematic nature of exploration underlies the long-run stability in the price of copper, he is able to conclude that, with respect to the response of long-run supply to demand, "copper does not appear to differ from commodities outside the mining industry."

The next selection is a book review, written in 1957, in which Herfindahl puts forward his view of an ore deposit as a form of capital and describes in some detail the difficulties this raises for measuring input and output in the mining industry. The review might well be read by anyone trying to apply statistics to this industry. Here again Herfindahl's knowledge of the mining industry and his ability to make that knowledge meaningful in an economic context is evident.

The last selection in this section is the text of a history of metal mining in the United States from 1839 to 1909, the period in which the United States emerged as a major world producer of metallic minerals. This study was originally published by the National Bureau of Economic Research and is still available; therefore the detailed appendix tables and notes are not reprinted here. In this work, more than any other, Herfindahl deals directly with the statistics of the industry and attempts to make long-term series showing output, employment, and productivity. He also discusses the technologic changes that have occurred in the industry and points out differences both among commodities and among regions.

### Supply of Natural Resource Information

As noted above, Herfindahl's work on the supply of natural resource information began with his trip to India in 1963. Of course, earlier studies on exploration had already involved him in a subject related to the acquisition of information. However, this trip, and subsequent shorter assignments with United Nations agencies, gave him the opportunity to organize his thinking further and prepared him for his South American assignments.

The culmination of this work was *Natural Resource Information for Economic Development* [5], in which Herfindahl treats the provision of information as an investment like other investments. As an investment, information costs money and also creates the opportunity to earn more money. If it is collected too early, money is wasted because it sits idle; if it is collected too late, returns on its use will be less than they might otherwise have been. Similarly, either too little or too much may be spent on information because its collection is subject to diminishing returns. All these considerations are treated in a fairly difficult and abstract chapter of the book. Together with the theory, however, is a great deal of data on the costs of obtaining information, on the sorts of information available in South America, and on the institutional structures that seem most likely to be effective and efficient in providing information. It is this institutional material that the selections in this section emphasize. In contrast to much of the theory of the long-run supply of minerals, it is difficult to think of ways to test the theoretical models here. To some degree they are formal representations of conclusions that can be obtained by simpler reasoning. On the other hand, as demonstrated by the experience of many countries and many projects, we have a great need for the institutional conclusions to which this theoretical approach led Herfindahl. Hence, the first selection is chapter 6, "Some Guidelines for Organization and Administration," reprinted in full with the exception of one appendix.

The appendix to chapter 2 of the same book, "The Question of Exploration Strategy," is also reprinted. This is a little-known but very useful attack on the idea that systematic drilling on some grid pattern would be an ideal method to gain geological information and locate mineral deposits. Such a view, Herfindahl points out, mis-conceives both the goal of an exploration program (which should be to increase the size of our real output, not simply to increase information) and the criteria for determining when enough exploration has been done (which is a matter of the net present value of ore found by successive unit outlays on exploration).

The final two selections are adaptations of the work on information. The first, "Economic Considerations in Assessing the Role of Remote Sensing in Country Development," applies the book's conclusions to a single exploration technique; the second, "The Value of Mineral Surveys to Economic Development," applies similar principles to a single industry. Herfindahl is really asking how the government of an underdeveloped country (or an agency advising that country) can make use of (1) remote sensing, or (2) mineral surveys to maximize the return to the country, given (a) its inherent endowment in mineral capital, plus (b) its willingness to invest in information-gathering techniques. In all these studies, Herfindahl carefully focused on the right questions, explicitly avoiding such questions as whether remote sensing or mineral surveys *would* lead to increased production. As he says in one paper, "To ask this question is something like asking, 'Does investment pay?' The answer in both cases is yes, if properly done."

## The Quality of the Natural Environment

As Orris Herfindahl turned in the last five years of his life to questions involving the natural environment, he was undertaking a labor of love. He once commented to me that he would have liked to have spent more of his time studying water resources instead of mineral resources. He might well have specialized further in these problems had it not been an area in which he was personally involved; I can also recall his stating that self-involvement was the death of sound analysis. Whether one agrees or disagrees with this principle, it is hard to deny that a source of strength he found it to be. In any event, after his return from Chile, he did focus extensively on this area in his writing, though in his thinking it goes back much earlier.

Although he would not have maintained that much of this work was original (nor indeed that his work on the economics of exhaustible resources was), he was among the first to understand the importance of externalities in a modern context and to unite material on economic relationships with that on physical-biological relationships. Almost all of the major principles detailed in weightier books on pollution and the environment can be found in a descriptive format in *Quality of the Environment* [3], the little book he coauthored with Allen Kneese.

This work modified to some degree Herfindahl's earlier optimism about market processes. Though it is never entirely explicit, he seemed to be working toward a distinction between two types of environmental problems: those such as the discharge of effluents into air and water and onto the land, with which the market system could (at least in principle) deal quite adequately; and those which involve such matters as preservation of natural beauty or congestion, as well as the possibilities for climatic disruption and destruction of life support systems, for which market processes seemed less than adequate. It is probably fair to say that natural areas in particular took on, for Herfindahl, the character of a merit good that ought to be provided by society. At the same time, he foresaw that the forces that would lead to recognition of natural areas as merit goods (e.g., the growing popularity of wilderness camping) could in themselves jeopardize the very values that the merit good was supposed to provide. Hence, he urged that a longer time horizon was appropriate for analysis of and policy concerning such issues than could be justified for, say, mineral exploration or investment in development.

To a greater extent than elsewhere, Herfindahl wrote about the environment for a general audience, not for his colleagues. Much of his work in this area, including the first two selections for this section, was presented orally and has been hitherto unpublished. The paper entitled "Effects of Resource Depletion and Economic Growth on the Quality of Life" is probably the best single expression of Herfindahl's personal views about appropriate environmental management, and one of the very few in which his biases show through clearly. Moreover, in translating significant portions of the work of Ortega y Gasset, he demonstrates both his inclinations toward philosophy and his knowledge of Spanish. The other paper, "Can Increasing Demands on Resources Be Met?" is included partly for comparison with the earlier excerpt on the conservation of minerals (selection 6), a topic Herfindahl dismisses in the first few pages of this paper in order to talk about what he now sees as the more important problems—the side effects of supplying natural resources. He also draws a distinction between various kinds of pollutants in terms of their dispersion and cumulative effects and in terms of the likelihood that market processes can be designed to cope with them. The final selection for this topic area is a short excerpt from *Quality of the Environment,* which captures some specific comments concerning natural areas. Here again, Herfindahl was thinking well in advance of others about a particularly difficult problem of environmental management and was searching for a policy approach consistent with individual choice and market processes.

PERSPECTIVE

Shortly after I was asked by Resources for the Future to compile this memorial volume, I began to wonder whether it should be a history of Herfindahl's ideas or a review of his most important contributions. The question seemed particularly relevant, since we wanted not simply a memorial on the bookshelf, but a volume that would serve as a reference and a guide to Herfindahl's work for students and resource specialists. It is a special tribute to Orris Herfindahl that, in the end, there was no conflict between the two conceptions of the book. His ideas were remarkably consistent over time and over a variety of topics. The main reason for this, of course, was that he brought a consistent philosophical framework to bear on all the problems he considered. This framework included both his ethical beliefs and neoclassical economic theory. Several themes derived from that economic theory run throughout Herfindahl's work.

First among these themes is the principle that no special discipline of resource economics or mineral economics is needed to deal with natural resources. Natural resources are economic goods, and therefore more or less conventional theoretical and empirical economic analysis can explain their supply and demand relationships. Moreover, and what is not entirely the same thing, Herfindahl made it clear that natural resources not only *can* be studied by methods of conventional economics, but *deserve* to be so studied. (One might argue that the latter was the greater contribution because natural resources, and particularly minerals, had been largely neglected by modern economists until about 1950.) At the heart of all Herfindahl's work is the belief that natural resources present problems worthy of an economist's attention and perhaps even requiring some specialized knowledge before analysis, but that the basic concepts are at most only special cases of the economic theories so usefully adapted to other sectors of the economy. For this reason, Herfindahl much preferred to be thought of as an economist, not as a resource economist, much less a mineral economist. From time to time he expressed the fear that he would be trapped in the field of mineral economics; that is, that the demands on his time as a result of his reputation in this one area would leave him no time to pursue newer and, for him, more interesting problems.

The second major theme is that of investment. Herfindahl was always interested in the process of investment, and he brought this

interest to bear on subjects that had previously received little systematic treatment. The first of these subjects was, of course, conservation, a field in which he knocked down a number of platitudes and
inserted some well-defined and operational propositions. He maintained that conservation was simply an investment process in which
some things were preserved for future consumption or future enjoyment; thus an action leading to conservation was, according to Herfindahl, neither good nor bad in itself, but could be either, depending
upon how one evaluated the resulting shift in the time stream of
benefits and costs.[6] He looked at the gathering of information in
much the same way. Again he cleared away misconceptions about
resource and mineral inventories, maintaining that expenditures on
data, particularly those oriented toward project construction or regional development, are investments and therefore subject to all the
pitfalls—diminishing returns, incorrect forecasts, and the like—that
surround other investments. Similarly, Herfindahl's ideas about investment in mineral exploration, evident in his early work, really make it
a form of information gathering. He was understandably proud of
having established that exploration could be viewed as systematic
investment in the production of ore deposits and that, though occasional accidental discoveries would continue to turn up, they by no
means dominated the normal market processes leading to discovery.
As with conservation and resource inventories, additional exploration
was neither good nor bad but was to be rationally evaluated by
comparison of costs and returns over time.

A third theme that runs throughout much of Herfindahl's work,
although only a few are specifically concerned with it, is the idea of
measurement. As emphasized above, Herfindahl was a master in seeing
behind statistics to the real goods and services they represented, a trait
that one reviewer attributed to his early experience in the National
Income Unit. Whatever its source, from his doctoral dissertation, in
which he measured changing concentration in the steel industry, to
his final works on environment, he felt that theory must eventually
be put forward in the form of testable propositions. He spent considerable time finding appropriate and adequate measures for the
propositions he himself put forward, no easy task, given the problems
of dealing with ore deposits and the natural environment. One of his

---

[6] See also Edward S. Mason's response to Ciriacy-Wantrup and Herfindahl in
"The Political Economy of Resource Use," *Perspectives on Conservation*, Henry
Jarrett, ed. (Baltimore: The Johns Hopkins Press for Resources for the Future,
Inc., 1958), pp. 161–162. Mason suggests that it is too late to make *conservation*
into a value-free term, though he accepts their view of its economic meaning.

last works is almost a catalog of possibilities for obtaining the data needed to test models of environmental pollution [25].[7]

The final theme is in some ways the most characteristic and the most difficult to treat—his insistence that economics must rest on explicit ethical principles. Thus, his work generally reflects the assumption that the market system is basically benign, a view that accorded well with his desire for systematically finding and providing orderly philosophies, as well as with his conservatism. Needless to say, he accepted such modifications of market results as were required by the existence of externalities and economies of scale, but for much of his career he believed that the market would provide, if not the best of all possible worlds, at least an economically and ethically acceptable one. The word *ethically* was of course critical, for he accepted the results of the market system only because he also accepted its ethical underpinnings, notably the lack of coercion of man by man, and the responsibility of each individual for his own actions. He consistently developed his models and policy conclusions within this framework. Additional ethical values were incorporated without difficulty in his early work by making adjustments in order to improve the distribution of income.

As Herfindahl's attention turned toward the environment and natural areas, and more generally toward the quality of life, he became less certain. In a 1972 memo to his colleagues at Resources for the Future, he wrote: "The events of the last decade or so have shown that the perennial apprehensions of many persons about the prospects of mankind for a long-continued enjoyment of a high standard of living were justified". In the face of this conclusion, he found it difficult to reconcile some of his personal values with the workings of the market system. On the one hand, he saw no way to avoid losing certain things he valued highly, unless individuals exercised self-restraint; on the other hand, he saw little evidence that self-restraint was growing any more common than it had ever been. Society could of course impose restraints (though Herfindahl was by no means sanguine about the politics of this), but this in turn challenged the individualistic values also critically important to him.

Such trends no doubt account for the note of pessimism that appears in some of his later work, notably in "Effects of Resources Depletion and Economic Growth on the Quality of Life" (printed as selection 17). And it may explain his return to theoretical work in the last years of his life, which can be seen as a retreat from policy

---

[7] Herfindahl was largely responsible for part 3 of this paper, entitled "Data Needs Suggested by the Models for Analysis of Environmental Pollution."

applications in order to find a new path that could circumvent the dilemma. One characteristic of nineteenth-century economic liberals (among whom Herfindahl numbered himself) and twentieth-century political liberals (with whose goals he had much sympathy) alike is a faith in and a mistrust of man. Orris Herfindahl was aware of his duality of thought in this regard; much of his study of philosophy and work in economics can be seen as an effort to reconcile the two.

Thus, the heritage that Orris Clemens Herfindahl leaves is to be found not only in his contributions to the study of natural resources, but also in the ethical precepts that were incorporated with them. His family and his associates received these directly. Others have the opportunity to learn of them through his writing.

# PART ONE

*The Nature and Scope of Resource Economics*

# SELECTION 1

# IS RESOURCE ECONOMICS
# UNORTHODOX?

On reading Professor Sargent's contention that resource economists are different from other economists, one of the members of this journal's editorial board experienced a twinge of disagreement. Thinking I might have the same reaction—and he was right—he asked me to express some of my thoughts on the relationship between resource economists and other economists, or better, between the economics of the two groups. My position is very simple. The relevant economic theory (and political theory) is the same for all applied fields of economics, of which natural resources may be viewed as one. The particular physical content of the applied fields obviously varies, however, and each will make use of some branches of theory much more than others.

Sargent's main contentions are that "other" economists believe (1) that the free market is the prime resource-allocating mechanism in our society and (2) that the market system in the long run gives results as good as or better than other systems.

To this economist, with one foot in each of the camps of orthodoxy and resources, these propositions seem to be well founded. Whatever may be thought of the results of the system, the economist who con-

Reprinted by permission from *Journal of Soil and Water Conservation*, Vol. 24 (January–February 1969), pp. 10–11.

tends that the market is not the prime resource-allocating system has his work cut out. Many economists of both varieties believe there is considerable empirical evidence for the second proposition.

In alleged opposition to these two general propositions, Sargent maintains that reliance on the market mechanism has made a mess of our use of natural resources (pollution, abuse, etc.) and that only the resource economist understands that allocation of natural resources to different uses must be accomplished through the political process. But surely to view the market system as the main allocation instrument in our society and a market system as having certain advantages over other systems does not entail the view that the market will solve all problems.

What is the situation in the "natural resource industries"? The fact is the market does perform the allocative function quite well in a number of them, subject to the legal restrictions (not all of which are undesirable) that have been imposed, including agriculture, forestry, and mining. Perhaps the main test of performance here is whether investment and output respond to changes in demand in response to changes in profits from "normal" levels.

Any "market" economist would agree with Sargent that pursuit of self-interest will yield less than desirable and attainable results in many cases, including many involving natural resources. Market-oriented economists have known for years that the presence of real external benefits and/or costs will result in misallocation in certain cases. To blame the market system for these misallocations is like blaming penicillin for failing to mend a broken leg when prescribed instead of a cast.

What is to be done about these cases? To say that the political process can solve all is too loose a prescription. The political process functions in many different ways, depending on the conditions that are set up for its functioning in the case at hand. The questions are: Who is going to participate in the process and how? What is the system? What are the rules for resolving conflicts in resource use?

At this point one ignores the market economist at his own peril. Demand for some of these commodities can be studied and estimated, contrary to Sargent's assertion. More important, it may be possible to suggest procedures that will enable us to reap some of the good results of reliance on market forces, such as adjusting supplies to willingness to pay, while avoiding some of the bad. Many "political" choices can be aided by quantifying costs and benefits, in some cases for different levels of "product" quality.

All of this is a far cry from the reliance Sargent would have us place on the "scientific" expert. The expert ought to and must participate in any practical problem to be sure that correct technical relations are being used, but his valuations of outcomes are on the same footing as those of anybody else. No expert can tell me or anyone else how much we are willing to pay for a bog. The futility of relying on the expert for the final choice is evident on asking, which expert's recommendation shall we follow? A system is needed for the rational resolution of competing demands, including those of different types of experts.

How is the strength of these competing demands to be measured in those cases where there is not a market for the good or service in question? In some cases indirect statistical measures based on observable transactions are possible. Where these are not feasible, the "conventional" economist certainly would not be opposed to any means that would throw some light on what the different sectors of the demand spectrum would be willing to give up in order to get the good or service in question. However, surveys of generalized goals do not appear to this economist to aid decision making on resource use, because they are not closely enough related to the all-important question of how much the individual is willing to pay.

This emphasis on willingness to pay does not mean that the "conventional" economist is insensitive to esthetic values or any other values. The point is that the satisfaction of any value requires the use of scarce productive services of some type, and we must necessarily have some way to allocate them. We can and do in many cases choose not to use willingness to pay as the criterion, but then some other method of rationing must be used.

Quite often information on willingness to pay will be of use in applying another method. A common case is that in which a public body undertakes to meet all demand for a service at a price of zero. The need to know the demand function in order to avoid supplying more than is demanded is just as great as if the price were positive and equal to cost.

Sargent's views on benefit-cost analysis differ from those commonly held by "conventional" economists largely because of semantic reasons. If benefit-cost analysis is taken to mean an attempt to take into account all benefits and costs (whether easily measurable in money terms or not) in a suitable decision-making framework, it seems to me that a denial of its universal applicability in allocation problems comes close to advocating irrationality. Some benefits and costs obviously may not be associated with money flows and may be difficult to measure, but no economist that I know has ever advocated that such benefits or costs should be neglected in making the decision.

Some of Sargent's warnings on the use of benefit-cost analysis are to the point, of course. The possibilities for managing a resource are rarely exhausted by comparing only two options. The fact that a certain option has a benefit-cost ratio greater than one is not a sufficient condition for choosing that option; another option may yield a greater gain to society.

To me the useful part of Sargent's position can be put in this way: The "conventional" economist who ventures to work on resource problems will sometimes err because he does not sufficiently understand the physical and biological relationships involved and because he is not accustomed to working with problems in which benefits and costs external to the decision-making unit occupy so prominent a place. The remedy is not to abandon conventional economic principles but rather to learn enough about the problem at hand to apply them usefully.

# IDENTIFICATION AND STUDY OF POLICY PROBLEMS IN THE MINERALS INDUSTRIES

## METHODS FOR IDENTIFYING POLICY PROBLEMS

The three methods for identifying policy problems to be discussed here are as follows: (1) examination of current status and outlook; (2) projections; and (3) the efficiency approach—that is, an attempt to identify obstacles to the maximization of social product.

One of the most popular methods for identifying presently or prospectively pressing problems of mineral policy is what is called here "examination of current status and outlook." Many people, both in and out of government, seem to feel that the way to locate problems is to go down the list of mineral commodities, one by one, look at production, sales, inventories, and price changes, and then try to see

*Editor's note:* This selection is the first part of a paper presented to the House Republican Task Force on Earth Resources and Population on May 22, 1969. The remaining two sections included a discussion of various measures of changes in the size of and production by the minerals industry between about 1955 and 1965, followed by examples of what were, to Herfindahl, among the more important and real policy issues involving the minerals industry: improving efficiency in the supply of crude oil, policy for minerals on federal lands, stockpiling of minerals, organization of minerals ventures abroad, and improvements in the location ("claim") system for awarding title to minerals.

what the immediate future holds in store, perhaps by simple extrapolation of certain key demands, estimation of excess capacity, and a totalling up of plans for expansion of capacity. For example, a substantial price change often is the signal for a flurry of such activity. Or, in the case of a proposed disposal from the stockpile, the question considered is how "disruptive" the disposal sale may be.

All too often such examinations of the current situation and outlook, made with the avowed purpose of changing policy or formulating new policy, result in nothing. In some cases there may be a good deal of hand wringing, but usually no one can find any handles to pull that will make the machine work differently. Sometimes actions will be advocated and perhaps taken that will suppress the undesirable symptoms.

Examination of the current situation and outlook is defective, in several ways, as a means of identifying policy problems. The fundamental weakness is that the method commonly is associated with a failure to be clear about the fundamental objectives of policy. The method seems to rest on the view that changes in price, production, and the like pose policy problems, but the mere fact of change indicates nothing of the kind. After all, there are many changes that are needed and beneficial. In most cases there is no need to watch the process of adjustment in the apprehension that the market will fail. Suppose, for example, that the production of a certain mineral has decreased. This is of no particular significance in and of itself so far as policy is concerned. On the other hand, suppose that things have been going along on an even keel in an industry, or that production and sales have been increasing handsomely. This happy state of affairs may conceal gross inefficiency or monopoly that a policy change might be able to remedy.

I am not arguing, of course, that examination of the current situation and outlook is a useless activity. Those who are engaged in making the production, inventory, and demand decisions that are the stuff of the market process had better keep their fingers on the pulse of things if they don't want to lose their shirts. My point is different—that this is not the route to the identification of policy problems. It is true, of course, that the perception of a trend or a large change may alter our evaluation of the importance or significance of a known policy defect or may stimulate the search for a gap in policy not previously identified.

A second method for identifying policy problems that enjoys considerable popularity involves the use of "projections." The implicit rationale involves, first, a prediction of demands in some future year on the assumption that long-run supply prices remain unchanged, that is, that relative prices of the various materials remain unchanged. In such a set of predictions, the factors that bring about absolute and relative change in the quantities of the different materials produced and consumed are change in per capita and total income, extrapolations of technological trends, extrapolations of trends in tastes, together with some degree of explicit or implicit consideration of income elasticities of consumer goods and services. Prediction systems of various degrees of complexity are possible.

These conditional predictions—or projections, as some people prefer to call them—are then confronted with information bearing on the supplies of the materials. This information may be of varying degrees of sophistication and adequacy. Whatever the situation in this respect, discrepancies between quantities demanded and quantities likely to be supplied under the assumption of unchanged prices are regarded as indications of problems that perhaps warrant a change in policy to deal with them.

This method for identifying policy problems suffers from the same defects as does the method of assessing the current situation and outlook. The main difference between the two is that the latter focuses on the present and the immediate future, whereas the method of projections commonly has a much longer horizon. In each case, however, the mere change of price does not indicate in and of itself the desirability of changing any aspect of policy. If the rise in price is associated with the most advantageous way of dealing with a changed situation, there is nothing to be done, granted that all would like to see a situation in which the prices of materials never rose, other things equal.

The most one might say for the projections method of identifying policy problems is that the likelihood of a large change in price—in either direction—may stimulate a searching examination into the need for policy change. In the case of a prospective large rise in price, it may be realized, for example, that the loss from a certain policy already known to be uneconomic has increased so greatly that stronger efforts must be made to change it.[1] This consideration, common to both methods of policy identification discussed so far, is involved in what might be called the dynamics of the process of policy formation, but it does not define or indicate the situation in which there is a genuine opportunity for beneficial policy modification. Still, the true believers in these two procedures as methods for identifying policy problems have more than this in mind. It seems likely that the exponents of each method share a somewhat indefinite criterion, namely, that the

---

[1] The usefulness of projections for purposes other than that of identifying policy problems is not discussed here.

existence of a policy problem is indicated by one or more of the following: cost and price increases, increases in imports, and declines in consumption or production. If the presence of one of these changes merely triggered a search for advantageous policy change, advocated changes could still be based on a relevant criterion, but, unfortunately, maintenance of the status quo seems to be the policy objective of many. The attempt to maintain the status quo in price, production, and imports necessarily will result in bad policy, however, for only a little analysis is necessary to show that maintaining the status quo in a world of change cannot be regarded as the fundamental objective of mineral policy.

So far as mineral policy is concerned, the basic objective to be served, in my judgment, is economic efficiency. That is, in view of the fact that the consumption of mineral products requires the use of productive services that could have been used to produce or buy other things, we should try to arrange things so that we do not use up more productive services in mineral production or procurement from abroad than the mineral products are worth to us. If opportunities to move toward this situation are neglected, real national income will be lowered. The notion of economic efficiency requires, of course, that proper account be taken of effects on other economic units that are external to the decision-making unit.

There is general agreement in our society that the basic instrument to be used in attaining the objective of economic efficiency is the market system. That is, investment in the different minerals industries and production of the different minerals is to be guided by demands expressed on markets by offers to buy. Profits over and beyond the necessary return to capital are the signal inviting expansion of production and investment, and losses are the signal for reductions. The implication is that investors in the minerals industries, like those in other industries, must bear the consequences of their decisions. If they and their operating agents anticipate demand correctly, they stand to make something more than the normal return on capital, although if the system is as competitive as we hope it is, the profits beyond this normal return will not continue, for additional investment will take place and eliminate them. On the other hand, investors must stand any losses resulting from their failure to forecast correctly. There is no such thing as insurance for all investors against risks of the market in our basic conception of the system. True equity holders stand to make the gains—*and* the losses. It also should be perfectly clear, on not more than a moment's reflection, that this basic conception of the operation of the market system does not—and this needs very strong emphasis— oblige the government to keep the output of any commodity from declining or to keep any industry from experiencing losses.

All this does not mean, however, that government should have no interest in the economic health of the minerals industries or in the terms on which users of minerals, which means all of us, can acquire them. The position is rather that the government should intervene or take positive action only if the market is functioning improperly in some way or if there are objectives we wish to attain which the unaided market will not attain. That is to say, the need for positive mineral policy arises in cases of market failure or where we have "collective" objectives. Bear in mind, however, that the mere existence of a "need" for positive policy is not by itself a sufficient justification for intervention.

### Policy Related to Efficiency

Positive mineral policy presumably designed to improve the functioning of the market takes, or might take, a number of forms. Very important among these is the provision of information by government to remedy what presumably would be a deficiency were the market left to its own devices. The two principal expressions of this aspect of policy are the economic information activities of the Bureau of Mines, some of its technical research (e.g., studies of specific mine operations and characteristics), and the topographic and geological mapping activities of the U.S. Geological Survey. In each of these cases the justification for the activity ought to have two parts: (1) the uses to which the information is put should be worth more than the cost of providing the information (and this should be true of the last $1,000 added to, say, the Bureau of Mines budget as well as of the total spent on information); and (2) private enterprise either would not develop the information, or would do so only at higher cost.

Though perhaps not usually thought of as involving a part of mineral policy, situations with so few sellers that a noncompetitive price results is another important possibility for market failure in the minerals industries, as is well known.

Nor will the market automatically take care of providing suitable conditions for the procurement of minerals from foreign countries. There are, in fact, various possibilities for government action that will improve the conditions under which U.S. companies are able to operate abroad and that will, at the same time, result in larger revenues for the host country and contribute to a greater assurance of regularity in mineral supply.

Another occasion for positive policy arises from the fact that the federal government is the owner of a very large quantity of sources of minerals. Since these properties, located in national forests, on the continental shelf, and elsewhere, are not automatically managed by the private market, the problem of administering these lands so as to secure the maximum social return from them is included here along with other cases involving a failure of the market to perform.

### POLICY FOR OTHER OBJECTIVES

National security is one of the main objectives of mineral policy, aside from economic efficiency. The supply of minerals and mineral products is one of many components contributing to our national security and must receive direct attention in policy.

A second major objective not directly encompassed in at least one version of allocative efficiency is fostering technological progress that will bring about a reduction in the costs of finding and processing minerals. In some industries, the job of fostering technological progress seems to be rather well taken care of by the firms within the industries and by activities in nonprofit institutions related to them, but in the case of every industry, and the minerals industries are no exception, we must ask whether there is some social return to be had from government actions that would advance techniques of production in these industries. The possibilities for action are numerous.

Still another objective not embraced within the idea of allocative efficiency is that of softening the blow of declines in demand for mineral products. In the view of some, there are problems here peculiar to the minerals industries by reason of the fact that some mineral-producing areas are dependent principally upon the production of minerals for their economic welfare. If the demand for a mineral declines, or perhaps a better example, if the quality of the deposits in the locality deteriorates so much in relation to prices that profitable operation is no longer possible, some argue that the blow of this decline in economic activity should be softened in some way, with benefits accruing to a mixture of the workers in the minerals industries, those in other local industries, and the owners of the enterprises of the area.

One final sphere of policy is the problem of the rate at which minerals are exploited over time. This should be regarded as a part of the problem of the rate of capital accumulation. Although these problems receive lip service attention in practical affairs, it seems fair to say that the rates of capital accumulation and mineral consumption over time are mainly the unplanned result of individual and corporate decisions on savings as influenced by a variety of policies directed at problems other than that of capital accumulation.

All policy measures will have effects on particular private interests. These effects of positive policy on different private incomes can be completely ignored only under circumstances so unusual or assumptions so special that they cannot be regarded as being universally applicable. Accordingly, policy formation must pay attention to effects on private incomes and wealth apart from public objectives, for two different reasons. On the one hand, governmental policy should not inflict serious financial injury on individuals without compensation. To say this is grossly to oversimplify a very complex problem, of course. Anticipation of possible injury is an important element here, and much will turn on the definition of *serious*. On the other hand, we must be vigilant to spot those cases where policy measures are proposed and argued for because of their supposed beneficial public effects but whose main effect will be the augmentation of private incomes and wealth in ways that do not require the rendering of service and production of equivalent value.

Particular policy measures may affect more than one of these objectives. The problem in developing mineral policy is to see whether we can conceive of actions that will improve our net position with respect to all these objectives. In some cases, actions will have effects on only one policy objective, or, if on more than one, the effects may be pretty generally in the same direction. In other cases, the promotion of one objective will require at the same time some sacrifice in the degree to which we have been able to attain another of the objectives in the list. In all these cases, the goal of research and analysis should be to identify possible changes in policy and to reveal their effects. For many measures, this will involve a calculation of the effect on social product as ordinarily measured, without reference to changes in private incomes. We have emphasized that for these types of proposed changes, analysis ought also to proceed to estimate the changes in private incomes that will follow.

In the case of objectives other than those related to the attainment of economic efficiency, research and analysis can often make an important contribution to the formation of policy by considering an array of possibilities for attaining provisionally fixed objectives. Although there is no calculus that permits us to put together in a single sum quantities of national security and the benefits flowing from a softening of the blow in the decline of demand for a mineral, we can talk about the cost of different ways of attaining, let us say, the same national security position with respect to certain specified aspects of mineral supply. If our interest is in the alleviation of human suffering, we can also talk about the cost of various ways of leaving disadvantaged people in a specified improved situation. It should never be sufficient justification for the adoption of a policy measure simply to assert that this measure serves important objectives shared by all of us. Thousands of undesirable policies do this. The problem is to select those policies which can give us a given quantity of progress toward objectives for the least possible cost.

Note that I have not made any mention of the stimulation of exploration as an objective of mineral policy. This, in and of itself, cannot be an objective of policy. If the performance of the function of exploration is unnecessarily hampered—i.e., if social costs are raised—by some factor under the control of government, then there may be a case for intervention. But there can be no thought of commending a measure just because it stimulates exploration, for to do this ignores or begs the question of the principles by which the economic system is to allocate productive services to different activities. If we apply these principles to the activity of exploration, we find that the volume of exploration activity should depend on the demand for mineral properties and the present stock of properties in relation to the supply function for mineral properties. The demand for mineral properties in turn is derived from the anticipated demand for the final mineral product. It would be undesirable to interfere with these demand and supply forces simply in order to increase the volume of exploration activity, for there is only one volume of activity that reflects a balancing of marginal costs against marginal values (prices). To stimulate a larger volume of activity involves a loss of social product. Stimulation of exploration by a subsidy would be like subsidizing the operation of sawing in a lumber mill. The obvious question is: Why stimulate one of a sequence of production operations? On the other hand, if there are institutional or other obstacles that can be shown to prevent the attainment of this volume, it is in order to begin a search for efficacious change.

To recapitulate: Positive mineral policy or change in it *may* be advisable where: (1) existing positive policy leads to misallocation or waste (unnecessary cost); (2) there is market failure (e.g., in the cases of information, government land, monopoly, external effects, conditions of operations abroad); (3) national security is involved; (4) promotion of technological progress is a problem; (5) there is local distress.

# TIME FOR STOCK-TAKING

## (*with* ALLEN V. KNEESE)

### THE ROAD WE HAVE TRAVELLED

In this last chapter we look back over the material we have covered in the context of a number of important general questions. What have we learned about economic theory that helps analyze problems in the management of natural resources? Where are the difficulties? Is economic theory of help in predicting what the future has in store for society? Can it help us to make decisions that will presumably affect future events or will we be swept along willy-nilly to unknown and perhaps terrible future states?

Our objective has been to provide an account of those parts of allocation theory that seem to be especially useful in the analysis of problems in the management of natural resources *and* which do not receive much attention in the usual courses in economic theory. The first step was a rapid review of the basic ideas of allocation theory, including the sources of market failure, this being central to the later concern with resource problems that are not wholly encompassed within private economic entities.

Substantial attention was given to the idea, and some of the basic techniques, of maximization subject to side conditions or restrictions. One of these techniques, linear programming, was given considerable

Reprinted by permission from Orris C. Herfindahl and Allen V. Kneese, *An Introduction to the Economic Theory of Resources and Environment* (Columbus, Ohio: Charles E. Merrill Publishing Co., 1974), chapter 12.

attention along with the closely related tool of input-output analysis, since these tools have and will play an important role in the empirical analysis of resource management systems. Although basic ideas are important, the reader will want to consult specialized sources to develop a certain amount of technical expertise in manipulating these tools.

Since some important natural resource problems are part of the more general problem of capital accumulation, far more space has been devoted to capital theory and related matters than in a conventional text. A simple model of capital accumulation was presented. Some of the implications of steady growth of various types were brought out. We have taken the liberty of giving considerable emphasis to our own comments on the problem of how rapidly capital should be accumulated and of how natural resources might be introduced into the problem. Two types of more specific problems involving management over time were discussed, each of them involving the economic system in interaction with a natural system. The first of these natural systems was the comparatively simple one of mineral depletion, the second was a simple example, cast in terms of a fishery, of the immensely more complicated problem of managing economic-biological systems.

In view of the tremendous importance of government investment related to natural resources, we gave detailed discussion to benefit-cost analysis, starting with basic ideas of discounting and optimizing the various features of an investment opportunity. Two basic problems were the selection of the rate of discount and the problem of multiple objectives. Here again we have not confined ourselves to a recounting of the views to be found in the literature but have discussed our own at length. In particular, we have been critical of the internal rate of return as a selection criterion, certain methods of cost allocation, and the routine inclusion of income redistributive effects as an element in project evaluation.

Various concepts in public investment theory were illustrated by applications, including "rescue" operations, flood damage control, recreation benefits, the analysis of options for managing water quality in a river basin, and inland waterways operation.

Problems of residuals management were discussed in terms of water quality management and from two points of view: one, the management of the external effects, and the other the management of the "asset" whose services are implicitly being utilized by the process of effluent discharge. The latter orientation led to the important conceptual device of the basin-wide firm. Concrete illustrations were provided by studies of water quality management in the Delaware and Potomac estuaries.

Some aspects of residuals management need to be approached comprehensively. A completely comprehensive residuals theoretical model was introduced in the form of a materials balance accounting. While the application of a complete materials balance scheme with attention to location would be extremely complex and beyond present capability, a more limited application is possible, involving only a partial materials balance and one region. A theoretical model of this type which will permit choices via linear programming was presented. A variant of this model is currently being applied to a concrete situation.*

In summary, we have found that many problems which otherwise seem capable of causing great confusion can be resolved by application of some of the most elementary and basic concepts of economics. The confusion concerning benefit-cost ratios is an example of this. On the other hand, we found as we pursued our discussion that some realistic elements of the natural resources situation were putting greater and greater strain on our usual theoretical equipment—especially the simpler versions of static or comparative static partial equilibrium theory. Problems of technological change and stochastic processes, not to speak of uncertainty of outcomes, were omnipresent. In the later stages we found it necessary to depart from the simpler partial equilibrium formulations of problems entirely in an effort to deal with the pervasive externality problems associated with residuals disposal and congestion phenomena resulting from increasingly heavy use of common property resources. While we feel that the introduction of general equilibrium theory is useful to aid understanding of these phenomena, the models we used still suffer from grave deficiencies. To a substantial extent these result from the simplifying assumptions which we made about production processes and the static character of the models.

In particular, a great deal of work needs to be done before we are in a position to assess the worth of input-output and feasible applications of the various types of programming to problems of effluent management. For example, consider the problem faced by the policy maker who would like to control a family of residuals by means of taxes imposed on their discharge. How can he discover this optimum set of taxes, taxes which ideally may vary according to effluent, location of discharge (this may imply variation by concentration of dischargers), location of those affected, and so on? One method would be experiment, with an attempt being made to estimate the net change in benefits with each small alteration in the set of prices. Clearly this

---

* See Clifford S. Russell and Walter O. Spofford, Jr., "A Quantitative Framework for Residuals Management Decisions," in Allen V. Kneese and Blair T. Bower, *Environmental Quality Analysis: Theory and Method in the Social Sciences* (Baltimore: The Johns Hopkins Press for Resources for the Future, Inc., 1972).—*Ed.*

option is out of the question since large adjustments of real capital might be involved ultimately, and these might take so much time that progress would hardly be visible. The problem must therefore be analyzed in some way to permit a search on paper for a set of prices that will at least yield a substantial improvement if not the optimum. But application of such analysis—whether by simulation, programming, or other technique—may involve such drastic simplification either because of the sheer complexity of reality or because of ignorance of relevant functions (especially damage functions) that important opportunities for economization are missed.

We have not attempted to give an account of the economics of particular resources except as seemed useful in order to provide an introduction to the application of theoretical ideas from allocation theory. In consequence, there has been no attention given to industrial organization, something that would have been essential had this been a text on the economics of the various natural resources.

### Preparation for the Long Term

By and large, the orientation of this book has been toward problems of the present and the immediate future. A number of problems, however, that involve action now will have important effects extending far into the future. How useful is our theory in the analysis of these problems?

In the most general terms, the problems of the future will involve the pressure of population on natural resources. This is also a way of characterizing the problems of the past, but the complexion of the problem has changed considerably. We shall still be faced with the possibility of increases in the cost of particular natural resource products or services—food, materials, energy—but in the future something new will have been added and is already here in some measure. Never before have problems of congestion confronted us in so ubiquitous a manner as now, and it is as certain as anything in human affairs can be that these will become far more severe in most countries within the coming decades. The other new element is effluents in such quantities and of such a nature as to impose increasing costs in deterioration of health and in destruction of natural beauty to the point of threatening changes in basic physical and biological processes on regional or global scales. The new element in the situation is not that man's activities are having region-wide effects. This has been happening everywhere human population has increased sufficiently, beginning with pastoral activities on so intensive a scale as to result in overgrazing and continuing with the clearing of forests and the extension of cultivation.

In some regions, the resulting change in the behavior of the ecosystems has been profound and costly to the people of the region. Much extension of cultivation has taken place without causing strongly adverse effects on humans—although cultivation obviously has changed the behavior of ecosystems in a fundamental way. What is new is an "unintended" flow of effluents resulting from new ways of conducting agriculture, of manufacturing, and of consuming that bring the possibility of *adverse* effects on a scale much larger than ever before. It behooves us to ask whether our intellectual constructs can contribute to understanding what may lie before us.

Economic theory has been formulated pretty much on the assumption of complete information or has incorporated certain stochastic elements only with considerable difficulty. Can it be applied to problems that involve not only stochastic elements, but that are shot through with basic uncertainties?

There is a six-way flow of substances and services between the various "environments," businesses, and households. Unfortunately, we are at this date very much in the dark as to the effects of each of these classes of flows. For example, cigarettes have been shown (obviously not with certainty) to be an agent of catastrophe for a large number of persons. How many more substances like this are we ingesting in water and food and breathing in the air? What kinds of physical and psychic difficulties will emerge in the future as the result of different types of congestion?

Alas, the unsuspected effects of our way of life are but one facet of our ignorance and uncertainty. Suppose that the *effects* were all measurable. We should like then to do something to reduce the more serious of them, but what should be done? What caused them? While there no doubt are many measures that could be taken with some considerable confidence of *their* effects, the unfortunate state of affairs is that many aspects of natural systems are so poorly understood that in many cases we should be at a loss to suggest remedial measures.

Here then is a different situation for which to devise economic theory. What constitutes economizing behavior in situations of this sort? What theoretical constructs seem to be especially useful in contexts characterized by massive uncertainties by way of directing our attention to strategic variables that we should attempt to estimate? Is the best we can do to suggest that we act in such a way as to insure against catastrophic effects? If this is the best, how do we decide that sufficient and appropriate action has been taken?

Perhaps the most serious difficulty in theorizing and trying to prescribe actions that affect the very long run is that of specifying the social welfare function. The difficulty, however, would seem to be less for the formulation of positive theory than for prescription, for any attempt to prescribe for the long pull ought to call attention to and deal with possible inconsistencies in the ruling social welfare function. These are more likely to be present in considering right action for the increasingly uncertain picture we see as our vision is directed forward in time. One of the difficulties may be viewed as revolving around two aspects of the population in the society—the identity of the persons included and the number of persons.

The reader will recall that for contemporaneous problems we urged a view that ascribed great importance to efficiency calculations based on market prices. This was done on the ground that it was possible to adjust public policy to take reasonably good account of other aspects of the social welfare function other than the benefits associated with efficient production. An individual experiences over a lifetime the results of a whole series of public decisions on many matters, made, we might imagine, in the name of efficiency, and with certain distributional consequences. These consequences will be largely offsetting, thus enabling him to find his place in the socially agreed distribution of income. Where large effects on personal income flow from a particular public decision, special attention is possible.

Unfortunately, the ideas of offsetting effects and consensus on distribution are not available in the case of members of the same society who are separated by a substantial interval of time. Offsets of effects of public decisions on particular individuals over a long period of time are not possible. What is more, the decisions in question do not constitute a set, each member of which is not very important, but rather they color and determine major features of the society at various points in time. They are of a class with the contemporaneous decisions on the income distribution aspect of the social welfare function.

What can the economic theorist do? On the one hand, he can accept the decisions made by the present society with respect to capital accumulation, present consumption and destruction of natural resources, and with respect to production and consumption activities carrying with them the possibility of future damage to natural resources as an expression of the social welfare function. In this case, his task will be to formulate theory that will facilitate the prediction of the successive states of the economy that will unfold as this social welfare function governs the society's responses to the changing stock of natural and man-made capital and to changes in the stock of knowledge.

On the other hand, if the theorist feels that there are defects in the process by which society determines courses of action having important effects on the distant future, perhaps even leading to actions that are seriously inconsistent, he may want to abandon his role as observer, point out the inconsistencies, and perhaps try to specify those aspects of the social welfare function that would be or ought to be adopted by society if the process of determination were "satisfactory."

Any attempt to summate utilities over time can be and probably should be viewed as following the latter course, since it implies a very special view of the social welfare function. The question must then be asked whether the particular manner of viewing the social welfare function is adequate from an ethical point of view or whether some other type of language might facilitate discussion.

The question of the number of people for which "we" are trying to maximize welfare is a question that involves the passage of time, since numbers can be changed only slowly. We have already discussed the conundrum of per capita utility versus total utility for the society. But suppose that problem is resolved. The proper economizing acts will depend on the size and growth of the population. Indeed, the growth of population may be one of the variables on which we can act. Here we encounter the unfortunate fact that there is no theory of population worthy of the name. All of the speculation on future population seems to be essentially an exercise in arithmetic calculation based on the inertia that is present in the rate of population growth stemming from the fact that it takes a fair number of years for people to grow to child-bearing age and pass on through it. As we pass through and beyond the influence of this inertia, the estimates become more and more speculative.

Most of the speculation about population problems has focused on the developing countries, with dispute over the role of population in economic growth. No real agreement has developed on this issue nor has the clarity of the discussion been enhanced by a persistent inter-mixing of issues concerning population *growth* and population *size*. Some have argued that population is a positive force in economic development because it permits specialization and scale economies (an issue of size). On the other hand, it is argued that rapid population growth is adverse because of the undesirable effect it has on age structure (an issue of rates of change). Large families have been considered conducive to economic development because dependency creates high motivation. One could continue to spell out issues that have been raised, but a firm conclusion one can draw from the discussion is that there is no *simple* relationship between population growth, rates of economic development, levels of per capita income, and other variables of interest to society.

To say that past attempts to add up the utilities of groups living at different times have not been very attractive does not mean we do not have obligations to those who will succeed us. It may be possible to clear the way for theorizing about such obligations by specifying a few limiting characteristics of the intergenerational social welfare function. Unfortunately, the attainment of even this modest goal is fraught with difficulty in a pluralistic society since even limited characteristics cannot be related to *agreed* fundamental philosophic positions. Indeed, one of the main difficulties here, we suspect, is that a far from negligible number of people entertain philosophical-religious positions that carry no implications whatsoever for our behavior as it might affect future generations.

Not very many are thoroughgoing individualists (in the worst sense of the word), however, and the number who are thoroughgoing "my-generationists," although not individualists, is probably similarly small. Still, there are surely many who would not dismiss as nonsensical the query: "Should we worry at all about the survival of future generations?" At the other end of the spectrum, there may even be a few whose position is implicitly rather similar to maximizing the undiscounted sum of utility of all persons existing from now on on the assumption that all have the same utility function of a specified form.

Our own entry for consideration as a modification of the social welfare function is a modest one that would be compatible with a variety of philosophic-religious positions: our actions should not be such as to foreclose the attainment of a position with respect to non-exhausting resources by future populations that is attainable by us. How limited this suggestion is can be indicated very briefly by noting that it says nothing about preserving exhausting resources nor does it say anything about the cost of attaining the position wanted. Perhaps this is merely a roundabout way of saying that doing things that foreclose return to the prior situation are to be avoided. Obviously, this notion would require considerable clarification, but we think exploration of its implications might yield something of interest.[1]

Perhaps some of the implications of this idea can be brought out by imagining ourselves to be in the shoes of those living in the future. We can then ask certain questions that they almost certainly will be asking. For example, "Do I regret that the goods and services I consume do not and cannot contain as high a material and energy content as those of the late twentieth century?" While the offhand answer of most people probably would be "yes," further reflection might well lead to a reply of "no" or "not very much." Technological progress between now and then certainly will have served to mitigate the effects

---

[1] Irreversibility has an important role in the work on conservation of S. V. Ciriacy-Wantrup. He advocates what he terms a "safe minimum standard of conservation." See his *Resource Conservation: Economics and Policies* (Berkeley: University of California Press, 1952), especially pp. 251ff.

of higher prices for energy and materials (if these have occurred, as seems likely). Just as important is the enormous flexibility with which consumers can reform their budgets so as to provide satisfying lives even with radical changes in the composition and/or level of consumption as measured in constant prices. With "adequate" food, clothing, shelter, and medical care, are high levels of materials and energy consumption necessary for a full life?

A second question might be: "Are the material 'essentials' of life limited by a population that is too large? Do I suffer from congestion because those living in the twentieth century and later failed to start limiting population?" The likely answer to this question is not nearly so clear as for the first. Even if those of the twentieth century failed to start limiting population by deliberately adopted measures, population in this country, at least, might have stopped growing because of endogenous forces. More disturbing, does the person born into a society of high congestion regret that his ancestors were so prolific or does he find himself unable to conceive that a less congested society would be more desirable?

A third question might be: "Are we poorer in services flowing from the 'environment' because of actions by the people of the twentieth century that could have been avoided, perhaps at very little cost to them? How many sources of natural beauty are gone that we might have enjoyed? Is the productivity of the land or water bodies greatly diminished?"

Note the difference between material flows and environmental flows. Maintenance of material and energy flows at high levels for a long period of time might present obstacles because of rising costs associated with the exploitation of lower grade deposits or because of difficulties associated with the disposal of residual products such as tailings and radioactive wastes. This would be likely to occur even with population held down far enough to avoid excessive congestion. In contrast, the alternative cost of maintaining environmental flows not only can be held down by a combination of population control and technological progress but may be quite small. It would seem that any theoretical approach to the problem of economizing in this situation which gave substantial weight to the well-being of those living later would end with very high valuations for actions that would avoid sacrificing environmental service flows. Let us try to put the point in another way. If we contemplate man in the future living in what in certain respects is a wasteland, it is hard to imagine that the possibility for "converting" environment into capital goods (which could be reproduced in part by recycling) could make up for the loss.

A number of specifications of at least some of the aspects of the social welfare function have been suggested. One that is enjoying considerable current attention is the "ecology ethic," a term that must have been used first by a person unacquainted with either ecology or ethics. Perhaps this point of view has something in common with Schweitzer's view of the sacredness of living things or with the concept of the Pueblo Indians and others of living in harmony with nature. The issue is posed perhaps most sharply in connection with the question of preserving endangered species. The California brown pelican is endangered by DDT, the whooping crane has been hunted almost to extinction, and the blue whale may not make it. Scientists often discuss the importance of the genetic material which might be lost for scientific research, ecological imbalances, etc. All of which may be important. But one can't help but suspect that underlying all of this is the feeling that there is something ethically wrong about man destroying a species of living things, especially among the higher life forms, whose destruction he should avoid or prevent *even if* the cost outweighs any foreseeable benefit in terms of direct human utility from the creature. While we must confess an emotional sympathy with this viewpoint, it does still leave us with an unanswered question. Presumably even the most dedicated ecologist would be unwilling to incur a great cost in human suffering to preserve an animal species with little direct utility to humans. On the other hand, if the cost of preservation were very small, presumably even the most devoted utilitarian would not wish to destroy the species for such a small gain. But the difficult questions lie in the middle ground and the ecology ethic, however attractive, seems to leave us without a criterion of choice, although it provides a partial guide.

The ecology ethic involves the idea of avoiding transition to states that can't be reversed (often termed irreversibilities), and this was true also of the suggestion we made. An important distinction can be made between the two, however. Many, if not all, supporters of the ecology ethic wish to avoid crossing these thresholds because they believe that Nature ought to survive, whether its survival is good or bad for humans. This probably would be the position held by a pantheist, for example, although no doubt many supporters of the ecology ethic are not pantheists and perhaps not theists of any sort.

Our suggestion, in contrast, viewed preservation of options as being desirable (to us) because of our concern for future humans. The question of why we should be concerned at all about humans of the future opens up even more fundamental questions which will not be discussed here.[2]

_____

[2] The reader interested in pursuing these matter further will wish to consult an

### Changing Preferences and Man's Adaptation

One of the basic assumptions which we as economists make in developing welfare economics models is that tastes and preferences are exogenously given. This effectively forecloses us from inquiring into the normative basis for the utility functions which we assume all consumers to have. Of course, economists realize that tastes are not immutable or God-given, but trying to introduce taste-formation into the corpus of economic theory would present us with complexities as yet unmeasured.

The idea behind the exogenously given tastes assumption is that fully informed consumers (the usual assumption of consumer welfare theory) will weigh off all alternative options available to them in a rational and intelligent manner. Perhaps a weaker but still possibly satisfactory version of this concept would be to assume that, even though the consumer is not fully informed, the gaps in his information are random and that he has an equal probability of becoming informed or educated about all things bearing on his welfare. Whether this assumption could be supported in fact is doubtful in view of the likelihood that there is a bias against acquiring information about and tastes for unowned and unpriced collective goods. Let us consider a specific instance. The automobile is a private good. It is in the interest of the automobile and fuel industries to cultivate a taste for new, elaborate, powerful, and expensive automobiles. These are large and economically potent industries whose advertising touches virtually every person in the country every day. It is, of course, possible that rather than more or larger cars being sold as a result of competitive advertising, the separate companies cancel each other's efforts. But it is hard to believe that all the glamour, sex symbolism, and other

---

article by Lynn White, Jr., "The Historical Roots of Our Ecologic Crisis," appearing in *Science*, Vol. 155, No. 3767, March 10, 1967, p. 1203. White asserts that the historical roots of the ecologic crisis are to be found in the anthropocentrism of Christianity, which resulted historically in man's indifference to the fate of things nonhuman and his unthinking exploitation of nature. He says that there can be no hope of solving the crisis without the diffusion of something like the spirit of St. Francis, who talked with the birds and animals. While his view of the role of Christian doctrine in the formation of attitudes toward nature no doubt has some historical validity, he does seem to neglect a major aspect of Christian (and Judaic) doctrine present from the earliest times, to wit, love thy neighbor. If love motivates us—and it surely does motivate many Christians and non-Christians alike—the perception that one's action toward nature is harming other people surely leads to the conclusion that something had better be done about the action. It appears to us that the strength and clarity of this perception are far greater now than at any time in the past, and for a very good reason. We rather clearly have it within our power to produce environmental changes on scales that did not appear to be possible before.

blandishments do not have some effect on the number and types of automobiles sold.

The other side of the coin is that the automobile is a notorious user of common property resources. It is by far the largest single source of air pollution in the United States and its rusting hulks render the landscape hideous over large areas of the country. It requires urban space to an extreme degree. Yet since everyone, and therefore no one, owns these common property resources, no one has much incentive to try to educate and propagandize the public about their value. Thus when we view taste and preference formation in a dynamic context, we find it hard to argue that there are no biases.

Another more physiological and deeply psychological way of viewing this phenomenon of taste change is the "man adapting" concept widely propounded by René Dubos. Dubos writes:

> The human saga has been the endless search for new environments; and each new move has required adaptive changes to the painful and dangerous. . . . The most a man can do is to make sure that the environmental changes he brings about do not outstrip his adaptive potentialities. . . .
>
> Some of [the] delayed and indirect consequences will naturally affect physical health and will therefore be measurable objectively. But others will be concerned with more subtle qualities of human life and will require qualitative value judgments. Because man is so adaptable, he can learn to tolerate murky skies, chemically treated waters, and lifeless land. . . .
>
> The most important values, unfortunately, are not definable in terms of specific qualities or characteristics of nature—they involve man's relation to his total environment.[3]

The essence of this thought is that while man may not on the surface be aware of any destructive effects of environmental deterioration, because his tastes adjust themselves, chronic physical and mental health problems are often the end result. If true, the implication of this for economic theory is that a consumer's choices at any moment of time cannot be taken as an expression of his best interest *as he would see it* if he knew what was happening to him. The difficulties this presents for economic welfare theory are serious.

Perhaps an even deeper question than that raised by Dubos is as follows: What if man adapts to what we would, from our present perspective, view as a badly deteriorated environment but with no manifestly harmful mental or physical effects—indeed, let us say he is very happy? This is what we might term the 1984 question.[4] We might

---

[3] René Dubos, "Air, Water, and Earth," *Looking Ahead*, Vol. 16, No. 6 (Washington: National Planning Association, September 1968).

[4] Some may already have adapted. Consider the following statement, said to have

visualize man living at very high densities, sealed off from any natural environment (because it is toxic), benignly stoned on much improved psychedelic drugs, resting on his effortless exerciser. Is there anything in a relativistic view of preferences which would provide grounds for judging such a state to be unwholesome? The answer appears to be no—but we shiver at the thought.

If good theory is to be formulated, it must be conceived with some image of the situation to which it applies. This is the main difficulty for the theorist thinking about the long run—our image of it is very hazy even with respect to its general outlines. Nevertheless, it may be worthwhile speculating a bit about the general characteristics that future development may have.

By now it should be clear to everyone that steady growth theorizing cannot possibly have more than a very partial relevance to the concrete problem of the future development of the economy and society. We have already seen how growth could conceivably come to a halt even if nature imposed no limitations whose impact would increase. The halt could result from either a consumer glut or the accumulation of a quantity of capital so great that there were no further opportunities for investment. Nor does it seem impossible that net savings might be zero before either of those limiting conditions was reached. If this did not happen, development of new opportunities for investment might be limited (not simultaneously) by a cessation of growth in the stock of technological knowledge. If the system as a whole should exhibit large diseconomies of scale, this too presumably would be reflected in the exhaustion of investment opportunities.

To many, however, it is becoming increasingly clear that limitations stemming from "nature's niggardliness" must have an important place in our thinking and probably will have a controlling influence on development long before any of the above conditions is realized. It is not so much that the cost of food may rise because of the comparatively fixed supply of agricultural land or that the cost of materials may rise because of exhaustion of good deposits. These may still turn out to be important elements in the picture, especially in some countries. In many countries, however, and even for all of them taken together, the limiting aspects of nature may first turn out to be limitations on her capacity to receive and absorb the many types of debris from human activities without serious deterioration.

One way to perceive some of the major adaptations which would have to be made is to imagine the evolution of a self-contained society. Let us assume away the problem of the intergenerational social welfare

---

been made in a smoggy state: "When you've seen one redwood tree, you've seen them all."

function by assuming that population is stable and that its members do not age or die. That is, "I" as I am now will continue. Let us suppose also that we understand the functioning of natural systems and how this is altered by various human activities.

Economizing considerations would require the gradual alteration of consumption patterns and production processes in response to pressures on natural systems as capital and output, and therefore returns to the environment, rose. The cost of newly mined mineral products very likely could be expected to rise as lower and lower grades were mined.[5] At the same time, the supply of material reclaimed from scrap would be increasing, since with a higher price it would pay to undertake the expensive collection activities required as scrap is assembled from more dispersed and scattered sources. In those cases where new production could take place from an "inexhaustible" source, such as sea water, without undue damage to the environment, there would be an upper limit to the increase in price, as noted earlier.

It might be noted that complete recycling of materials in the sense of recovering all of the materials input for reprocessing and use is impossible. Many materials are dispersed so widely in the course of use (e.g., paints, thinners, solvents, fuels and other materials converted to gases, cleaners, etc.) that collection is impossible. Even for those which appear to be of a more fixed nature, such as metals in formed shapes, the ubiquitous processes of oxidation and friction insure a partial dispersal that cannot be avoided. Also, recycling requires the input of other materials and energy, and may in fact produce its own pollutants. Thus, the optimum extent of recycling depends on the circumstances of the moment and requires a calculation of all of the relevant costs. It is likely, of course, that at the present time recycling of certain materials is below optimum because of deficiencies in the cost calculations. Some social costs are not properly reflected in decisions.

In the case of energy, the costs of the "inexhaustible" sources (breeder fission reactors and fusion) and the costs of energy from mineral sources (petroleum, coal, etc.) would be expected gradually to converge and then diverge, with energy from fossil fuel sources becoming less and less important and perhaps eventually disappearing altogether. Given our assumption of a constant population, food production certainly would pose no problem, since we should be able to do at least as well as we are doing now.

With increasing output, we would be putting greater and greater strains on the environment. As these strains developed, the idealized

---

[5] Recall that the mining of one-half percent copper ore requires the mining and grinding and disposal of a little more than twice as much barren rock as for one percent ore.

society we are considering would take steps to reduce the demands on the services of the environment. If the inventory of radioactive substances escaping to the atmosphere as the result of energy from fission rose to the danger point, effective steps would be taken to economize on this form of energy and perhaps to reduce the escape of radioactive material to the atmosphere. If pesticides finding their way to soil and water bodies threatened permanent damage, their use would be reduced. In sum, as the pressures mounted, the ideal adjustment would involve a combination of a number of measures, including adjustment of the consumer budget away from products whose production entailed dangerous or damaging effluents, and the redesign of products and processes to reduce the activities producing damaging effluents and to reduce the flow of certain effluents to places where they can produce damage. A similar readjustment would take place to reduce the impact of congestion effects.

These alterations of the consumer budget and production processes would take place in such a way as to maximize product, taking into consideration all service flows from the environment, including those not now appropriated, whether those flows go directly to enterprises or to individuals. We would have made a rational sacrifice in the "quality of the environment" up to the point where this sacrifice was balanced by satisfactions from the extra flow of *particular* types of goods made possible by this sacrifice.

It is likely that it would take a very long time before this society would approach a "steady state" very closely, but it would be highly likely that the primary production of *certain* substances would be greatly curtailed or even eliminated. These curtailments could easily be so important or so pervasive as to require large changes in consumption patterns and production methods, but even with these the general style of life might be similar to that of the present. Perhaps the factors most likely to result in great change would be the possible need to restrict the production of atomic electric power (presumably from breeder reactors) in order to control the stock of dispersed radioactive material in the atmosphere and on the surface of the earth and in water bodies, or local and regional heat disposal problems arising from the large consumption of energy.

If the assumption of a constant population is abandoned, even the most general outlines of the future are greatly obscured. The inertia inherent in the present age distribution of this country's population would insure continued growth for several decades to come even if the net reproduction rate were to drop to maintenance level tomorrow (an average of a little more than two babies during a lifetime for each female born). While it appears to us that our institutions function well enough to cope with our growing difficulties even if population continues to grow for some time, failure to curb this growth rather soon would subject our system to increasing strains since the need for radical readjustments in certain directions would be more likely. The age distribution of a stable population would be quite different from the present and past distributions in this and many other countries, however, and these also would require important changes in many aspects of economic and social life.

In the United States, the natural increase in population from 1968 to 1969 was about 0.8 percent per year. Net civilian immigration added another 0.2 percent, giving a total increase of about 1.0 percent. If the decline in the net reproduction rate from about 1.7 in 1960 to about 1.1 a decade later should continue (where 1.0 would indicate age-specific fertility rates which, if continued, would eventually stabilize the population), U.S. population could stabilize in several decades or perhaps even decline, not because of any act of positive control but simply because of the unfolding of the determining forces.

The picture is entirely different for the world as a whole, and especially so for the less developed countries. After making estimates of future birth and death rates, the United Nations concludes that world population will almost double between 1969 and 2000, with the rate of growth being about 2.2 percent per year in the less developed countries as against 1.0 percent for the developed countries. The ratio of the populations in the less developed countries to those of the developed is estimated to be 10:3 in 2000. And if governments do not attain positive control over population growth by that time and growth still continues, the disparities and the pressures on available resources will continue to mount until finally growth is brought to a grinding halt by increases in death rates.

In the face of the uncertainty surrounding population growth, economic theory could proceed to analyze problems of capital accumulation and resource degradation on the basis of various assumed patterns of population growth. This of course is what has been done in the past, with population growth usually assumed to be a constant, including zero growth, a popular assumption. We should like to be able to put the theory to work, however. But how does a catalogue of paths and outcomes help if there is no way to make an effective choice of any particular one? It would be very useful, of course, to have a theory of population growth that would in fact enable prediction, a theory that indicated the important variables involved, and thereby would permit the elaboration of various possibilities for control.

Control of population may be possible, however, without having a complete theory of population growth at hand. Although it may be impossible to predict what would happen to population in the absence of deliberate societal control measures, control measures are available which may be sufficient to limit growth. Whether positive control in the sense of being able to move population up or down as wished is achievable is far from certain.

Here we encounter the need to inquire into the formation of societal consensus. If this is strong enough, methods adequate to the task probably could be put into effect. But will society do so? Does today's society really care if it and the immediately following generations build up a population inertia that in turn will result in a path for society that will be very painful for later generations? Certainly the economist is under an obligation to try to make sure that present society is aware of the likely future results of its present actions bearing on population growth. Thus the catalogue of possible paths is of some use after all!

In elaborating these possibilities, it probably would be useful to experiment with more specific forms of the social welfare function, partly to make ethical implications more explicit. One possible modification, already hinted at in earlier pages, would be to abandon the monotonic relation between welfare and goods, perhaps thinking of the same level of welfare as attainable with widely different quantities of goods and services, provided certain specific minimum requirements are met. Another modification involves the "environment." At the conceptual level, service flows from the environment to households are an element of welfare and of course the service flows from the environment to businesses also affect welfare indirectly. Finally, it would seem that the conundrum of whether to maximize per capita utility or total societal utility might be resolved by including population itself or its derivative effects in the welfare function.

An even more difficult puzzle is how to incorporate the people of other societies, present and future, into the analysis. While a social welfare function can be conceived that incorporates them, the possibility of specifying a function on which there might be agreement among the different societies seems even more remote than for a single society.

Another possible route for analysis in the face of this difficulty would be that of international trade theory. The new element in the analysis would be real external diseconomies among the traders (nations). This factor would extend the range of outcomes considerably. Differences among the social welfare functions of the various societies, especially with respect to their views on future generations, would be an important element in determining the range of outcomes. For example, certain types of national behavior could bring all systems to a halt rather than merely altering the terms of trade, as in the usual analysis.

### Envoi

Economic theory is unique among social science theories. Its strength arises from its strong devotion to the concept of an interdependent system and from the effort to be reasonably precise in formulation. As a result of these features the theory has a built-in tendency to consider alternatives and tradeoffs and has yielded useful theorems and hypotheses. Finally, the relatively rigorous formulation of the theory has made it comparatively easy for economists to explain it to other scientists and to work in interdisciplinary relationships with them.

Thus our criticisms and reservations are far from a call to abandon the inherited body of theory or to try to make discontinuous jumps to other formulations. Rather, it is to be hoped that economists and other scientists will be moved to build on the theory, to extend it, to improve it, and to make it an even more useful tool than it now is for decision making in the interest of society.

# PART TWO

*Natural Resources Supply and Conservation*

SELECTION 4

# SOME FUNDAMENTALS OF

# MINERAL ECONOMICS

It is the purpose of this paper to provide a simple account of some processes involved in the economics of exhausting assets, especially an account of exploration. The resulting analytic framework should be helpful in evaluating recent suggestions on materials policy and also in thinking about currently pressing problems flowing from widely advertised "shortages" of certain minerals.

Some of the elements involved in the exploration process have been discussed in two of the leading articles in this field, but they leave the role played by exploration essentially untouched. The elementary economics of the mining firm was given a very satisfactory exposition in 1913 by L. C. Gray.[1] Eighteen years later, Hotelling analyzed competitive and various non-competitive situations in exhausting assets, but his work involved the assumption that it is known that all deposits of the mineral have been found.[2] A description of the exploration process requires examination of the mineral industry as well as the firm and introduction of the assumption that more mineral deposits can be found at some cost. We shall proceed by discussing first the

Reprinted by permission from *Land Economics*, Vol. 31 (May 1955), pp. 131–138.

[1] L. C. Gray, "Rent under the Assumption of Exhaustibility," *Quarterly Journal of Economics*, Vol. 28, 1913–14, pp. 466–89.

[2] H. Hotelling, "The Economics of Exhaustible Resources," *Journal of Political Economy*, April 1931, pp. 137–75.

competitive minerals firm, following Gray, and then the competitive minerals industry. The analysis will be applied to a problem in mineral taxation and to some exploration data for petroleum.

### THE COMPETITIVE MINE

The competitive mine operator is faced with the problem of determining how rapidly to extract a mineral from the ground. In the discussion of this problem it is assumed that (1) the anticipated price of ore is constant, (2) the ore is of uniform quality, (3) the contents of the mine are known to the operator, and (4) marginal cost in any given year and the corresponding average variable cost are a function only of the rate of output in that year. The investment in mining equipment is assumed to have been made, and marginal cost, as here used, contains no element of revenue foregone by producing a unit of output in one period rather than another. The resulting quasi-rent goes to cover the cost of reproducible mining equipment and the investment in the mineral deposit. For other purposes more elaborate assumptions might be desirable; for example, making marginal cost in any period dependent in some way on the set of outputs over the life of the mine or on the cumulated output from the mine. The simple assumptions used here will serve well enough, however, to illustrate the problem confronting the mine operator.

To choose the mine's output schedule, each period's marginal net return (price minus marginal cost), in dollars of present value, must be compared with the marginal net returns of the other periods. It is immediately evident that it is necessary that the marginal net return be the same in every year of the mine's life, for otherwise profits could be increased by shifting output from one year to another. Comparison of the present values of marginal net returns will be facilitated by the diagrams in figure 1 showing demand and cost curves for successive years of the mine's operation.

In figure 1, price is assumed to remain at six dollars and all dollar values are measured from this level. Hence the zero on the vertical scale corresponds to a level of six dollars. There is no discount factor applied to year one, but in year two the line from which cost is measured (in present value) is moved up so that the distance to the line indicating price is equal to $\$6/(1+r)$, where $r$ is the rate of discount. In the diagram a discount rate of thirty percent has been used to make its effect easily visible. Costs in year three are similarly discounted and are measured from the third abscissa. Thus the cost curves flatten out and move up for more distant years, but any portion of a cost curve below the price line in year one will also be below it in any later year.

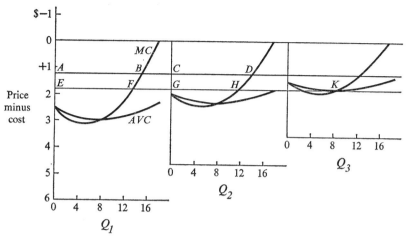

FIGURE 1. *Price minus cost measured in present value.*

This representation is equivalent to plotting the present value of price minus cost for successive years, as is indicated by the label for the vertical axis. For every year, equal vertical distances represent the same number of present dollars.

To illustrate the equating of marginal net returns in the years of the mine's operation, suppose, first, that the length of the period over which the mine is to be operated is dictated by a wise government (hypothetical) and is set at two years, with the further requirement that the mine be operated at a uniform rate of output throughout any single year. With the present value of the difference between price and marginal cost the same in each year, that level of (P—MC) is selected which will enable the contents of the mine to be extracted within the dictated period.[3] If the contents of the mine are twenty-nine units, the operator selects outputs of approximately fifteen units (AB) for the first year and fourteen units (CD) for the second year. Any shift of outputs will reduce profits, as is evident on inspection of the diagram.

If the directive is changed to permit any length of life for the mine, the operator must decide whether it is profitable to extend the life of the mine by transferring output from earlier to later years. In the example, he will transfer output from years one and two to year three

---

[3] If the contents of the mine are large enough, this condition may involve operation at outputs with marginal cost greater than price. If the mine operator is required to exhaust the contents in two years, he will operate at these outputs, with the second year output greater than the first; but, if the government permits him to abandon part of the mine's contents, he will produce equal outputs in the two years with marginal cost equal to price.

in such a way as to leave the present values of marginal net revenue equal for the first two years. The net revenue loss on units transferred from the earlier years is approximately equal to the change in output times marginal net revenue. The net revenue gain from the additional output of the third year is equal to output transferred times price minus minimum average variable cost. In the example this minimum is attained at an annual output rate of eight. He may, of course, operate at this rate for only a part of the third year.

So long as maximum average net revenue in year three is greater than marginal net revenue in the first two years, it will pay him to transfer more output to the third year. In the present example the finish of this adjustment process is indicated by line EK. The present value of the marginal net revenue in each year is equal to the maximum average net revenue in the last year of operation, with outputs in the three years of approximately 13.5 units (EF), 11.7 units (GH), and 3.9 units. The output of 3.9 units in the third year is produced in a little less than half a year at an annual rate of eight units. It would not pay to transfer any output to the fourth year unless the contents of the mine were somewhat greater than 33.2 units ($=13.5+11.7+8$), that is, unless the present value of marginal net revenue, adjusted to a three-year plan of operation, is less than the present value of maximum average net revenue in the fourth year.

### THE LONG RUN: CONSTANT COST OF EXPLORATION

The preceding section has not involved the problem of adjustment in the number of mines. The possibility of finding new properties by exploration makes the analysis of this problem for the exhausting resource quite similar to that of industries using only reproducible assets. It is only at a late stage in the history of an exhausting resource that the problem takes on peculiarities that distinguish it from the case of reproducible assets.

The first long-run case to be considered is the simple one in which the quality of ore discovered remains constant, on the average, and the average cost of discovering a ton of metal (or ore) remains constant. It is immediately evident that the long-run equilibrium, after proper imputation of returns, will be characterized by zero profits for the industry in both exploration and mining. The "profits," or rent, on the deposits discovered will be entirely consumed by the cost of exploration. If true profits do appear for the industry as the result of an increase in, say, demand, exploration activity will increase, resulting in a larger stock of known properties. Since no property will be held idle if the industry is competitive (unless costs are too high for properly defined variable costs to be covered), current output will increase, the price of metal and ore will decrease to the original level, and exploration activity will then decrease, but not to its original level.

From this simple schema it is evident that the stock of known properties is not a matter of happenstance but is determinate and governed by economic forces. Proximately, the stock of properties in long-run equilibrium is related to the output of the industry and the rates at which properties are exploited. The governor that brings about changes in the stock of properties is profits after allowing for exploration costs.

The principal variables lying behind the industry's rate of output and the rate of property exploitation are the following:

1. *Demand.* If demand increases, price goes up, producing profits and an increase in exploration activity. The stock of properties is increased, current output increases, and the price of ore declines to its original level. The stock remains greater, industry output is higher, as is also the volume of exploration activity in order to maintain the larger stock of properties.

2. *Cost of exploration.* If the cost of exploration declines, profits appear in exploration. Exploration activity increases the stock of properties, and the prices of metal and ore decline in response to a greater output of ore and metal until, on the average, profits from exploration are zero. The stock of properties is permanently larger, as is also the rate of exploration.

3. *Economics of scale in mining.* The larger the output at which diseconomies of scale appear in mining, the more rapid will be the rate at which a particular property will be exploited, and the lower will be the supply price for ore.

4. *The rate of discount.* The higher is the rate of discount, the more rapid is the rate of exploitation, and the higher will be the supply price for ore.

5. *The average size of property.* If the typical mining operation incurs increasing costs after a certain output if it increases output per year, an increase in average size of deposit will lead to an extension of mine life and an increase in the supply price of ore. With a larger size deposit the mine operator could keep the same mine life, but he can escape some of the diseconomies of scale by extending mine life and increasing his annual outputs by a smaller quantity than if life was left unchanged.

The above five factors are the principal ones affecting the industry's rate of output and the rate of property exploitation. This is not a complete catalogue, and an analysis of the factors considered here could easily be quite complex, but at the least it should be clear that the stock of known properties is a determinate result of demand and cost conditions in exploration and mining.

### THE LONG RUN: RISING COST OF EXPLORATION

On the assumption that the cost of exploration rises with the cumulated discoveries of the industry, we now examine relations among cost of exploration, price of ore, rate of exploration, and the stock of properties, following the course of the mineral industry to the end of its life.

Changes in the number of mines are brought about by the presence of profits or losses in exploration, that is, by the difference between the value of a typical known property and the cost of discovery. The present price of ore and the cost of mining together with prices and costs anticipated over the life of a mine determine the present value of a typical deposit of ore in the ground, and the difference between this value and the cost of discovering a typical deposit determines the direction that will be taken by the volume of exploration activity, with the usual short- and long-run adjustments when the output of the exploration industry changes.

With a shift from constant to rising cost of exploration, the life of a mine will be lengthened, and the stock of properties will decrease with further rises in price. The stock of properties will decrease because a negatively sloped industry demand curve and a rising cost of exploration will result in losses if the stock is not diminished. At all times the quantity of ore coming on the market in any year will be equal to the quantity of ore discovered plus the decline in the stock of properties and, when the system is moving along in equilibrium, the value of known deposits will be rising, the discovery rate and the stock of properties will be declining with the quantity of ore placed on the market, resulting in a price that fulfills price expectations in the sense that the value of ore in ground moves up with the cost of exploration. While the price of ore in ground moves up with the cost of exploration, the rate at which the cost of exploration rises depends on the cumulated discoveries of the industry, which in turn depend on the rate at which price rises. This interrelationship may be clarified by considering what would happen if further discovery is impossible.[4]

If further discovery is impossible, the price of ore in ground will rise at a rate equal to the rate of discount. If it were anticipated that price would rise faster than this, properties would be withheld from current production to take advantage of the higher future prices and vice versa.

<hr />

[4] This is the case that was examined by Hotelling in 1931.

With price rising each year by the rate of discount, the time at which a property is exploited would be a matter of indifference for any single operator. The date of complete exhaustion of all reserves will depend on the complete demand curve.

Suppose next that further discovery is possible, but only with rapidly rising exploration cost. Under these circumstances, the bulk of current supply will come from reduced stock, but exploration will take place as price moves up, preventing price from rising as rapidly as the rate of discount but with exploration still not in sufficient volume to maintain the stock of properties. Exploration will continue, at higher and higher cost, until price finally gets so high that nothing is purchased, and the "day of judgment" for this mineral will have been reached. The mineral will almost surely not be completely exhausted but, given demand, it simply will not pay to continue looking for it.

The above discussion has proceeded on the assumption that the economy in question is isolated. If this is not the case and the mineral can be imported, the situation is quite analogous to the domestic case where different producing regions are involved, a problem that has been avoided in this discussion by the implicit assumption of a uniform average cost of exploration throughout the country. With this restriction removed, the regulator of exploration activity in each region or country is still the gap between average price of ore in ground (price of metal less smelting and mining cost) and the cost of exploration. In equilibrium, cost of exploration, though not necessarily the same in each region because of transportation and other cost elements, will move up by the same amount in all regions as time progresses, although regional differences in the behavior of the exploration cost functions may produce shifts in the relative quantities supplied by the different regions. If a new producing region is discovered, there are two effects as its output increases: the price of metal is pushed down, though very little if the region is unimportant relative to total supply, and the cost of exploration in the new region rises until it is "equated" with the cost of exploration elsewhere, that is, until there is no gap between price of ore in ground and cost of exploration in the region. Finally, mention should be made of the influence of scrap recovery. The effect of the scrap component of supply is to reduce the demand for primary metal. The supply curve for metal from scrap will depend on the stock of metal in use, its age distribution—though this is not of much importance for the long-run problem—the scrap rate, and collection and processing costs. In those cases where irretrievable losses in use are low, scrap can act as a powerful factor to cut down the rate at which reserves in the earth are exploited. This is obviously not true for fuels, but the recovery rate is significant for many metals.

The preceding discussion has covered only the competitive firm and industry. In addition to the non-competitive situations, there are many factors that have not been considered, two of which are mentioned here. First, technological development at the several levels of production can stave off long-run difficulties and, for considerable periods of time, actually overcome them. Second, the analysis has proceeded as if metals are independent in production. This is not true in many cases. Copper, lead, zinc, gold, and silver, for example, are often associated in various combinations in the same ore. Because of association of metals in ores and also because an explorer is often uncertain of what ore he will find, exploration activity is also likely to involve more than one metal and more than one type of ore. Some of the modifications necessitated by these factors are clear enough. Others would require much development. A simple account of the exploration process has been presented here, however, in the belief that it will be of some service in the consideration of minerals problems.

## An Application of the Analysis

One of the important problems to which the preceding discussion of the exploration process can usefully be applied is capital recovery in the minerals industries for tax purposes. In the case of reproducible assets, the basis for capital recovery under federal income tax law is the cost of the asset. If the tax laws are to leave investment in minerals industries just as attractive as in other industries, neglecting the problem of risk aversion or preference, what should be the capital recovery provisions for minerals?

The statement is often made that since a miner is using up his capital with every ton of ore taken from the ground, he must be allowed to deduct the value of the ore mined (presumably value in ground) as an expense if he is to have adequate funds to acquire another deposit and continue operation. If this is permitted, however, investment in minerals will be favored over investment in other industries. If the minerals industries are in long-run equilibrium, it is true that capital recovery equal to value of mineral in ground would provide a sum equal to the cost of finding the properties. There are difficulties, however, resulting from the fact that some firms spend money on exploration without results. If they are permitted to deduct these expenditures, as they should be, and at the same time the successful firms are permitted deductions equal to the value of known mineral in ground, the total deductions allowed the industry will be greater than the expenditures incurred in finding the properties, contrary to the practice for other industries where deductions may not exceed the cost of acquiring the property. To put it simply, the lucky firms should not be permitted to make capital recovery deductions for capital invested by the unlucky firms, which is what they would be doing if they deducted the full value of the ore they mine rather than the cost incurred in finding it. If the firms are restricted to deduction of actual costs incurred, as they should be, deductions will not be sufficient to provide for replacement of each property when the cost of exploration is rising. This is, of course, a desirable result.

The writer hastens to add that market value of ore versus cost as the basis for capital recovery is not a live issue in the politics of mineral taxation. Actual deductions go far beyond either standard. The problem has a measure of current interest, however, because the assertion that market value is the correct basis for capital recovery is sometimes used, illogically, to support the percentage depletion system.[5]

### EXPLORATION FOR PETROLEUM

It may be objected that the hypothesis under consideration, that the volume of exploration activity depends on the anticipated profit from exploration, cannot adequately describe the operation of minerals industries, because exploration is so uncertain an activity that it will not respond systematically to changes in profit. It is the purpose of this section to see whether exploration for petroleum responds to variables that may be taken to represent changes in average expected profit. Oil is selected for examination because some relevant data are available over a long period of time, especially a measure of exploration activity.

The mere existence of exploration activity that is unrelated to expected profit is not sufficient to invalidate the hypothesis that the volume of exploration depends on expected profit. Although some or even a large amount of exploration may take place in ignorance of profit prospects or because of risk attraction, activity that is geared to profit may still dominate the behavior of the total volume of exploration.

The annual number of wells drilled in the United States is used as a measure of petroleum exploration activity.[6] The deflated price of

---

[5] The time pattern of deductions for depletion can usefully be regarded as a separate issue from the problem of the total amount of deductions allowable over the life of the property.

[6] *Petroleum Facts and Figures, 1950* (New York: American Petroleum Institute), p. 121. This series embraces dry holes and all successful oil wells, including development wells and gas wells. Service wells are excluded. Some writers would probably wish to exclude development wells (those drilled within one mile of a producing well) leaving only the exploration wells. Although the probability of

crude oil [7] and deflated private final product [8] will be used as indicators of anticipated profit. The data cover the period from 1909 to 1949, with 1917–18 and 1942–45 omitted because the variables were not free to move in their usual fashion in these years. All variables are expressed in deviations from trend rather than in absolute values.[9]

Trends have been eliminated to prevent them from dominating short-term changes in the variables. The long-term changes in these and related variables are, of course, of great interest. The wells-drilled series has a substantial upward trend over the forty-year period, the trend value increasing from eighteen thousand in 1909 to thirty thousand in 1949, an increase of two-thirds. The deflated price of crude, with sizable fluctuations, has very little trend over this period, with a 15 percent increase from $1.25 per barrel to $1.43 (deflated price). At the same time, the increase in crude production was enormous. The 1949 trend value of 1.90 billion barrels was eleven times the 0.17 billion barrels produced in 1909. The much smaller increase in wells drilled is the result of declines in two ratios, the ratio of reserves to annual production and the number of wells drilled per unit of discoveries and new developments. Both of these series declined during the first half of the period from 1909 to 1949 and were roughly constant in the last half. The ratio of reserves to annual production fell from about twenty-two to around thirteen. Thousands of wells drilled per billion barrels of discoveries and new developments fell from roughly forty to around eleven.[10] The changes in these two ratios are probably to be accounted for mainly by technological developments in search, drilling, and production.

With trends eliminated, the following correlation results are obtained:

$X_1$ Wells drilled (deviations from trend)
$X_2$ Deflated price of crude (deviations from trend)

---

success is quite different, both types are open to the influence of changes in anticipated profit, and both types of drilling result in the verification of deposits whose presence was suspected but not known with certainty.

[7] Ibid., p. 121. The price of crude was deflated by the B.L.S. wholesale price index.

[8] Deflated gross private product for 1929 to 1949 was extended back to 1909 by a deflated net private product series. The deflated gross private product series is from p. 146, *1951 National Income Supplement* to the *Survey of Current Business*. The deflated net private product series is taken from p. 544 of A. G. Hart's *Money, Debt, and Economic Activity*.

[9] A linear trend was eliminated from the wells-drilled and price series. Deflated private product was expressed in deviations from a linear logarithmic trend.

[10] The data from which the two ratios have been calculated are from *Petroleum Facts and Figures, 1950*, pp. 121 and 182.

$X_3$ Deflated private product (deviations from trend)

| | | | | | |
|---|---|---|---|---|---|
| $r_{12}$ | .70 | $r_{13}$ | .56 | $r_{23}$ | .06 |
| $r_{12 \cdot 3}$ | .81 | $r_{13 \cdot 2}$ | .73 | $R_{1 \cdot 23}$ | .87 |

Both the price of crude and private product contribute substantially to explaining the variation in wells drilled. The price of crude plays an obvious role as an indicator of anticipated profit, but the interpretation of private product is less clear. It might be viewed as an indicator of shift in the demand curve or may indicate a combination of availability of funds, the elusive element of confidence, and estimates of shifts in the demand curve.

A check on these results is possible for the period after World War I by using profits after taxes in the crude oil and natural gas industry as an indicator of anticipated profit from petroleum exploration.[11] The variables considered here for the years 1919–41 and 1946–49 are as follows:

$X_1$ Wells drilled (deviations from trend previously calculated)
$X_3$ Deflated private product (logarithmic deviations from trend previously calculated)
$X_4$ Deflated profits (deviations from linear trend)

The simple correlation between wells drilled and profits after taxes is moderately high ($r_{14} = .74$). The partial influence of private GNP with the influence of profits "eliminated" ($r_{13 \cdot 4} = .45$) is much lower than it was with the price of crude as the third variable ($r_{13 \cdot 2}$ was .73). Consequently the multiple coefficient, $R_{1 \cdot 34} = .80$, is not much higher than the simple correlation between wells drilled and profits after tax ($r_{14} = .74$). Profits, a most reasonable indicator of anticipated profit, do appear to play an important role in explaining the variation in wells drilled.

These data as well as those for the longer period from 1909 to 1949 do not suggest that all exploration for petroleum is systematic but only that the systematic portion is large enough to dominate the behavior of total wells drilled.

The hypothesis that exploration responds to anticipated average

---

[11] The profits series is taken from *Statistics of Income* and is deflated by the B.L.S. wholesale price index. After 1937 the Bureau of Internal Revenue has separated field services from the oil and gas industry, but I have included field services over the whole period. For the present purpose this industry and some others should be excluded from the profits series, but the difficulties in doing so are very great. The series suffers from another defect in that the capital recovery deductions allowable for tax purposes are not closely related to deductions that are relevant to determining the profitability of crude oil production for the purpose of investment.

profits has here been applied only to petroleum. Unfortunately, measures of exploration activity are not yet available for other minerals. If such measures become available, it is the writer's view that exploration for these minerals will be found to be systematically related to variables reflecting anticipated profit. The joint product aspect of mineral exploration and production will considerably complicate matters, of course.

The contrary hypothesis, that exploration in total is not systematically related to profits, is not attractive for either petroleum or other minerals. The important condition necessary to attract "rationally" managed funds to exploration is that the dispersion in the success attending the repeated investment of a given sum of money not be too high. There are two reasons for believing that this condition is widely met. If by exploration is meant an attempt to get additional information on the presence or absence of a mineral deposit, then much of it is not a matter of search in unknown areas with a low expectation and high dispersion of success for repeated efforts of limited size, but rests instead on relatively good prior knowledge and a fairly high expectation of success. This view seems reasonable because so much exploration activity apparently is based on contiguity and extension.

From the viewpoint of the investor, another source of stability in the success of investment is the availability of devices for spreading risk, such as the corporation. This factor is independent of the preceding one and can operate even though the expectation of success for exploration efforts of small size is very low and the dispersion of results is high. In this way the problematical success of limited exploration operations can be overcome, with the investor remaining exposed to much the same kinds of uncertainty that accompany investment in firms outside the minerals industries.

# SELECTION 5

# *WHAT IS CONSERVATION?*

A discussion between two conservationists who are interested in conserving different things often degenerates into polite name calling or worse. Smith will tell Jones that he doesn't know what *true* conservation is. And Jones will reply acidly that what Smith proposes—far from being conservation—is profligate waste. Finally the discussion ends from boredom or exhaustion, with each conservationist walking away shaking his head and saying to himself that he doesn't see how anyone could hold such inane views. The outsider viewing this fruitless exchange is puzzled. If both parties are for conservation, which everybody seems to think is a good thing, what are they quarreling about?

One of the difficulties is that the word "conservation" is used with varying meanings, often without telling the other party to the discussion what one's own definition is. But the confusion is not simply a matter of failing to let the other fellow in on one's private definition, for many users of this term seem to have no clear definition of their own and seem to prefer the ambiguity that results.

The imprecision surrounding use of the word "conservation" has been associated with widespread attempts to appropriate its persuasive sound for special interests. If a certain proposal is labeled a conservation proposal, or to go even further, if the proposal is said to represent *true* conservation—implying that there is a subtle but compelling case

Reprinted from *Three Studies in Minerals Economics* (Washington, D.C.: Resources for the Future, Inc., 1961).

for its adoption—there is probably a tendency for more favorable reaction than if a less emotive term is used. After all, if a person is asked whether it is better to conserve or not conserve, he no doubt will vote for conservation. Of course it would be unthinking of him to vote at all since he didn't ask the questioner what meaning was to be given to conservation, but the point is that the mere mention of the word tends to stimulate favorable response rather than a search for meaning.

The confusion surrounding use of the term "conservation" and the attempt to appropriate favorable reaction to it for special interest proposals and programs is readily apparent to even the most cursory examination. It is an interesting exercise to go over speeches or writings on conservation matters and to ask what definition of conservation the person might have had in mind. Quite often it turns out that he believes his policy should be adopted *because* it will conserve (that is, save for future use or preserve for use) a *particular* resource product, for example, water for irrigation. But confusion arises when the city dweller insists that the water should go to the city for drinking, cooling, etc., because *that* is really conservation.

Sometimes general definitions are given. A widely favored one is the following: "Conservation is the use of natural resources for the greatest good of the greatest number for the longest time." This is the definition that Gifford Pinchot, the founder of what historians are wont to call the Conservation Movement, was fond of using. Pinchot credits the definition to W J McGee (who insisted on no periods after the initials), a freewheeling intellect of very wide interests and great ability who worked with John Wesley Powell and later with Pinchot.[1]

When this definition is read off rapidly—conservation is the use of natural resources for the greatest good of the greatest number for the longest time—the three superlatives have a delightful ring. If this is conservation, how could anyone be opposed to it? No one could be, of course, unless he stops to ask himself how three variables can be maximized at the same time. Imagine a father trying to distribute a bag of candy to his children so as to maximize the amount of candy received by each child who gets candy *and* the number of children receiving candy *and* the length of time the candy will be visible.

Still another general formulation has enjoyed great popularity with politicians for over half a century, and with others whose audiences are of opposing minds. Again let us take Pinchot's formulation, which may have been fathered by him: "Conservation implies both the development and the protection of resources, the one as much as the

---

[1] Gifford Pinchot, *Breaking New Ground* (New York: Harcourt, Brace and Co., 1947), p. 326.

other. . . ." [2] On the surface, this should command general assent, for who among us is opposed to development? Who is opposed to the protection of resources? The trouble comes when the blanks are filled in. Suppose that development means covering a canyon with a lake for purposes of power and irrigation while preservation means leaving the canyon alone so that its beauty can be seen. An excellent example is provided by the Echo Park controversy. It was indeed impossible both to develop the dam site and at the same time preserve one of the products of this natural resource, namely, the beauty of Echo Park and the nearby canyons. Unfortunately, a verbal incantation that reconciles the irreconcilable does not in fact resolve the very real conflict between development and preservation. There is no inconsistency between development and preservation, however, if one's objective is the "conservation" of only one of the uses of the resource.

In the case of mineral resources, the stock of which is used up in the act of consumption—perhaps with some recirculation—the injunction to develop and preserve simultaneously is even more mystifying than it was in the preceding case. Development in the case of minerals means production, but preservation presumably means postponement of consumption. How can both be done simultaneously except by accumulating an ever larger inventory of metal above the ground?

Pinchot's casual approach to the problem of definition is even further illustrated on the same page where we are admonished both to develop and to preserve. For example, "The essence of conservation is the application of common sense to the common problems for the common good." Or, "Conservation is simple, obvious, and right." Comment would be superfluous.

Slackness and confusion in definition, so clearly exemplified in the writings of Pinchot and his contemporaries, have continued down to the present. It is only the exceptional writer on conservation whose use of the word is not self-contradictory or a mere camouflage, whether deliberate or not, for the promotion of some special interest such as special wilderness areas, irrigation, power, and so on. The definitions of Pinchot's time, perhaps better called slogans, have been repeated ever since. "The greatest good for the greatest number for the longest time" will be with us for a long time to come. And almost any speech on natural resources coming out of the Department of the Interior contains the contradictory admonitions to develop and to preserve within the same sentence.

What is the origin of this confusion in definition? Why has it con-

---

[2] *Proceedings of the Joint Conservation Conference,* Sen. Doc., 60th Cong., 2nd Session, Vol. 10, p. 123.

tinued for so long? In my view this indifference to clarity of definition rests in considerable part on the existence of deep underlying conflicts among various interest groups in the area of conservation policy, by which I mean the policy problems involved in determining how natural resources are to be used. Proponents of special conservation interests, in their zeal to alter governmental policy, have made clarity and consistency of definition a secondary consideration. Indeed, clear definition might lose all the advantage to be gained from using so fine sounding a word as "conservation" or the related "develop and preserve." Clarity about real intentions might unnecessarily antagonize those who otherwise would not press home to the real meaning behind generalities.

Certainly one of the dominant conflicts in the field of conservation was and is the conflict between development and what I shall call nature preservation. By "development" is meant the use of natural resources in such a way as to involve the construction of auxiliary capital goods such as dams, roads, processing plants, hotels, etc. "Nature preservation" is a term which embraces the whole spectrum of groups interested in preserving various aspects of nature as she is (Or is it with some "development"?) for the direct enjoyment of individuals. Such diverse things are involved as birds (to be preserved for eye, ear, and palate), solitude, scenery, trees, flowing water, naturally still water (that is, natural lakes), etc. This is sometimes said to constitute the birds and bees school of conservation, a phrase that can be uttered with a tone of either affection or derision, depending on whether one is in or out of the group.

The antagonism between development and nature preservation has always been present in the field of conservation. Even the founder of the movement in the United States, Gifford Pinchot, was not disposed to ride both these horses at the same time. It is quite clear on reading his writings that he was a developmentalist first and a preservationist only secondarily, if at all.

For example, in 1903 Pinchot made the following statement in an address to the Society of American Foresters: "The object of our forest policy is not to preserve the forests because they are beautiful . . . or because they are refuges for the wild creatures of the wilderness . . . but . . . the making of prosperous homes. . . . Every other consideration comes as secondary." [3] It is not surprising that the nature preservationist groups became increasingly dissatisfied with Pinchot's views on what conservationists should be doing, and that they came to feel he

---

[3] Quoted in Samuel P. Hays, *Conservation and the Gospel of Efficiency* (Cambridge: Harvard, 1959), p. 41.

was using the Conservation Movement to promote policies to which they were strongly opposed. This divergence in points of view was an important factor in bringing about the disintegration of the Conservation Movement.[4]

The conflict between development and nature preservation has erupted from time to time in pitched battles. For example, New York's constitutional provision requiring the Adirondack State Park lands to be kept "forever wild"—that is, with no lumbering—was the subject of intense controversy in the constitutional revisions of 1895 and 1915, and there are always attempts to nibble away at it. Most recently the nature preservationists tilted with developmentalists who wanted a thruway constructed to pass through the eastern part of the Park. This controversy is especially interesting for our purposes because it also provided an example of the conflict between development and preservation *within* the ranks of the preservationists. That is to say, the preservationists were divided, with one group, whose *bona fides* is not open to question, supporting the thruway partly on the ground that it would not prevent the preservation of anything worth preserving. The constitutional amendment required to allow construction of the thruway (called the Northway) was passed, and construction is in progress.

The Hetch-Hetchy controversy, involving construction of a dam across a beautiful valley to supply water for San Francisco, is still remembered by many. The establishment and the regulations governing the uses of wildlife refuges, national parks, and national forests have been and continue to be the source of controversy between the two groups. Recently an intense struggle has been going on over a bill that would establish wilderness areas on certain parts of Federal land holdings.

These few brief references give only a hint of the depth and pervasiveness of the perennial conflict between development and nature preservation. It should be emphasized again, however, that this is not the only controversy within the groups who call themselves conservationists. Various types of development often turn out to be incompatible with each other: irrigation versus urban water supply, for example. And within the nature preservation group there are latent conflicts that come into the open every now and then. The split over construction of the Northway has been mentioned, but there are many more. For example, the National Park Service—certainly a nature preservationist organization—frequently comes under fire because it concedes too much to development in the form of roads, accommodations, and so on. Struggles within the preservationist group frequently involve a

---

[4] Ibid., passim.

difference of view in the amount and type of development in the form
of facilities that should accompany "preservation."

It is these conflicts, then, which are an important source of uncritical
or intentional usage according to which the statement that a certain
action or policy is conservative in nature (in the everyday meaning of
conserve) is meant to imply the desirability of that action or policy.
"Build the dam, because that will *conserve* water and prevent its waste
in spring floods." Or, "It is only by not building the dam that the
natural beauties of the valley can be *conserved*." Each side has tried
to wrap itself in the favorable reaction surrounding the word "conservation."

Broadly speaking, there are two ways by which usage can be brought
to heel so that it will aid rather than hinder understanding. One way
is to say that the goal of conservation policy is to adjust outputs
through time in such a way as to maximize the return from *all* resources at the disposal of society. In the process of doing this, some
resources will be used up, perhaps "completely," and there may be a
gradual transformation of "natural" resources into man-made capital
"goods" of many different types. To put it differently, this view of
conservation policy equates it with "wise use of resources."

This is a view that enjoys considerable currency. If carefully adhered
to, it avoids what we have called the main difficulty in usage, for on
this view you cannot say that a certain policy represents "true conservation" until a *complete* economic analysis of its effects has been attempted, and no reasonable person can ask for more than that. But to
equate conservation with "wise use" is to attain a defensible usage only
by assimilating the problem of conservation completely into the general economic problem of maximizing output and by departing radically from the everyday meaning of the word "conserve."

It is preferable, in my opinion, to preserve common usage and to
agree that a conservative act is one which saves something for future
use instead of present use or which saves something for use instead of
nonuse. This usage leaves open the possibility that the conservation
of one resource may entail the sacrifice of another resource which others
may want to conserve. Thus there is *no* justification for concluding
that a certain policy should be adopted simply because it conserves
some resource, for it may involve so much cost either in the form of
current productive services required (e.g., to build a dam) and/or in
the destruction of *other* resources that it is not justified. A proper
usage, if the everyday meaning of "conserve" is retained, should *not*
involve the implicit view that conservation is always desirable. Sometimes it is, but sometimes it is not. The question always is whether the
gains outweigh the costs.

If this obvious but important point is neglected, the way is open to advocate policies that make no economic sense at all. An extreme example is provided by those who have been able to conclude—without examining costs—that government policy should be directed to the *full* regulation of nearly all the nation's streams over the long run. (Full regulation means the complete or nearly complete evening out of flow on a stream. The usual means for doing this is to build storage capacity behind dams.) Other cases of error resulting from neglect of costs may be more subtle. For example, no satisfactory argument can be constructed for an indiscriminate policy of maximum sustained yield from "forest lands." Nor can a satisfactory argument be made for a policy to conserve coal by requiring coal operators to mine 100 per cent or any other percentage of the coal in a deposit. Such questions cannot be discussed usefully without reference to costs.

Conflicts within the conservation area will not be eliminated even if the term "conservation" is used in a proper way; that is, without pretense that a particular conservation policy is desirable, *ipso facto,* without reference to costs. But clear usage is a tool which at least will not hinder—and probably will aid—the resolution of conflicts over the use of resources. It is likely that a clear usage, always with the realization that conservative action is desirable only if benefits exceed costs, will be of increasing importance, for the intensity of conflicts over the use of certain resources probably will increase as time goes on.

In the future as in the past, however, many conservation problems will continue to be settled for us by the working of the private market system. This is especially true of the minerals industries. By and large, we accept the price system as the arbiter between the present and the future, and there is little prospect that this practice will be abandoned. We do not, for example, impose a tax on the production of copper in order to save copper for use by future generations. The problem of the level of recovery is left to the mining company, the smelter, and the refiner. The reason why the price system can be trusted to yield a suitable solution to many of the conservation problems involving minerals is that costs and benefits involved in mining and related activities effectively enter into the calculations of private firms to a greater extent than is true for the exploitation of other natural resources.

The petroleum industry in the United States constitutes a notable exception, of course. The fact that single ownership was not coextensive with oil pools required some sort of action to prevent the needless multiplication of oil wells and to prevent economically wasteful loss of oil underground. Our attempts to cope with these problems seem to be running into increasing difficulty, however, not because the problem

of rational exploitation of an oil pool has suddenly become more difficult from a technical point of view, but because the particular method
of control in vogue is yielding some undesired results.

The elements of our control system are, first, control (actually only
partial) of total production of the industry. The objectives are mixed,
of course, being both conservation and control of price. If control of
price were not involved there would be no restriction of production of
individual wells below "efficient capacity" or perhaps MER (maximum
efficient rate). The second element of the system is spacing regulation.
A third element is limitation of imports. An additional point, so
important it must be called a fourth element of the system, is that there
is essentially no restriction on the development of new producing
capacity other than the test of profitability. The combined effect of
these factors is the development of capacity to produce far in excess of
current production, as could easily have been predicted.

The difficult conservation problems—and this includes U.S. petroleum production—arise in those cases where relevant costs and benefits
are not united in the calculations of a single economic unit. In some
cases, the benefits from a certain action cannot be appropriated by the
business that would have to pay for the action. Elimination of stream
pollution is a case in point. Or the benefits from a certain action may
be worth the cost to a firm, but perhaps this action imposes costs on
others for which the firm does not have to pay. Logging and grazing
may increase the rapidity of runoff, for example, an effect that may be
of no concern to the logger or grazer but of prime importance to
downstream users of the water. Sometimes a governmental decision-
making unit may neglect certain costs or benefits because it is engaged
in stimulating one type of resource use. This may even be viewed—
in practice if not legally—as its official mission. Sometimes certain costs
or benefits are not brought to bear on a decision because they cannot
be quantified in money terms or can be described only in vague non-
quantitative terms.

It is likely that in the natural resource area this type of problem will
become more pressing as time goes on, both because demands for each
of the possible uses of some resources are growing relative to supply,
and because new rival demands are rising rapidly whereas before they
may have been inconsequential.

Consider, for example, just a few of the various parties with at least
partially conflicting interests in the way land and streams are used.
There is irrigation vs. power, irrigation vs. domestic and industrial
water use, uses requiring dams vs. the scenery, fishing, etc., associated
with flowing streams, in particular the whole complex of benefits associated with flowing streams vs. domestic and industrial water use.

There is the sand and gravel pit or the clay pit with its ugliness and sometimes dangerous pools of water vs. the residential area with its small children, logging vs. scenery, highways bringing a greater density of people to remote areas vs. solitude, logging and grazing vs. the people downstream who want a slower runoff, and so on.

There are two factors that will tend to intensify these conflicts as times goes on. One is the increase in population, with its obvious effects on the demands for the many different uses of water and on the supply of open space. The other factor is what appears to be an increasing per capita demand for many particular forms of outdoor recreation and for outdoor recreation in general. A number of these forms of recreation do require extensive space and a low density of people. The changing structure of demands for services of resources arising from these two factors suffices to insure no easing of problems in the conservation area.

Exploitation of minerals may be less affected than will be the use of other natural resources, but even here the increased density of population will have its effect—by zoning or otherwise—especially on the ubiquitous minerals. And even in areas where population density remains low, mineral operations will experience more frequent collisions with the various forms of outdoor recreation activity. This will not be a new problem, but it will arise more frequently.

How are the conflicts to be resolved? A first step has already been suggested, namely, to stop pretending that a policy is desirable just because it entails the conservation of something.

Some conflicts can be solved easily since they involve situations in which all the potential users of a resource can *effectively* voice their demands in monetary form. In such cases the presumption in our society (but perhaps rebuttable in some instances!) is that the highest bidders should win, whether the resource is in public or private ownership. It is highly desirable that an effort be made to develop new forms of organization and procedure to permit more extensive use of the market to resolve questions of resource use.

But in many cases there are serious difficulties standing in the way of a thoroughgoing market solution of the problem of rival demands. While interference with and modification of the market's solution will not necessarily yield a better result, the possibility is open. Regulation of the way a resource is used may be desirable where the private user does not take account of significant costs or benefits that his action imposes or gives to others. Some decisions have long-lasting consequences requiring an estimate of demands and costs far into the future, with some cases involving social penalties for underestimate (or overestimate) that may not effectively enter into the private decision. Some benefits and costs do not yield easily, if at all, to valuation in terms of money, even for current flows of benefits and costs, let alone those of the future. Here we must analyze and calculate as best we can, trying to search out *all* benefits and costs, some of which may have to be measured and described in nonmonetary terms. It should be recognized that there *are* benefits flowing from natural resources for which individuals cannot express their preferences in money terms, simply because there is no feasible way for this to be done. In particular, it will not do to argue that society "needs" lumber or minerals but that scenery, etc., can always be dispensed with. This is an unreal choice, for the problem always involves a specific location. If consumers could express their preferences in economic terms, they might well indicate they want a particular slope to be forested rather than bare.

A consequence of the fact that some flows of benefits and costs do not receive effective expression in monetary terms is that some of the decisions about the use of natural resources inevitably involve substantial redistributions of real income. The losers from the destruction of the beauties of nature are rarely compensated. The point is not that they should be compensated or that "nature" must always be preserved. The point is that, at a minimum, those whose responsibility it is to make decisions on the use of certain resources should be aware that attention to total costs and benefits may not be enough, for the effects on the real incomes of particular individuals may be substantial.

Unfortunately there is no magic formula that will resolve these problems. The "multiple use" solution, for example, is certainly applicable in many cases, but in some cases it turns out to be just a slogan serving to camouflage the complete sacrifice of one use to others. For example, a reservoir may yield multiple uses including certain forms of recreation, but it is also true that construction of a reservoir entails the complete sacrifice of all uses that depend on the presence of a flowing stream. Once again the lesson is that no slogan, not even one so appealing as multiple use, can resolve all the conflicts present in resource use. Some uses are simply inconsistent with some other uses.

In any particular decision involving incompatible uses, one or the other must be sacrificed, of course. But for a group of decisions involving different projects, uses need not be inconsistent for all projects in an area taken together. It is only by paying close attention to the evolving pattern of use decisions that it is possible to give recognition and at least partial satisfaction to incompatible demands. An indiscriminate application of a multiple-use slogan runs the danger that certain uses which are inconsistent with "multiple use" will get neglected in decision after decision, thus securing no recognition in the final picture that emerges.

In many cases the instrument for resolution of conflict will have to be the political process. The participants include not only those ordinarily thought of as politicians, but the varied types of participants in any significant political problem, such as interested voters, government employees, lobbyists, journalists, and so on. Obviously *some* sort of resolution comes out of the process, but the question is how to make the results better. Certainly information and understanding of effects are necessary. Apart from this we need ingenuity and imagination in the formulation of new or variant solutions—new compromises, if you like. And in this area, as in many others, the majority ought to take very seriously its obligation not to trample unheedingly over the minority. In the case of nature preservation issues, especially, certain segments of the population may receive an important part of their real income—measured in satisfaction—from publicly or privately owned resources in which they have no legal interest.

If this advice is taken to heart by the participants in these conservation problems, a change in posture will be required in some cases. While it may seem tactically wise—and may even be pleasant—to oppose all dam construction or to damn the wilderness enthusiasts as a minute nonworking portion of the population with perverted tastes, any progress toward a more suitable resolution of conflicts as they arise is going to be made by those who are less inflexible. An abandonment of fixed positions would be helpful.

The main burden of this discussion perhaps will not be attractive to those who believe that greater conservation of some one thing is always desirable, whether that be songbirds, irrigation water, trees, or grass for sheep, for we have downgraded the term. As often used, it is taken to imply sufficiency for action. The view suggested here, on the other hand, is that a conservative act may or may not be desirable, depending on all the associated benefits and costs and perhaps on the redistribution of real incomes involved. But this downgrading of the term, if it should be called that, does not carry with it any implication that conservation issues are unimportant. Rather, insistence that acts of conservation should not be undertaken simply because something is conserved reflects a view that conservation problems are so important that it is unwise to deal with them on the basis of slogans.

# GOALS AND STANDARDS OF PERFORMANCE FOR THE CONSERVATION OF MINERALS

## CONSERVATION OF MINERALS WITHOUT MORE RAPID ACCUMULATION OF CAPITAL

Up to this point the problem of the rate of use of mineral deposits has been treated as a part of the more general problem of the rate at which capital should be accumulated. It was emphasized that however rapidly it was decided to accumulate capital, minerals should be used so that the rate of return on the value of the mineral deposit equaled the rate of return on capital. But what about acting on minerals alone?

Excerpt reprinted by permission from *Colorado School of Mines Quarterly*, Vol. 57, No. 4 (October 1962), pp. 153–171.

*Editor's note:* In the first part of the full paper, Herfindahl maintains that, since minerals are a form of capital, conservation of minerals for future generations is only a subtopic of the more general concern of providing for the future by general capital accumulation. He states: "One facet of the problem of conservation of minerals overshadows all the others: Are we and each of the generations that will follow us leaving enough minerals for later use? Most of our discussion will be devoted to this problem—whether a goal for conservation can be formulated, applied and attained. The route to consideration of mineral conservation will be indirect, however, with attention being given first to the more general problem of capital formation. This arises from the fact that the goal of society is certainly not to leave future generations 'enough' minerals simply to insure that they have minerals, but rather to leave them in a position to enjoy 'adequate' incomes. Hence our primary concern must be with the quantity and composition of capital

Suppose it is not feasible to accumulate capital more or less rapidly than is done through the forces of the market. Should minerals still be conserved as compared with the market result or not?

There are three questions to be considered: (1) What circumstances would conceivably justify changing the rate at which mineral deposits are used without changing the rate at which capital is being accumulated? (2) What are some of the difficulties that would be encountered in trying to change the rate at which mineral deposits are used? (3) Does the actual situation warrant a change in the rate of use of mineral deposits?

In view of our previous insistence that the rate of use of mineral deposits (and therefore their prices) should be adjusted so that the rate of return on the value of the mineral deposit is the same as the return on capital, any justification for trying to change the rate at which minerals are consumed must be along these lines: First, if the market inaccurately forecasts prices—whether because of errors in forecasting demands or costs—there is a possible case for intervention. A special instance is a "strategic" defense material. It might be undesirable to "run out" of a material before rivals do. Second, the process by which the return on the value of a mineral deposit is adjusted to the productivity of capital may work imperfectly. In this case, intervention may be justified. We shall concentrate our attention on the first possible justification for intervention, inaccurate forecasts of future demand, since it presents the more important problem.

Suppose that "we"—presumably the government—decide that the market is underestimating future demand. The market, for example, may not accurately visualize the costs of adapting to higher fuel costs rapidly. If we believe this is the case and wish to conserve minerals, what are some of the problems that would be encountered?

An obvious difficulty is to gain support for measures that would slow down mineral consumption, for there is a plausible case for the view of the market at any time even though it conceivably may be erroneous.

More important, it takes strong measures to make much difference in future rates of consumption of a mineral, especially if demand is increasing because of population and income growth. If demand were

left to them with the conservation of minerals constituting a part of this more general problem." Herfindahl first reviews capital accumulation under a market system and then looks at various theoretical proposals, especially that of Frank Ramsey ("A Mathematical Theory of Saving," *Economic Journal*, Vol. 38 [1928]), for increasing the rate of accumulation so as to maximize utility or consumption of all individuals, including those who will live in the future. Herfindahl contends that this line of approach is of very limited use, not only because it is so difficult to define utility and consumption over time, even in the absence of technological progress and population change, but also because it is ethically unsatisfactory once "some imprecise minimum level of income" has been reached.

not growing, restriction of consumption in the early years by imposition of a tax would extend the period of consumption much further into the future. But we are in a situation where there is a possibility for tremendous growth in the demand for minerals, with the actual outcome depending very importantly on the degree of success enjoyed by the underdeveloped countries in raising the level of their income. In this situation, even very heavy levels of taxation are likely to have only a small effect in extending the period of consumption.[1]

[1] Suppose that the demand for a mineral is growing at, say, 1 per cent per year. There is a known quantity of the mineral to be produced over a certain period of time, which period is determined by the conditions that: (1) the price of mineral in the ground (*i.e.,* the "royalty") rises at the market rate of interest, assumed to be 5 per cent; and (2) the total quantity demand in all periods be equal to the quantity in existence "now."

If a tax is now imposed on production, the total period of exploitation is increased by what seems to me a rather small amount. The numerical example summarized in the following table serves to illustrate the argument. From the values assumed for the various constants we are able to calculate that total production of this mineral product over all time is 5,678 if the imagination is used in reading the slide rule. The whole period of exploitation turns out to be about 226 years. Quantity consumed per year starts out a hair below 8, rises to 44.7 in the 190th year and around that time begins to fall, reaching 0 in the 226th year. The price of metal starts out at approximately 2 (the cost of mining and processing is assumed to be 2), reaches 4.21 in year 200, and 26 years later reaches the maximum of 10, at which price demand is 0.

Now suppose that a tax is imposed on the production of the mineral. The table shows that even very heavy levels of taxation, sufficient to raise the initial price by as much as 50 to 100 per cent, have quite a small effect in extending the whole period of consumption.

*Effect of a Per Unit Tax on Production and Consumption of a Mineral over Time*

| Tax per unit: | 0 | 1 | 2 | 4 | 6 |
|---|---|---|---|---|---|
| $T$ [a] | 226 | 236 | 253 | 290 | 356 |
| $P_0$ | 2.0 | 3.0 | 4.0 | 6.0 | 8.0 |
| $P_{100}$ | 2.0 | 3.0 | 4.0 | 6.0 | 8.0 |
| $P_{200}$ | 4.2 | 4.1 | 4.4 | 6.0 | 8.0 |
| $P_{290}$ | — | — | — | 10.0 | 8.1 |
| $q_0$ | 8.0 | 7.0 | 6.0 | 4.0 | 2.0 |
| $q_{100}$ | 21.7 | 19.0 | 16.3 | 10.9 | 5.4 |
| $q_{200}$ | 42.9 | 43.3 | 41.2 | 29.3 | 14.8 |
| $q_{290}$ | — | — | — | 0 | 35.0 |
| $\bar{q}_0$ [b] | 8.0 | 7.0 | 6.0 | 4.0 | 2.0 |
| $\bar{q}_{100}$ | 8.0 | 7.0 | 6.0 | 4.0 | 2.0 |
| $\bar{q}_{200}$ | 5.8 | 5.8 | 5.6 | 4.0 | 2.0 |
| $\bar{q}_{290}$ | — | — | — | 0 | 1.9 |

*Note:* Demand: $q_t = e^{rt} (a + bP_t) = e^{.01t} (10 - P_t)$

Price over time: $P_t = k + Le^{it} = 2 + .0001 \, e^{.05t}$, where $L = .0001$ is royalty on metal in ground at $t = 0$, $i = .05$, $k = 2$, and $b = -1$.

Total quantity in deposits at $t = 0$, is 5,678. $P_T$ is always 10, and $q_T = 0$.

[a] Total period of exploitation.

[b] Per capita consumption on the assumption that demand and population each grow at 1 per cent per year.

Nationalism raises difficulties for the conservation of minerals just as it does for an attempt to alter the rate of savings. Can we envision all nations agreeing to put on a tax or adopt some other measure that would restrict present consumption? This hardly seems a live possibility. Suppose, then, that we approach the problem on a purely nationalistic basis. Is it conceivable that we would act to conserve domestic supplies for use at a later time—either for consumption or for trading for other goods—on the grounds that the market is underestimating the strength of future demand? Does it seem likely that we could get sufficient support for a measure that would tax domestic production very heavily but that would not tax consumption or imports? To ask the question is to answer it.

Just as we did for the problem of altering the rate of saving, we must also ask how much difference further conservation of exhausting minerals would actually make to the welfare of future generations over a very long period of time. If the market is underestimating the future demand for minerals, or, alternatively, some of the costs associated with adjustment to higher relative prices for minerals, a slowing down of the present rate of consumption would permit stretching the adaptive process over a longer period of time and would start it in operation somewhat earlier than otherwise would be the case. But once again, any easing of the situation which could be brought about by reducing present consumption or production of minerals could easily be overwhelmed by a slight change in population growth over what was anticipated or by comparatively small changes in the rate of increase in productivity.

*An Appraisal of the Present Situation*

Over the long pull a going society cannot possibly rely on or "require" minerals which will "run out." Either they run out or the rate of consumption is almost zero. Since low-cost minerals inevitably will run out, world society must increasingly rely on two sources for energy and materials: (1) mineral sources so plentiful that the possibility of "running out" is very, very far in the future, that is, the very plentiful but very low-grade sources; and (2) flow resources and renewables.

Now let us turn our attention to energy. Without atomic energy, costs of energy from present conventional sources (e.g., oil, coal) would probably start to rise within a period of time measured in a comparatively few hundred years or less.[2] As the price of energy rises relative to other prices, economizing on energy consumption would take place at every point of consumption, whether in production processes or by consumers. Producers would substitute those processes that consume

[2] This is deliberately vague with the object of discouraging debate about numbers which at best could be only highly imaginative guesses.

less energy but more of other inputs. At the consumer level, similar shifts away from direct energy consumption and from products "embodying" a great deal of energy would take place.

Possibilities of this sort are so extensive that it is difficult to form a coherent view of how far we could go in cutting energy consumption. As time went on, we would act to decrease heat loss in space and process heating, use lighter and less powerful automobiles, do less aimless driving, and perhaps eventually see a renaissance of bicycling and walking. The pattern of movement required to pursue the tasks of daily living—going from home to work, returning from work to home, shopping, amusements—would be altered so as to result in a lower draft on energy materials. In some locations use of solar heat would begin to pay. Eventually our present conventional sources of energy would be used for energy purposes hardly at all; most of our energy supply would have to come from sunlight, either directly or through some intermediary such as falling water, wind, or plants, and a small quantity from the internal heat of the earth.

Under such circumstances life would be radically different from what it is now, at least in its external manifestations. Ought we to reduce our consumption of presently conventional energy materials (recall that we are assuming no atomic energy and no prospect for such a development) to permit some, but not all, later generations to have an easier time of it? Our answer must involve an estimate of what difference our action would make, as this information must be fed into the system of ethics that is guiding us. Suppose that population does not become excessive so that our action has some chance of making a perceptible difference. If one feels that multiplication of goods and services beyond a certain point quickly becomes pointless so far as satisfaction from life is concerned—phrase it in whatever way is congenial to your intellectual background—we must ask whether our failure to conserve energy sources would prevent the attainment of this "basic" level of living or not. Our conservative action would start the transition to unconventional sources of energy earlier but continue it to a later point in time. Presumably the accumulation of technological knowledge would make this transition easier the later it took place.

My own feeling is that our failure to take conservative action would not prevent the attainment of this basic level of living even if the transition had to come quite soon. Actually the transition would not seem to be soon or even particularly revolutionary if compared with the extensive technological changes that have taken place over recent decades and the last few hundred years. Consequently, I do not feel it would be a catastrophe if my descendants had to get along on sunlight and falling water. If they would not be too numerous, their lives could be quite satisfying.

Some believe that the multiplication of energy-consuming goods and services to quite high levels is important in terms of satisfaction or quality of life—put it as you will. For them, the conservation of energy sources would be, in the situation under discussion, more attractive than to me.

Whether for good or ill, the day of transition to energy from the current flow of sunlight has been postponed, perhaps even permanently, by the advent of atomic energy and the likelihood of suitable progress on the problems of breeding neutrons and disposal of fission waste products. Whatever the justification for conservative measures in the absence of atomic energy, the case is far weaker now. Energy is no longer in a special class by reason of the magnitude of the transition required as the switch is made from exhaustible to flow sources of energy. Energy and materials are now in the same boat; there will be a gradual transition to higher-cost sources required as time goes on, but a definite slowdown in the rate of deterioration of resources used because low-grade sources are very plentiful.

Thus the countries which have been and are chewing up high-grade mineral deposits have purchased an easy conscience. They have done this by advancing knowledge to the point where future generations will not have to worry about "running out." Surely the greatest contribution we can make to their material welfare is by continuing to advance and extend this knowledge rather than by attempting to restrict the rate at which high-grade mineral deposits are being consumed.

# DEPLETION AND ECONOMIC THEORY

The standard analysis of a static economic system deals with flows of commodities and services that are uniform through time. The properties of this system are customarily described by assuming a change in some condition and then comparing the resulting equilibrium situation with that before the change. This procedure has proved to be enormously useful in thinking about and working with all industries, including the mineral industries.

Everyone is aware, however, that over longer periods of time some of these flows could not remain uniform. This is not the case even with agriculture, although under certain circumstances the changes can be quite slow. The changes are even more evident in the case of mineral products, for the conditions affecting their costs of production may be fairly rapidly changed by the very act of producing them. Indeed, in some cases it may be useful to think of the mineral as subject to exhaustion.

These phenomena are usually characterized by the term *depletion*. The essence of the concept of depletion is not a sudden running out of something but rather a progressive change in the quality of a resource, or in the current costs (outlays made approximately at the time of production of the mineral product) of producing the resource product. Sudden running out is included in this more general conception as the special case in which current cost is constant up to true exhaustion. It is more likely, though, that current cost will rise with approach to a limit—a very important case, as we shall see. There may be some cases, however, in which we shall be unable to discern any limit.

The objective of this paper is to show how some simple but fundamental economic theory can aid in explaining the course of price and production in situations characterized by depletion. The cases to be considered are simple in that they abstract from a number of complicating factors present in the real world. The propositions arising out of analysis of these simple situations are useful and essential in considering depletion problems in their full complexity, however.

Most of the discussion assumes that demand for the mineral product in question, present and future, is known by all participants in the market. Unless otherwise specified, the demand function is assumed to stay constant through time. Production functions[1] are assumed to remain unchanged through time.

It should be clearly understood that the problem explored involves the price and *industry* outputs of the depletable commodity over time. Specifically, we abstract from the problem of the manner and rapidity with which a profit-maximizing mining firm will exploit its mineral deposit. If an intuitive device is needed to make this abstraction plausible, a convenient one is to think of the unit time period as being of the same order of magnitude as the life of a mine. Generally speaking, this is short compared with the period during which the mineral will be mined anywhere.

The basic theoretical ideas discussed here are not new. They are all embedded in the basic and definitive treatment given this subject by Harold Hotelling in 1931 (4) and, of course, have an extensive antecedent history, although not with specific reference to minerals, so far as I am aware. Because we restrict ourselves here to the simplest but still powerful tools, only competitive situations are examined. Even though the simplicity of our tools requires some of the problems to be given a discrete formulation, it is possible to go through a number of exercises of a comparative-statics type. Most important, the simple formulations to which we restrict ourselves contain and make accessible elements of economic theory that are essential for interpreting the realities of mineral supply.

It seems especially appropriate to extend acquaintance with this body of theory, for the factual situation to which it is applicable has changed in many ways from what it was thirty-four years ago. What is left in the earth is quite different and is increasingly better known.

---

[1] To be thought of as an implicit function relating quantity of product (products if a multi-product firm) and quantities of the inputs of the various productive services.

What we are able to do to obtain these products is also very different. There is, therefore, an opportunity to improve our understanding of the problem of mineral supply over the long run.

### THE BASIC PROBLEM—ALL DEPOSITS KNOWN, CURRENT COST CONSTANT

It is assumed that all deposits are known and that their quality is uniform in the sense that current cost per unit of metal recovered (outlays made at the time a deposit is exploited) is the same for all of them. It is assumed that quantity demanded is zero at some finite price. This seems reasonable for any particular product in view of the substitution possibilities that exist and that become increasingly attractive as the price of a metal rises.

In this situation (see fig. 2), the course of price must be such that at each point in time production will be induced at just the rate demanded so long as there are any unexploited deposits or unsatisfied demand. If each year during the period of exploitation (i.e., the period of time over which the mineral is being produced and sold) is to have some production, no year can be more attractive to an owner of a deposit than another, for if it were, he and all this brethren would shift production to that year.

We conclude that the present value (PV) of the royalty at different points in time must be the same: [2]

$$(P_{t_j} - C)\, e^{-rt_j} = (P_{t_i} - C)\, e^{-rt_i}$$

That is, the royalty $R$, which is the price of the metal (price per unit metal recovered) *in the ground,* must rise at the rate of interest or discount, $r$. Thus $P_t = (P_0 - C)\, e^{rt} + C$ where $C$ is the current cost of mining and processing. Note that $P_t$ does *not* rise at the rate of $r$ per unit time. The relative rate of increase of $P_t$ does approach $r$ as a limit, however, as $P_t$ becomes large in relation to $C$.[3]

We know that the royalty must rise at the rate of interest. But at

---

[2] Under competition the royalty $(R_t)$ will be equal to price of the metal $(P_t)$ minus the current cost $(C)$ of getting it out of the ground and processed.

$e^{-rt}$ is approximately the equivalent of $(1 + r)^{-t}$.

In $e^{-rt}$, the annual rate of interest, $r$, is continuously compounded. That is, if $n$ is the number of times $r$ is compounded per year and $n = mr$, then $(1 + r/n)^{nt} = [(1 + 1/m)^m]^{rt} = e^{rt}$ as $n$ becomes indefinitely large.

Thus there is a rate of growth which, if compounded only once a year, will grow as does the continuously compounded rate, $r$. If $(1 + r_a)^t = e^{rt}$, then $\log_e (1 + r_a) = r$. For small values of $r$, $\log_e (1 + r_a)$ is approximately equal to $r_a$; that is, $r_a \cong r$.

[3] The price curve is rising and convex to the time axis:

$$P_t' = r(P_0 - C)e^{rt} > 0$$
$$\text{and } P_t'' = r^2(P_0 - C)e^{rt} > 0$$

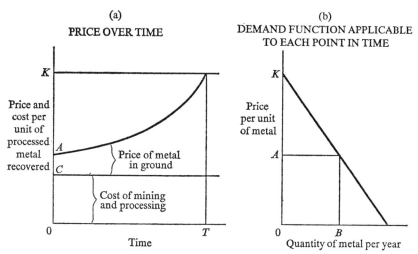

FIGURE 2.

what level is the initial price? If the participants in the market foresee the future correctly, an initial price of $OA$ will yield production and sales of $OB$ per year. As price increases, production and sales will decrease—the metal will no longer be used in less important uses—until finally at $P_T = OK$ nothing will be produced or demanded and all the deposits will be used up. We shall call $T$ the period of exploitation. If the initial price is too low, the deposits will be used up before price has reached $OK$, the maximum that buyers are willing to pay. And too high an initial price will result in the maximum price being reached before the deposits are exhausted.

There are several important points to be noted about this simple situation, which is instructive even if not very realistic. First, production and consumption in any one period depend on what happens in all other parts of the period of exploitation. If consumers feel that a deposit should be used up later rather than earlier, as indicated by the price they are willing to pay for metal in the ground being higher for the later than for the earlier period (with both prices discounted to the same point in time), the time of exploitation will be shifted. In this way uses at different times come to be balanced.

Note also that the determination of the rate of use of the mineral deposits is integrated with the whole investment process in the economy

The curve of log price is also rising and convex to the time axis:

$$(\log_e P_t)' = \frac{r(P_t - C)}{P_t} > 0$$

and $$(\log_e P_t)'' = \frac{rC\,P'_t}{P_t^2} > 0.$$

by reason of the fact that holding a mineral deposit is an alternative to holding other forms of capital and to consumption. Hence, as with all problems involving the balancing of economic magnitudes at different times, a discount process is necessary to perform the comparison simply because of the existence of the option to invest and secure a net return over time. That is, there is a possibility that by using the services of a mineral deposit now the outlay on other current productive services to produce the same amount of product (as measured by market value) can be reduced. This saving can be used to produce either capital goods or consumption goods. The equation of the value of these opportunities at the margin is automatically secured by the profit-seeker making his choices on the basis of present values calculated by using the market rate of return on investment. The price of metal in the ground will be such as to bring equilibrium in the market for mineral properties to enable mineral deposits to play their proper role in the "maximization of income over time." [4]

From the point of view of society or the firm, a mineral deposit is best viewed as a piece of capital that can yield a flow of services which represent its consumption, just as with a machine that wears out.

### Change in the Rate of Interest

With this bit of apparatus at our command, we can show the effect of changes in the fundamental conditions of the problem. For example, what would be the effect of a lower rate of interest (fig. 3)? As in figure 2, the initial solution with $r_0$ is represented by the solid curve, with the time of exhaustion at $T_0$ when the maximum price of $OK$ is reached.

If a lower interest rate, $r_1$, were associated with the same initial price, the course of price through time would be the dashed curve below curve $r_0$. But if price is lower at each point in time than in the other situation, the quantity purchased at each point in time would be larger, and the deposits would be exhausted before the maximum price is reached, say at $T_1'$. Thus the new solution must start at a higher price. But if earlier prices are higher, later prices must be lower if the maximum price $OK$ is not to be reached before exhaustion. Hence, the new price curve must cross the first and the period of exploitation is lengthened, as indicated by the curve, $r_1$.

With a lower rate of interest it is no longer so urgent to use the services of the deposits early—the cost of not using them is lower. Or,

---

[4] But note that this paper is concerned with market behavior. To discuss the welfare problem of maximizing income over time even very sketchily would extend this paper unduly. The problem is discussed in my "Goals and Standards of Performance for the Conservation of Minerals" (3, p. 78).

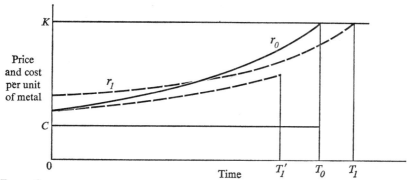

FIGURE 3.

think of the effect of the decrease in $r$ on the present value of the royalty, $(P_t - C)\, e^{-rt}$. For early $t$'s there is little effect, but the increase is more for later $t$'s. Hence it pays to shift production and consumption to the future.

### Increase in the Quantity of Deposits

The effect of an increase in the quantity of deposits is obvious: price is lower at each point in time, royalties are lower, quantities consumed are higher in all periods, and the period of exploitation is lengthened.

### Change in Current Cost

If current cost is reduced, say to $C_1$ as in figure 4, retention of the same initial price would result in a higher price at all later points in

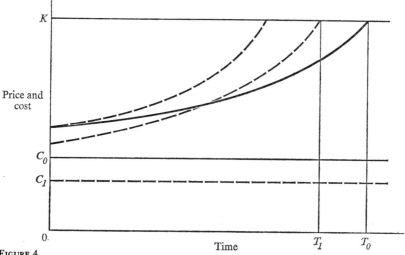

FIGURE 4.

time (indicated by the dashed curve) because the initial royalty, which increases at the rate of interest, would be larger. But this would result in zero sales at price $OK$ before the deposits are exhausted. Hence initial price and early prices must be lower and later prices must be higher if exhaustion is to coincide with price $OK$. The new price curve (dotted) will cross the solid curve associated with cost $C_0$ and the period of exploitation is *shortened*. This requires that the initial royalty be higher, that is, the initial price does not decrease by so much as the reduction in cost. The effect of the cost reduction on the PV of royalties is greater for early $t$'s. Hence it pays to shift production and consumption to the present.

The same diagram can be used to show the effect of imposing a severance tax on each unit of product produced. $C_1$ and the corresponding price curve now represent the initial situation. Imposition of the tax raises current cost to $C_0$. The effect of the tax on the PV of $(P-C)$ can be reduced by shifting production to the future, a process that stops when price prospects are those of the solid curve. Early prices are higher, later prices lower, and the period of exploitation is lengthened. These are the effects of any uniform cost increase.

One type of tax will have no effect on output, prices, or consumption, however—namely, a royalty-based severance tax which takes a constant percentage, $k/100$, of the realized royalty. To see why the production schedule is unchanged, consider a mineral for the exploitation of which there is a certain solution, that is, exhaustion occurs at the right time and it is impossible to increase the royalty on any unit of product produced by shifting its production to another time. This stability of the production schedule is the result of a certain set of relationships between the present values of every pair of royalties: [5]

$$(P_{t_i} - C_{t_i})\, e^{-rt_i} \gtrless (P_{t_j} - C_{t_j})\, e^{-rt_j}$$

A tax of $k/100$ per cent changes the PV of each royalty to $(1-k)(P_t - C_t)\, e^{-rt}$, but this leaves the relationship between every pair of royalties the same as before. If $R_i$ was greater than $R_j$ before tax, it will still be greater after tax. The consequence is that there is no inducement to alter the schedule of output over time.

*Increase in Demand*

The effect of an increase in demand depends on the precise way in which the demand curve shifts, but I surmise that price will be higher

---

[5] In the basic problem under discussion so far, the current costs are the same and the PV's of all royalties are equal. In more complicated cases to be discussed later, the PV's of many pairs of royalties are unequal.

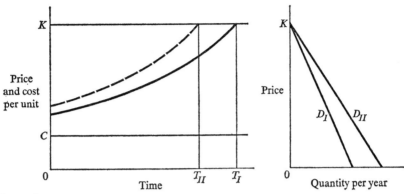

FIGURE 5.

in each period in all cases where the new demand curve does not lie to the left of the old at any point. Three specific cases are considered here, the first being an increase in quantity demanded at each price by a constant percentage, leaving price elasticity of demand the same at each price. The maximum price is unchanged.

After the increase in demand, the former price curve associated with demand curve $D_I$ (fig. 5) would result in premature exhaustion. Hence initial price must be higher and so also price and royalty at each point in time. The period of exploitation is shortened. The impact effect of the change on the PV of royalties is greater for early $t$'s, both because of discount and because of the particular change in demand that was posited.

Now consider a shift such that price is higher by the same absolute amount at each quantity demanded (fig. 6). The initial situation is represented by curves $I$. A new price curve (dashed curve $II_a$) through time that is higher by the upward shift in the demand curve would

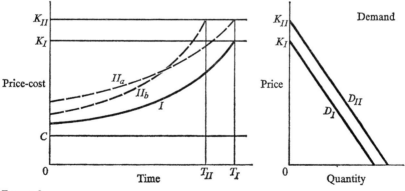

FIGURE 6.

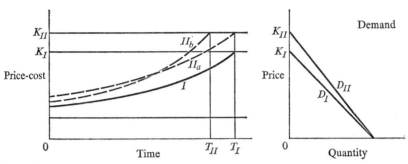

FIGURE 7.

result in exhaustion at $T_I$ as before, but the royalty would be increasing at less than the rate of interest.[6] The solution curve ($II_b$) will have to start lower and cross the dashed curve. Prices and royalties are higher than before (curve $I$) and the period of exploitation is shortened.

This is true even in the case where the demand curve shifts so that the price associated with each quantity increases by a constant percentage, as in figure 7. If price is higher in each period by this percentage (see curve $II_a$), exhaustion will occur at the same time as with demand curve $I$, but the royalty then would be increasing more slowly than the rate of interest.[7] Hence the solution curve must start below the dashed curve, cross it, and end up shortening the period of exploitation as shown by curve $II_b$.

For some, the shortening of the period of exploitation will seem to conflict with intuition, for if demand is greater, shouldn't use be shifted from present to future in the sense of extending the period of exploitation? The answer is no, as we have seen. Perhaps there is a tendency to forget that the urgent demands as expressed by the demand increase are urgent now as well as in the future, and that the discount process applies to them as well as to the less urgent demands at lower prices.

## ALL DEPOSITS KNOWN, QUALITIES DIFFERENT, QUANTITIES LIMITED

As soon as differences in the quality of deposit are introduced, we are exposed to the full complexity of the problem of exploiting min-

---

[6] Increasing the price by a constant also raises royalty by a constant: $R_t + a = (P_0 - C)e^{rt} + a$. Hence, $1/(R_t + a) \cdot d(R_t + a)/dt = rR_t/(R_t + a) < r$.

[7] With $D_I$, $_IP_t = {}_IR_0e^{rt} + C$. If $_{IIa}R_t = k_IP_t - C = k_IR_0e^{rt} + kC - C$ with $k > 1$, as with the dashed curve $II_a$, then

$$\frac{1}{{}_{IIa}R_t} \cdot \frac{d_{IIa}R_t}{dt} = \frac{r\,k_IR_t}{k_IR_t + C(k-1)} < r.$$

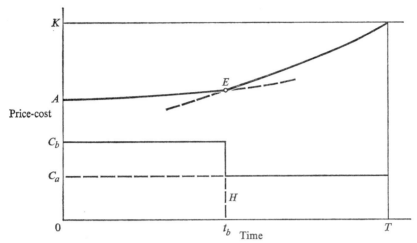

Price-cost

FIGURE 8.

erals over time under conditions of certainty. To simplify exposition, assume that there are two grades of deposit with different current costs. Within each grade deposits are of uniform quality.

Under the assumptions made here, both grades cannot be exploited simultaneously. (Under different assumptions they may be; see following section on exploration.) Since the price of metal must be the same no matter what its source, simultaneous exploitation would require that the absolute growth in price be equal to the absolute increases in the royalties on the two different grades which are growing at the same relative rate but which are of different sizes. Suppose both grades are being exploited at $t_0$. At $t$, it would be necessary that $P_t = (P_0 - C_a)e^{rt} + C_a = (P_0 - C_b)e^{rt} + C_b$ where $C_a$ and $C_b$ designate current costs of the two grades, $a$ and $b$. But this is impossible, since $e^{rt}(C_b - C_a) \neq (C_b - C_a)$ if $r$ is greater than zero.

In which order will the two grades be exploited, then? There are two possibilities, one of which is unstable. Suppose the poorer deposits are exploited first. This situation is shown in figure 8. The royalty $C_b A$ rises at the rate of interest and so also does $EF$, the royalty on the better deposits. $OC_a$ is current cost per unit for the better deposits and $OC_b$ for the poorer.

This is not a stable order of exploitation, for it would now be possible for the owner of a higher-grade deposit to get a higher royalty (in present value) by working his deposit earlier. Consider a better deposit being worked at $t_b$, the time of transition from grade $b$ to grade $a$. The PV at $t_0$ of the royalty earned at $t_b$ is $(P_{t_b} - C_a)e^{-rt_b}$. But if he exploits at, say $t_0$, his royalty will be higher since $(P_0 - C_a =$

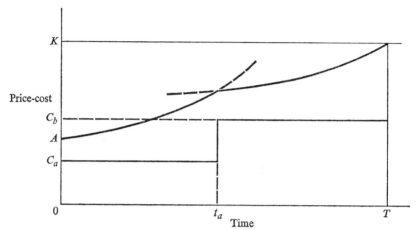

FIGURE 9.

$[(P_{t_b}-C_b)e^{-rt_b}+C_b]-C_a>(P_{t_b}-C_a)e^{-rt_b}.$ That is, $(C_b-C_a)>(C_b-C_a)e^{-rt_b}.$

We conclude that the better deposits will be exploited first, with the configuration of price and cost that of figure 9. From society's point of view, the productive services saved while using the better deposits can be put to work producing either capital or consumer goods.

Within each grade's period of exploitation, the royalty rises at the rate of interest. Price rises at a slower relative rate which gradually increases toward the rate of interest but never reaches it (see note 3, above). At the transition point the rate of price increase becomes lower and begins its increase toward the rate of interest anew.

It will not pay to shift the time of exploitation of a given deposit to the period when another grade is being exploited. Suppose a poorer deposit exploited at $t_a$ is shifted to, say, $t_0$. The new royalty would be less than the former; hence the shift will not be made. That is, $(P_0-C_b)<(P_{t_a}-C_b)e^{-rt_a};$ $[(P_{t_a}-C_a)e^{-rt_a}+C_a]-C_b<(P_{t_a}-C_b)e^{-rt_a}$ since $(C_b-C_a)e^{-rt_a}<(C_b-C_a).$ Similarly, it will not pay to shift a better deposit to the period when the poorer deposits are being exploited.

While the present value of the royalty received by each grade diminishes as we pass from one grade to another (this is obvious, since $_bR_{t_a}<_aR_{t_a}$), it is possible for the *undiscounted* royalty of a poorer grade, say, $_bR_{t_a}$, to be greater than that of the preceding grade at the beginning of its period of exploitation, say, $_aR_{t_0}$. Not only this, it appears possible for the relative rate of price increase to grow even though we pass from better to poorer grades. This is not very surpris-

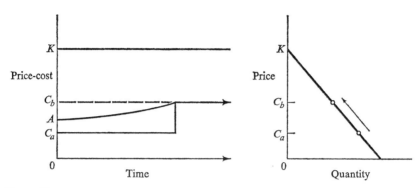

FIGURE 10.

ing, since this is the predicted result when there is only one grade.[8]

An important special case of this situation is that in which the quantity of metal in the lower-grade deposits producible at a current cost of $C_b$ is extremely large, for example, a metal extracted from sea water. In this case $C_b$ is the price reached at the end of exploitation of the better deposits (fig. 10). Thereafter price stays at $C_b$ and does not rise. Production and consumption are higher while the better deposits are being exploited than if the quantity of poorer deposits is limited, as it is in figure 9.

### Change in the Relative Quantities of Grades

Suppose we start with a situation in which there are two grades, $a$ and $b$. The initial course of price over time is shown by curves $I_a$ and $I_b$ in figure 11. Assume that low-grade deposits are increased and high-

---

[8] Consider the following hypothetical numbers, which show price, royalty, and cost for grades $a$ and $b$ at three points in time. The rate of discount is 100 per cent per unit time.

|  | $t = 0$ | $t = 1$ | $t = 2$ |
|---|---|---|---|
| $P_t$ | 2 | 3 | 4.9 |
| $_aR_t$ | 1 | 2 | (3.9)* |
| $_bR_t$ | (.9)* | 1.9 | 3.8 |
| $C_a$ | 1 | 1 |  |
| $C_b$ |  | 1.1 | 1.1 |
| PV *as of* $t = 0$ of: |  |  |  |
| $_aR$ | 1 | 1 | .975* |
| $_bR$ | .90* | .95 | .95 |

* If exploited at the time indicated at head of column.

Price increases by 50 per cent between $t = 0$ and $t = 1$, but by 63 per cent between $t = 1$ and $t = 2$. Even so, the PV of $R$ decreases as you move from grade $a$ to $b$, $R$ within each grade increases at $r$, and the PV's of $R_a$ and $R_b$ are reduced by switching to later or earlier exploitation, respectively.

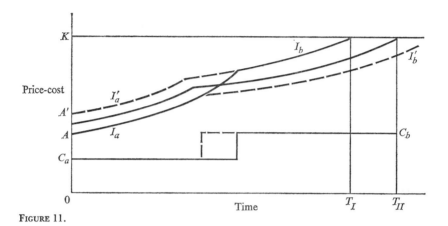

grade deposits are decreased by equal amounts as measured by recoverable metal. How will the course of price and production through time be changed? If the initial price is the same as before, grade $b$ would come into production earlier than before and its price curve would be lower than before (see $I'_b$). But with price the same or lower at each point in time, deposits will be exhausted sooner than before, and price will not have reached $OK$, the maximum price. On the other hand, a new price curve, $I'_a$, that intersects $I_b$ extended will result in price $OK$ being reached before exhaustion, since price is the same or higher in each period with the same total quantity to be sold over the period of exploitation. The solution curve, therefore, will start between $A'$ and $A$, and the period of exploitation for grade $b$ will be extended forward and backward, the total period of exploitation thus being extended. Early prices are higher and later prices are lower. Consumption and production thus are shifted from the present to the future. The present value of the per unit royalty is reduced on the lower grade and increased on the higher grade.

*Cost Reduction in Current Cost of Poorer Grade*

Suppose the current cost of producing grade $b$, the poorer grade, is reduced but with no expectation of further change. The initial solution with cost $C_b$ is indicated by curves $I_a$ and $I_b$ (fig. 12).

If the same initial price were maintained, the price curve for grade $b$ would be $I'_b$ because the initial royalty on grade $b$ at $t_{I_a}$ would be higher than before. Maximum price $OK$ would be reached before exhaustion. Consequently initial price must be below $OA$, but later prices will have to be higher than before if exhaustion is to coincide with price $OK$. Curves $II_a$ and $II_b$ represent the solution. Early prices are

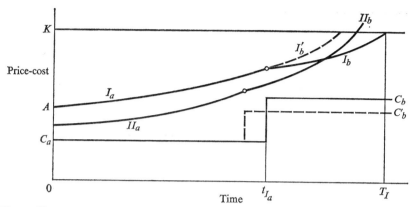

FIGURE 12.

lower, later prices higher, and the whole period of exploitation is reduced. The present value of the royalty is reduced on both grades, but
at $t_{I_a}$ the reduction for the poorer grade is less than the cost reduction,
for otherwise $I_b$ and $II_b$ would not intersect.

### Increase in Quantity of Lower-Grade Deposits

Suppose the expected quantity of low-grade deposits (held with
certainty) is increased. Retention of the initial price curves (fig. 13)
would result in price $OK$ being reached before exhaustion. Initial price
must therefore be lower. Price is lower at all points in time, the period
of exploitation of grade $b$ extended forward and backward, and the
whole period of exploitation is lengthened.

The result is similar if the quantity of grade $a$ deposits is increased:

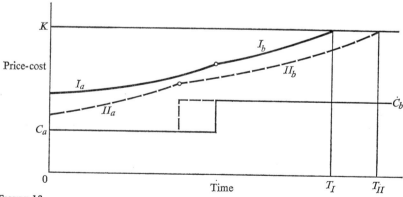

FIGURE 13.

price is lower at all points in time and the total period of exploitation is increased.

EXPLORATION

Up to this point, it has been assumed that the location and quality of all deposits are known. How would the analysis be changed if deposits have to be found?

### Exploration for Different Minerals Independent, Deposits of Uniform Quality

Consider first the case in which exploration for each mineral is independent of search for any other. That is, if you look for copper, you find copper; if you look for iron, you find iron. Suppose, further, that exploration is not always successful, but that the deposits that are found are of uniform quality. If the dispersion of returns to expenditure on exploration is small enough to enable the investors and/or firms in the field to effectively consolidate risks, there will be an economically effective cost of exploration. By effective, I mean that an increase in the price of mineral properties above this level will bring additional exploration effort and success and vice versa. Furthermore, if we take a very long view, the outlays on exploration can be thought of—at least for the purpose of developing some usable analytical apparatus—as being made approximately at the time of production. In this case, the conclusion is that exploration outlays can be regarded as a part of current costs. No modification of the preceding analysis is called for.

### Deposits of Different Qualities

Suppose that exploration efforts, when successful, uncover deposits of *different* qualities. What difference does this make to our analysis?

To see what is involved here, suppose that the deposits found are of two different qualities and that they are found in a fixed ratio. Suppose that a certain schedule of production is to be met over time. Consider two ways to meet this schedule:

1. Work both grades of deposit as they are discovered.
2. Increase the exploration effort so that the production schedule can be met from only the higher-grade deposits so long as any remain to be discovered. From then on, work the lower-grade deposits.

Option two involves higher exploration outlays now; other current outlays are lower now and higher later as compared with option one. Given the relative frequency with which the two grades are found, the rate of discount, and the total quantity of mineral to be found, which option requires the lower PV of outlays depends on the size of exploration cost as compared with the difference between other current outlays for the two grades and on their distribution through time. Competition will insure that the cheaper method of exploitation (in terms of PV) will be adopted. Whether this turns out to be simultaneous or sequential, the price of metal in potential mineral-bearing lands (unexplored) will rise at the rate of discount. In terms of our earlier formulation, the relevant current cost will be equal to current outlays, including exploration, if exploitation is simultaneous. With sequential exploitation the price of mineral-bearing land, which will rise at the rate of discount while exploration is taking place, will be made up of price of mineral produced from the better deposits minus current outlays including exploration plus the appropriately discounted value of the royalty that poorer land will earn later. Appropriate adjustments must be made here to express values per unit area. After exploration has been completed and exploitation has shifted to the poorer land, the royalty per unit of mineral will rise at the rate of discount as in the case of known deposits of uniform quality.

In a very special case of joint discovery of two grades of deposits in fixed proportions relations are very simple. Symbols are as follows:

$E$ = Cost of exploration per unit of metal found,
$a$ = Fraction of metal found that is in the richer type of deposit,
$A$ = Current outlay to produce metal from the better deposit,
$B$ = Current outlay to produce metal from the poorer type of deposit.

Assume that:

1. Output of mineral is constant.
2. The total period of exploitation for the two grades of deposits is long and the rate of discount is not extremely low.
3. $a$, the fraction of discoveries in better deposits, is not very small.

Assumptions two and three make it possible to neglect the costs that would be incurred in working the lower-grade deposits under sequential exploitation because their present value is insignificant. In this case, costs will be lower when both grades of deposit are worked simultaneously if: [9]

---

[9] If we regard exploration and production outlay as simultaneous, the present value of costs for simultaneous production is

$$\int_0^T [E + aA + (1-a)B]\, e^{-rt}\, dt.$$

Present value of costs for sequential production is

$$\int_0^{aT} [(E/a) + A]e^{-rt}\, dt + \int_{aT}^T B\, e^{-rt}\, dt.$$

Recall that output is uniform through time, say, at level one. If $arT$, and thereby

$$E+aA+(1-a)B<(E/a)+A$$

that is, if          $$(1-a)(B-A)<E[(1-a)/a]$$

or                   $$B-A<E/a.$$

In the general case where the quality of deposits found forms a continuous distribution with a substantial range, exploitation will always
be sequential in the sense that some deposits will be held for later
exploitation. In the long view, these deposits which are found but not
exploited right away are a significant product of the exploration process and some day may be explored further and perhaps exploited. As
time goes on, this buildup in our inventory of knowledge of potential
mineral-producing lands changes considerably the circumstances in
which the exploration function is carried out.

### SUBSTITUTION

Suppose two metals are substitutes. Metal $A$ is derived from deposits
so plentiful that its price is expected to remain constant for a very long
time to come. Metal $B$ is expected to be exhausted much earlier. The
initial situation is depicted for metal $B$ by curves $I$ in figure 14.

Now suppose that the advance of technique makes it easier to substitute these metals for each other so that, given the price of metal $A$,
the demand curve for $B$ becomes more elastic at each price. With the
same initial price of $OA_I$, the new maximum price, $K_{II}$, would now be
reached before exhaustion. Hence initial price will be lower and price
will rise more slowly. Early consumption will be increased and later
consumption decreased.

A more complex case is that of two metals, each of which increases
in price at rates of the same order of magnitude.

Assume that curves $A_I$ and $B_I$ of figure 15 represent a course of
prices through time that meets the required conditions.

Now assume that $A$ and $B$ become better substitutes for each other
in the sense that a given change in the ratio of their prices results in a
larger shift in relative quantities purchased than before. As the price

---

$rT$, is large enough, the second term may be neglected and the relationship in the
text will hold approximately.

The same variables will be related as an equality in the case where deposits
found form a continuous distribution by grade of deposit, but the quantities must
be properly interpreted.

In equilibrium, the cost of working the marginal grade of deposit is $B$. This
must be equal to the cost of producing another unit of metal by exploring and
increasing the outputs of all grades down to the marginal grade, with the increases
summing to one unit. $A$ is the average cost of working deposits down to the
marginal grade as distributed in the discovery distribution. The fraction of metal
found that is in the deposits actually worked is $a$.

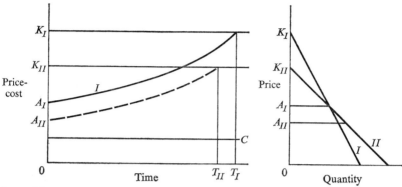

FIGURE 14.

of $B$ increases relative to the price of $A$, smaller quantities of $B$ and larger quantities of $A$ will be taken than before. $B$ will now be exhausted too late and $A$ too early.

The solution requires that the initial price be lower for $B$ and higher for $A$. The relative rate at which the price of $B$ rises will be lowered and that of $A$ raised. Consumption in the early years will be reduced for $A$ and raised for $B$.

The effect of easier substitution among a group of commodities that are being exhausted may be summarized by saying that the rates at which their prices increase become more uniform. This is true for both of the two commodity cases examined here. The prices of the commodities tend to behave more like the prices of one commodity, and they will behave as one in the limiting case where the metals become perfect substitutes.

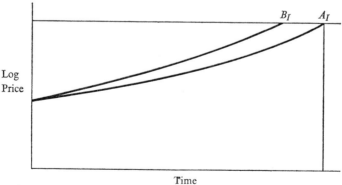

FIGURE 15.

## JOINT PRODUCTION

Joint production is an important aspect of the supply of some mineral products. The joint supply of deposits of different grades has already been mentioned, but quite often more than one metallic element is found in the same deposit. In some cases, e.g., lead, part of the supply of a metal will be joint with another while the remainder is not. The relative importance of receipts from the different elements in joint supply vary enormously. In some cases each element is of substantial importance (co-products), but in other cases some elements are of minor importance (by-products).

Joint production poses no special problems for the long-run theory of minerals; standard economic theory applies. It is mentioned here simply as a reminder that it is an important element in the case of some commodities.

## MINERAL SUPPLY IN LIGHT OF THE THEORY

There are widely different ways in which the prices of mineral products could behave. Each of these might be compatible with the theory discussed here, but the implied views about mineral supply would be quite different. In this section we shall ask what the apparent long-run price behavior of mineral products implies for the views held on basic supply conditions when this price behavior is interpreted in the light of the theory. That is, we seek some indication of the views held by market participants on the nature of the depletion situation, as defined earlier (see p. 64).

It will be helpful to try to categorize some different types of long-run price behavior. In the first category there is no exploration in response to economic incentive, because the sum of exploration and other current costs is above the maximum price. If other current costs are low enough, however, there may be an industry based on discoveries made for reasons other than profit or based on supplies that exist for other reasons—perhaps because they are found with other elements that do warrant exploration. If supplies are based only on accidental discoveries and are infrequent enough, there would be interruptions in production, with each interruption preceded by maximum price. If more frequent, we could expect a fluctuating price around a long-run course reflecting estimates of demand and the very long-run supply of accidental discoveries. In the case of by-products, supplies are connected with the supply of the major metal.

In the second category there is an increasingly rapid rise in price until the maximum price is reached or the industry gets along on accidental discoveries.

In the third category there is a slow rise, or even no rise in price.

In the fourth there is a rise in price to a level where a higher-cost source of "unlimited" supply is available. This might be the same mineral found in lower-grade deposits or it might be another commodity that is a very good substitute. If it is not a good substitute in all uses, however, we shall simply have one commodity in category two and the other—once its exploitation begins—in the third category.

The first category contains few, if any, commodities dependent entirely on accidental discovery unrelated to economic incentive. The point is not that there are no such discoveries, but that they do not account for the whole supply of the deposits of any commercially important mineral product.

Category one does contain many products (by-products) whose source material is dependent on the output of some more important product with which they are found, and it is to these that we now turn.

As far as I am aware, category two—substantial and increasingly rapid rise in price—is empty. The point is not that there have been no changes or movements in price which appear to have been of a long-term nature. Indeed, they seem to have been fairly numerous.[10] It is my impression that in most cases the changes in level or the trend observed is substantially accounted for either by technological progress, which can bring about sizable changes in comparatively short periods of time, or by the opening up of new and perhaps richer major sources of supply.[11] Many such developments must be regarded as accidental from the point of view of the theory discussed here, since they had origins much more complex than simply the supply response to the prices of mineral products.

In sum, I see very little that looks like persistent price rise based on estimates that we shall run out or that costs will rise a great deal in the comparatively near future.

If this view is right, how is it to be accounted for in terms of the theory? The simplest explanation is that the participants in these markets do not believe costs are going to rise substantially at any time early enough to make an appreciable difference after a discount factor of, say, $(1/1.10)^t$ has been applied to expected price and expected current cost. For $t$ as low as 50, this discount factor is .0085 and for $t = 100$ it is less than .0001. This means, going back to the basic situation explained at the outset, that a large quantity of deposits must result in

---

[10] Prices of a number of the more important mineral products relative to the Bureau of Labor Statistics General Wholesale Price Index are conveniently plotted in Neal Potter and F. T. Christy, Jr., *Trends in Natural Resource Commodities (8)*.

[11] These questions were investigated in some detail in my *Copper Costs and Prices: 1870–1957 (2)*.

a price very near to current cost and that there will be no perceptible rise in price because of depletion for a very long time.

It is important to understand that expected current cost is much influenced by the expectation of future cost reductions flowing from technological progress. In the absence of this, expected current costs as we move down to the much more plentiful lower grades would have been and would be much higher. These relations are schematized in the diagrams in figure 16, the first of which shows the relationship between current cost and cumulated production and the second the course of price and cost over time.

Curves $I$ refer to a situation in which there is no expectation of technological progress. Cost rises as the industry moves to poorer deposits and both cost and price rise through time with production ceasing at $T_I$ when cost is at the maximum price $OK$. With technological progress, expected cost rises less rapidly as production takes place and might even be constant, as with curve $II$. In this case price and cost will be constant (and equal) through time.

With this interpretation, it can be seen why the economic activity of the minerals industries proceeds in much the same way as that of

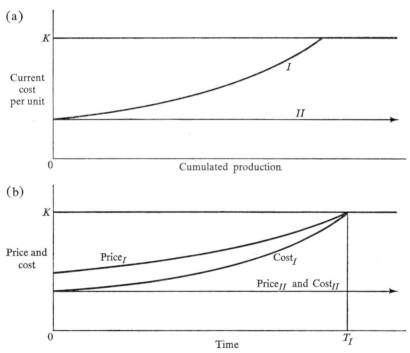

FIGURE 16.

other industries. We do *not* observe the managers of mineral corporations wondering how rapidly and when the production of the industry will be drawing to a close. True, the mine must look forward to its death, and the corporation may choose not to replace its exhausted deposits, but the very real problems they face are seldom considered in the context of depletion for the world industry as a whole.

A very large quantity of deposits exploitable at expected costs within reach of those now current is an observable feature of this world. In part this is a consequence of the fact that the earth—up to now, at least—has been very large in relation to the volume of materials-consuming activity. Of equal importance, however, has been technological advance, which has relentlessly lowered costs, sometimes slowly but occasionally rapidly, making it possible to exploit the enormously greater quantities of materials available as we move to lower grades at costs which often are comparable with past costs for considerably higher grades.

It does not appear possible to determine with any precision the relationship between grade of deposit and total quantity of contained metal or other element for any mineral product. There are numerous estimates of reserves, potential reserves, or potential resources, but such estimates appear to be tied quite closely to the existing stock of knowledge about presently known mineral deposits and therefore should not be viewed as attempts to estimate the complete cumulative distribution by grade [12] for a whole country or the world.

A compilation of the most all-embracing estimates that have been made appears in Bruce Netschert and Hans H. Landsberg, *The Future Supply of the Major Metals* (7). A few points on a cumulative distribution of contained metal by grade can be derived from tables therein for United States iron ore, United States manganese, and world manganese deposits. The logs of grade and cumulated quantity of metal in the deposits of the specified or higher grade appear to be linearly related for United States iron with $d \log Q/d \log$ grade around $-5$. A linear relation means that a given percentage change in grade is associated with an unchanging percentage change in cumulated quantity over the range involved. In this case, a 1 per cent decrease in grade (say, from 40.0 to 39.6 per cent) is associated with a 5 per cent increase in quantity of that grade or higher.

For world manganese a 1 per cent decrease in grade is associated with a decreasing per cent increase in cumulated quantity over the range from 52 per cent to 25 per cent (true for both absolute and relative

---

[12] Obviously such a distribution would require some constraints on what constitutes a deposit. One possible constraint would be depth.

decreases in grade), but the curvature appears to be reversed as grade moves from 25 per cent to 20 per cent—according to the estimate.

For world copper, estimates prepared for the President's Materials Policy Commission show a constant relative increase in contained metal as grade decreases absolutely (9).

The view that available quantities of contained metal increase rapidly as grade decreases is clearly held by the group of experts who prepared the reports on potential resources of metals and minerals for the President's Materials Policy Commission (9). While the underlying data are very incomplete and imprecise, it is fair to say that these experts believe that deposits exploitable at costs that are, say, two times present costs are very large relative to current rates of exploitation.

The resources situation for fossil fuels is somewhat different. The high rates at which they are and will be consumed suggest that major adjustments in sources of supply will have to be made comparatively soon. It is still the case, however, that very large quantities of fossil fuels as a whole are available.

Ultimate resources of crude oil have been estimated by A. D. Zapp to be 300 billion barrels for the United States and 2,250 billion for the world as compared with 1963 production of 2.8 and 9.5 billion, respectively. These estimates are tied to current technology and prices, however. More liberal assumptions raise the estimates to 590 and 4,350 billion barrels, respectively.[13]

Estimates of total recoverable resources of petroleum, natural gas liquids, oil shale, and tar sands vary widely, depending on assumptions about costs and technology. If we take estimates by members of the U.S. Geological Survey which are tied to current prices and technology for crude and which are conservative for the other sources, the world total of recoverable resources is 3,300 billion barrels with a little over 600 billion of this shale. In 1963 world production of crude was 9.5 billion barrels. Estimates based on more liberal assumptions with respect to cost and development of technology are far higher, of course, totalling about 13,000 billion barrels.[14]

Similarly, coal reserves are very large in relation to present production. In the United States, for example, recoverable coal reserves have been conservatively estimated to be 830 billion short tons (1). Allow-

---

[13] See A. D. Zapp, "World Petroleum Resources" (11, p. 3). These estimates include past production, which was 65 billion barrels for the U.S. and 122 billion for the world as of 1960.

[14] The petroleum and natural gas liquids estimates are by A. D. Zapp, the tar sands estimate is by H. L. Berryhill, Jr., and the oil shale estimates is by D. C. Duncan (11). I have reduced the estimated oil content of shale by one-half to allow for oil not recovered for both the conservative and liberal totals. Natural gas is not included in either total.

ance for undiscovered deposits might add another 1,500 billion tons to this (*6*, table 1), giving a total of some 2,300 billion tons as compared with a 1963 United States production of 0.478 billion tons. The corresponding figures for the world are a conservative estimate of recoverable reserves of 2,600 billion short tons (*1*). A less conservative estimate might add another 15,000 billion tons (*6*, table 2) as against a 1963 world production of 3.92 billion short tons.

To summarize, the price behavior of mineral commodities is consistent with the view that quantities will be available for exploitation near present costs that are large in relation to present consumption. This view is well supported by the extant estimates of mineral resources, and applies to the energy commodities as well as to the others, but not necessarily to any one country.

## Shall We Run Out in the Very Long Run?

The purpose of these paragraphs is very limited—to stress three considerations which seem especially important in studying problems of mineral supply over the very long run. One of these has received much stress in our previous discussion. The other two need mention because our discussion has deliberately abstracted from them.

*The idea of the cost limit.* The fourth category of price behavior— rise in price to a limit imposed by the cost of exploiting a very plentiful source of supply—would seem to be especially applicable to the problems of very long-run supply, for these successive cost levels set limits on the amount of price rise that is possible. The notion of cost limits is very useful in thinking about energy commodities over the very long run. The current supply situation notwithstanding, demands now met by petroleum products from the usual source will have to be met comparatively soon (decades?) from other sources, that is, from shale, tar sands, coal, atomic energy, and, to a limited extent, from sources related to the current flow of sunlight such as rivers, tides, and plants. As we move toward the higher-cost sources, quantities available become large, and the question of the cost of exploiting the more plentiful source is all-important in shaping the course of price to that level.

If we succeed in making breeder reactors, the notion of cost limits will be the dominant feature in price determination for a long time to come, for that situation will involve not only costs that are within reason by present standards but very large quantities of source material for both energy and materials, that is, country rock and sea water.

*Changes in demand.* Our discussion has had almost nothing to say about changes in demand. For the most part attention has been concentrated on supply, with the demand curve assumed to be fixed. There are two general points to be made that are especially pertinent to the problem of very long-run mineral supply. First, quantities of new mineral products demanded cannot and will not continue to grow for even a few centuries at substantial relative rates of growth. The reason is very simple—we would have chewed up the earth's surface to a depth of a mile or so (5). An analogous statement could be made about population growth. Present relative rates of growth cannot continue for a long period of time.

Valuable though it is to understand that $(1+i)^t$ is not useful for the description of some phenomena, this doesn't begin to touch the interesting problems involving the forces and the processes by which these rates of growth will be decreased over the very long run.

In the case of mineral products, one important element of the process by which demand for new production will be reduced over the very long run is scrap. As prices rise, it will become profitable to recover and sell for use again a larger and larger portion of each year's purchases, thus reducing the demand for newly produced mineral products. It may turn out that for some products we shall be able to approach what might be called a steady-state position [15]—either with supply coming from scrap or in some cases with production from practically inexhaustible sources such as sea water.

So far as scrap recovery is concerned, we are already reusing a number of commodities. In 1963, for example, the following percentages of gross supply were furnished by secondary production in the United States: antimony, 52 per cent; lead, 42 per cent; iron, 30 per cent; tin, 22 per cent; copper, 19 per cent; magnesium, 16 per cent; mercury, 15 per cent (10).

The fraction of a year's purchases that will be recovered is probably a good deal larger than these percentages, for they represent recovery from *past* and lower levels of purchase divided by present sales.

In the case of energy the possibility of reducing demand by use of scrap is not open to us. Here a steady state may be approached if demands do not grow too much and if we succeed in learning how to "burn" rock and mine sea water, supplementing this with some combination of the current flow of energy from the sun.

### REFERENCES

1   Paul Averitt, "Coal Reserves of the United States and the World," in *Domestic and World Resources of Fossil Fuels, Radioactive*

---

[15] To be thought of as involving the absence of cumulative change in economic magnitudes.

*Minerals, and Geothermal Energy,* preliminary reports of members of U.S. Geological Survey for Natural Resources Subcommittee of Federal Science Council, November 28, 1961, mimeo.

2  Orris C. Herfindahl, *Copper Costs and Prices: 1870–1957,* Baltimore: Johns Hopkins Press, for Resources for the Future, Inc., 1959.

3  Orris C. Herfindahl, "Goals and Standards of Performance for the Conservation of Minerals," *Quarterly of the Colorado School of Mines,* 57, No. 4 (October 1962), 153–71. Reprinted in *Natural Resources Journal,* 3 May 1963), 78–97. [Excerpt reprinted as selection 6 in this volume.—*Ed.*]

4  Harold Hotelling, "The Economics of Exhaustible Resources," *Journal of Political Economy,* 39 (April 1931), 137–75.

5  M. King Hubbert, *Energy Resources,* National Academy of Sciences–National Research Council, Publication 1000-D, Washington, 1962.

6  Vincent McKelvey, "Synopsis of Domestic and World Resources of Fossil Fuels, Radioactive Minerals, and Geothermal Energy," in *Domestic and World Resources of Fossil Fuels, Radioactive Minerals, and Geothermal Energy,* preliminary reports of members of U.S. Geological Survey for Natural Resources Subcommittee of Federal Science Council, November 28, 1961, mimeo.

7  Bruce Netschert and Hans H. Landsberg, *The Future Supply of the Major Metals,* Baltimore: Johns Hopkins Press, for Resources for the Future, Inc., 1961.

8  Neal Potter and F. T. Christy, Jr., *Trends in Natural Resource Commodities,* Baltimore: Johns Hopkins Press, for Resources of the Future, Inc., 1962.

9  President's Materials Policy Commission, U.S. National Security Resources Board, *The Outlook for Key Commodities,* Vol. II of *Resources for Freedom,* 5 vols., Washington: U.S. Government Printing Office, 1952.

10  U.S. Bureau of Mines, Department of the Interior, *Minerals Yearbook, 1963,* Washington: U.S. Government Printing Office.

11  A. D. Zapp, "World Petroleum Resources," in *Domestic and World Resources of Fossil Fuels, Radioactive Minerals, and Geothermal Energy,* preliminary reports of members of U.S. Geological Survey for Natural Resources Subcommittee of Federal Science Council, November 28, 1961, mimeo.

# PART THREE

*Application of Economics to the Minerals Industry*

# SELECTION 8

# THE PROCESS OF INVESTMENT
# IN THE MINERAL INDUSTRIES

For this study, a basic question is whether investment in the finding and development of copper deposits will respond systematically to signals of profit and loss and whether there will be resulting real changes in product to an extent sufficient to make useful the conception of a stable long-run supply curve. If the conception of a stable long-run supply curve (that can be moved by long-run forces) is warranted, it can be used to interpret the record of price (cost) changes. It is sometimes contended, however, that the common view that investment responds systematically to profit is not applicable to the mineral industries, because of certain characteristics peculiar to them. These alleged special features usually reduce to two. First, mineral deposits are depletable. Second, the risk involved in the search for minerals is far greater than that encountered in other industries.

The fact that mineral deposits are subject to depletion is not sufficient to destroy the usefulness of the usual theory of investment in analyzing the problems of the mineral industries. Many types of mineral deposit can be replaced by investment in the same way as can durable assets subject to depreciation. In the first case, money must be invested in finding another deposit; in the second, money is invested

Reprinted from *Copper Costs and Prices: 1870–1957* (Baltimore: The Johns Hopkins Press for Resources for the Future, Inc., 1959), chapter 3.

in making another durable asset. So far as the economic aspects are concerned, there need be no essential difference between the two. The physical differences are very great, of course, but this is true also of different depreciable assets.

Risk in the search for mineral deposits is a more difficult problem. The question considered here is not whether higher risk, assuming risk is in fact higher, deserves a higher reward than in industries where risk is lower. Rather, the issue is whether it is useful to think of a stable supply-relation governing investment in minerals. If it is not, interpretation of the past record of price (cost) and thinking about future possibilities will be radically different. On this view, successful finds of mineral deposits would have to be regarded as largely accidental. Even so, this would not necessarily mean that the price of the mineral would behave in an erratic fashion over the long run, for a rather steady stream of accidental small finds might match a regularly changing long-run demand. It is even conceivable that the conditions determining the volume of accidental finds [1] might have produced a gradually increasing number of finds to match rising long-run demand. This happy result, however, would require an unusual amount of coincidence.

It would seem more likely that if the volume of mineral deposits found is independent of the price of the mineral product, the supply of new deposits would fluctuate in a rather erratic fashion. Changes in the flow of accidental finds relative to long-run demand would be reflected in very sizable fluctuations in the payment, or rent, going to deposits good enough to be exploited. And, looking to the future, if private investment had been unable to organize the supply of new mineral deposits under the conditions that have prevailed up to now, it would be unlikely that it could succeed in doing so under conditions even more unfavorable, for example, running out of easily observable outcrops. [2]

Perhaps the idea that new mineral deposits are mainly the result

---

[1] That is, factors such as the number of people exposed to mineralized areas, the state of transportation, the diffusion of knowledge of geology and mineralogy could produce a certain volume of finds that are accidental from the point of view of economic process.

[2] According to the President's Materials Policy Commission, geologists "agree that extensive new discoveries [in the United States] of traditional materials will call for new methods. Prospectors already have combed nearly every square mile of the continental United States and large areas of Alaska. Not much more can be expected from the search for outcroppings of minerals that have long been commercially important. From now on, the search for these minerals must be directed toward deposits hidden in the earth." See *Resources for Freedom, Volume I, Foundations for Growth and Security* (Washington, D.C.: U.S. Government Printing Office, 1952), p. 27.

of accidental finds is too simple a way of looking at the problem. What would the process of finding look like if it were on the whole a systematic economic process? How would accidental finds fit into it? Under what circumstances would they dominate the finding and development of new mineral deposits? Some light may be thrown on these questions by a general examination of a systematic process of investment in the finding of minerals.

### INVESTMENT IN MINERALS

In the systematic investment process described here, investment is guided by the expected return. This does not mean that a particular act of investing a certain amount of money will receive the expected return. Success in any one act of investment is not assured, but the rate of return is predictable with smaller and smaller error as the number of acts of investment of a given size increases. It is presumed that devices are available for consolidating, or averaging together, the risks of failure,[3] and that they are used to an extent sufficient to make investment change in response to differences between the expected rate of return from, say, copper investment and investment elsewhere. A mineral deposit is here viewed as a capital good that is produced and that yields a flow of productive services. Some deposits are much better than others; that is, they yield a larger flow of productive services. As soon as this view of the mineral deposit is adopted, it is appropriate to inquire into its cost of production and the factors that determine cost.

If mineral deposits are like other capital goods in that they have a cost of production, what does it mean to produce a deposit in view of the fact that the deposit was there all the time? By "producing" a deposit is meant all the activities involved in finding it, in determining its size and other physical characteristics (which in turn affect the cost of producing the mineral product from that deposit), and in developing the deposit to the point where mining can begin. A part of these investment activities precedes actual mining from a particular deposit. But investment in the deposit continues after mining has begun, since knowledge of the deposit continues to be accumulated during the process of mining. It is never feasible to investigate com-

---

[3] Such devices are available and are widely used. The most important device is the corporate form, which works in two ways. First, it permits the volume of investment for one corporation to be large enough to get a substantial consolidation of risk. Second, individuals may spread their investments among different corporations, thus diminishing the impact on the individual of failure in any one investment project. Spreading of risk does not require the corporate form, of course, as is observable in exploration for petroleum, especially.

pletely the physical characteristics of a deposit before mining begins. Instead, mining will begin as soon as enough data on the deposit have been accumulated to warrant the further investment in equipment and structure required to start exploiting the deposit. Then, as mining proceeds, additional data on the deposit will be accumulated, in part as a result of mining activities, and in part as the result of additional finding activity that is not related to current mining operations.

An important part of producing a deposit, then, is the accumulation of knowledge about pieces of land. And much of the expenditure required will result in negative statements to the effect that on a certain parcel of land there is not enough mineral to warrant further investment.[4]

## A Picture of Investment in Mineral Deposits

At any given point in time, potential investors are aware of certain facts relevant to the prospects for finding minerals on each acre of land. Suppose that the investor classifies all the acres of land into different types by making use of these facts. The acres in any one type will be similar in that the facts known about them, and therefore the prospective cost of producing the mineral product from them, are approximately the same. The facts include location, transportation facilities and rates, geological structure (ranging from general knowledge of the area all the way to detailed information about quantities, location, and configurations of the commercial minerals), facilities and availability of other productive services, and so on. There will be many types into which land can be classified, since the number of characteristics and their significantly different values is very large. Very little will be known about some types; a great deal about others.

Now suppose that a fairly large number of acres in a particular type is under common ownership. The owner can formulate various programs of investment with the object of producing whatever minerals are present. The program which will produce the highest rate of return on investment will be the one followed. That program

[4] The accumulation of this sort of knowledge of the physical characteristics of pieces of land is to be distinguished from the kind of knowledge that is viewed in economics as a part of the state of the arts and which is open for use by all. A close analogue is found in surveying, where the principles of surveying are a part of the state of the arts and may be used by anyone. But the metrical properties of a plot of ground may be found out only by spending the money required to apply the principles of surveying and get the wanted facts. So, also, the principles of the geology of ore deposits and other relevant disciplines are available for use by anyone, but to determine whether or not ore is present on a particular plot of land requires the expenditure, or investment, of money on the application of the geological and other knowledge.

will start out with expenditures of a certain type, perhaps a quick surface reconnaissance, in the first year. On the basis of this, it will be decided that certain acres are poor prospects and do not warrant further expenditure. But some acres will remain good prospects and further investment will take place. This process will continue until actual mining and sale of minerals finally begin on the few acres left in the running, and eventually these deposits will have been exhausted. Now the owner can look over the years of investment and production activity and be able to calculate the rate of return on investment over the whole period. This is the *expected rate of return* on investment in acres falling in the specified type at the beginning of the whole process. There will be a corresponding expected rate of return for each of the other configurations of information into which the acres of land are classified. The expected rate of return is the first variable with respect to which acres of land of a given type are classified.

The second variable with respect to which the acres of land are classified is the *dispersion in one-year rates of return* on invested capital. Consider the acres of land of a given type (these are acres about which the known relevant facts are similar) under common ownership. The investment plan, determined as described above, calls for so much investment per acre during a period, say, a year. At the beginning of the period, there was a certain price per acre for the mineral rights on this type of land. As a result of the investment activity during the year, these acres of land move to other classes of land. For each of these classes there is a price for mineral rights per acre. At the end of the year, a rate of return can be calculated for each acre by relating the change in the price of the mineral rights for an acre (decreased by the amount of investment on the acre) to the price of the mineral rights at the beginning of the year plus the money invested.[5] These rates of return for the acres in a given type class at the beginning of the year form a frequency distribution with a certain dispersion. That is, on a few acres the increase in price resulting from investment during the year will be very great, but for many others the price per acre will decline as the result of the new facts. Thus, it is this dispersion in annual rates of return which is the second variable according to which land of a given type is classified.[6]

---

[5] The rate of return can be negative. At the end of this year, the acres of land will again be reclassified as the result of additional knowledge accumulated from the investment of the preceding year. On the basis of the new classification of acres, investment will again take place.

[6] Dispersion could be measured by the standard deviation of the rates of return.

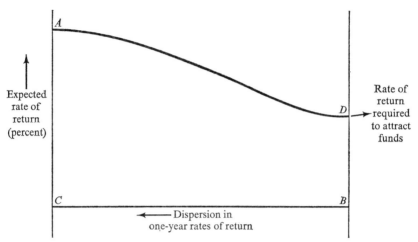

FIGURE 17. *Schematic illustration of the process of investment in finding minerals.*

The classification of land of the different types according to the expected rate of return and the dispersion in one-year rates of return is shown schematically in figure 17, which indicates the situation at the beginning of a given period of time. Certain acres about which the known facts are similar are designated as type *A,* which has the indicated expected return and dispersion in one-year rates of return. Similarly, there are other types, such as *B, C, D,* and so on.

Investment will be undertaken on land of type *A* during the coming period, for the ultimate expected return is high enough to attract the funds. Profitability of the investment is far from assured for a small operation, however, for the high dispersion in one-year rates of return (dispersion increases from right to left) indicates that a small operation that has only a few acres of type *A* land may be wiped out early in the process if it happens to have no plots of land on which continued investment is warranted.

Land of type *C* shows a high dispersion of one-year rates of return, and investment will not be undertaken because the expected rate of return is too low.

Nor will investment be undertaken on type *B.* Enough is known about this type to be quite sure of the ultimate rate of return on even a small number of acres, but the return is too low to warrant investment. For example, the rate of return on investment in exploration on, say, land of the type found in northern Iowa would have very little dispersion. But it would not be a paying proposition, for the prospective return is negative, let alone being high enough to match the return obtainable elsewhere.

Land of type $D$ will attract investment in finding. Acres on which mining is currently taking place would fall in this area on the diagram, since the dispersion in rates of return would be comparatively low, indicating that a great deal is known about production potentialities, and the expected rate of return is high enough to induce investment. The rate required to attract funds for investment in type $D$ has been drawn at a level lower than that for type $A$ to suggest that the market may require a premium for extra risk. There is no contention, however, that this is in fact true.

Now consider what happens to the acres of a given type from one period to the next. At the end of a period, acres of, say, type $A$ will move to new types because more has been found out about them. On the whole, it can be expected that the dispersion of one-year rates of return will be less within these new types of land than it was for type $A$ (although it conceivably could be greater for a few classes), since more is known about the characteristics of these acres. It is this additional knowledge that forms the basis for the reclassification. Some of the acres in type $A$ will move to types that would yield an expected return below the current rate required to attract funds. Some will move to types of land with an expected return above that of type $A$, and so on. In general, there will be a movement of type $A$ acres to the right.

The same kinds of movement will take place for other types of land in which investment is taking place. Particular acres move to the right, with many of them going to a class of land below the line of profitable investment as more is found out about them.

This introduction to the process of investment in finding highlights two problems: (1) the determinants of the distribution of acres by types of land at a given time, and (2) those forces that cause an acre and also types of land to change positions in the diagram. The first problem is so complex that only the most simple statements can be made about it here. Briefly, the present distribution of acres by types of land is the outcome of the natural features of the earth plus a large part of human history. The course of human migration over the face of the earth, the growth of systematic knowledge, and other human activities, in the form of investment and otherwise, are the determinants of this distribution. In terms of present stocks, the distribution depends on the state of the arts, the natural features of the earth, and the stock of capital (including men) used in productive activity. But the second problem is narrower and can be discussed in greater detail. What causes particular acres to change position, with types staying fixed? And what causes the location of types in the diagram to change?

Investment is perhaps the main force that moves particular acres of land from one type to another, but it affects only those plots above the level of the current return on investment. Investment in finding does not end with the beginning of current production, however. Mining activity itself provides a large amount of data bearing on the extent and other characteristics of the property.

Another force that will move acres from one to another type is the noneconomic find. Some finds are "accidental" in the sense that the finder was not engaged in the economic activity of finding. Noneconomic accretions to knowledge of deposits would include finds or facts accumulated in the course of other activities (both economic and noneconomic) ostensibly not related to exploration and the results of nongovernmental and governmental investigations of a wide variety aimed at accumulating data on particular plots of ground. These studies in applied geology and so on may be indirectly influenced by economic considerations of various sorts. The relation between these noneconomic finds and systematic investment in finding is left for later attention.

Particular plots of land move from one land class to another as more data are accumulated on these plots. This process can take place under constant demand and cost conditions. In contrast, the distribution of types of land will remain the same under constant demand and cost conditions, but may change when demand and cost conditions change.

The influence of changes in the state of the arts on the expected return for different types of land is obvious. Technological advance in finding, mining, and extraction (including advance in the science of geology and related disciplines) may make investment in certain types of land profitable where it was not profitable earlier. It may also, it should be noted, make further investment in some types of land unprofitable. For example, the development of methods of mass mining undoubtedly had this effect on investment in many types of land not suitable for the newer methods of mining.

As the process of investment moves particular acres of land from left to right and they move into production, the price of mineral rights for those types just below the line of current return eventually will rise in the absence of technological progress. The necessity of going to poorer deposits constitutes an increase in cost, and will cause the prices of mineral products and of these types of land to rise. The movement of types of land from below to above the line of current return will take place all the way across the curve representing the required rate of return. Some of the types that move up will contain acres of land that earlier had moved down into these types because they were judged not to warrant further investment at the time. Consequently, there will be cases where investment is resumed in acres of land once rejected as not warranting additional investment. The density in types of land immediately below the line of current return may be very high, with the result that only a small rise in price will suffice to move a number of types above the line.

Putting together the movements of types and of acres among types, as time goes on an upward movement could be expected for types of land (and of the acres within them) in the absence of technological change. At all times, there will be a movement of acres to the right and generally downward from one type of land to others. The downward movement would reflect the fact that one of the results of investment is to find that certain acres of land are poorer than they earlier were thought to be.

### Type of Ore and Investment in Finding

The discussion so far has been concerned with investment in finding without reference to the particular mineral to which the finding is directed. For each type of land, a probability distribution of acres among the various minerals can be constructed. The nature of these distributions will vary greatly for the different types of land. In general, the distribution will be less concentrated on any one of a few minerals for those types of land that signify little knowledge— that is, for those types with a high dispersion in one-year rates of return. As more is found out about the characteristics of a plot of land, the accuracy of predictions about the mineral that will be found will tend to increase. In many cases, the kind of commercial mineral that may be present (although it may be present only in small quantities) can be predicted with a high probability of success at a rather early state in the finding process. There are not many cases where the driller of an alleged oil well has been troubled with the problem of disposing of metallic minerals. But at the earliest stages of finding, there can often be considerable uncertainty about the identity of minerals that may be present.

### Equilibrium in the Process of Investment in Finding

Actual mineral operations provide a confusing picture that obscures the nature of equilibrium in the process of investment in finding. Deposits that are currently being exploited come in all grades, with costs of production (excluding royalties) ranging from market price on down. Chance elements appear to play a large part in determining the success of mineral enterprises—or so one would be led to believe from journalistic comment on the fortunes and prospects of mining companies.

From at least some points of view, this picture of chance and confusion is correct. Prospecting is a risky business, and penny stocks are not a suitable investment for a person especially fearful of losing capital. Stockholders and company officials are happily surprised when the presence of ore on a property is verified. But although the influence of chance may appear to the outsider to be rampant, the conclusion that the process as a whole should be so characterized is unwarranted, for averaging out may be possible in a way that will permit the idea of equilibrium to apply over long periods. If this is the case, then in the long run and on the average, a dollar of investment in finding (applied in the currently appropriate manner) will result eventually in producing properties, some good and some poor, that together yield the current annual rate of return on the dollar invested.[7]

Equilibrium in this sense does not require any particular distribution of investment expenditure among types of land. That is, there are a number of ways to find out enough about properties to bring them to the producing stage. At one time, the cheapest pattern of finding may involve a chain of operations that extends all the way back to properties about which very little is known. At another time, the cheapest pattern may involve a greater concentration of investment on properties about which a considerable amount is known. But in either case, a constant market level of return on investment will indicate satisfactory adaptation to long-run forces.

The definition of equilibrium, however, could exclude this type of situation, with the result that an equilibrium situation would then involve investment in properties along the whole range of dispersion in one-year rates of return. But it seems more useful to restrict the equilibrium concept to the situation involving adjustment of only the quantities in control of the investors in the long run. Large-scale accidents of finding, for example, are not subject to investors' control and by definition are not foreseen.

To recapitulate, the uncertainties inherent in the process of finding minerals enter into the economic aspects of the finding process at three points. First, uncertainty that is predictable in the large is taken into account in the formulation of systematic investment programs. Second, even if the uncertainties are predictable, there can be investment in finding that is not systematically related to expected returns

---

[7] Investment in finding will also result in the tentative conclusion (tentative because subsequent events may cause it to be revised) that some properties do not contain exploitable mineral.

(risk attraction). Third, some finding will take place without any investment in finding. That is, finding can take place in conjunction with some activity—economic, recreational, and so on—that is not intentionally related to finding.

The second and third types of finding—providing they are fairly well predictable—need not make it inappropriate to view the total supply of producing properties as responding on a long-run supply curve to changes in the prices of minerals, for that portion of the supply that comes into being without regard to the price of mineral commodities simply forms an inelastic component of total supply. To take an example from another industry, if the government were to grow wheat on a fixed number of government-operated farms and put this wheat on the market regardless of price, the amount of wheat coming from farms that *do* respond to price would be smaller, but the total quantity of wheat coming on the market would still respond to the price of wheat.

But suppose that the finds that come without regard to price are not in fact very predictable. Is it still useful to think of investment in finding as responding to price signals? Erratic and large-scale finds have no place in the system which is being elaborated here, of course. That is, such finds must be regarded as a change in the given conditions of this explanatory framework, since systematic adjustment forces do not encompass these finds. Instead, the erratic finds are a part of the underlying conditions to which systematic adjustment takes place. Their effect on cost levels current at the time can easily be exaggerated, however, in view of the continuing nature of the process of investment in finding. On the whole, it seems better to view accidental finds, whether large-scale or not, as substituting for only a small part of this investment process.

How do the finding activities of government (for example, its geological work) fit into the above discussion of finds which are not motivated by price? Again, the effect depends on whether the government activity is extensive enough to dominate the total supply of the activity at this level of finding activity. If the government conducts finding activity for a mineral on a few pieces of property, carrying this activity up to a certain stage, but leaves the market to organize the bulk of it, finding activity can still be regarded as tied to price. Someone simply receives a subsidy, whatever may be the noneconomic justification for it.

If, however, government activity dominates the total supply of finding activity at a certain level, with the results of this activity offered for use free of charge, this stage of activity will be independent of price, and prices of mineral commodities will be lower than they otherwise would have been. Such activity is common at the earliest stages of the finding process, where the dispersion of returns is very great and where it may be difficult to organize private activity in such a way as to enable the business or individual to appropriate the results of his investment. This is especially true in the United States, where preliminary finding activity is difficult to organize because of private property in mineral rights involving many individuals over areas that are small in relation to finding techniques.

### THE CUMULATIVE SUPPLY CURVE

The results over time of the process by which investment in finding increases knowledge of potential mineral properties to the point where actual production of the mineral can begin can be summarized with the aid of the concept of a cumulative supply curve.

### A Single Region

Suppose, for example, that there is one region producing a mineral commodity and that there is no foreign trade. In the production of this mineral, the short-run period will have its usual meaning. The short-run cost, or supply, curve will be the one resulting from changing output within a period that will permit changing the quantity of some inputs—such as labor, energy, materials, and so on— but one that is too short to permit alteration of mine structure and to find and develop new properties. This cost, or supply, curve is a function of the industry's rate of output in, say, tons per year.

While there are many short and long runs, depending on the inputs whose quantities can be varied, it is possible to schematize by characterizing the long-run period as one long enough to permit variation in all of the inputs subject to control by the firms in the industry. It is a period long enough to disinvest in mineral properties or to permit the construction of various mine structures and transportation facilities. It is also long enough to permit investment in finding and to develop these properties all the way to production.

Assume that these production activities are carried on under a situation in which there are no innovations in technology and in which the finding of deposits takes place under constant conditions. Then the cost, or supply, curve resulting from different annual rates of output may be regarded as an increasing function of this industry's rate of output. Cost will increase with output because a higher output will require higher prices in order to bid labor and other productive services away from other industries. If the output of the industry is small, however, this long-run cost curve can probably be taken as

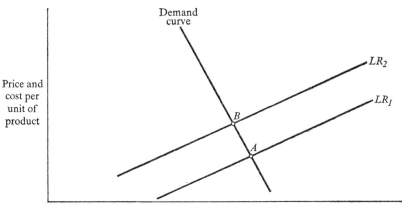

FIGURE 18.

approximately horizontal (that is, cost does not rise with increase in the industry's output), for in this case the industry is likely to use only a small part of the total supplies of each of its productive services. In any case, this long-run supply curve will be less steep than the short-run supply curve, for greater freedom in planning inputs means a smaller increase in cost to attain any specified increase in output.[8]

But suppose that the conditions under which finding of deposits takes place are not constant, but deteriorating, and that there still are no offsetting improvements in technology. It may be necessary to go farther from markets to find new deposits, or the frequency with which a deposit of a given grade is found may be declining simply because we are, in a sense, running out of the more accessible and richer deposits. In this case, the cost of producing the mineral product will be rising over time, and the long-run cost curve of the previous paragraph will be shifting upward along its whole length. With a constant demand curve, the successive equilibrium positions will be as depicted in figure 18.

The demand curve shows the quantities per year that will be bought at various prices. $LR_1$ shows the long-run average cost in year one of producing various quantities per year of the commodity under *constant* finding conditions. Equilibrium is at point *A*, with

[8] It is precisely this difference between the short-run and the long-run supply curves that forms the major part of the explanation for the large increase in the prices of many mineral products in the face of the sudden and sizable increase in demand on the outbreak of the Korean affair in 1950. Rapid and sizable increases in the outputs of these commodities could be obtained only at substantially higher prices (and marginal costs).

price and cost equal and the quantity supplied equal to the quantity demanded. With a deterioration in finding conditions, the whole long-run average cost curve moves upward, say to $LR_2$, with a resulting increase in price and decline in output and consumption of the commodity.

If this deterioration in what might be called the natural resource situation is assumed to take place in a regular fashion, it is appropriate to view cost as a function of the *cumulated* annual outputs (that is, total production from some base date) of the industry as well as of the annual rate of output at a given time. With a given demand curve, one could plot the successive average costs as a function of cumulated output of this product. Such a curve would reflect both the influence of deterioration in the natural resource situation *and* the movements to the left along the successive long-run cost curves resulting from the entire conjunction of demand and cost conditions.[9]

To simplify exposition from here on, suppose that average cost is a function only of cumulated output, rather than of both cumulated output and the annual rate of output. In this case, the long-run supply curve, given the finding conditions, may be viewed as a horizontal line rather than as rising. Now cost will rise with cumulated output, as in the more general case just discussed. But the increase in cost will reflect only the steady deterioration in finding conditions, and not changes in the annual output of this industry in relation to the rest of the economy. This situation is depicted in figure 19.

At time-1, equilibrium is at point $t_1$ in the diagram showing price as a function of annual output and in the diagram showing price as a function of cumulated output. But at this annual rate of output, deterioration in finding conditions is proceeding at such a rate that when time-2 is reached equilibrium is at $t_2$ in each diagram and cost has moved up. But as the rate of output declines as price moves up the demand curve, a wide variety of cost conditions will probably yield the result that the rate at which price and cost rise over time

---

[9] All of this can be formulated mathematically, if desired. Average cost is a function of cumulated output and the derivative of cumulated output with respect to time. The long-run supply curve, as a function of annual output, given conditions for finding, loses its precision in this formulation (strictly speaking, it is not reversible through time), but it may be thought of as the average cost function with cumulated supply held constant. Price is a function of annual rate of output (i.e., the derivative of cumulated output with respect to time). Setting cost equal to price yields a differential equation in cumulated output and time, the solution to which will give the course of cumulated output, annual output, price and cost over time.

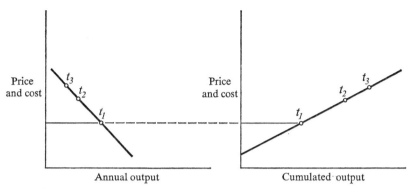

Price and cost — Annual output

Price and cost — Cumulated output

FIGURE 19.

decreases. That is, $t_3$, representing the situation at time-3, is closer to $t_2$ than was $t_2$ to $t_1$.

It should be noted that the intensity of demand for newly mined copper will be affected, first, by the supply of copper coming from articles that are scrapped and, second, by the price of close substitutes, notably the price of aluminum. Thus these two factors will affect the rate at which the price and cost of copper move up the cumulative supply curve through time.

### More than One Region

Now consider the case of a mineral product produced in two regions. It is assumed that in each region cost rises, not necessarily at the same rate, as cumulated production increases. That is, the basic natural resource situation is deteriorating as production proceeds. For simplicity, it is assumed again that cost does not vary with the industry's output under constant finding conditions.

In an equilibrium situation, cost per unit of output—assuming proper values are put on deposits—must be the same in each region at any given time, and cost including return on capital must be equal to the market price. This means that the rates of production in the two regions must be such that they result in cost rising at the same rate per unit of time. Consequently, if the rate at which cost rises as cumulated output increases is twice as great in region $A$ as it is in region $B$, then the rate of output per year in region $A$ can be only one-half that in region $B$. If this is not the case, cost will not be rising at the same rate per year in each region.

In general, the outputs of the different regions will be divided in inverse proportion to the slopes of their respective cumulative supply curves. If these curves are linear, relative outputs of the different regions will be constant over time, and cost in each region will be changing at the same rate through time. If these curves are not linear, relative outputs may have to change through time in order to preserve a uniform rate of increase in cost through time.[10]

### The Meaning of "High-Cost Region"

No region can have higher costs (delivered to the same market) than another in a situation of long-run equilibrium as defined here. If there is a difference in cost, it will be eliminated by a slowing of investment in the one higher-cost region and an increase in investment in the other. This will continue until the cost difference is eliminated, after which cost will move up through time at the same rate in each of the regions.

This is not to say that there can be no such thing as a higher-cost region. First, if the two regions are not in long-run equilibrium, costs can differ until a state of equilibrium is reached. Second, even though there may be no long-run cost difference if "cost" is defined as cost of the commodity at a given market, other definitions may result in a showing of cost difference even in a situation of long-run equilibrium. For example, costs of the commodity at the mine, with or without royalties, will surely show differences.

But the idea of higher- and lower-cost regions has an important meaning even in the context of long-run equilibrium. Even though cost may be the same in each region at each point in time in a situation of long-run equilibrium, *that region in which cost rises more rapidly with respect to cumulated output may be called the higher-cost region.* Under conditions of long-run equilibrium and no change in technology, this greater rapidity of rise in cost will be reflected in a proportionately lower annual rate of output.

### The Quantity of Resources

The ideas developed here may be of some aid in clarifying the concept of the quantity of resources. Although the quantity of, say, copper in a region conceivably can be described by a single number to express the tons of copper in the ground (how far down?), such a figure would have little relevance to any human problem at this

---

[10] The general relations are as follows. Symbols: $Q_i$, cumulated production in region $i$ ($i = 1, 2$); $c_i$, average cost in region $i$; $p$, price. Cumulative supply curves of the 2 regions: $c_1 = f_1\ (Q_1)$, $c_2 = f_2\ (Q_2)$. Demand curve: $p = h\ (q_1 + q_2)$ where $q_i = dQ_i/dt$. Since costs and price are equal at every moment of time, $dp/dt = f'_1(Q_1)\ dQ_1/dt = f'_2(Q_2)\ dQ_2/dt$. I.e., the ratio of the two annual rates of output is $q_1/q_2 = f'_2(Q_2)/f'_1(Q_1)$.

point in history. In the system of ideas used here, direct quantification of natural resources has been avoided, and changes in the "quantity" thereof are expressed through the shape and position of the cumulative supply curve. More accurately, quantification of natural resources in any sense relevant to economic problems is dependent on man's estimates of what it costs to produce different quantities of certain commodities with the use of these natural resources.

These remarks pertain to attempts to quantify resources over a large area. They are not meant to deny the possibility of direct quantification for, say, the mineral contents of deposits that fall into the same class with respect to such characteristics as depth, grade, kind of country rock, and so on. In this case, cost per unit will be about the same for different deposits. Hence, the "quantity of natural resource" present in deposits can be described by one number, namely, the mineral contents of the deposit. Even this has its difficulties, for the physical boundaries of a deposit often are not sharp.

Nor are these remarks intended to deny the possibility of physical description of certain pieces of earth. Geologists and others do exactly this, and these descriptions are indispensable for making economic decisions about the use of natural resources. But estimates of either quantities or cost without the other are of very limited usefulness for making economic decisions.[11] Both costs and quantities of product are required to convey an idea of the "quantity" of a natural resource that is available from an economic point of view. The quantities of a natural resource of a particular type thought to be present in different regions can be roughly compared in one dimension by such devices as comparing the quantities that can be produced at or below a specified cost.

### Change and the Cumulative Supply Curve

The long-run cumulative supply curve has been defined on the basis of a constant state of the arts. Since this curve is the result of systematic finding activity conducted under a profit system, and since supply is cumulated over time, the curve rises—because recourse must

---

[11] The writer is not aware of any estimates of cost without at least implicit reference to quantities, but the application to economic problems of estimated quantities of natural resources without reference to cost has been and continues to be a popular waste of time. Two relatively recent reports have marked a notable advance over this widespread error. These are *Resources for Freedom, op. cit.,* and *Mineral Resources of the United States,* by the staffs of the U. S. Bureau of Mines and Geological Survey (reprint; Washington, D.C.: Public Affairs Press, 1948). In each case, both quantity and cost are emphasized.

be had to poorer natural resources—and is not reversible. But abrupt progress in any part of the processes involved in producing this commodity (including processes in other industries whose products are purchased by this mineral industry) introduces a break in the cumulative supply curve. A succession of such changes may even leave the historical course of cost at an approximately constant level, as is illustrated schematically in figure 20.

Now suppose there are two regions. With progress in the production of the mineral taking place in each region, in what sense can a historically constant ratio between their outputs be said to indicate the relative rates of deterioration in the quality of the resources in the two regions? Difficulty arises here because the rate of deterioration in resources—measured by the rate at which cost increases with cumulated output—is defined only for a constant state of the arts. In the face of technological changes, it cannot be said that constancy in relative outputs of the two regions implies that the rate of deterioration would have been constant if there had been no changes in the state of the arts, although that might have happened. Nor can it be said that deterioration in resources goes on independently of technological changes. While deterioration will occur under any given state of the arts, there is no measure of deterioration that will give the same result under all. Unfortunately, the measure here has to be tied to a given state of the arts.

The consequence is a limitation on the significance of an observed constancy in relative rates of output of different regions. However, certain conclusions can be drawn in a situation where (1) technological changes produce a succession of changes in the cumulative supply curves and (2) where there is a constant adaptation of annual outputs to changes in the slopes of the cumulative supply curves. In general,

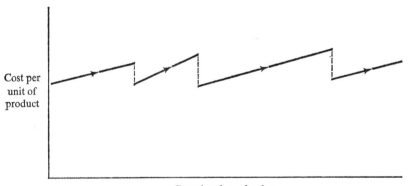

Cost per
unit of
product

Cumulated production

FIGURE 20.

a constant ratio between regional outputs means that the successive slopes of the cumulative supply curves have stayed constant relative to each other. That is, the succession of relative rates of resource deterioration in the two regions—with each segment of each cumulative supply curve referring to a different state of the arts—has stayed the same.

If technological change is posited to offset the cumulative supply curves in a certain way, then constancy in the ratio of regional outputs has a somewhat clearer significance. For example, if progress displaces either or both of the two regional cumulative supply curves by a constant amount, slopes of the two curves at equal costs will be unchanged. If only one is displaced, there will be a period of disequilibrium until cost is equalized. In this case, the time pattern of cost increase, assuming no further changes in the curves, will be the same as it would have been from a similar starting position before the change, but the whole upward procession of cost over time will take place later than it would have if there had been no progress. Deterioration in the resources of one region as compared with the other, as measured by the ratio of the slopes of the curves, would be constant.

Or suppose that progress causes a horizontal displacement of the regional cumulative supply curves in such a way as to keep the ratio of the slopes at each price the same as before the change took place—for example, an equal proportionate movement to the right. Again, the ratio of annual outputs will be the same at each level of cost as in the original situation, but the displaced time pattern of cost increase will in all likelihood be different.

But technological progress may not affect the slopes of the cumulative supply curves in these simple ways; it may change their relative slopes from what they otherwise would have been. For example, the rate of resource deterioration under a given state of the arts may require an increase over time in the ratio of the outputs of two regions, but progress may favor one of the regions in such a way as to result in a historically constant ratio.

Observation of the ratio of outputs cannot unravel this kind of situation, for the ratio reflects the combined influence of resource deterioration and progress. Therefore—to repeat a related point— observation of historical data cannot reveal how rapidly resource deterioration (meaning deterioration apart from progress) really was taking place. The only way to do this is to make estimates of cost behavior over time on the assumption of a constant state of the arts or to make some restrictive assumption about the effect of progress on costs over time.

## Summary

A basic question for this study is whether investment in copper production, especially at the exploration and development stages, systematically responds to profit and loss signals. In this chapter, a general description of a systematic process of investment in minerals has been developed. This framework was then extended to develop the idea of a cumulative supply curve, a device that is of some use in thinking about cost changes of a mineral through time. It should be useful in considering the material on the behavior of the price of copper that is to follow. At a later point, it is argued that the record of copper price and output on the whole is consistent with the view that investment in copper is systematic, and that it responds reasonably well to the signals of profit and loss.

SELECTION 9

# CHANGES IN THE SIZE
# OF COPPER MINING COMPANIES

Data on changes in the location of copper production are consistent with the view that development of new sources of output and the decay of old sources have been an obstacle to significant collective restriction of output over any substantial period of time. This view is supported, in a general way, by study of the size distribution of copper mining firms, although it is only feasible to cover a considerably shorter period. That is to say, the shifts in the relative importance of different countries and different states within the United States are associated with a substantial movement within a relatively stable size distribution of copper mining companies.

In addition to confirming the presence of disruptive shifts in position, study of the changes in size distribution yields several other results that are of aid in assessing the intensity of competition in this industry. First, the distribution by relative size, to judge from the thirty largest firms, has been rather stable since the twenties; but from 1912 to the twenties there was a definite increase in concentration. Second, the study of firms enables a comparison of the size distribution of the copper mining industry with other industries, a

Excerpt reprinted from "A General Evaluation of Competition in the Copper Industry," *Copper Costs and Prices: 1870-1957* (Baltimore: The Johns Hopkins Press for Resources for the Future, Inc., 1959), chapter 7, pp. 164-171.

comparison that will be helpful in gauging the intensity of competition in this industry.

The shares of world output of thirty leading copper mining firms for selected years from 1912 to 1956 are shown in table 1. There was a definite increase in concentration from 1912 to 1923. This increase took place mainly because of growth in the share of the top four firms (from 39 to 51 per cent of world output), but also because of growth of firms ranking five to eight (from 10 to 13 per cent of world output). Taking the two groups together, there was a sizable increase in the share of the first eight for the period (49 to 64 per cent).

A characterization of change in concentration since the twenties depends on the measure of concentration that is used. If the percentage for 1947 is disregarded because distorted by World War II, there seems to have been a small decline in the share of the top four since 1928. However, this decline was more than offset by growth in the share of firms five to eight, with the result apparently an increase in the share of the first eight firms from the mid-sixties to seventy per cent. The share of firms ranked nine to thirty declined from 23 per cent in 1912 to 20 per cent in 1923. In 1956, it was at about the same level. The combined effect of these movements has been a rapid increase in the share of the top thirty firms from 1912 to 1923 (72 to 84 per cent), with perhaps an increase of a few percentage points in the following years.

A more comprehensive measure of concentration, labeled C, shows an increase from .05 in 1912 to .093 in 1923, and then a decline to .081 in 1956. This measure of concentration combines into a single figure the two main components of the concept of concentration, namely, the number of firms in the industry and the "inequality" of the distribution of their outputs or size. If, on the one hand, the outputs of all the firms are equal to each other, this measure will be equal to the reciprocal of the number of firms. On the other hand, if the distribution of outputs for a given number of firms changes in such a way as to increase the coefficient of variation,[1] the measure will increase.

To gain some impression of the significance of this output distribution and the changes that have taken place in it, table 2 compares measures of concentration for the copper mining industry with those for other industries. This comparison is very loose for a number of reasons. The measures for other industries are for the

---

[1] Equals the standard deviation of the outputs divided by the mean of the outputs. That is, it is equal to a measure of the dispersion of the outputs taken relative to the mean output. The standard deviation is divided by the mean output since, for example, a range in outputs of different firms of fifty tons a year is far more significant if the average output is forty tons a year than if it is 400 tons.

TABLE 1. *Annual Mine Production of the Leading Thirty Copper Firms as a Percentage of World Output in Selected Years, 1912–1956*

| | Percentage share in | | | | | | |
|---|---|---|---|---|---|---|---|
| Rank of firms | 1912 | 1923[a] | 1928[a] | 1935[a] | 1939[a] | 1947[a] | 1956[a] |
| First | 15.5 | 21.2 | 21.1 | 16.9 | 16.7 | 22.3 | 17.6 |
| Second | 11.3 | 19.0 | 19.5 | 13.4 | 16.6 | 19.3 | 15.3 |
| Third | 8.0 | 6.2 | 6.5 | 7.7 | 7.2 | 10.7 | 8.3 |
| Fourth | 4.0 | 4.4 | 5.9 | 7.5 | 6.8 | 7.3 | 8.2 |
| Fifth | 3.1 | 3.5 | 3.5 | 6.6 | 6.5 | 5.9 | 6.6 |
| Sixth | 2.4 | 3.3 | 3.4 | 5.6 | 5.9 | 4.9 | 6.5 |
| Seventh | 2.1 | 3.2 | 3.1 | 4.3 | 3.9 | 4.4 | 4.3 |
| Eighth | 2.0 | 2.9 | 2.6 | 2.7 | 2.9 | 2.4 | 3.1 |
| Thirtieth | 0.7 | 0.5 | 0.4 | 0.4 | 0.3 | 0.3 | 0.4 |
| Firms 1 to 4 | 38.9 | 50.8 | 52.9 | 45.6 | 47.4 | 59.6 | 49.4 |
| Firms 1 to 8 | 48.6 | 63.6 | 65.4 | 64.7 | 66.6 | 77.1 | 69.9 |
| Firms 1 to 30 | 72.0 | 83.6 | 84.8 | 86.6 | 84.0 | 93.1 | 89.0 |
| Firms 5 to 8 | 9.6 | 12.8 | 12.5 | 19.1 | 19.2 | 17.5 | 20.5 |
| C, a coefficient of concentration [b] | .05 | .093 | .096 | .071 | .077 | .114 | .081 |
| Ratios of outputs of firms 9 to 30 to outputs of firms 1 to 8 | .48 | .31 | .30 | .34 | .26 | .21 | .27 |
| Ratios of outputs of firms 5 to 8 to outputs of firms 1 to 4 | .25 | .25 | .24 | .42 | .41 | .29 | .42 |

*Note:* The underlying data have been assembled from various issues of a number of sources, among which are the following:

*Yearbook* of the American Bureau of Metal Statistics, New York.

*Minerals Yearbook* [formerly *Mineral Resources of the United States*], U.S. Department of the Interior, Bureau of Mines (Washington, D.C.: U.S. Government Printing Office).

*The Mineral Industry*, annual statistical supplement to *Engineering and Mining Journal* (New York).

*Moody's Manual of Industrials* (New York: Moody's Investors Service).

Walter E. Skinner, *The Mining Year Book* (London).

Walter Harvey Weed and Horace J. Stevens, *The Copper Handbook* (Houghton, Michigan); later *The Mines Handbook* (New York).

*Mines Register*, successor to *The Mines Handbook* (New York).

The percentages are based on the recoverable copper content of mine output. In some cases, mine output is unobtainable and smelter output must be used. Where this is necessary, the difference from mine output is not sufficient to change any of the conclusions.

In resolving problems of corporate control, majority ownership of voting stock has been taken to constitute control. Where less than a majority is owned, an attempt has been made to resolve these questions by following competent contemporary opinion on whether there is effective control. The main problem here is the Guggenheim interests (later Kennecott) where the views of Weed and Stevens have been followed. That is, Utah Copper, Nevada Consolidated, Chino, Ray, Kennecott, National Metallurgical, Braden, Mother Lode (1918), and Chile (up to 1923) have been combined. The pattern of control is clearer in later years because stock acquisitions and mergers have cleared up problem cases.

The following companies have been assigned to Anaconda: Andes (1916), Chile (1923), Walker (1918), Utah Consolidated—Utah Delaware—(1924), Cananea, Inspiration, Mountain City, and National Tunnel.

*Notes to table 1 (continued)*

Phelps Dodge has been assigned Arizona Copper (1921), Calumet and Arizona (1931), New Cornelia (1931), Moctezuma, and Old Dominion.

In accordance with the generally accepted view on control of Roan Antelope, it has been counted as a part of American Metal Climax, Inc., which owns a 33 per cent direct interest through its majority-owned Rhodesian Selection Trust. American Metal Climax is also assigned Chibuluma, Mufulira, and Matahambre (until 1955).

Rhodesian Anglo-American includes Rhokana—B'wana M'Kubwa and N'Changa —and Kansanshi (1953).

Howe Sound includes Chelan, Brittania, and Carmen.

Newmont includes Magma (1921), Sherrit Gordon (1956), O'Okiep, and Idarado.

Noranda includes Horne, Waite Amulet, and the Mining Corporation of Canada— Normetal and Quemont—(1948), and Gaspé—(1955).

Ventures, Ltd. includes Falconbridge, Opemiska, and Frobisher—Kilembe—(1940).

Miami and Tennessee are combined under the Lewisohn interests.

American Smelting and Refining includes Northern Peru, Corocoro (1934–55), Buchans, and Mt. Isa (1956).

Turkeye Bakir includes Ergani and Murguel.

[a] In 1928 and later years Russian output has been excluded entirely. Russian output was negligible in 1923, 1.2 per cent of the world total (including Russian output) in 1928; 4.2 per cent in 1935; 4.9 per cent in 1939; 7.4 per cent in 1947; and 11.7 per cent in 1956. The percentages for 1947 and 1956 include the output of East Germany. If Russian (and East German) output were considered as the output of a firm in, say, 1956, it would be the third largest "firm." The top four firms would still account for 44 per cent of the output, and the top thirty firms would account for 89.5 per cent of the total as against 88.2 per cent without Russia included in the calculation. C would be lowered to .077.

[b] This coefficient of concentration, C, combines into a single figure the two main components of the concept of concentration, namely, the number of firms in the industry and the "inequality" of the distribution of their outputs or size. Various specific measures of concentration can be shown to involve these two main elements. This particular measure involves the number of firms, N, and uses the coefficient of variation of outputs, C.V. (or whatever variable is selected as a measure of size) as a measure of inequality. That is,

$$C = (1/N)(1 + C.V.^2) = \sum_{i=1}^{N} (P_i/100)^2$$

where P is the firm's percentage share in the industry total. Thus, an industry with ten firms of equal size would show

C = 0.1 = (1/10)(1 + 0), since the coefficient of variation is zero.

The coefficients on this line have been calculated on the basis of the top thirty firms' outputs by squaring their P/100's and summing. The number of firms in the industry is not known, but the true C can be bracketed as follows: (1) The true C cannot be less than the value calculated for the top thirty firms. (2) The highest possible value for C, given the P's for the top thirty firms, would be obtained if the remaining unlisted firms were of the same size as the thirtieth firm (none of them can be larger than the thirtieth firm if the top 30 have been picked successfully). In no case would this raise the calculated total for thirty firms by more than .002. For more detailed discussion and application of this measure of concentration, see *Business Concentration and Price Policy* (New York: National Bureau of Economic Research, 1955), especially "Measures of Concentration," by Gideon Rosenbluth, pp. 57–99. See also Rosenbluth, *Concentration in Canadian Manufacturing Industries* (New York: National Bureau of Economic Research, 1957); and O. C. Herfindahl, "Concentration in the Steel Industry," a Ph.D. dissertation on file at Columbia University (New York, 1950).

TABLE 2. *Concentration in World Copper Mining and Selected Products of U.S. Manufacturing Industries*

| Product | Percentage accounted for by leading four firms | Percentage accounted for by leading eight firms | Value of shipments (*billions of dollars*) |
|---|---|---|---|
| World (1956): | | | |
| Copper mining | 49 | 70 | 3.21 a |
| United States (1954): | | | |
| Passenger cars | 98 | 99 | 9.47 |
| Gypsum products | 89 | 97 | .27 |
| Cigarettes | 82 | 99 | 1.62 |
| Metal cans | 81 | 89 | 1.29 |
| Canned milk | 79 | 86 | .34 |
| Tires and inner tubes | 78 | 91 | 1.62 |
| Truck tractor, chassis, and trucks | 77 | 93 | 1.73 |
| Refined cane sugar | 67 | 86 | .86 |
| Bottled liquors | 67 | 82 | .54 |
| Antibiotics for human use | 67 | 89 | .25 |
| Biscuits and crackers | 66 | 73 | .79 |
| Pig iron | 65 | 82 | 2.49 |
| Glass containers | 63 | 78 | .63 |
| Household mechanical washing machines | 62 | 84 | .44 |
| Household refrigerators (electric and gas) | 62 | 83 | .57 |
| Sanitary tissue health products | 57 | 71 | .43 |
| Truck trailers | 56 | 65 | .26 |
| Shortening and cooking oils | 55 | 79 | .89 |
| Flour mixes | 54 | 67 | .40 |
| Still picture equipment | 54 | 64 | .17 |
| Wool carpets and rugs | 50 | 71 | .34 |
| Candy bars (except solid chocolate) | 49 | 62 | .23 |
| Cold-rolled steel and strip | 49 | 70 | 1.64 |
| Canned meats (except dog and cat food) | 46 | 63 | .58 |

*Note:* The data for copper mining are from table 1. Concentration percentages for all the other products are from Report of the Subcommittee on Antitrust and Monopoly to the Committee on the Judiciary, *Concentration in American Industry,* 85th Congress, 1st Session (Washington, D.C.: U.S. Government Printing Office, 1957), table 41, p. 166. Note that these percentages are based on *product* shipments rather than on total shipments of firms in the specified industry.

a World output multiplied by "average price" per U.S. Bureau of Mines.

United States only, while the copper measures are for the world. More important, the degree of concentration in the relevant market is not related to market performance in a simple way, for there are many other factors involved.

These comparisons with manufacturing industries do not warrant the conclusion that concentration in copper mining is so low that the industry is bound to show highly competitive behavior regardless of other factors. What is suggested is that copper mining is not highly concentrated as compared with a number of other industries. Rather, it concentration of output is lower than that of a good many industries whose behavior is widely regarded as strongly competitive. In appraising the data for these industries, which have not been selected for inclusion on a systematic basis, factors other than size structure as characterized by the shares of the top firms may be important, notably, import competition, ease of entry into the industry, and elasticity of demand for the product.

Two important factors that further limit the exercise of monopoly power do not show up in the measures of concentration in the production of copper used in this study. They are the production of copper from scrap and the competition provided by aluminum for a substantial part of the demand. One expert estimates that about 30 per cent of the free world's consumption of copper is supplied from scrap. A part of the scrap component of total supply, that is, a part of new scrap, is controlled by the producers of newly mined copper through fabricating subsidiaries.[2] But the fact still deserves emphasis that the measures of concentration used here do not reflect an important independent component of the supply of copper, or, alternatively, do not reflect a factor serving to increase the elasticity of demand facing the producers of newly mined copper.

---

[2] See estimates of Jean Vuillquez, as reported in the *American Metal Market*, May 16, 1957, p. 1. A substantial part of this presumably is new scrap. (New scrap is generated in the fabrication of products containing copper. Old scrap is generated when the products are finally scrapped after being worn out.) In the United States in recent years, new scrap (including copper content recovered in alloys) has been running about 20 per cent of total copper consumed, which may be approximated by apparent withdrawals of new refined copper on domestic account plus copper recovered from new and old scrap. Old scrap has been supplying about the same percentage. That is, new and old scrap together supply about 40 per cent of U.S. copper consumption as defined here. See U.S. Department of the Interior, Bureau of Mines, *Minerals Yearbook* (Washington, D.C.: U.S. Government Printing Office, various issues).

# DETERIORATION, OUTPUT, AND THE PRICE OF COPPER

### HAVE COPPER RESOURCES DETERIORATED?

At first blush, it appears that the factual results obtained in this study should be able to throw light on the question of whether the resources from which copper is produced have deteriorated over time. It turns out, however, that this is a subtle and difficult question, as has already been indicated in the discussion of the theoretical framework underlying this study.

One way of dealing with the question of deterioration would be in terms of an absolutely complete physical inventory—an inventory that cannot possibly be taken. Then if the inventory of copper in the ground had declined between two dates the answer would be that resources have deteriorated—again, so far as deposits in the ground are concerned. This inevitably would be the case in any period during which actual mining of ore had occurred, but there might well have been no deterioration so far as the recoverable stock of copper above the ground is concerned. Here the production and use of copper do not result in a deterioration of this part of the physical resources, but

Excerpt reprinted from "Conclusions and Summary," *Copper Costs and Prices: 1870-1957* (Baltimore: The Johns Hopkins Press for Resources for the Future, Inc., 1959), chapter 8, pp. 220-235.

rather an increase to the extent that the copper placed in use is recoverable to be used again.

But this type of answer to the question of whether resources have deteriorated is clearly unsatisfactory. It would be much better to have an answer in economic terms. What the writer would like to know is the impact on production cost of changes in the physical environment within which copper is produced. And these changes would of course be attributable to the productive activity of man, since geological processes resulting in the formation of new deposits of copper may be considered at a standstill. Unfortunately, the relative price changes observed in this study measure the *combined* effects of "deterioration" in resources and of changes in the state of the arts—not only in copper mining, smelting, and refining, but elsewhere in the economy where progress has been made in the production of goods and services that in turn are used in the production of copper. The answer to the question of the differential effect on cost of deterioration in resources must, then, be in the nature of an estimate of what would have happened to the cost of producing copper in the absence of technological progress.

Following this approach, assume that the state of the arts is held constant and also specify the size and nature of the stock of capital goods. Then, starting from the natural resource position as it was in, say, 1870, how would the cumulative supply curve have behaved if copper had been produced at the 1870 annual rate until the total amount of copper produced was equal to the quantity actually produced between 1870 and the present? The quantity produced is very important, of course. Suppose, for example, that there had in fact been very great resource deterioration over a certain period. By reducing the total quantity to be produced in this hypothetical calculation, the amount of deterioration (as measured by the rise in cost under the constant state of the arts) could be brought as close to zero as wished.

Specifically, suppose that the calculation is started from the position of 1870. The capital equipment in existence in all the various industries of the world's economy is as it was in 1870, and no progress is made in the state of the arts. Suppose that the production activities in all the different industries of the world's economy in the year 1870 keep on repeating themselves without growing. Imagine that the net new capital formed each year is thrown away at the end of the year so that the next year can be a duplicate of the activities of 1870, with the one exception of those changes that are necessary in the copper industry to take account of the fact that production has used up some of its resources and has required that the copper industry move on to the exploitation of other resources. Now, let the production activities of 1870 be repeated over and over again, with the copper industry producing its 1870 output in each year until it has ground out as much copper as it in fact produced in the years between 1870 and the present. Under these conditions, which have had to be specified in order to isolate the effect on cost of deterioration in the resource position, what would have happened to the cost of copper? The writer presumes that the cost of producing copper would have gone up very much.[1] Indeed, it may well be that the quantity of copper involved could have been produced under the 1870 state of the arts only with costs so high that the impact on the rest of the economy would make the experiment conceptually impossible.

Now, start with the natural resource position in 1870 so far as the production of copper was concerned but with 1958 techniques and the capital equipment in existence in that year, and ask the same kind of question as in the situation just considered. What would have happened to the cost of copper with the 1958 production activities being repeated over and over again and with the copper industry producing its 1958 output until it had produced a quantity of copper equal to the total amount produced between 1870 and 1958? Just as in the former case, the cost of producing copper would no doubt have gone up, but the amount of rise in absolute terms would certainly be much less. Indeed, it couldn't possibly be much more than, say, 15 cents a pound. From the vantage point of 1870, however, the increase could be many, many times larger.

Perhaps there is not very much to be learned from speculations of this sort, but they serve to emphasize two points. First, any simple notion of resource deterioration is likely to be useless without a considerable explication of what one chooses to mean by this phrase. Second, and very important though perhaps obvious, deterioration in the various physical aspects in terms of which resources can be described are less significant the more advanced the state of the arts and

---

[1] Compare the statement of C. E. Julihn and H. M. Meyer in *Mineral Resources of the United States, 1928—Part I* (Washington, D.C.: U.S. Government Printing Office, 1931), p. 713: "Repeatedly in the past a critical stage in the copper industry has been reached at which there was, in fact, some likelihood of a dearth of copper due to more rapid increase in consumption than in production. This has generally been reflected in the price of the metal, although new discoveries of ore deposits and improvements in technology have thus far prevented the development of any very acute situation. For example, it is now recognized that such an acute situation was averted by the technologic developments in mining, milling, and smelting related to the opening of the so-called porphyry coppers. Without the contribution of metal from these low-grade mines the world could not have had for some years past anything like the tonnage of copper it has actually consumed, even at much higher prices for the metal than those that have prevailed."

the greater the quantity of capital (since capital can be substituted for so-called resource products).

But why cannot a decline in the grade of ore be taken as a conclusive indicator of deterioration in the resources from which copper is produced? The basic fact involved here is that the grade of ore (that is, its copper content) is only one of many circumstances that determine the cost of producing copper from a particular deposit. Hence, the techniques of production and the types and locations of deposits may in fact be such that the more expensive deposits to produce are those with a higher grade of ore. If the state of the art of finding deposits is in a reasonably good condition, then some low-grade deposits will be exploited before higher grade deposits. Nor can changes in the grade of ore over time be taken to indicate the course of the historical cost of producing copper or any other mineral product. Again, it could be that an advance in technique has made it possible to use a lower-grade ore at no increase in price or even at a lower price than the higher-grade ore that was used earlier.

To return to the original question: have the resources from which copper is produced deteriorated? If changes in the price of copper were measured in a situation where there was no increase in productivity in the rest of the economy, the answer would be easy. The level price for copper resulting from a situation in which there had been technological advance in the production of copper would necessarily involve deterioration in the resources—whether this deterioration is measured with reference to an early or a later point in time. But the comparatively level price for copper over long periods of time is a price that is roughly constant relative to the prices of other goods, with all prices affected by technological advance. Hence, a level price for copper in and of itself does not permit the conclusion that there has been deterioration of the natural resources from which copper has been produced. Under the circumstances, there could have been an increase in the relative price of copper without deterioration in the resources if there had been a slower advance in productivity in processes affecting the price of copper than in processes affecting the prices of other goods.

However, deterioration in some degree is certainly suggested by the earlier hypothetical calculations for the period from 1870 to 1957. Furthermore, deterioration, as defined above, probably has taken place in the period after World War I. This is suggested, but not established, by the figures given in table 3 showing a decline in the grade of ore in the United States. If it is true that deterioration (in the sense specified here) has taken place in the worldwide environment in which copper is produced, then the rapidity of movement up the

TABLE 3. *Grade of Copper Ore Mined in the United States, 1880–1956*

| 1880 | 3.0% | 1921–30 | 1.6% |
|------|------|---------|------|
| 1889 | 3.3 | 1931–40 | 1.6 |
| 1902 | 2.7 | 1941–50 | 1.0 |
| 1906–10 | 2.1 | 1951–56 | 0.8 |
| 1911–20 | 1.7 | | |

*Sources:* Figures for 1880 to 1936 from Y. S. Leong et al., *Technology, Employment and Output in Copper Mining* (Philadelphia: Works Projects Administration, National Research Project, and U.S. Department of the Interior, Bureau of Mines, February 1940), p. 220. Those for 1937 to 1956 from U.S. Department of the Interior, Bureau of Mines, *Minerals Yearbook* (Washington, D.C.: U.S. Government Printing Office, various issues).

cumulative supply curve (which has been lowered by technological progress) has been affected by the size of the demand for copper. That is, the greater the demand for copper, the more rapid will be the upward movement in the price of copper, provided the rate at which cost-reducing improvements are introduced is independent of cost increases caused by a deteriorating copper-producing environment.[2]

In the case of copper, the observed prices reflect a worldwide demand whose relative rate of growth has been declining, as shown in table 4. From 1881 to World War I, the long-term percentage growth in production was about constant with no indication, to the eye at least, of increase or decrease. The retardation has come since that time and has involved a persistent decline in growth of demand (production) rather than a drop to a lower level of growth after World War I. The tentative conclusion suggested by these data is that the stable long-run price of copper after World War I is attributable in part to the decline in the growth of the demand for copper. If this decline had not occurred, the interpretive model developed in this study suggests that the deflated long-run price of copper would have been increasing after World War I.

Two factors have played a part in the declining rate of growth in the demand for newly mined copper. One is the increasing importance of copper recovered from old scrap; the other is a large decline in the price of aluminum relative to the price of copper. The importance of the first factor for the world as a whole cannot be established directly.

---

[2] It is conceivable that moderate and slow cost increases would stimulate increased applied research to reduce costs, research which no doubt would enjoy some success. The writer, however, is not aware of any evidence that would confirm or even suggest such a relationship for the copper industry as a whole. What happens in individual companies when their costs go up is another, and no doubt easier, question.

TABLE 4. *Annual Rates of Growth in World Primary Copper Production between Selected Periods, 1881–1957*

| | |
|---|---|
| 1881–90 to 1905–14 | 5.5% |
| 1905–14 to 1923–29 | 3.6 |
| 1923–29 to 1936–39 | 2.5 |
| 1936–39 to 1947–57 | 1.9 |

*Note:* These percentages are the continuously compounded annual rates that will yield the actual relative production totals for the adjacent periods indicated. The first two rates are based on smelter output; the last two on mine output. Data are from U.S. Department of the Interior, Bureau of Mines, *Minerals Yearbook* (Washington, D.C.: U.S. Government Printing Office, various issues), and from U.S. Department of the Interior, Bureau of Mines, *Summarized Data of Copper Production*, Economic Paper No. 1 (Washington, D.C.: U.S. Government Printing Office, 1928). For years after World War I, the smaller periods have been chosen to exclude obviously abnormal years. Similar retardation in the relative growth of production is present between the peacetime "peak" years of 1884, 1912, 1929, 1937, and 1957. The percentages are 5.4 per cent; 3.8 per cent; 2.2 per cent; and 2.0 per cent.

However, data for the United States alone show the following levels for copper recovered from old scrap as a percentage of apparent consumption: 1908–14, 18 per cent; 1919–29, 29 per cent; 1930–39, 39 per cent. In the years after World War II, 1947–56, old scrap was only 26 percent of apparent consumption.[3] But the years after World War II brought a very large fall in the price of aluminum as compared with the price of copper. In 1936–40 the ratio between the prices of aluminum and copper was about the same as in the years 1919–29. Between these two periods and 1947–57, the ratio between the two prices fell by 58 per cent.[4] There can be little doubt that this change played a large part in checking the rate of growth in the demand for copper. Indeed, in the United States, apparent consumption in 1957 was about at the same level as in 1947, and may actually have been lower.

[3] These percentages are calculated from data in U.S. Department of the Interior, Bureau of Mines, *Minerals Yearbook* (Washington, D.C.: U.S. Government Printing Office, various issues). Data for 1908 to 1947 are summarized in Charles White Merrill, "The Accumulation and Conservation of Metals-in-Use," *Proceedings of the United Nations Scientific Conference on the Conservation and Utilization of Resources, Volume II, Mineral Resources* (New York: United Nations Department of Economic Affairs, 1951), p. 34. Apparent consumption is the sum of apparent withdrawals of new copper on domestic account and copper recovered from old scrap. The latter includes both refined copper and copper recovered in alloys.

[4] The price ratios are calculated from prices in *Metal Statistics, 1958* (New York: The American Metal Market), pp. 355, 617. These are published prices, of course, and at times may not reflect actual prices very closely. See the remarks of Donald H. Wallace on aluminum prices in William Y. Elliott et al., *International Control in the Non-Ferrous Metals* (New York: Macmillan, 1937), p. 254.

### Deterioration of Resources and the Cumulative Supply Curve of Different Regions

The earlier discussion of the cumulative supply curve * suggested that an examination of the relative outputs of different sectors of the world would permit certain restricted statements about the rates at which these sectors are advancing along their cumulative supply curves. It will be recalled that in the simplest situation where there is no technological progress the shares in total production are inversely related to the rates at which cost is rising with respect to cumulated output in each of the regions.

Where technological progress lowers the cumulative supply curves for both regions by the same amounts, the relative shares of the different regions can be interpreted in the same way. But if this does not take place and if stable shares in total output are interpreted as above, the indicated rate at which cost is increasing along the cumulative supply curve for the region with the slower rate of progress will be exaggerated. It is important to realize in this connection that progress is a very comprehensive concept and includes all elements that affect cost, not only those that are operating within mines and plants but also those outside. Thus, an improvement in the stability of government, which in turn may lead to a reduction in the expected reward that investors demand, is a kind of progress that will affect cost.

Within the United States and other producing regions of the world, the reductions in cumulative supply curves are a result of technological progress and other "developmental" progress. In addition, the relative shares between two points in time will also be affected by governmental subsidies which permit a lowering of selling price without any actual reduction in economic cost. Again, a candidate for consideration here is the special tax privileges accorded mining activities in the United States. This study, however, has not assembled evidence to permit an evaluation of changes in the relative importance of subsidies between various points in time as between the United States and other producing regions. Nor is the writer in a position to make even a judgment in terms of "greater than" or "lesser than" on the amounts by which the cumulative supply curves of the United States and the rest of the world have been lowered between various points in time as the result of progress. Thus, interpretation of table 5, along the line suggested by the analysis of comparatively simple situations is subject to the qualifications flowing from different downward shifts in the cumulative supply curves.

---

* See selection 7.—*Ed.*

TABLE 5. *Ratio of Copper Output outside the United States to U.S. Output,*
*1881–1956*

| 1881 | 4.06 | 1901 | .93 | 1921 | 1.43 | 1941 | 1.95 |
|------|------|------|-----|------|------|------|------|
| 1882 | 3.46 | 1902 | .87 | 1922 | 1.02 | 1942 | 1.74 |
| 1883 | 2.88 | 1903 | .88 | 1923 | 0.90 | 1943 | 1.73 |
| 1884 | 2.38 | 1904 | .79 | 1924 | 0.87 | 1944 | 1.86 |
| 1885 | 2.05 | 1905 | .75 | 1925 | 0.97 | 1945 | 2.09 |
| | | | | | | | |
| 1886 | 2.06 | 1906 | .74 | 1926 | 0.93 | 1946 | 2.37 |
| 1887 | 1.76 | 1907 | .83 | 1927 | 1.04 | 1947 | 1.89 |
| 1888 | 1.60 | 1908 | .74 | 1928 | 1.10 | 1948 | 2.05 |
| 1889 | 1.57 | 1909 | .67 | 1929 | 1.16 | 1949 | 2.29 |
| 1890 | 1.35 | 1910 | .75 | 1930 | 1.52 | 1950 | 2.04 |
| | | | | | | | |
| 1891 | 1.23 | 1911 | .79 | 1931 | 1.92 | 1951 | 2.12 |
| 1892 | 1.04 | 1912 | .77 | 1932 | 3.21 | 1952 | 2.26 |
| 1893 | 1.03 | 1913 | .78 | 1933 | 5.06 | 1953 | 2.29 |
| 1894 | 1.00 | 1914 | .79 | 1934 | 4.96 | 1954 | 2.71 |
| 1895 | 0.94 | 1915 | .68 | 1935 | 3.27 | 1955 | 2.40 |
| | | | | | | | |
| 1896 | 0.84 | 1916 | .58 | 1936 | 2.10 | 1956 | 2.39 |
| 1897 | 0.84 | 1917 | .67 | 1937 | 2.06 | | |
| 1898 | 0.83 | 1918 | .65 | 1938 | 3.08 | | |
| 1899 | 0.83 | 1919 | .70 | 1939 | 2.32 | | |
| 1900 | 0.80 | 1920 | .75 | 1940 | 2.03 | | |

*Note:* The ratios for 1881–1921 are calculated from U.S. Bureau of Mines estimates of smelter production; those for 1922–56 are calculated from its estimates of
mine output. See U.S. Department of the Interior, Bureau of Mines, *Minerals Yearbook* and *Mineral Resources of the United States* (Washington, D.C.: U.S. Government Printing Office, various issues).

The interpretation of the relative shares of total output of copper
within and outside the United States along the lines of the cumulative
supply curve must refer to the long run. The actual ratios (fig. 21) reflect, however, many short-run influences. The rapid decline in this ratio from 1881 to around 1900 is probably better interpreted in terms of
getting to a position of long-run equilibrium on the cumulative supply
curve, rather than as indicating the rate at which the United States
was moving up its cumulative supply curve as compared with the rate
at which other producing regions were moving up theirs. When a new
producing region was opened up whose characteristics had not been
well known, the ratios between the output of the area containing the
new producing region and the output of the rest of the world probably
would change very rapidly until completion of the region's initial burst
of exploitation.

Moving on through time, the relative shares of the United States
and other regions were about constant up to the twenties. Once again
a fundamental change, the nature of which has already been discussed,
seems to have occurred around World War I. The very large rise in

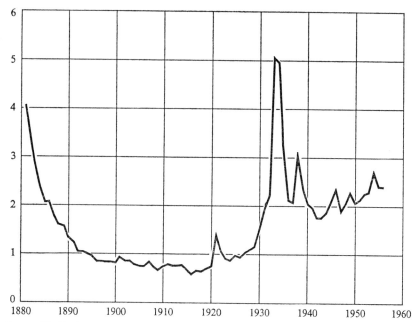

FIGURE 21. *Ratio of copper output outside the United States to U.S. output, 1881–1956.*

the ratio in the years immediately following 1929 is attributable to events associated with the depression, notably the efforts at restriction of output from 1932 to 1934. The response of the ratio to business cycles in the United States seems to be much greater after 1930 than was true before that time.

If we look at the whole period after 1920, there appears to have been an upward drift in the ratio, interrupted by the temporarily high ratios of the thirties. This is the result of a roughly constant level of output in the United States as against a rising output in the rest of the world. The ratio in the last few years has been over two. The simple interpretation, discussed earlier, would mean that the United States is moving up its cumulative supply curve at a rate over twice as fast as is the rest of the world. Again, however, this does not mean that cost in the United States is moving up through time at a rate twice as great as that of the rest of the world. According to this study's interpretative schema, costs in the United States and in the rest of the world are moving up at the same rate through time, this equality being preserved through a difference between the shares of the two areas in total output.

### The Significance of Long-Run Stability
#### in the Price of Copper

After elimination of the abnormal years before World War I, copper prices seem to have been comparatively stable over a long period. There are sizable gaps in the record of normal years after World War I, but, even here, the years that remain yield no suggestion of upward or downward drift over the period as a whole. And the history of the industry does not suggest that there were fluctuations in long-run cost in the periods separating the normal years. The constancy of long-run price points to an important conclusion about the process of finding, developing, and producing copper: investment in these activities responds in a systematic way to long-run profit prospects.

It is sometimes argued that two characteristics allegedly peculiar to mineral industries—(1) that mineral deposits must be replaced on exhaustion by exploration for new deposits and (2) that success in the search for new deposits is very uncertain—sharply differentiate their functioning from, say, that of manufacturing industries. In manufacturing, so the argument goes, you can readily replace a worn-out machine simply by going out and buying one; you don't have to look very hard to find it. In manufacturing, the investment of $10 million in a new plant will, if you have been reasonably prudent, result in a plant that is worth about $10 million. The consequence of these differences, runs the argument, is that the functioning of a mineral industry is somehow different from manufacturing. Some cite this difference in turn as justification for special treatment by government. In the case of copper, evidence indicates that the existence of these differentiating characteristics has not sufficed to differentiate the long-run response of investment to profit prospects in the mineral industries from the response in manufacturing or other industries. If this were not the case, a type of price behavior over long periods of time different from that which actually took place could be expected.

The stability of the long-run price can be thought of as a result of the relation between, first, the rate and variation from year to year in the accidental finds of copper deposits,[5] and second, the size of the demand for copper relative to the rate at which accidental finds are made. That is to say, the constancy of the long-run price over time depends on the size of the "field" (or environment, or matrix) in which systematic exploration and development activity (that is, systematic

---

[5] "Accidental finds" are finds that are made not as the result of finding activity that is systematically related to the price of copper.

from the point of view of the whole industry) can take place. Three general cases of this relationship should be distinguished.[6]

First, there is the case in which the exploration and development activity that responds systematically to profit prospects is present in such volume as to dominate the accidental finds that are made. In this situation, the stock of known properties grows as demand grows, and new properties regularly replace old properties as they decline, but the stock of properties never gets very far ahead of production. There may be accidental finds, but their disruptive effects are diminished by reason of the fact that the volume of systematic finding and development activity will adapt itself to unexpected changes in the volume of accidental finds.[7] In this kind of situation, it may be said that the field in which exploration, development, and production activities take place is large in the sense that it provides a stable or only slowly changing set of natural obstacles to the process of production. Specifically, if the areas in which copper deposits may be found are large and there is sufficient knowledge of the general characteristics of these areas to permit reasonably good prediction of the success of the exploration efforts of the industry as a whole, then the finding and production of copper will be taking place in a relatively stable environment. For example, if the outstanding characteristics of the environment in which finding activity takes place consist in general geological knowledge that there are some unexplored regions or areas with relevant characteristics similar to those where ore has already been found, long-run variations in price should not be expected because of variability in the rate at which deposits are found. In this type of situation, then, the production of copper would, in its general aspects, be similar to the production of "ordinary" goods, for neither one would be confronted with erratic natural shifts in the environmental obstacles to production. But in the cases of both copper and other goods, there are shifts in the force of environmental obstacles to production arising from technological progress.

A second general case would be that in which there is no systematic finding activity and in which there is no accidental finding activity. That is to say, successful exploration is so difficult and so costly—perhaps even impossible—that the price of the commodity (given the substitutes for the commodity) does not justify looking for additional deposits. In this case, if no additional deposits happen to be found,

---

[6] It is assumed that the magnitude of the effects of technological progress on price remains roughly constant through time.

[7] See O. C. Herfindahl, "Some Fundamentals of Mineral Economics," *Land Economics*, Vol. 31, No. 2 (May 1955), p. 131. [Reprinted as selection 4 in this volume.—*Ed.*]

price fluctuation would not be expected over the long term either; analysis of the behavior of price over time would take the form of a fixed stock analysis, as has been done by Hotelling.[8] The essential feature coming out of this analysis is a regular rise in price over time.

The third case would be that in which the field where exploration and development activity takes place is very limited, but every now and then is enlarged by accidental finds or other factors. An accidental find, for example, may result in the realization that deposits can be found in a region hitherto thought to be barren. If this knowledge is significant with respect to the total volume of production of the commodity, it becomes necessary to view production of the commodity as taking place under a new and different set of basic conditions. It would be expected that the long-run price of the commodity would be marked by periodic falls coming about as a result of accidental discoveries that are significant relative to the size of the industry, followed by slower increases during those periods when the stock of properties is not enlarged through systematic finding activity.

The copper industry has developed rather clearly along the lines of the first case and not the second or third. That is, there probably was only one decline in price (before the mid-eighties) that would be associated with accidental finds that were large relative to the size of the industry as in the third case. But it is very clear that systematic exploration activity does take place in the copper industry, thus precluding the applicability of the second and third cases.

There is some direct evidence that the environment within which copper deposits are found and exploited is very extensive. Informed guesses of the potential copper resources of the world show over 200 million tons of copper in 2 per cent ore or better and about 450 million tons of 1 per cent ore or better. World production of new copper at the time these estimates were made was about 3 million tons per year.[9]

If it is the first case that is applicable to the development of the copper industry, at least over rather considerable periods of time, the implication to be drawn is that the process of finding and developing new deposits to replace the old deposits as they decline is systematic from the economic point of view. That is to say, there is an effective

---

[8] See Harold Hotelling, "The Economics of Exhaustible Resources," *Journal of Political Economy*, Vol. 39, No. 2 (April 1931), p. 137.

[9] See The President's Materials Policy Commission, *Resources for Freedom, Volume II, The Outlook for Key Commodities* (Washington, D.C.: U.S. Government Printing Office, 1952), pp. 136–37 and 143–45. The amounts cited here have been read off the graph on p. 144. While these estimates are subject to a large error and are confined to present major producing districts, there is little doubt that potential copper resources are very large as compared with present production levels.

cost of exploration and development; if demand increases relative to the producing stock of properties, the increase in price effectively induces additional finding and development.[10]

This view may appear to be in conflict with the common opinion that the finding and developing of mineral deposits is in fact a very risky business. Risk and chance are certainly important, and it is necessary to explain how they fit into the view taken here. To the extent that risks are effectively consolidated, they do not prevent a systematic relation between investment (that is, investment that is successful on the average) in the finding and developing of deposits on the one hand and price on the other. It should be noted that effective consolidation of risks from the point of view of the operation of the industry is quite consistent with ineffective consolidation from the point of view of an individual, a joint venture, or even a corporation. That is, if the number of these small units which expose themselves to financial ruin responds to movements in the price of copper, and if increased (or decreased) finding activity does result in an increased (or decreased) volume of finding and development activity, then from the point of view of the operation of the industry there is a systematic investment response to price. The industry operates as if there were an effective consolidation of risks, which may in fact be true, especially at the level of the individual investor.

This is not to say that there has been a steady flow of new copper-producing properties year in and year out. Even if there is a stable *response* of investment in exploration and development to long-run prospects for profit, changes in demand over the business cycle would

---

[10] A test of this conclusion by direct examination of discovery rates cannot be made because the relevant data do not exist. W. E. Wrather, who retired from the directorship of the U.S. Geological Survey in 1956, has said, "Unfortunately, except for the United States petroleum industry and for iron mining in the Lake Superior region, no sort of reliable statistical data from which to determine that rate [the rate of discovery] have as yet been compiled for this hemisphere. The reason for this is that national and international estimates of reserves did not really begin until the 1930's; moreover, such estimates included only proved material and material commercially mineable at the time. . . . As improved technology made this submarginal material available, it became included in subsequent estimates, so that greater estimates of reserves did not necessarily mean new discoveries." See *Proceedings of the United Nations Conference on the Conservation and Utilization of Resources,* p. 48.

In the writer's view, the feasibility of direct verification would be doubtful even if reserve estimates of the quality of those made currently were available for a long period of time. This doubt rests on difficulties inherent in the definition of discovery and on the magnitude of errors present in current estimates. The "margin of error" is said by the U.S. Geological Survey and Bureau of Mines to be at least 50 per cent for estimates of the total of measured, indicated, and inferred ore. See *Resources for Freedom,* p. 137.

be sufficient in themselves to cause fluctuation in the actual flow of investment. Such accidental finds as there have been have not exerted major effects on the long-run price of copper by virtue of their infrequency combined with the importance of the subsequent investment required. It is important to understand that the initial cost of finding is the cost of establishing that there is some ore at a certain location plus establishing inconclusive indications that additional quantities may be present. But this provides only a small part of the knowledge of the deposit required for the production of copper, and it provides none of the physical capital. Consequently, the bulk of the investment activity involved in exploration and development comes after the point where uncertainty of results is a dominant feature of the activity. In addition, the volume of systematic finding activity surely adapts itself to the volume of accidental finds.

If these views are correct, accidental finds are not going to have much effect on price, and the observed behavior of the long-run price of copper will not be disturbed simply because a lucky find has been made. Insofar as the response of long-run supply to demand is concerned, copper does not appear to differ from commodities outside the mining industry.

SELECTION 11

# REVIEW OF

# "CAPITAL AND OUTPUT TRENDS IN

# MINING INDUSTRIES, 1870–1948"

The major finding of this paper is a rise in the ratio of capital to output in the mining industries over the period 1870 to roughly 1919; the rise was followed by a decline in the ratio from about 1919 to 1948. The period over which the ratio increased was marked by a more rapid growth in mineral output than the period over which the ratio fell. The rise and subsequent fall in the capital-output ratio are found to characterize each mineral industry, although the amounts of rise and fall are not uniform for the different industries. The estimates of capital for 1870, 1880, 1890, 1909, and 1919 are based directly on replies to questions on capital in the mineral censuses for those years. Capital estimates for 1929, 1940, and 1948 are derived by applying ratios of capital to output derived from corporate income tax data to total U.S. output for the different industries.

Although these findings are carefully qualified, in my judgment the author is inclined to overrate their reliability. A large amount of the

Reprinted by permission from the *Journal of the American Statistical Association* (March 1957), pp. 119–122. The book under discussion, written by Israel Borenstein, was published as Occasional Paper 45 by the National Bureau of Economic Research in 1954.

rise in the ratios from 1870 to 1919 is probably attributable to under-reporting of capital in the early censuses and perhaps to the possibility that revaluations following tax law changes got into the amounts reported for the 1919 census. It is more likely that the results reported for the period following 1919 do reflect a genuine decline in capital-output ratios, but until it can be more firmly established that certain factors did not cause a spurious decline or until the real factors "causing" the decline are more clearly identified, the results should be regarded as decidedly tentative.

There are two matters of concept that a reader of this paper should keep in mind. First, the paper is concerned with the quantity of capital used in the industry and not with the flow of services from the capital goods. The difference can be substantial for both different industries and different periods of time.

Second, it is useful to distinguish between current production of a mineral product (such as copper ore) and production of a capital good used in current production, namely, the mineral deposit. On the output side, the problem of measuring the output of the capital good (the mineral deposit) is especially difficult. On the input side, measurement is complicated by the fact that some of the activities of a mineral firm jointly produce both kinds of product.[1] The definition of capital used in the paper includes, for firms classified in the minerals industries, the capital goods used in producing both kinds of output, but the output definition does not include the capital goods part of the output.

An attempt is made to separate "land" from other capital, apparently on the ground that "land" is not involved in the demand for savings (p. 42). The usefulness of this separation seems doubtful, for what gets recorded in the land account depends in part on accidents of market turnover, as is recognized on p. 43. More important, it is difficult to see why a mineral deposit should be treated differently from other capital goods. And in the long run the value of a mineral deposit does tend to reflect real expenditures on discovery and development (as is recognized for oil on p. 42).

The author is of the opinion that use of census data for both capital and product insures a high degree of comparability in the measures of capital and output (p. 63). He recognizes the possibility of error in capital data (p. 75), but is willing to rely on them because of their consistent behavior. But the consistency may reflect consistent changes

---

[1] One of the more important aspects of "producing" a mineral deposit is finding out more about its extent and other characteristics. Current production activities play a part in this accumulation of information.

in sources of bias. Specifically, I suspect radical under-reporting of capital in the early censuses with fuller reporting as time went on, although it would be a mistake to think that the report on capital in mining ever was satisfactory.

For example, in the Census of 1880 [2] the Special Agent stated that the result of changing the capital question "has been to increase very greatly the amount returned as 'capital of the mining establishments' . . ." (as compared with 1870).

In the Census of 1890 in the iron ore section it is said that assessed valuations were sometimes used.[3] In the section on petroleum it is said that the average value of a well reported for the Census was $1,839, ". . . which, for what is stated above, is evidently very low." [4]

In 1902 the capital questions were omitted in view of the past experience with them, and we are told, "A careful study of the statistics for the different censuses leads to the conclusion that there are no reliable comparative data for all mines and quarries other than the quantity and value of products." [5]

The following statement appears in the 1919 Census, the last mineral census to contain a capital question: "The reports received in respect to capital, however, at both censuses [1909 and 1919] have in so many cases been defective that the data compiled are of value only as indicating very general conditions." [6]

In addition to fuller reporting of capital in successive censuses, the 1919 values received an additional boost because of revaluations permitted by new tax laws. First, under the income tax law the taxpayer's basis for his properties was the higher of cost or fair market value on March 1, 1913. Second, the discovery depletion provisions in the Revenue Act of 1918 (passed in 1919) were open to properties discovered after 1913 and resulted in extensive revaluations, especially in petroleum. It seems likely that the 1913 revaluations reached books of account and hence got in the Census. Since the administrative organization for discovery depletion was not set up until late 1919, it is less clear that these revaluations affected replies to the Census, but some probably did.[7]

Capital for 1929 and later years is estimated by applying ratios of capital to receipts (taken from corporate income tax balance sheet

[2] *Report on the Mining Industries of the United States* (1886), p. xxvii.
[3] *Report on Mineral Industries in the United States at the Eleventh Census: 1890* (1892), p. 15.
[4] Ibid., p. 433.
[5] *Mines and Quarries, 1902* (1905), p. 9.
[6] *Mines and Quarries, 1919*, p. 15.
[7] See Douglas Eldridge, "Federal Income Taxation of Mineral Resources" (1949), a Ph.D. thesis on file at the University of Chicago.

returns) to value of product based on censuses and Bureau of Mines data. At this point an important step in the argument is omitted, namely, to establish that the reserve for depletion and depreciation (and hence the net assets) tends to reflect depletion and depreciation taken for business purposes rather than depletion and depreciation taken for tax purposes. If this were not the case, the assets as recorded in balance sheet returns would have become a progressively smaller part of the business accounting asset value because tax depletion is a good deal higher than cost depletion and is not limited to the cost of the asset. In addition, a substantial amount of capital outlays is expensed in tax accounting that is capitalized under "sound" accounting principles.[8] Balance sheet data in *Statistics of Income* commonly reflect "business" rather than tax depletion and depreciation,[9] but even so, it is problematical whether "sound business accounting practice" in these industries will yield results that fit the economist's concepts very closely.

One of the main problems resulting from using data from *Statistics of Income* arises from the basis on which firms are classified by industry. Mining and oil companies whose principal activity is considered to be smelting or refining—and this would include many of the major companies—are classed in manufacturing rather than in mining.

In assessing the importance of this difficulty, the author notes a fairly close agreement between his petroleum capital estimate and two independent estimates for 1940 and 1948. He also compares the capital-product ratios for the appropriate groups in manufacturing with those in mining, but this is inconclusive, for what is needed is a comparison of this ratio for the mining activities of firms classified in manufacturing with the ratio for mining activities of those classified in mining.

The potential importance of these classification difficulties is indicated by the percentage of total corporate depletion taken by corporations classified in mining and quarrying. In the thirties this percentage ranged from 40 to 60, but in recent years it has run around a third.[10]

---

[8] According to one estimate, half of the outlays for finding and developing oil are expensed under "financial" accounting; three-fourths of these outlays are expensed under tax accounting. See J. G. McLean and R. W. Haigh, *The Growth of Integrated Oil Companies*, p. 251.

[9] The method of estimating the value of "plant" (a step in deriving "land" as a residual for 1929 and later years) is not independent of tax depreciation and depletion, however. The procedure described on page 72 seems to be equivalent, except for averaging, to extrapolating 1919 improvements and equipment by net fixed assets to 1930, and extrapolating beyond 1930 by depreciation taken on tax returns. The question is how well tax depreciation reflects the movement of the "plant" component of non-land.

[10] See Joseph Lerner, "A Discussion of Extractive Industries and National In-

Thus more than half of the corporate mining activity appears to be classified outside the mining and quarrying industry.

The decline in the ratio of capital to output is especially large for the petroleum industry. From 1919 to 1948 the ratio fell by 70 per cent, and from 1929 to 1948 by 50 per cent.[11] These results can be roughly tested by working with data for the domestic production activities of the large oil companies.[12] My calculations, in which I tried to duplicate Borenstein's procedures with the addition of a correction for years of low output, indicate a fall in the capital-output ratio from 1934 to 1948 of 23 per cent, but the ratio appears to have risen after 1948, so that from 1934 to 1953 the ratio fell by only 8 per cent. The annual rate at which Borenstein's series falls appears to be some two and a half to three times greater.

I would not urge that any great reliance be placed on these calculations—they are weak at a number of points—but the contrast with Borenstein's results is sufficient to warrant close attention to factors that might explain the behavior of these two series. What portion of the observed declines represents a real decline in the ratio of capital to output in petroleum production? What portions of the observed declines is the result of inadequacies of data and necessary departures from proper definitions? Some of the factors that may be involved can only be listed here.

The first possibility is that the minor industry of crude petroleum, etc., in *Statistics of Income* does not properly represent oil production activities because of the classification of many large oil companies in manufacturing. This may account for a substantial part of the difference.

Other factors that may be involved, some involving real change and some not, cause both series to change in the same direction, but the size of the effects may well have been different.

That a genuine decline in the ratio of capital to output has occurred is suggested by the decline in the ratio of proved reserves to annual production of crude oil from 21 in 1909–1918 to 12 in 1946–1955.[13]

Because dry holes tend to get expensed, an increase in the ratio of dry holes to wells drilled would tend to decrease the ratio of capital to

---

come Accounting," a paper given at the Conference on Research in Income and Wealth, Nov. 18–19, 1955, revised (mimeographed), p. 26.

[11] These ratios are calculated from values for both capital and output expressed in 1929 prices.

[12] See the annual financial analysis of 30 or more large oil companies published by the Chase National Bank (now The Chase Manhattan Bank). Titles and authors vary.

[13] American Petroleum Institute, *Petroleum Facts and Figures*, various years.

output. Dry holes as a percentage of wells drilled has increased by about a half from 1920 to the period after World War II.[14]

Other factors that may be involved include vertical disintegration, the development of spacing and production regulations, and the question of the adequacy of business accounting for the economist's needs, including the possibility of over-expensing, over-depreciation, and over-depletion. The first of these warrants some comment here.

Vertical disintegration of field services (notably well drilling) would progressively lower the capital figure (but not output) from what it otherwise would be, since the capital for well drilling by firms that are classified in the minor industry, crude petroleum, would be reduced as drilling activity was transferred from these firms to firms classified in the field service industry.[15] There has been an increasing tendency to hire well drilling rather than do it yourself. The percentage of total footage drilled by contractors was 68 in 1935, 82 in 1948, and 92 in 1955.[16] A substantial amount of money is involved, as is suggested by the fact that in 1953 about $2.5 billion was spent in the U.S. on well drilling.[17]

Borenstein's Occasional Paper is, of course, preliminary and brief. We look forward to his full analysis of findings in the more detailed monograph that is to follow.

---

[14] Ibid.

[15] Firms engaged *primarily* in providing field services, including independent drilling contractors, are not included in the *Source Book* data from which the ratio of capital to output is taken. If field service firms were included in both capital and output, the ratio of capital to output in, e.g., 1948, would have been 1.22 instead of 1.40. Field services had a capital-output ratio of only .64.

[16] The data are from the American Association of Oilwell Drilling Contractors.

[17] News release of the American Petroleum Institute for January 27, 1956.

SELECTION 12

# DEVELOPMENT OF THE MAJOR METAL MINING INDUSTRIES IN THE UNITED STATES, 1839–1909

The United States' rich endowment of mineral deposits made possible an enormous expansion in the output of metallic minerals from 1839 to 1909. The expansion of output was far from uniform in time or space, however. This paper develops the industry's statistical record of output and employment, by region and by mineral product. Some of the factors that produced the expansion are also briefly discussed.

Since this group of industries showed substantial changes in rate of output growth and large regional shifts, both among already producing regions and from them to new regions, the effects of some of the causal factors are shown more clearly here than in an already settled country with long-established mineral industries. In many cases, the record of output and employment gives some indication of the influence of the location of existing markets and economic activity, of changes in the

Reprinted by permission from *Output, Employment, and Productivity in the United States after 1800*, Studies in Income and Wealth, Vol. 30 (New York: National Bureau of Economic Research, 1966). Copyright © 1966 by the National Bureau of Economic Research. The appendix tables have not been reprinted here.

*Note:* I wish to acknowledge the valuable work of Selma Rein in investigating and evaluating a very extensive body of source material for output estimates and other data on the development of the mineral industries. Jerome Milliman and

TABLE 6. *U.S. Mine Output as Percentage of World Mine Output: Copper, Lead, Zinc, Gold, and Silver,*[a] *1849, 1879, and 1909*

|  | 1849 [b] | 1879 [c] | 1909 [c] |
|---|---|---|---|
| Copper | 1 | 15[d] | 60 |
| Lead | 16 | 22 | 30 |
| Zinc | 0 | 12 | 35 |
| Gold | 24 | 30 | 17 |
| Silver | 0.3 | 44 | 27 |

[a] Metal content.

[b] World output is from J. D. Whitney, *The Metallic Wealth of the United States, Described and Compared with that of Other Countries,* Philadelphia, 1854. U.S. output is as estimated in the present paper.

[c] World output is from the various *Economic Papers* of the U.S. Bureau of Mines, except for copper in 1879. U.S. output is as estimated in the present paper.

[d] World output is Henry R. Merton's estimate in *Mines and Quarries, 1902,* Census Bureau, Washington, 1905, p. 491.

cost of transportation, of technological change within the mining industries and, above all, of the quality of natural endowment and changes in it resulting from mining activity. A few comments are possible also on the bearing of the record of the mineral industries on some general issues of economic development.

The major metallic mining industries, which are the subject of this paper, constitute almost all of the industry—98 per cent or more if measured by value of output. This group is defined to include iron ore, copper, lead, zinc, gold, and silver. But major metal mining has been only a minor part of all the mineral industries, which include coal, petroleum, sand and gravel, and clay products, among others. And even this minor share was declining throughout much of the period under study—from one-third in 1870 to one-fifth in 1910, if measured by employment.

All mineral industries have been quantitatively unimportant for the United States as a whole—probably accounting for less than 3 per cent of total employment during the period under study. But in certain regions the mineral industries, and metal mining in particular, have been of far greater importance, and an examination of the record reveals their influence on the timing and pace of regional economic development and especially on the location of certain types of economic activity.

Until the beginning of metallic mining in the West, U.S. production of nonferrous ores was only a small part of the world total, except for lead. In the years that followed, however, the United States came to produce the sizable fractions of world output shown in table 6.

Sam Schurr have given me the benefit of their helpful comments on an earlier draft of this paper.

The U.S. mine output of copper was sufficient to provide a sizable surplus over consumption of primary copper from about the 1860s on. Mine production of lead, however, was closer to apparent consumption over most of the period under study. Zinc mine output was roughly equal to consumption after 1879; in the 1850s none at all was produced.

In this study, the base year data are derived mainly from the various Censuses, supplemented in earlier years by Whitney's comprehensive account of the mineral industries [1] and in later years by the data collected by the U.S. Geological Survey. It is perhaps not surprising that the Census data are defective in important ways. The 1870 Census was the first to make much effort to collect data for the mineral industries. The 1840 and 1850 Censuses are very doubtful, so much so that they seem unusable for our purposes. We have found it better to ignore them and to extrapolate employment back from 1860, by our estimate of output. Throughout the Censuses, the data on number of mines are particularly poor. [2]

The statistical record is not useless, however. It reveals faithfully the general movements of output, by commodity, and the fortunes of the different regions in the production of the various commodities. Less reliance can be placed on its employment data—though even here the general outlines of what happened are evident—and some reliance can be placed on even the more detailed quantitative aspects of the general picture.

### OUTPUT BEHAVIOR, 1839–1909 [3]

Within only seventy years, the mine output of the major metals grew to 117 times its 1839 level, a rate of growth averaging about 7 per cent

---

[1] J. D. Whitney, *The Metallic Wealth of the United States, Described and Compared with that of Other Countries,* Philadelphia, 1854.

[2] It was difficult to get data and even to find mines in the areas of the Rocky Mountains, the Southwest, and the Pacific Coast. For example, the Census of 1880 explains that the collection of statistics was hampered by, among other things, "the assassination of Colonel Charles Potter, the expert in charge of this territory" (*Census of 1880, Precious Metals,* p. 100).

[3] In this section and in the rest of the paper it is necessary to speak of changes in the output of a "commodity" that in fact is made up of several commodities—iron in ore, copper in ore, etc. These must be combined by some weighting scheme. Since our interest is in mine output, it would be preferable to use as a weight the price of a "real" unit of value added, but this has not been feasible. Instead, 1879 market prices have been used as weights throughout.

However, the market prices used were the prices of metal for copper, lead, zinc, gold, and silver ores, but the price of ore for iron ore. While any weighting scheme other than the value-added one is arbitrary, it is true that the weight of one commodity, iron ore, is taken at the mine level but at the metal level for the others. The problem here is that the ratio of the price of metal to the price of the "ore" of that metal ("ore," because of the joint product problem at the ore per annum.[4] That growth, while exhibiting considerable steadiness in the aggregate, was punctuated by a number of large and sudden changes, both in the geographical location of production and also in the commodities produced. The two types of rapid change, clearly evident in tables 7 and 8, are related, of course. We shall see that there have been two major initiators of change: (1) discovery of large mineralized areas with deposits far richer than those previously exploited; and (2) development of cheaper transportation which permitted the exploitation of extensive deposits where in many cases the grade of ore was only reasonably good.

The most obvious change in the location of mineral output over the period was the shift, just before the Civil War, from complete dominance by the East to a marked dominance by the West (including the Southwest, the Rocky Mountains, and the Pacific Coast), and to the West's continued but less imposing dominance at the end of the period (table 8). In 1839 the share of the East in the total was 100 per cent, but by 1859 the precious metal discoveries in the West had reduced this share to 20 per cent. Thereafter, the share of the East increased to a level of 43 per cent by the end of our period in spite of the great development of mining in the West. Within the eastern region, the major shift was a steady increase in the share of the north central area (which in our classification includes, among other states, Michigan, Minnesota, and Missouri) from a share of one-third in 1839 to 84 per cent in 1909.

In 1839 iron ore and lead dominated major metal mining and continued to do so until the great precious metal discoveries gave gold and silver mining the leading position from 1849 to 1869. Since that time, the relative importance of the other four metals—especially of copper and iron ore—has increased considerably.

Changes in the fortunes of the different regions and the different commodities are so closely intertwined that they must be examined together in order to be understood. Table 8 indicates that the north-

---

level) was considerably higher in 1879 for iron than for copper, gold, silver, zinc, and probably lead.

If the price of iron—about 3.7 times the price of the same quantity of iron in ore in 1879—had been used to weight iron ore output in our tables, a number of statements in the paper would need extensive alteration. For example, all statements about the relative importance of iron ore compared with the other mine products would be liable to change. So also would all statements about movements of a composite that contained iron ore, provided the movement of iron ore differed substantially from the movements of the other members of the composite.

The weighting scheme that uses the price of pig iron instead of the price of ore as a weight will be called the "alternative weighting scheme." As we go along, some effort will be made to indicate the effect of using this scheme.

[4] All relative rates of growth in this paper are continuously compounded.

TABLE 7. Indexes of Value of Mine Output of Major Metals, by Region and Commodity, 1839–1909 (in 1879 prices, 1909 = 100)

| | 1839 | 1849 | 1859 | 1869 | 1879 | 1889 | 1902 | 1909 | Relative percentage share, 1909 |
|---|---|---|---|---|---|---|---|---|---|
| **Region** [a] | | | | | | | | | |
| New England | — | — | — | — | — | — | — | — | |
| Middle Atlantic | 12 | 20 | 35 | 54 | 80 | 76 | 67 | 100 | 3 |
| South Atlantic | 21 | 34 | 28 | 43 | 61 | 81 | 132 | 100 | 1 |
| North central | 0.8 | 1.3 | 2.2 | 4.6 | 11 | 25 | 69 | 100 | 36 |
| South central | 2.5 | 2.6 | 3.9 | 2.3 | 6 | 35 | 80 | 100 | 4 |
| East | 2.0 | 3.1 | 4.8 | 8.0 | 16 | 30 | 71 | 100 | 44 |
| Southwest | — | — | 0.6 | 13.0 | 20 | 20 | 35 | 100 | 19 |
| Rocky Mountain | — | — | 1.0 | 5.9 | 18 | 47 | 92 | 100 | 32 |
| Pacific | — | 29.0 | 130.0 | 56.0 | 57 | 43 | 71 | 100 | 6 |
| West | 0.9 | 2.9 | 15.0 | 14.0 | 23 | 38 | 71 | 100 | 57 |
| United States | | 3.2 | 11.0 | 11.0 | 20 | 34 | 71 | 100 | 101 |
| **Commodity** | | | | | | | | | |
| Iron ore | 1.9 | 3.2 | 4.7 | 7.4 | 14 | 28 | 69 | 100 | 26 |
| Copper | — | 0.1 | 1.4 | 2.6 | 4.7 | 20 | 58 | 100 | 37 |
| Lead | 4.5 | 6.1 | 4.3 | 4.5 | 24 | 40 | 71 | 100 | 6 |
| Zinc | — | — | 1.7 | 4.1 | 9.4 | 24 | 71 | 100 | 5 |
| Gold | 0.6 | 14.0 | 60.0 | 43.0 | 43 | 41 | 85 | 100 | 14 |
| Silver | b | 0.2 | 0.7 | 16.0 | 61 | 90 | 98 | 100 | 11 |
| | | | | | | | | | 99 |

*Note:* All tables with no source given are derived from one of the basic tables in the appendix. [Not reprinted here.—Ed.]
If the alternative weighting scheme had been used (see text fn. 3), the following indexes would have resulted:

| | 1839 | 1879 | 1909 |
|---|---|---|---|
| United States | 1.3 | 16 | 100 |
| Middle Atlantic | 20.0 | 128 | 100 |
| North central | 0.3 | 8 | 100 |

[a] The following states (or predecessor territory) are included in the regions. *New England:* Me., N.H., Vt., R.I., Mass., Conn.; *Middle Atlantic:* N.Y., N.J., Pa.; *South Atlantic:* Del., Md., Va., W. Va., N.C., S.C., Ga., Fla.; *West north central:* Minn., Iowa, Mo., N.D., S.D., Neb., Kan.; *East north central:* Ohio, Ind., Ill., Mich., Wis.; *South central:* Ky., Tenn., Ala., Miss., La., Ark., Okla., Tex.; *Southwest:* Ariz., N.M., Nev.; *Rocky Mountain:* Mont., Idaho, Wyo., Colo., Utah; *Pacific:* Calif., Ore., Wash.; *West:* Rocky Mountain, Southwest, Pacific; *East:* all regions not in the West.
b Less than 0.5 per cent.

TABLE 8. *Percentage Value of Mine Output of Major Metals, by Region and Commodity, 1839–1909 (in 1879 prices)*

|  | 1839 | 1849 | 1859 | 1869 | 1879 | 1889 | 1902 | 1909 |
|---|---|---|---|---|---|---|---|---|
| **Region** | | | | | | | | |
| New England | 4 | 1 | a | a | 1 | a | — | — |
| Middle Atlantic | 36 | 17 | 9 | 13 | 10 | 6 | 2 | 3 |
| South Atlantic | 15 | 6 | 2 | 2 | 2 | 1 | 1 | 1 |
| North central | 34 | 15 | 8 | 15 | 20 | 26 | 35 | 36 |
| South central | 10 | 3 | 1 | 1 | 1 | 4 | 4 | 4 |
| East | 100 | 42 | 20 | 31 | 34 | 37 | 43 | 43 |
| Southwest | | a | 1 | 22 | 19 | 11 | 9 | 20 |
| Rocky Mountain | | | 3 | 17 | 29 | 44 | 41 | 32 |
| Pacific | | 57 | 76 | 30 | 18 | 8 | 6 | 6 |
| West | 0 | 58 | 80 | 69 | 66 | 63 | 57 | 57 |
| United States | 100 | 100 | 100 | 100 | 100 | 100 | 100 | 100 |
| **Commodity** | | | | | | | | |
| Iron ore | 60 | 27 | 12 | 17 | 18 | 22 | 26 | 26 |
| Copper | | 2 | 5 | 8 | 9 | 22 | 30 | 37 |
| Lead | 30 | 11 | 2 | 2 | 7 | 7 | 6 | 6 |
| Zinc | 0 | 0 | 1 | 2 | 3 | 4 | 5 | 5 |
| Gold | 9 | 60 | 79 | 53 | 30 | 17 | 17 | 14 |
| Silver | a | 1 | 1 | 16 | 34 | 30 | 16 | 11 |
| Total | 100 | 100 | 100 | 100 | 100 | 100 | 100 | 100 |
| Iron ore, copper, lead, zinc | 90 | 39 | 20 | 30 | 36 | 54 | 68 | 75 |
| Gold and silver | 10 | 61 | 80 | 70 | 64 | 46 | 32 | 25 |
| Total | 100 | 100 | 100 | 100 | 100 | 100 | 100 | 100 |

*Note:* If the alternative weighting had been used, the following percentage distributions would have resulted:

|  | 1839 | 1879 | 1909 |
|---|---|---|---|
| New England | 6 | 1 | 0 |
| Middle Atlantic | 53 | 24 | 3 |
| South Atlantic | 12 | 3 | 1 |
| North central | 15 | 25 | 55 |
| South central | 14 | 2 | 6 |
| Southwest | 0 | 13 | 11 |
| Rocky Mountain | 0 | 19 | 19 |
| Pacific | 0 | 12 | 4 |
| Total, U.S. | 100 | 99 | 99 |
| Iron ore | 85 | 45 | 57 |
| Copper | — | 6 | 22 |
| Lead | 12 | 4 | 3 |
| Zinc | — | 2 | 3 |
| Gold | 4 | 20 | 8 |
| Silver | — | 23 | 7 |
| Total | 101 | 101 | 100 |

a Less than 0.5 per cent.

east region was of minor importance in 1839 and thereafter dwindled to practically nothing as far as major metal minerals were concerned. The middle Atlantic region was the dominant iron ore producer in 1839 and accounted for a little over one-third of the total major metal mineral output. The output of iron ore in this region increased steadily until 1879, after which it fell. After 1879, the region's output of zinc increased substantially, but neither these changes nor those in the output of iron ore were sufficient to prevent the region's decline to a comparatively low level until by the end of the whole period it was decidedly a region of little importance for the major metallic minerals.

The south Atlantic region, which started off in 1839 with 15 per cent of the total metal ore output—a total made up of iron ore and gold in roughly equal parts—enjoyed a small spurt in iron ore output after 1869, but in every decade after 1839 it must be reckoned a region of practically no importance for major metallic mineral production.

The south central region, whose output of iron ore gave it about 10 per cent of the total in 1839, also enjoyed a rather greater increase in this output after 1869 but, sizable as it was, it was far from sufficient to give the region any more than minor importance in the total.

The remaining regions—east north central, west north central, and the West (the Southwest, Rocky Mountains, and Pacific Coast)—are ones in which spectacular development in metal ore output took place. This can be seen in the top panel of table 9, since most of the asterisks,

TABLE 9. *Growth of Value of Mine Output of Major Metals, by Region and Commodity, 1839–1909 (% per year in 1879 prices)*

|  | 1839–49 | 1849–59 | 1859–69 | 1869–79 | 1879–89 | 1889–1902 | 1902–09 |
|---|---|---|---|---|---|---|---|
| **Region** | | | | | | | |
| New England | 1.3 | 0 | −7.2* | 19.0* | −11.0* | | |
| Middle Atlantic | 5.5 | 5.5 | 4.3 | 3.8 | −0.5 | −1.0 | 5.8 |
| South Atlantic | 4.6 | −2.1 | 4.3 | 3.7 | 2.8 | 3.8 | −4.0 |
| North central | 5.0 | 4.9 | 7.5* | 8.8* | 8.0* | 7.9* | 5.2 |
| South central | 0.4 | 4.4 | −5.6 | 9.5* | 18.0* | 6.4* | 3.2 |
| East | 4.6 | 4.2 | 5.2 | 6.8* | 6.3* | 6.7* | 4.9 |
| Southwest | — | — | 31.0* | 4.4 | −0.4 | 4.1 | 15.0 |
| Rocky Mountain | — | — | 17.0* | 11.0* | 9.5* | 5.2 | 1.2 |
| Pacific | — | 15.0* | −8.5* | 0.3 | −2.8 | 3.9 | 4.8 |
| West | — | 15.0* | −0.8 | 5.3 | 4.8 | 4.9 | 5.0 |
| United States | 13.0* | 12.0* | 0.7 | 5.8 | 5.3 | 5.6 | 4.9 |
| **Commodity** | | | | | | | |
| Iron ore | 5.1 | 3.7 | 4.7 | 6.2* | 7.1* | 6.9* | 5.3 |
| Copper | — | — | 6.3* | 6.0* | 15.0* | 8.2* | 7.7* |
| Lead | 3.0 | −3.6 | 0.6 | 16.0* | 5.2 | 4.5 | 4.9 |
| Zinc | — | — | 8.8* | 8.4* | 9.3* | 8.4* | 5.0 |
| Gold | — | 15.0* | −3.0 | 0 | −0.6 | 5.7 | 2.3 |
| Silver | — | 15.0* | 32.0* | 13.0* | 4.0 | 0.6 | 0.4 |
| Gold and silver | | 15.0* | −0.7 | 4.9 | 2.1 | 2.8 | 1.5 |

* Indicates rate of growth over 6 per cent per year.

indicating an annual rate of growth over 6 per cent per year, are found in these regions. The rates of growth for New England are of no significance, since they are based on very small outputs. The north central area enjoyed an early specialization in lead. Although its initial share of output declined because of the tremendous growth of output in the West, output in the north central area increased steadily and sizably after Michigan began to produce copper. Iron ore also enjoyed a steady and an even larger growth, first in Michigan and later in Minnesota. Added to these were the smaller but still significant increases in the outputs of lead and zinc after 1869 and of gold in South Dakota. The result of the growth in output over the whole range of ores was to make the north central region the leading metal ore producer by 1909.

The discovery of gold in California in 1849 opened the great metal mining era of the West. The gold deposits of California were so rich that in 1859 the Pacific region was producing three-quarters of the country's total metal ore output. After the peak Census year of 1859, however, the region declined in relative importance (6 per cent of the U.S. total in 1909), although its 1909 output was only 23 per cent below that of 1859. After 1890, copper increased to account for about one-third of that share, the remainder being made up of gold and a small quantity of silver.

Metal mining in the other two regions of the West—the Rocky Mountains and the Southwest—began on a significant scale a decade later than it did in California with the 1859 discovery of gold and silver in Nevada and Colorado. Initially, the output was made up almost entirely of gold and silver, since only their values could support the very high cost of moving concentrate or metal out of the producing areas. As time went on, transportation improved with the steady spread of railroads, and it became profitable to mine for products associated with the gold and silver, that is, copper and lead and, to a lesser extent, zinc. This is reflected in a steady decline in the importance of gold and silver in the outputs of those regions, as shown by table 10.

The bulk of the absolute growth of metal mine output is shown by table 7 to have taken place in the last two or three decades of the period under review. Although the annual rates of growth were very high for the country as a whole from 1839 to 1859—mainly because of gold—the absolute quantities involved were quite small. After a pause during the Civil War decade, metal mine output grew steadily for the country as a whole but with considerable variability among commodities and regions. For example, total metal mine output in 1889 was only one-third of the 1909 level. Southwest output was only one-fifth of the 1909 level. So also was copper output. Even gold in 1889 was only 41 per cent of the 1909 level, although it had been 60 per cent some twenty years earlier.

TABLE 10. *Value of Gold and Silver as Percentage of Total Metal Ore Output of the Western Regions, 1869–1909*

|      | Rocky Mountain | | Southwest | | Pacific | |
|------|------|--------|------|--------|------|--------|
|      | Gold | Silver | Gold | Silver | Gold | Silver |
| 1869 | 90 | 10 | 36 | 64 | 98 | 2 |
| 1879 | 19 | 70 | 24 | 65 | 93 | 6 |
| 1889 | 11 | 55 | 24 | 41 | 91 | 8 |
| 1902 | 22 | 32 | 13 | 18 | 72 | 7 |
| 1909 | 17 | 25 | 19 | 15 | 61 | 7 |

In summary, the period 1839–1909 began with all ore produced in the East—iron ore and a little gold on the eastern seaboard and lead in the upper Mississippi valley. In the East, iron ore output increased in the middle Atlantic region until the north central area (Michigan) began to displace it. The spectacular bursts of precious metal output in the West began in 1849, first in California and a decade later in Nevada and Colorado. As transportation improved in the West, the relative importance there of gold and silver declined and that of lead, zinc, and particularly copper increased. The north central region, an important early producer of lead, became the country's leading mineral producing region with the tremendous development of copper in Michigan after 1850 and of iron ore in the Great Lakes states after 1875. The period began with the middle Atlantic and north central regions as the main mineral producers and ended in 1909 with the north central, the Rocky Mountain, and the southwestern regions as the main producers. In 1839, iron ore and lead accounted for most of mineral output (60 and 30 per cent, respectively). In 1859, four-fifths of the country's metal ore output was in the form of gold and silver, practically all of which was gold. By 1909, copper was the leading mineral, accounting for a little over one-third; iron ore accounted for one-quarter and gold and silver together for one-quarter of the major metal ore output.

## EMPLOYMENT

Our estimates of employment are based mainly on Census data. There have been special mineral Censuses of widely varying worth beginning with the year 1879. In 1869, minerals were given a separate section in the *Census of Industry and Wealth,* but before that time minerals received no special attention. The treatment of minerals in the 1840 and 1850 Censuses is so poor that no useful estimates of employment—or output, for that matter—can be made from them.

Census employment data are for establishments, that is, for industries. While mining industries are identified by the names of commodities, a commodity with a particular name is not necessarily produced entirely within the industry of the same name, nor is an industry with a particular name restricted to production of the commodity of that name. For this reason, it was necessary to consolidate lead and zinc into a single industry and to do the same for gold and silver. In the latter part of the nineteenth century the discrepancy between commodity and industry became wider. In the Rocky Mountain and southwestern regions copper, lead, and zinc began to appear in considerable quantities although employment in these industries was often recorded by the Census in the gold and silver mining industry.

One of the major Census mysteries, especially in 1839, 1849, and 1859, is the definition of mining. A number of nonmining activities closely associated with mining appear to be included in Census tabulations for mining. The iron mining figures seem to be fairly comparable after the 1860 Census in which iron mines were classified with blast furnaces when owned by the same firm, and the noncaptive mines were tabulated separately. For gold and silver, the Census employment estimates definitely contain more than mining operations, but the nonmining operations included have always been closely associated with mining itself. The data for Michigan copper almost certainly include a considerable amount of smelting. This may also be true for some parts of the West in the later decades of the century, although the Census employment data probably exclude smelting more thoroughly in the West than in Michigan. Employment data for lead and zinc are obscure; a substantial number of smelter workers is probably included in the nominal mining employment.

With time, a somewhat clearer line has developed between mining and smelting operations, both in actuality and in the successive Censuses. This has caused "mining employment" to be lower in the later years than it would have been otherwise. Hence an observed decline in the ratio of employment to output is probably somewhat larger than it ought to be.

### Distribution of Employment by Region and Industry

There is naturally a rough correspondence between the distribution of employment among regions and among products and the distribution of output, but a comparison of tables 11 and 8 reveals numerous departures from this conformity. The differences are all reflected in the ratio of employment to output, examined in detail later.

Because of the similarity between the distribution of employment

TABLE 11. *Percentage Distribution of Employment in Major Metal Mining, by Region and Commodity, 1839–1909*

| | 1839 | 1849 | 1859 | 1869 | 1879 | 1889 | 1902 | 1909 |
|---|---|---|---|---|---|---|---|---|
| Region | | | | | | | | |
| New England | 3.6 | 1.3 | 0.5 | 1.0 | 1.3 | 0.4 | — | — |
| Middle Atlantic | 43.0 | 22.0 | 11.0 | 23.0 | 19.0 | 9.0 | 4.1 | 3.0 |
| South Atlantic | 24.0 | 12.0 | 3.1 | 3.4 | 4.3 | 5.3 | 5.2 | 2.7 |
| East north central | | | | | 13.0 | 20.0 | 24.0 | 21.0 |
| West north central | | | | | 9.6 | 7.9 | 16.0 | 21.0 |
| North central | 19.0 | 11.0 | 8.8 | 17.0 | 23.0 | 28.0 | 40.0 | 43.0 |
| South central | 10.0 | 4.2 | 1.9 | 1.7 | 1.8 | 5.1 | 7.0 | 5.2 |
| East | 100 | 50 | 25 | 46 | 50 | 48 | 55 | 54 |
| Southwest | 0 | 0.2 | 1.4 | 7.3 | 12.0 | 8.6 | 6.3 | 11.0 |
| Rocky Mountain | 0 | 0.0 | 1.6 | 15.0 | 15.0 | 28.0 | 26.0 | 23.0 |
| Pacific | 0 | 50.0 | 72.0 | 32.0 | 23.0 | 16.0 | 13.0 | 13.0 |
| West | 0 | 50 | 75 | 54 | 50 | 52 | 45 | 46 |
| United States | 100 | 100 | 100 | 100 | 100 | 100 | 100 | 100 |
| Commodity | | | | | | | | |
| Iron ore | 59.0 | 31.0 | 14.0 | 32.0 | 33.0 | 35.0 | 35.0 | 32.0 |
| Copper | 0 | 3.3 | 8.5 | 9.2 | 6.4 | 5.8 | 19.0 | 28.0 |
| Lead and zinc | 25.0 | 8.9 | 2.1 | 2.9 | 7.8 | 5.8 | 7.0 | 11.0 |
| Gold and silver | 16.0 | 57.0 | 75.0 | 56.0 | 53.0 | 53.0 | 38.0 | 29.0 |
| Total | 100 | 100 | 100 | 100 | 100 | 100 | 100 | 100 |

and output, the general movements over time are much the same. Major metal employment was entirely in the East at the beginning of the period, with the middle Atlantic region dominating. During the next few decades, the initial distribution was radically changed because of the influx of workers into gold and silver mining, first in the Pacific Coast area and then around the beginning of the Civil War into the Rocky Mountain and southwestern regions. By 1902 Michigan copper and Lake Superior iron ore had brought the north central region to a leading position. In the West, development of the base metals limited the decline in the region's relative employment position.

## Major Metal Mining Employment Compared with All Mineral Employment

The major metal mining industries do not, of course, constitute the whole mineral industry for, as table 12 shows, they have accounted for less than one-third of all U.S. mineral employment since 1870. In addition to the major metals, the mineral industries include the comparatively unimportant minor metals, the so-called nonmetallics (e.g., sand and gravel, clay), and the very important category of mineral fuels, coal and petroleum.

While the regional percentages differ considerably even in the earlier years, there clearly has been an increasing regional specialization on

TABLE 12. *Comparisons of Employment in Major Metal Mining, All Mineral Industries, and Total Employment, by Region, 1870–1910*

| | 1870 | 1880 | 1890 | 1900 | 1910 |
|---|---|---|---|---|---|
| Major Metal Mining as Percentage of All Mineral Industries | | | | | |
| New England | 11.0 | 17.0 | 4.5 | 0 | 0 |
| Middle Atlantic | 23.0 | 19.0 | 6.3 | 2.2 | 1.7 |
| South Atlantic | 27.0 | 32.0 | 21.0 | 16.0 | 5.5 |
| East north central | 28.0 | 33.0 | 26.0 | 26.0 | 22.0 |
| West north central | 20.0 | 48.0 | 22.0 | 37.0 | 51.0 |
| South central | 28.0 | 27.0 | 22.0 | 15.0 | 11.0 |
| Southwest | 42.0 | 125.0 [a] | 71.0 | 52.0 | 68.0 |
| Rocky Mountain | 48.0 | 29.0 | 59.0 | 48.0 | 62.0 |
| Pacific | 41.0 | 45.0 | 54.0 | 36.0 | 54.0 |
| United States | 32.0 | 32.0 | 24.0 | 21.0 | 20.0 |
| Major Metal Mining as Percentage of Total Employment [b] | | | | | |
| New England | 0.04 | 0.07 | 0.02 | 0 | 0 |
| Middle Atlantic | 0.48 | 0.49 | 0.19 | 0.08 | 0.07 |
| South Atlantic | 0.10 | 0.15 | 0.18 | 0.19 | 0.10 |
| East north central | 0.31 | 0.35 | 0.53 | 0.60 | 0.58 |
| West north central | 0.09 | 0.46 | 0.28 | 0.64 | 0.93 |
| South central | 0.04 | 0.05 | 0.15 | 0.17 | 0.14 |
| Southwest | 6.9 | 20.0 | 9.0 | 6.5 | 8.4 |
| Rocky Mountain | 12.0 | 7.6 | 7.5 | 7.1 | 5.2 |
| Pacific | 6.7 | 4.8 | 2.1 | 1.8 | 1.3 |
| United States | 0.47 | 0.56 | 0.47 | 0.50 | 0.51 |
| All Mineral Industries as Percentage of Total Employment | | | | | |
| New England | 0.40 | 0.46 | 0.46 | 0.34 | 0.31 |
| Middle Atlantic | 2.1 | 2.6 | 3.1 | 3.8 | 4.2 |
| South Atlantic | 0.37 | 0.48 | 0.86 | 1.2 | 1.8 |
| East north central | 1.1 | 1.1 | 2.0 | 2.3 | 2.6 |
| West north central | 0.49 | 0.95 | 1.3 | 1.7 | 1.8 |
| South central | 0.17 | 0.21 | 0.69 | 1.1 | 1.3 |
| Southwest | 17.0 | 16.0 | 13.0 | 13.0 | 12.0 |
| Rocky Mountain | 26.0 | 26.0 | 13.0 | 15.0 | 8.5 |
| Pacific | 16.0 | 11.0 | 3.9 | 5.1 | 2.4 |
| United States | 1.5 | 1.7 | 2.0 | 2.4 | 2.5 |

*Source:* Major metal employment is our estimate. 1870–90 are from table A-4, and 1900 and 1910 (1902 and 1909) are from table A-5. All mineral industries and total employment are from H. S. Perloff et al., *Regions, Resources and Economic Growth*, Baltimore, 1960. [Appendix tables not reprinted here.—*Ed.*]

[a] Obviously incorrect. The estimate for employment in all mineral industries is probably too low.

[b] Employment data from table A-4 are used below to calculate major metal mining employment as a percentage of total employment, with the latter assumed equal to all males (including slaves) 15–60 years of age as recorded in the population Censuses.

| | 1840 | 1850 | 1860 | 1870 |
|---|---|---|---|---|
| New England | .04 | .03 | .03 | .06 |
| Middle Atlantic | .22 | .25 | .31 | .56 |
| South Atlantic | .15 | .19 | .13 | .14 |
| East and west north central | .14 | .15 | .20 | .28 |
| South central | .08 | .07 | .07 | .06 |
| Southwest | — | .26 | 2.9 | 7.2 |
| Rocky Mountain | — | — | 2.4 | 13.0 |
| Pacific | — | 11.00 | 18.00 | 6.6 |
| United States | .14 | .30 | .67 | .57 |

major metallics since 1870. In 1870 major metal employment accounted for no more than 48 per cent of all mineral employment in any region, but in 1910 four regions had over half of their mineral employment in the major metal mining industries. In 1870 no region had less than 11 per cent of its mineral employment in the metal mining industries, but in 1910 four regions were below that level. In the western regions major metal employment is a more important part of all mineral employment than it is in the East. Indeed, in one year a ratio of major metal employment to all mineral employment of 1.25 was obtained for the Southwest. No attempt has been made to correct this, since the more defective estimate is probably the estimate for all mineral employment, a series which is not the main concern of this paper. Still, taking the whole group of percentages for the western region, there can be little doubt of the dominant position held by major metals in the whole field of mineral employment.

## Mineral Employment Compared with All Employment

Mineral employment has always been a small part of total employment in the United States, although there has been a substantial increase from the 1.5 per cent level of 1870, shown in table 12.[5] Regional differences are very great, reflecting the rich deposits of minerals in some regions and the other opportunities for economic activity in each of the regions. The regions best endowed with metallic minerals are perhaps less well endowed in other respects. The theory of ore genesis indicates that this is not entirely a matter of chance. The consequence is that in the southwestern and Rocky Mountain areas metallic mineral employment was 5 per cent or more of total employment in each of the five Census years from 1870 to 1910, and even in the Pacific Coast region was 5 per cent or more in two of the five years. In the other regions, major metal employment is a much smaller part of total employment, being under 1 per cent in all cases, even in the west north central region, whose major metal components are lead and zinc, Minnesota iron ore, Michigan copper and iron ore, and South Dakota gold.

The middle Atlantic region emerges as the third most specialized mineral region when all mineral employment is compared with total

---

[5] It should be borne in mind that our estimates of employment are based upon the mineral Census and refer, in most cases, to average employment during the year of operations covered by the mineral Census. I believe the year of operations actually covered by most reports to the Census was the year preceding the nominal year of the Census. Thus the 1870 mineral Census, for example, very likely collected reports on calendar year 1869 from most of the reporting units. The occupational data on which the total mining employment estimates and the total employment estimates are based refer in all cases to the spring of the Census year.

employment. In 1910 the middle Atlantic region had over 4 per cent of its employment in mineral industries compared with about 2 per cent for the north central region, which is specialized in metallic minerals rather than the nonmetallic minerals that are important in the middle Atlantic area.

In the Rocky Mountain and southwestern regions, mineral employment as compared with all employment was still very high in 1910, 12 and 8 per cent, respectively. In the earlier years, as many as one out of every four employed persons was working directly in a mining industry in the Rocky Mountain area.

These percentages are high for a developed region. Nevertheless, the picture of the West as completely dominated by metallic mineral mining is so strong that many may be surprised that they were not higher there. The circumstances under which major metallic employment could be close to 100 per cent would be most unusual. If a wholly empty region is entered for the first time by prospectors, all of whose activities—including shooting, preparation, and cooking of game—are regarded as part of mining, then employment in the major metallic industries in that area would equal total employment. (The probability would be, of course, that the Census taker would not be able to find the prospector.) But as soon as the region under scrutiny is enlarged, there are necessarily many kinds of activity other than metal mining, even though the mining industries may be the main or even the sole reason for them. Mining must be supported by industries that supply materials and equipment. Equipment, mineral products, food, and other consumer commodities must be transported. Men and their families must be fed, housed, and clothed. And in many mineralized areas there are other bases for economic activity, some of which would be carried on even in the absence of any mineral industries. The consequence is that throughout the whole of the period measured here metallic mineral employment and all mineral employment have been greatly outweighed by employment classified in other industries. Nevertheless, the existence of ghost towns and ghost areas proves that in many smaller areas almost all employment was derived from the major metallic industries. With the development of activity around other economic opportunities, later data show that mineral employment has declined relative to total employment. In 1950, for example, all mineral employment was 3.4 and 3.5 per cent of total employment in the Rocky Mountain and southwestern regions, respectively, compared with 26 and 17 per cent in 1870.

### RATIO OF EMPLOYMENT TO OUTPUT

The behavior of employment in relation to output is summarized in table 13. The ratio of employment to output $E/O$ "eliminates" the

TABLE 13. *Indexes of Employment Divided by Output, by Region and Commodity, 1859–1909 (1889 = 100)*

| | 1859 | 1869 | 1879 | 1889 | 1902 [a] | 1909 [a] |
|---|---|---|---|---|---|---|
| New England | — | — | — | — | — | — |
| Middle Atlantic | 144 | 193 | 182 | 100 | 60 | 46 |
| Iron ore | 133 | 173 | 164 | 100 | 94 | 88 |
| Lead and zinc | 275 | 618 | 411 | 100 | 20 | 17 |
| South Atlantic | 95 | 66 | 95 | 100 | 81 | 74 |
| Iron ore | 99 | 169 | 105 | 100 | 91 | 102 |
| North central | 181 | 159 | 148 | 100 | 63 | 63 |
| Iron ore | 57 | 178 | 155 | 100 | 48 | 40 |
| Copper | 484 | 205 | 151 | 100 | 104 | 108 |
| Lead and zinc | 112 | 112 | 234 | 100 | 63 | 93 |
| Gold and silver | | | 55 | 100 | 70 | 86 |
| South central | 174 | 278 | 186 | 100 | 69 | 64 |
| Iron ore | 183 | 402 | 202 | 100 | 80 | 75 |
| Southwest | 314 | 69 | 121 | 100 | 58 | 46 |
| Copper | | | 112 | 100 | 112 | 117 |
| Gold and silver | | 51 | 100 | 100 | 68 | 38 |
| Rocky Mountain | 147 | 241 | 123 | 100 | 63 | 70 |
| Copper | | | | 100 | 131 | 213 |
| Gold and silver | 107 | 175 | 99 | 100 | 64 | 65 |
| Pacific | 81 | 83 | 98 | 100 | 65 | 61 |
| Gold and silver | 82 | 84 | 99 | 100 | 80 | 81 |
| United States | 175 | 161 | 148 | 100 | 64 | 60 |
| Iron ore | 131 | 189 | 168 | 100 | 55 | 46 |
| Copper | 752 | 427 | 267 | 100 | 96 | 111 |
| Lead and zinc [b] | 212 | 202 | 228 | 100 | 73 | 106 |
| Gold and silver | 149 | 116 | 111 | 100 | 67 | 64 |

*Note:* The employment estimates do not attempt to take into account changes in hours worked per year. If it had been possible to take account of the decline in the number of hours, the measures of $E/O$ would have declined considerably more than they actually did.

1839 and 1849 are not included in the table, since employment in those years was estimated by extrapolating the 1859 quantity by output. Nor does table 13 include all the possible $E/O$ ratios that could be computed. It includes the regional $E/O$ ratio (equivalent to a weighted average of the industry ratios within a region weighted by output in the given year divided by the same weighted average for the base year) for all regions having production in 1909, all, that is, except New England. The U.S. values of $E/O$ are included, as are the U.S. industry averages, which may be viewed as equivalent to a weighted average of the regional industry ratios weighted by output in the given year divided by the same weighted average for the base year. Estimates have been included for individual industries within regions where these industries were of substantial size. Where outputs are very small, estimates of $E/O$ are not to be relied upon, for the estimates of both output and employment for those states of minor importance in the industry are subject to sizable error, both because of undercount of employment and the independence of the regional distributions of output and employment. For example, $E/O$ for middle Atlantic lead and zinc in the table exhibits a most unusual behavior. Another case of a very sharp change is that of the Southwest from 1859 to 1869 to 1879.

Each industry except iron ore is afflicted by a lack of correspondence between the definitions of output, which is measured on a commodity basis, and of employment, which is measured on an establishment basis. This lack of correspondence affects the estimates of $E/O$ in various ways. The most important case is that of lead and

*Notes to table 13 (continued)*

zinc. The lead output of the West (produced from silver and lead ores) is included in the lead and zinc industry's output, but the number of mines classified in the lead and zinc industry in the West is very small throughout the whole period. Zinc adds to the problem to a lesser extent since the West's zinc output was a smaller part of the U.S. total. On the other hand, the distortion introduced into the gold and silver series is much less, for the lead omitted from the output of this industry was only a small part of the total output of the industry. Lead and zinc outputs of the West as a percentage of the U.S. total were as follows:

|      | Lead | Zinc |
|------|------|------|
| 1859 | 0    | 0    |
| 1869 | 1    | 0    |
| 1879 | 70   | 0    |
| 1889 | 81   | 0    |
| 1902 | 72   | 11   |
| 1909 | 57   | 15   |

The change in the percentage of lead coming from the West caused $E/O$ for the United States to fall more (or rise less) from 1859 to 1889 and to rise more (or fall less) from 1889 to 1909.

A less important problem is caused by the transfer of establishments from the gold and silver industry to the lead and zinc or copper industries. As copper, lead, and zinc became the major parts of the output of a number of mines in these regions, the Census Bureau began to recognize the mines as something other than gold and silver mines, even though gold and silver were contained in the ores. Hence the employment formerly attributed to the gold and silver industry was shifted, in part, to the other major metal industries.

In a number of cases, Census output of a commodity is greatly below our estimates of output based on other and presumably better information, and the Census ratio of employment to output has been applied to our estimate of output. There has been no attempt, however, to correct and make sense of every case of odd behavior in the employment-output ratio. Hence there are many anomalies in the behavior of employment in relation to output, especially where the quantities involved are small. These arise in part because the regional estimates of output are based in some cases on sources that may differ substantially from the regional distribution of output contained in the Census.

[a] 1902 and 1909 Census employment data (see table A–5) have been adjusted in an attempt to make them comparable with 1889 data. 1909 was first put on a 1902 basis by calculating average monthly employment (which was 11 per cent below the Dec. 15 figure used in the 1909 Census for major metallic minerals). 1902 and 1909 state figures were then multiplied by the following factor derived from 1889 data, to get to the 1889 basis:

$$\Sigma \, (\text{employment})_i \Big/ \left[ \, \Sigma \, (\text{employment})_i \times \frac{(\text{days worked})_i}{300} \, \right]$$

where $i$ is the skill level or occupational group. This method of adjustment is suggested in *Mines and Quarries, 1902*, p. 90. 1902 employment in all major metallic minerals for the United States on the 1889 basis is 22 per cent above 1902 employment reported in the Census. I am indebted to Neal Potter for reminding me of this problem of consistency.

[b] See the second paragraph of the Note above.

size of the industry and can thereby show clearly one important aspect of the production structure. The ratio $E/O$ for minerals is likely to vary more among industries, among regions, and over time than might be expected in the nonmineral industries. The factors that tend to produce this result are discussed below. Their effects are obscured by the fact that our data are sometimes grossly inadequate measures of the quantities we would like to measure. The reasons for this are explained below before we turn to the "real" factors making for variability in $E/O$. It should be borne in mind that $E/O$ is not the inverse of total factor productivity in any meaningful sense but is simply the ratio of employment to output. In particular, it would be quite possible, though perhaps not likely, for $E/O$ to increase from one period to the next even though a proper measure of the total productivity of an industry would show an increase. It would be desirable to discuss productivity, its variation among industries and regions, and its variation over time, but estimates of inputs other than labor have not been possible for these industries.[6]

We should like also to measure long-term changes, but our data refer to particular years and sometimes to particular dates. The level of output or of employment may be distorted in any one year by forces that are temporary and will therefore prevent the data from revealing in full clarity the long-run changes that are taking place.

In the mineral industries, the measurement of output is complicated by the fact that the labor force is engaged in producing two types of goods—a "current" good, which comes out in the form of concentrate or ore, and a capital good, which is visible as a developed mineral deposit. It would be desirable in the study of $E/O$ to separate the two types of product and to separate the amount of labor used to produce each or—this not being very feasible even in principle—to make certain that the output measured includes the capital good part of the output as well as the current product. We have not been able to do this but wish to call the difficulty to the reader's attention. In some years the capital good part of output can be very important. Some mines in any year are nonproducing, for instance, although not necessarily dead or even poor mines, for they may have a substantial labor force at work with little evidence of product visible above the ground. Hence, the labor force is engaged in developing the mine, that is, in producing a capital good. In the nonmining industries, on the other

---

[6] For comments on the problem of extracting measures of capital used in mineral industries from the Censuses, see my review (*Journal of the American Statistical Association*, March 1957, p. 119) of Israel Borenstein's *Capital and Output Trends in Mining Industries, 1870–1948*, Occasional Paper 45, New York, NBER, 1954. [Reprinted as selection 11 in this volume.—*Ed.*]

hand, there is usually a rather clear separation between operations on "current account" and operations on "capital account," although in agriculture and some industries the labor force does indeed engage in the production of capital goods to be used by the industry itself.

## The Behavior of E/O

The interpretation of table 13 presents great difficulty both because of the large number of factors affecting the behavior of the ratios and because of the largely unknown errors reflected in the estimates of output and employment. There are many puzzling features of the table that raise the possibility of systematic error in the estimates of employment or output, and also the possibility of fundamental changes in the conditions of production. Unfortunately, possible explanations abound.

*1859–69.* One of the puzzles is that E/O rose from 1859 to 1869 in two of the four eastern regions and in two of the three western regions. In the two eastern regions, a factor in this behavior is probably the estimate of employment in iron ore. Since the Census data on iron ore employment cover only a small portion of all the iron ore mined, we have been unable to find a satisfactory basis on which to construct an estimate. There are real factors that conceivably could explain the behavior of the ratio, such as that during the Civil War resort to lower grades of ore could have produced an increase in the ratio.

*Rate of change of E/O.* The data for the United States as a whole show that E/O declined more rapidly from 1879 to 1902 than in the periods before or after (table 14). This pattern is much less clear for industries within regions, however; in part, the movements of the weighted averages for the United States reflect shifts among regions and among industries. But the maximum annual rate of decline in E/O occurs in one or the other of the two "decades" from 1879 to 1902 in five of the seven regions shown in table 14.

The annual rate of decline for the United States is less rapid from 1902 to 1909 than from 1889 to 1902. This is also true of each of the seven regions, although for only eight out of the eleven industries within regions included in table 14. Although the leveling off of the rate of decline in E/O may reflect in part the adjustment to the employment data for 1902 and 1909, these two years should be reasonably comparable if the Census adjustment for 1902 resulted in annual data equal to the average of monthly data. The adjustment of 1889 and 1902 to a common basis offers greater possibility for error.[7]

[7] See n. a to table 13.

TABLE 14. *Annual Rate of Change in Employment Divided by Output in Major Metal Mining, by Region and Commodity, 1859–1909 (% per year)*

|  | 1859 to 1869 | 1869 to 1879 | 1879 to 1889 | 1889 to 1902 | 1902 to 1909 |
|---|---|---|---|---|---|
| Middle Atlantic | +2.9 | −0.6 | −6.0 | −3.9 | −3.8 |
| Iron ore | +2.7 | −0.5 | −4.9 | −0.5 | −1.0 |
| South Atlantic | −3.6 | +3.5 | +0.6 | −2.1 | −1.2 |
| Iron ore | +5.4 | −4.8 | −0.5 | −0.8 | +1.7 |
| North central | −1.3 | −0.7 | −4.0 | −3.6 | 0 |
| Iron ore | +11.5 | −1.3 | −4.4 | −5.7 | −2.4 |
| Copper | −8.6 | −3.1 | −4.1 | +0.3 | +0.6 |
| Lead and zinc | 0 | +7.3 | −8.5 | −3.5 | +5.5 |
| South central | +4.6 | −4.0 | −6.2 | −2.9 | −1.0 |
| Iron ore | +7.9 | −6.9 | −7.1 | −1.8 | −0.8 |
| Southwest | −15.2 | +5.9 | −1.9 | −4.2 | −3.2 |
| Copper | — | — | −1.1 | +0.9 | +0.7 |
| Gold and silver | — | +6.8 | 0 | −2.9 | −8.5 |
| Rocky Mountain | +4.9 | −6.8 | −2.0 | −3.6 | +1.5 |
| Copper | — | — | — | +2.1 | +6.9 |
| Gold and silver | +5.0 | −5.7 | 0 | −3.4 | +0.3 |
| Pacific | +0.2 | +1.6 | +0.2 | −3.3 | −0.8 |
| Gold and silver | +0.2 | +1.7 | +0.1 | −1.8 | +0.2 |
| United States (total) | −0.8 | −0.9 | −3.9 | −3.5 | −0.8 |
| Iron ore | +3.7 | −1.2 | −5.2 | −4.6 | −2.5 |
| Copper | −5.7 | −4.7 | −9.8 | −0.3 | +2.1 |
| Lead and zinc | −0.5 | +1.2 | −8.3 | −2.4 | +5.3 |
| Gold and silver | −2.5 | −0.5 | −1.1 | −3.1 | −0.7 |

*Note:* See note to table 13.

## Factors Affecting E/O

In view of the uncertainties in the data, especially the levels and allocation of the employment data and the lack of correspondence between product and industry, any discussion of the factors affecting $E/O$ must be tentative. However, some of the factors involved have left their traces even in our rough data.

*Quality of deposits.* The decline in $E/O$ for the period from 1879 to 1902 for the United States as a whole is explained in part by a shift of output to regions with lower ratios of $E/O$. For example, middle Atlantic $E/O$'s for iron ore were considerably higher than those for the north central region, as can be seen below:

|  | *1869* | *1889* | *1909* |
|---|---|---|---|
| Middle Atlantic | 1.76 | 1.02 | 0.89 |
| North central | 1.46 | 0.82 | 0.33 |

Similarly, the $E/O$ ratio for copper in the West was considerably below that for copper produced in the north central region, as seen in the following figures:

|              | 1869 | 1889 | 1909 |
| ------------ | ---- | ---- | ---- |
| North central | 0.85 | 0.42 | 0.45 |
| Rocky Mountain | —    | 0.10 | 0.22 |
| Southwest    | —    | 0.17 | 0.20 |

And the $E/O$ ratio for gold and silver for the Rocky Mountain region was well below that for the Pacific Coast region. The main shift in output from 1879 to 1902 was between these two regions:

|              | 1869 | 1889 | 1909 |
| ------------ | ---- | ---- | ---- |
| North central | —    | 0.60 | 0.52 |
| Rocky Mountain | 0.85 | 0.48 | 0.32 |
| Southwest    | 0.30 | 0.59 | 0.22 |
| Pacific Coast | 0.97 | 1.16 | 0.94 |

Not all of the observed differences among the regional ratios are attributable to differences in the metal content of deposits, however, for the richness of the deposit is only one facet of quality. Perhaps even more important are size of the deposit and ease of working it.

*Transportation and exhaustion.* For gold and silver it seems possible to see the effects on $E/O$ of the discovery-exhaustion sequence and associated changes in transportation. When a new mining region is opened up, the heavy load of development work as new mines are brought to the point of production would tend to raise $E/O$. Independently of this factor, if the richest mines are discovered first, we should expect a later rise in $E/O$. On the other hand, if the richer discoveries came later, $E/O$ would decline, to rise at a still later point in time. What happened in the West was that both rich and poor deposits were discovered in these great mining regions. The factor that exerted the dominant influence on $E/O$ probably was transportation. As transportation improved, it became profitable to work leaner and poorer deposits, and we should expect an increase in $E/O$, especially with improvements of the magnitude represented by the change from pack train and wagon to rail transport.

Something of this effect may be visible in table 13. We do observe an increase in $E/O$ in the gold and silver industry of the Southwest from 1869 to 1879. The change from 1859 to 1869 is unreliable because 1859 was the first big year for mining in the Southwest. Similarly, in the Rocky Mountain area, which opened up in 1859, we observe an increase in $E/O$ for gold and silver. The Pacific Coast region had been producing since 1849, but here also an increase in $E/O$ is shown from 1859 to 1869 and from 1869 to 1879.

TABLE 15. *U.S. Railroad Mileage in the Western States, 1870–1910 (thousand miles)*

|  | 1870 | 1880 | 1890 | 1900 | 1910 |
|---|---|---|---|---|---|
| Southwest | 0.6 | 1.8 | 3.3 | 4.2 | 7.4 |
| New Mexico | — | 0.8 | 1.3 | 1.8 | 3.0 |
| Arizona | — | 0.3 | 1.1 | 1.5 | 2.1 |
| Nevada | 0.6 | 0.7 | 0.9 | 0.9 | 2.3 |
| Rocky Mountain | 0.9 | 3.2 | 9.3 | 11.6 | 15.5 |
| Idaho | — | 0.2 | 0.9 | 1.3 | 2.2 |
| Wyoming | 0.5 | 0.5 | 0.9 | 1.2 | 1.6 |
| Utah | 0.3 | 0.8 | 1.1 | 1.5 | 2.0 |
| Montana | — | 0.1 | 2.2 | 3.0 | 4.2 |
| Colorado | 0.2 | 1.6 | 4.2 | 4.6 | 5.5 |
| Pacific region | 1.1 | 3.0 | 7.6 | 10.4 | 14.9 |
| Washington | — | 0.3 | 1.8 | 2.9 | 4.9 |
| Oregon | 0.2 | 0.5 | 1.4 | 1.7 | 2.3 |
| California | 0.9 | 2.2 | 4.4 | 5.8 | 7.8 |

*Source: Statistical Abstract of the United States, 1920,* Census Bureau, Washington, 1921, table 226, p. 333.

*Note:* Table 10 shows the decline of gold and silver relative to the total output of these regions.

The effects of improved transportation on the composition and level of output in the West are much clearer than the effect on $E/O$. When transportation is costly—as it was in the West until the development of the rail network—mining is restricted to ores that have a high value per unit weight of the material to be transported any distance. The products that met this requirement best were gold and silver, while the other metal products with lower value per unit weight were of no importance until 1879 and even then only small.[8] Ten years later, the "cheaper" commodities were considerably more important, and by 1902 they were more important than gold and silver in the Southwest and nearly so in the Rocky Mountain region. The close association between the development of the rail network and the growth of the base metal commodities is suggested very clearly by table 15 which shows rail mileage by states at decadal points.[9] The association is much poorer for the Pacific Coast region than for the other two. Placer deposits (gold only) were far more important in California than in the states of the other two regions.

According to the 1880 Census, wagon haulage rates were seldom as low as 1 cent a pound for the trip from the mine and were as high as

[8] But gold and silver were not the only commodities to get over the transportation barrier. Furs succeeded in an earlier period, as did cattle and sheep during the time when mining was spreading throughout the Rocky Mountain and southwestern regions.

[9] See note to table 15.

6 to 8 cents a pound for the more distant mining camps.[10] In the same Census it is observed that Arizona produces chiefly gold and silver, "though lead and copper, particularly the former, are rather abundant, and will, no doubt, be exploited on a large scale when the railroad system is further developed." [11] When mining first began in Arizona, some of the mines were as much as 300 miles from the nearest railroad. The only way to transport concentrate was by wagon or pack train. Even in 1880, no mine could be worked in Arizona unless its ore contained products worth at least $150 a ton. As late as 1885, some ores in Colorado bore freight charges ranging from $50 to $100 a ton before reaching a railroad, but, by the turn of the century, all important mining camps were connected by rail with the main railroad lines.[12] Indeed, the Census report observed in 1880, ". . . now not only are there practically four great railway systems crossing the mountains from east to west, but a great number of short lines, generally narrow gauge, penetrate them in every direction, reaching mining towns which not many years since were only accessible by pack trains or saddle animals." [13]

*Technological change.* To link major changes in technology with changes that have taken place in our data from 1859 to 1909 appears to be impossible, except, of course, for the persistent and very sizable decline in $E/O$ for the United States as a whole and for each industry taken separately. It has not been possible, for example, to link definitely any particular change or set of changes with the accelerated declines in $E/O$ in the two decades from 1879 to 1902, although some suggestions can be made. Fortunately, there are available two helpful examinations of technology in metal mining. One, by Lucien Eaton, is a straightforward account of changes in mining technology from 1871 to 1946.[14] The other is a survey of the long sweep of changes in technology in mining by C. E. Julihn.[15] It is on these two expert accounts of changes in mining technology that the following remarks are based.

Julihn's view is that over most of the period there were many small advances with significant cumulative effect but nothing that could be characterized as a major improvement. Toward the end of the century,

[10] *Census of Minerals, 1880*, p. ix.

[11] *Census of Precious Metals, Statistics and Technology, 1880*, 1885, p. 44.

[12] *Census of Mines and Quarries, 1902*, 1905, p. 577.

[13] *Census of Precious Metals, 1880*, p. xii.

[14] See his "75 Years of Progress in Metal Mining," in *75 Years of Progress in the Mineral Industry*, A. B. Parsons, ed., American Institute of Mining and Metallurgical Engineers, 1947, p. 40.

[15] See his "Copper: An Example of Advancing Technology and the Utilization of Low-Grade Ores," in *Mineral Economics*, F. G. Tryon and E. C. Eckle, eds., New York, 1932, p. 111.

however, a major change was in the making—abandonment of the selective, small-scale methods of mining where the miner had to make sure the ore he mined was not diluted or lost on the way to the smelter, and development of nonselective, large-scale, mass production methods of mining. This shift in attitude and in method developed almost automatically as it became necessary to go to lower- and lower-grade ores during the latter part of the century. By using cheaper methods for breaking and handling large volumes of material, it was profitable to mine ores in which the desired mineral was diluted by large quantities of waste material, which could by then be cheaply separated from the desired mineral.

There were, of course, many developments in technology during the last half of the nineteenth century, but not all constituted improvements. Many of the changes were associated with development of new regions which contained new types of deposits or deposits of sizes different from those in the older producing regions. Other changes represented not innovations but rather adaptations to improved transportation. All that can be done here is to enumerate some of the more significant changes and recall that no single one or set of them was powerful enough to leave traces in the data at our disposal.

One of the more significant changes was the introduction of dynamite around 1870. Drilling, formerly done by hand, gradually came to be carried on by compressed air. Steam power gradually became generally used for lifting—electric power not becoming a significant factor in metal mining until after the turn of the century. There were constant advances in the arts of breaking and grinding ore, one of the most important being improvements in the processes available for separating minerals from each other but, of course, the array of sink and float methods now in the mining engineer's repertoire came into use only after the turn of the century. Surveying and mapping became more accurate and helped to cut costs in developing and in working mines. The steam shovel came into general use in the last quarter of the century in open-pit mining. Loading became mechanized. And even in so simple a thing as the design of the hand shovel, abandonment of the old long-handled shovel was a significant improvement. Along with these narrower aspects of changing technology came a series of gradual advances in mining methods, such as the sequence of operations, the spacing of shafts and drifts, and so on. There were two innovations that had their origin in the United States: the square-set system developed on the Comstock lode and hydraulic mining.[16]

If this study had been carried beyond 1909, the major innovation involved in shifting to nonselective mass methods of mining would

---

[16] *Census of Precious Metals, 1880*, p. vii.

TABLE 16. *Number of Iron Ore Mines and Output per Mine, by Region, 1869 and 1909*

| | Number of mines | | Annual output per mine (thousand short tons) | |
|---|---|---|---|---|
| | 1869 | 1909 | 1869 | 1909 |
| Middle Atlantic | 265 | 48 | 8 | 53 |
| South Atlantic | 51 | 89 | 2 | 24 |
| East north central | 89 | 88 | 12 | 164 |
| West north central | 3 | 144 | 60 | 221 |
| South central | 8 | 98 | 7 | 58 |
| United States | 420 | 483 | 8 | 76 |

have been evident in copper.[17] In iron ore, methods of mass mining were applied in Michigan and Minnesota long before their use in the rather different problems of copper and other nonferrous ores. In mining districts in which lead and zinc deposits were sizable the impact of the change in method should also be apparent.

### Number of Mines and Output per Mine

The factors influencing $E/O$ discussed above have had substantial effects on the number of producing mines and on the average product per mine. These effects have been concentrated on iron ore and copper and, to a smaller extent, on lead and zinc. While the number of gold and silver mines was quite different in 1909 from the number in 1869, the change in output per mine was much smaller than in the other three consolidated industries.[18]

Table 16 shows that the number of iron ore mines was about the same in 1909 as in 1869 for the country as a whole, although there were very large changes within regions. In the middle Atlantic region the number declined to less than one-fifth of its 1869 level, while in the west north central (Minnesota) and south central regions the numbers increased from a few in 1869 to over a hundred in 1909. Accompanying these shifts in the number of iron ore mines within regions were marked changes in output per mine. In the country as a whole, output increased about tenfold. Within each of the regions the increase was sizable, somewhat more than tenfold in the east north central region but decidedly less than tenfold in the west north central

---

[17] My study of the copper industry led to the conclusion that this development was clearly evident in the behavior of the price of copper *(Copper Costs and Prices: 1870–1957*, Baltimore, 1959).

[18] All data on number of mines and output per mine are from the various Censuses. The data in tables 16 and 17 are not consistent with the output data in table A-2 but suffice to give a rough indication of change.

region. From the start iron ore mining was on a rather large scale in the west north central region.

In the lead and zinc industry, unlike the iron ore industry, there was a large increase in the number of mines from 1869 to 1909—from 127 to 1,213. As in the iron ore and copper industries, there appears also to have been a substantial increase in the value of output per mine. In the west north central region (Missouri) the increase was of the order of sevenfold; in the east north central region (Wisconsin and Illinois) the increase was of the order of fourfold.

Gold and silver mines present a considerably more complex picture, partly because they consist of two different groups of mines, deep mines and a combination of placer and hydraulic operations. Between 1869 and 1909 the number of deep mines in operation increased very substantially, an increase which in absolute numbers took place mainly in the Rocky Mountain area, with the southwestern and the Pacific Coast regions also involved. The number of placer and hydraulic operations, on the other hand, declined to less than half its 1869 level, the decline taking place in absolute terms about equally in the Rocky Mountain and the Pacific Coast areas. Placer operations in the Southwest were never of any importance. Output per deep mine declined in every region which was in operation in both periods. With the placer and hydraulic operations, on the other hand, output per mine— which was only $5,000 in 1869—slightly more than doubled over the forty-year period, with almost all of this increase taking place in the Pacific Coast region.

Copper production in 1869 was an unimportant industry in every region with the exception of east north central (Michigan). As shown in table 17, in this region, which had almost as many producing mines

TABLE 17. *Number of Copper Mines and Output per Mine, by Region, 1869 and 1909*

| | Number of mines | | Annual output per mine (thousand dollars) | |
|---|---|---|---|---|
| | 1869 | 1909 | 1869 [a] | 1909 |
| Northeast | 2 | — | 97 | — |
| Middle Atlantic | 2 | — | 2 | — |
| South Atlantic | 4 | — | 24 | — |
| East north central | 27 | 21 | 86 | 1,430 |
| South central | 2 | — | 84 | — |
| Southwest | 3 | 120 | 6 | 308 |
| Rocky Mountain | — | 137 | — | 400 |
| Pacific | — | 23 | — | 232 |
| United States | 40 | 301 | 70 | 438 |

[a] Value of output per mine in 1869 was multiplied by the ratio of the price of copper in 1909 to the price of copper in 1869.

in 1909 as in 1870, output per mine in the later year was almost seventeen times that of the earlier year. In 1909, output per mine in the western areas was considerably lower than in the east north central region. Note, however, that we are dealing here with averages and with highly skewed distributions. An examination of the frequency distribution of mining enterprises in the copper industry by number of employees for Michigan, Arizona, and Utah in 1909 reveals that the largest mines were comparable in size to those in Michigan, but that in the western states there was a much larger number of very small mines than in Michigan.

<h3 style="text-align:center">MINERALS AND REGIONAL ECONOMIC DEVELOPMENT</h3>

The metallic mining industries played a major role in the westward spread of organized economic activity over the period of this study. Most important of all, they provided an export base for regional development and in some cases the only one. An export base is an essential part of the explanation of regional development where expansion of output and geographical expansion are associated, for, without it, there would be no reason to incur the locational disadvantage involved in moving away from established centers of activity. This economic opportunity often takes the form of an abundance of appropriable natural capital—forests, mineral deposits, or agricultural land. The richness of these pieces of natural capital permits higher costs for transportation to be incurred and thereby ensures the geographical expansion of production. The pace of this expansion then depends on the quality of the natural capital, the periods of gestation of man-made capital, the arrangements for spreading information about new economic opportunities, and the complicated mechanism governing the response to such opportunities.

The mere fact that minerals were produced, however, does not entail the conclusion that those deposits constituted valuable natural capital. The question is whether the amount of money spent in finding, developing, and producing the minerals was less than the cost of acquiring the products from the available alternative sources. The iron ore and copper deposits of the Lake Superior area and the coal deposits in all the areas where they were found were, in fact, valuable natural property, for the cost of finding and developing them was extremely low. As for gold and silver and the other metallic mineral deposits of the West, the size of the social surplus is more uncertain. If foresight were perfect, there would be no doubt about the answer, but the fact that the outcome of a mineral enterprise is uncertain opens the possibility that, from the point of view of society, the net rent earned was not large. This is quite different from saying that nobody made enormous profits on these deposits.

There is little possibility of estimating the net rent earned on the western deposits during the nineteenth century. The problem is very complicated from a conceptual point of view and involves expenditures not recorded in mining censuses. The impression, however, is almost universal that a substantial net rent was earned from the point of view of society as a whole. But even if net rents were negative, the fact that the activity was undertaken obviously exerted a profound influence on regional development. During the heyday of gold mining in California, gold was an important part of total economic activity, although there were other locational bases present before 1849. In parts of the Southwest, minerals furnished absolutely the only reason for settling there. In time, locational bases other than mining—agriculture, forestry, and lately "amenities"—developed, and mining diminished in relative importance both over the period under consideration and on down to the present.

Minerals were an export base with a peculiarity which aided regional development in another way. Since they had to be found, prospecting was an important means of accumulating knowledge of the different parts of the West. Assessment of the economic possibilities of a region—a necessity for all types of investment decisions—requires that a large stock of information of many kinds be at the command of many people, not just a few. The West was not unknown to a few white men who, before the Civil War, had roamed over most of the land as trappers. But the knowledge they had amassed was not comprehensive or systematic, and it provided only the bare essentials for the treks to Oregon and California. The extent of the ignorance of the West and the unreliability of what knowledge there was can be seen from the fact that even as late as 1867–79 the national government was induced to spend its money on four surveys of the West (King, Wheeler, Hayden, and Powell). Bartlett, in his account of those four surveys, sums up the situation as follows: "In 1867 men had asked, 'What lies out there?' By 1879, thanks to the work of the Great Surveys, their question had been answered. Now a new question was on men's lips: 'When shall we go there?' " [19]

*Is the Process of Mineral Development Systematic?*

A fundamental problem in the organization of the mineral industries is whether the finding and development of mineral deposits ex-

[19] Richard A. Bartlett, *Great Surveys of the American West*, Norman, Oklahoma, 1962, p. 376.

hibits a systematic response to economic incentive. Our survey of the spread of metal mining across the continent is relevant to this important question, and I believe the evidence supports the conclusion that for fairly large areas the search and development do respond in a systematic fashion to economic incentive, once it is widely understood that mineral deposits are probably present in the region. The actual pace of search and development and the actual growth of output do require other preconditions, the main one being transportation. For example, it was impossible for low-value ores of copper, lead, and zinc to be developed in the West until a rail network provided a cheap means of getting these mine products to market. It is true that, if we look at small areas or at the efforts of the lone prospector or even a single corporation, chance—from their point of view—plays an important part in success or failure. But if we step back and look at a larger area and a larger number of prospectors or corporations, the chance element begins to recede and a pattern of relentless expansion in response to economic incentive emerges in region after region.

The presence of copper in Michigan was known from very early times. The Smithsonian Institution has exhibited a large mass of native copper called the Ontonagon Boulder which had rested on the bank of the Ontonagon River in Michigan from prehistoric times until it was moved to Washington, D.C., in 1843. With knowledge of the presence of copper generally available, modern copper mining began in Michigan quite early, in about 1845. It expanded rapidly, and the search for additional deposits was conducted in an intensive manner. A similarly systematic and intense expansion of iron ore mining is observable in the Lake Superior deposits in Michigan and later in Wisconsin and Minnesota.

The presence of silver in what later was to be the southwestern United States was known for a long time. Indeed, the hope of finding large deposits of gold and silver had stimulated some of the earliest explorations in the Southwest—if they can be so dignified—but for a long time the presence of really rich deposits of gold or silver was hoped for rather than suspected. The well-known discovery which opened up the West for mineral exploitation was of California gold, a fortuitous discovery not to be ascribed to any economic activity in search of gold. But once the news of gold in large quantities in California was definite, the search was extended, covering more and more ground as time went on and alerting people to the possible presence of gold in areas far removed from California. The discovery of the Comstock lode in 1859 was an outgrowth of the California activity, and so probably, at a much greater distance, was the discovery of gold in Colorado the same year. After that, the process of combing the West for mineral deposits began. What prospectors and others were looking for depended naturally enough on what they could do with the mineral if they found it. This meant that in areas very far from the more settled ones attention was limited for a long time to ores containing large amounts of gold and silver. But with the development of the rail network, which was significant by 1880 but far more extensive by 1890, mining ores containing much smaller amounts of the precious metals began to pay.

# PART FOUR

*The Supply of Natural Resource Information*

# SOME GUIDELINES FOR ORGANIZATION AND ADMINISTRATION OF INFORMATION ACTIVITIES

Our search for guidelines for the management of information activities rests on a general view about the role of information in economic decisions about natural resources. The goal is not the amassing of "complete" information, nor is it particularly advisable to move toward this goal as "rapidly as possible," for what sensible meaning could these goals have? In the most general terms, we want information that will permit suitable investment decisions in the years immediately ahead—suitable, that is, in view of the fact that information has a real cost and that the course of economic development is powerfully constrained by forces whose operation is not going to be upset by the generation of any quantity of information whatsoever. Not only may more of one type of information mean less of others, but we run the risk of accumulating information, not for the solution of an actual problem by use of a complete information model, but for the sake of information itself, that is, for the accumulation of information that may never be used. We cannot collect all the informa-

Reprinted from *Natural Resource Information for Economic Development* (Baltimore: The Johns Hopkins Press for Resources for the Future, Inc., 1969), chapter 6.

tion "necessary" to solve a specified list of problems, partly because the particular problems to be solved "now" depend on information gathered earlier and partly because it pays to have only enough information to reach an acceptable solution.

How can we proceed to our rules for economizing? A conceivable method would be to emulate the agricultural economist who, together with his technical brethren, may be able to tell us how to handle the application of a certain type of fertilizer. On the basis of experiment or by statistical analysis of (varied) non-experimental fertilizer applications, he can say that with soil of a certain type, a certain pattern of rotation, and with certain climatic conditions, it will pay to apply a certain quantity of fertilizer per acre per season with present costs and prices.

For obvious reasons, no procedure very close to this is now possible with natural resource information, nor does such a procedure seem feasible on a large scale in the future. The benefits flowing from natural resource information are often quite diffuse. Not only that, but much information activity must anticipate the time of its use. And, unlike the case of the fertilizer, it is not easy to specify the product of some types of information. Superficially, some types of information may seem less than valuable because their collection serves only to cull out losing prospects—prospects, however, which could have absorbed a lot of investment funds had they been continued.

However difficult it is to make numerical estimates of the value of a little more or a little less information, two procedures are within our power. First, it is possible to make some suggestions for economizing which, while they do not result in a fine adjustment of outlays in the light of product produced, can be of help in preventing some gross misallocations of funds. Also it should be recalled that in many situations it is possible to be reasonably sure that a certain increase in expenditure will result in a product whose value is greater—or less— than the outlay in question.

The second possibility for dealing with the allocation problem involves a search for forms of organization and types of relations among organizations that will facilitate the making of judgments about marginal changes in information and its benefits. Even though we can't estimate the value of information, we may be able to specify some of the features of an organization that will enable improved evaluation of marginal changes in the information programs as time goes along.

The suggestions that are made here have two general characteristics. First, they look toward specialization and a full use of the specialist in the execution of natural resource information programs. But the specialist must be constrained to operate within the system by which investment and operating decisions in the natural resource field are reached. He is the servant of this system.

Second, the goal should be a system in which information programs are adjusted to the needs and demands of the governmental agencies and private entities that use natural resource information. It is to be expected that the balance of the programs and their content will change as time goes on.[1]

## How Much Information?

Our first guideline is obvious and perhaps rather formal, but it needs to be pointed out and kept clearly in mind.

*The quantity of information collected should be increased so long as the present value of the investment opportunity (or cost savings if this is the use to which the information is put) is increased by more than the cost of the information.*

This problem has been discussed at considerable length elsewhere.* Here the discussion is simply a reminder of the main lines of the argument but cannot very well be passed over, for the general orientation toward the management of information as a part of the process of maximizing the present social value of the investment opportunities undertaken is essential if we are to avoid uneconomic accumulation or failure to accumulate information.

Our analysis began by considering the simple case in which we suddenly become aware of an investment opportunity with constant demand and cost conditions after construction is completed. The proper size depends on one or more aspects of the behavior of a natural resource stochastic variable, for example, the flow of a stream. We can estimate the relevant characteristics of the behavior of this variable only on the basis of observed data. The problem is, how long can we afford to wait for data to accumulate before constructing?

The main problem here is the estimation of a function which relates

---

[1] Two authors have written on these problems with an approach similar in some respects to the one in this document, although there are numerous divergencies. See Estevam Strauss, "Algunos aspectos de la investigación y explotación de recursos naturales en América Latina relacionados con la planificación económica, Parte I," July 1965, mimeo.; and "Recursos naturales y planificación económica en América Latina, Parte II," November 1965, mimeo. (Santiago: Instituto Latinoamericano de Planificación Económica y Social). Part I also is available in English. See also Leon Laitman, "El desarrollo de datos sobre recursos naturales para la planificación económica: Un método integral," in *Temas Geográficos-Económicos,* Proceedings of Unión Geográfica Internacional, Conferencia Regional Latinoamericana, Vol. II (Mexico City: Sociedad Mexicana de Geografía y Estadística, 1966), p. 19.

* *Natural Resource Information,* chapter 5.—*Ed.*

expected present value of the investment opportunity at time $t$ to the number of years of data available, where $t$ is also the number of years of data available at the time of construction, $t$. We may think of $t=0$ as "now," the moment in which the investment opportunity is perceived.

The expected value of the investment opportunity will be low with little data available, but will rise with more data available. With little data available, the structure often [2] would be too large (resulting in unused capacity) or too small (resulting in lost opportunity for product or structural failure), thus reducing the expected present value of the opportunity. For small enough quantities of data, the expected value will be negative.[3] As the quantity of data increases, expected value (always as of time $t$) will rise, but at a decreasing rate. With our assumption of constant price and cost conditions, expected value will approach a maximum as our estimates of the values of the relevant parameters of the distribution involved approach the true values.[4]

We can go immediately to the conclusion that construction should take place when the cost of getting one more year of information is equal to the resulting increase in expected present value. The cost of getting one more year of data is made up of two elements, the outlay during the year to get the data, $k$, and interest on the expected present value of the opportunity we would have experienced if we had not waited one more year. That is, if $V(t)$ is the basic function, we should wait until its rate of increase, $V'(t)$, is equal to $[rV(t)+k]$, where $r$ is the rate of discount (the rate of return on investment).

Several conclusions are evident. First, it never will pay to wait for "complete" information. Second, an extremely important element of the problem is the cost coming from postponement of the stream of net revenues from the project. This factor means it does not pay to accumulate data until the increment in expected value is equal to the annual cost of the data. The percentage/100 rate of increase per year in expected value $V'(t)/V(t)$ must not be less than $[rV(t)+k]/V(t)=$

---

[2] We must imagine what would happen if many structures of this type were constructed with estimates based on the availability of, say, ten years of data. Then the same question must be asked for many cases of eleven years, and so on.

[3] Alberto Martinez has pointed out that in many parts of South America lack of climatological data makes it impossible to determine whether climate rules out the use of a foreign plant. He characterizes as innumerable the cases in which dams have been too large or too small, in the one case never filling and in the other in danger of failure. All types of works within reach of a river are frequently damaged because design has not been able to take into account the likely flows. They often are just not known. See his "Informe sobre clima y meteorologia de sudamérica" (UNESCO/CASTALA/2.1.2 II.1), p. 13.

[4] For example, the payoff may depend on the frequency of floods over a certain level, average annual flow, average flow during a certain part of the year, the dispersion of monthly flows, or other aspects of flow of the stream.

$r+k/V(t)$.[5] This means the effect on expected value of one more year of data must be quite sizable to justify waiting.

Now let us change the problem to a form that corresponds better to the problem facing information agencies. Suppose we are aware of the existence of a possible investment opportunity which will become viable some day because demand is growing.

The simplest case of demand growth is very unrealistic but still instructive. Assume that demand explodes into existence full blown at a certain time. How many years ago should we have started collecting data? If we are free to choose the time for construction, it is obvious that this should be when the demand comes into existence. What we must compare is the cost of reaching *back* in time for one more year of data (accumulating this cost to the date of construction at the rate of discount) with the resulting increase in expected value. In this case, one more year of data does not require postponing the stream of net rents, but, on the other hand, we incur an interest cost, which reflects real opportunities for investment that have been given up, on the funds spent on developing information.

For more realistic cases in which demands grow from year to year, the problem is more complex. We may think of the immediately preceding question—by how many years should the data program anticipate construction—as being analyzed separately for each possible date of construction. For each of these cases there will be a maximum expected value (discounted to the date of construction) associated with a certain number of years of data. The maximum of these maxima, with all of these discounted to a common date, represents the best time for construction and will also indicate the time when the data program should be begun. It should be possible to make estimates of this type, at least retrospectively.

Quantitative estimates of the sort required by these simple models are not feasible for many problems of information. In some cases there is difficulty in quantifying the information. In others the benefits are very diffuse or hard to measure. In all cases, however, the simple model poses the relevant questions. We should be trying to judge the product that will result from more information and should bear in mind the powerful role that should be played by the rate of discount in making these judgments. Postponement of a stream of net rents is very costly, as is also the premature assembly of information. These are not "merely financial considerations" but reflect the fact that capital goods have a return in real product.

---

[5] Note that what is involved is the ratio of *k* to *V(t)*, not the ratio of *k* to the capital cost of the project.

## What Areas Are Suitable?

*For the most part, natural resource information programs should be concentrated in or near the areas already being exploited.*

Although this suggestion may seem surprising, the considerations supporting it are quite compelling if expenditure on information is to be evaluated as a public investment. There are some partial exceptions, however.

First of all, as economic product and population grow in settled areas, it will pay to increase all the inputs that are used with natural resources, and for certain types of resources one of these inputs is information about the resource. One may think, for example, of soil and information about it. In this particular case, and in some others, too, the capacity of the owners or managers of natural resources to use information grows over time. The level of education may be rising, the extension service may have become more effective, or they simply may have learned how to put the available information to work and are now ready to use more detailed and more sophisticated information. Thus the need for information about natural resources does not vanish just because the natural resources of an area are being exploited. The emphasis may change as among resources and also the type of information may change, but the demand or need will remain.

But not only do there continue to be opportunities to invest in more information in areas already under exploitation. The very fact of the present locational pattern of economic activity implies that entrepreneurs have found the obstacles to the extension of economic activities to other areas to be insuperable, given the alternative investment opportunities available and the necessity of covering costs. In parts of some countries there are areas so disfavored that economic activity in them is not only sparse but nonexistent for all practical purposes.

Natural resource survey information is not likely to diminish the impact of the forces that have resulted in some areas having little or no productive activity in the natural resource industries. The extension of economic activity to very far distant or idle areas has two strikes against it, and in some cases more.

First of all, thanks to indivisibilities that are present in the construction of many types of infrastructure, it is certain that the cost of infrastructure services will be higher in areas with a low density of economic activity. It is not possible to construct a 100-mile highway for a flow of $k$ ton-miles per year at one-thousandth of the cost of a highway for a flow of $1,000 k$ ton-miles per year. Nor can one family have one-thousandth of a physician residing within walking distance of their plot in the newly exploited area.

Second, transportation is especially important in raising the cost of economic activity that is far distant from established centers, not only because of underutilization of capacity, the factor just discussed, but because of distance itself. For example, in the case of ore of various types, rail and port charges are sometimes 75 per cent of the cost of the ore delivered on board an oceangoing vessel.[6] In the case of the Pine Point lead-zinc development on the south side of Great Slave Lake in northern Canada, extension of the existing railway line accounted for two-thirds of a total investment of $128 million.[7] Or consider the prospects for a lumber operation on one of the Amazon tributaries. Assuming some reasonably homogeneous stands of marketable timber could be found, the transport handicap is simply gigantic, involving not only the handicap of distance but the obstacle posed by rapids and other hazards. What is more, it may be possible to exploit similar stands much farther downstream, where the transport problems are of a more routine nature and can be solved at a much lower cost.

There appears to be a strong tendency to suppose that programs to develop information about natural resources should involve extensive efforts in areas with little or no economic activity, if there are such areas in the country in question. Often the task seems to be conceived as one of filling in a *tabula rasa*. Actually a great deal is known about areas not now intensively exploited, granted that this may not amount to much in comparison with what could be known. But, more significant, the present pattern of economic activity and the present boundaries of economic activity imply the possession of a very useful type of information—that an important obstacle to the extension of economic activity has been encountered. This factor is strongly emphasized by the Paddock brothers in their recent study of agricultural development problems, and their viewpoint is buttressed by many examples from extensive experience.[8] Time and time again, someone has thought that he perceived a production opportunity that had been neglected, only to have his subsequent failure bring to his attention an unfavorable aspect of the opportunity that he either had not seen or had brushed aside as unimportant.

[6] Myles A. Walsh, "Development and Mechanization of Small Mines," in *Natural Resources*, Vol. II, U.S. Papers prepared for the United Nations Conference on the Application of Science and Technology for the Benefit of the Less Developed Areas (Washington: U.S. Government Printing Office, 1963), p. 238.

[7] *Mining Journal*, August 27, 1965, p. 143.

[8] William and Paul Paddock, *Hungry Nations* (Boston: Little, Brown, 1964).

The possibility of colonizing new lands no doubt accounts in many cases for the pressure to survey natural resources in such areas. In Latin America, for instance, many countries have such rapid rates of population growth that the task of creating productive jobs for the growing numbers presents many difficulties. In this situation, the tremendous areas of Latin America that are not now exploited for crops or grazing seem often to be thought of as a fine opportunity for colonization. Only 5 per cent of the total area of Latin America is presently used as arable land, and only another 20 per cent is used for pasture.[9]

While there seems to have been remarkably little attempt to make comprehensive economic evaluations of past colonization projects, the verdict of those who have studied the question is that projects in recent decades have been marked by many failures. It seems fair to say that they do not view future colonization as an important outlet for future population.

For example, Christodoulou, in a general review of colonization problems, writes, "The high proportion of failures in colonization projects certainly would have been lower if a thorough evaluation of past experience had been made and if norms and directions for future programs had been drawn from this evaluation." [10] Barraclough and Domike emphasize that colonization projects have incurred very high capital costs, sometimes more than twenty times the annual income of local small producers. This does not necessarily indicate economic failure, of course, for net income conceivably could be large enough to cover interest on investment and leave a net income for the producer. They seem to say this has not been the case, however. They judge projects with foreign colonists to have been more successful than those with domestic colonists because of better education and better social organization, among other factors. They do not view colonization as being able to take care of the "excess" population produced in rural areas.[11]

The argument for the development of survey type information on

---

[9] See Carlos Plaza V., "Los recursos naturales en la integración latinoamericana" (Santiago: Instituto Latinoamericano de Planificación Económica y Social, October 1966), mimeo, preliminary version, p. 20.

[10] D. Christodoulou, "La colonización de tierras: Algunos aspectos fundamentales que suelen descuidarse," *Boletín Mensual de Economía y Estadística Agrícolas* (FAO), Vol. 14, No. 10 (October 1965), p. 1 (my translation).

[11] Solon Barraclough and Arthur L. Domike, "La estructura agraria en siete Países de América Latina," *El Trimestre Económico*, Vol. 33 (2), No. 130 (April–June 1966). See especially pp. 261–63. See also the series of papers on colonization projects in various parts of Latin America presented at the 1966 meeting of the Unión Geográfica Internacional, Conferencia Regional Latinoamericana held in Mexico City, *La geografía y los problemas de población*, Vol. I. The papers and proceedings were published by La Sociedad Mexicana de Geografía y Estadística (Mexico City, 1966). The following are of special interest: Craig L. Dozier, "Problemas para la coloniza-

uninhabited areas would seem to rest on the presumption that without this information we are missing some valuable production opportunities that can be brought to light in no other way. Insofar as these areas are humid forest areas, the difficulty to be overcome does not appear to be one of locating rich areas exploitable with present techniques and large enough to stand the handicap of distance. Instead, so far as agricultural use of these areas is concerned, the problem appears to be one of developing methods for using these areas.

Many experts have examined the obstacles confronting exploitation of the hot humid areas and have found them to be very serious indeed. John Phillips, drawing on his experience in many countries, has emphasized three types of problems. First is an impressive array of health problems, not necessarily insuperable but as of now serious in many areas, and the prospect for rapidly reducing them to tolerable levels is not bright. The severity of the health problems is closely connected with the second type of problem emphasized by Phillips—securing the adoption by colonists of "best practice," both with respect to matters bearing on health and in production activities. The third type of problem is perhaps most fundamental, however, namely, the lack of understanding on a technical level of methods of exploitation which will yield enough to make settlement feasible. His assessment of the difficulties deserves quotation in full:

We are still ignorant about the technique and economy of the thinning or the complete removal of woody growth, for the purpose of utilizing the ground for the growing of annual and perennial crops. This is true for cocoa, coffee, pepper, banana and sundry food crops which may be grown in suitable association with indigenous trees and shrubs left *in situ,* and for those like oil-palm, tea, rubber, cotton, sisal and plantation banana and annuals suitable for mechanized cultivation requiring almost complete removal of the woody growth above and below ground.

The history of each and every larger-scaled enterprise, attempted on land where removal or thinning of woody growth has been a preliminary requirement, reveals how serious a problem is the effective clearing or thinning of such growth—compatible with satisfactory protection of the soil and the economy of investment. Instructive examples of what not to do are seen in experiences gained in the wooded savanna of Tanganyika (East African Groundnuts Scheme), the jungle of the Dry Zone of Ceylon (Gal Oya

ción efectiva de tierras nuevas en América Latina: Algunos ejemplos actuales" (p. 229); Alejandro Medino Valderrama, "El estudio de geografía regional, síntesis de la colonización de la Selva Peruana" (p. 247); Ulv Masing, "San Vito de Java: Análisis del éxito y fracaso de una colonia de agricultores inmigrantes en el bosque lluvioso de Costa Rica" (p. 267); Gottfried Pfeifer, "Observaciones a lo largo de las nuevas fronteras de colonización en Paraná y Matto Grosso" (p. 267); David E. Snyder, "Realidades geográficas de la colonización fronteriza contemporánea en América del Sur" (p. 329).

Irrigation Scheme) and in the humid *selva* of Peru (*vide* the valiant efforts of a well-known and philanthropic American, Mr. R. Letourneau . . . to clear land for pasturage). To these spectacular examples could be added many a small project by both governments and private enterprise from Latin America, through Africa to India and South-East Asia.[12]

Stamp places a similar emphasis on the technical difficulties of using the hot humid areas for agricultural purposes. While the growth of trees is indeed remarkable, the large excess of rainfall over evaporation results in rapid impoverishment by leaching of soil near the surface as soon as the tree cover is removed. He concludes, "By and large, if cleared, equatorial forests would provide vast areas of poor or indifferent soils, liable to become still further impoverished, and further liable to marked soil erosion." [13] He observes that in the equatorial regions that have proved to be productive, the soil and terrain conditions are often rather special (e.g., clay which can be worked into a water-holding layer for rice culture or a climate that is monsoonal).

It should also be noted that the transportation obstacle to the extension of economic activity by jumps from present activity, while it operates in all types of regions, becomes an even more important obstacle in the case of the hot humid areas, reaching its acme when excess water is combined with a rough terrain. Dozier's description of the 195-kilometer road from La Paz to the colonization project on the upper Beni River vividly illustrates the difficulties. The real trouble comes in the last 75 kilometers—a mere 47 miles. This stretch has an abundant rainfall, concentrated in half of the year but with plenty of rain in the so-called dry months, too. The road is constructed, not on a natural rock base, but on clay easily exposed on the mountainsides. Wherever natural drainage is insufficient, during and after rains the road becomes a quagmire of unbelievable proportions. For all practical purposes mobility stops, except for the most powerful road construction trucks and tractors. An ordinary four-wheel-drive vehicle can cover the 47 miles in a day—if it is lucky. In this particular case, the better quality of the first 120 kilometers from La Paz has resulted in spontaneous settlement on this stretch around Caranavi—with better economic success than is being enjoyed by the organized colonization project on the Beni.[14]

So far as agricultural and forest development products are con-

---

[12] John Phillips, *The Development of Agriculture and Forestry in the Tropics* (London: Faber and Faber, 1961), p. 83.

[13] L. Dudley Stamp, *Our Developing World* (London: Faber and Faber, 1960), pp. 47–51.

[14] Dozier, *La geografía y los problemas de población*, Vol. I, pp. 238–39.

cerned, then, the conclusion seems reasonable enough that viable investment opportunity is the more unlikely the bigger the jump (in economic terms) from present activity, and all the more unlikely if the jump is to the warm humid areas. This generalization seems applicable also to forest development projects. With little prospect for viable investment, natural resources information activity can well be concentrated in areas of present economic activity and those immediately adjoining. Note two particular implications. Where transportation routes are extended for non-economic reasons—for example, the development of a highway for military purposes—natural resources information activity immediately becomes appropriate, for one of the principal handicaps to investment, the cost of transportation, has been removed. In the evaluation of investment opportunities in such a case, the opportunity should be charged (or private investors should be charged) only with the additional transport costs occasioned by the investment. Secondly, the development of resource information for areas near those presently exploited will ensure the development of information for areas in which spontaneous settlement is taking place.[15] The monitoring and understanding of this process is of great importance for a variety of reasons. So far as natural resources are concerned, the settlement is often in areas susceptible to erosion damage from the methods of production used. Although the economic and social results of these settlements are of great importance to various governmental programs—for example, public works and governmental services of various types—the matter apparently is receiving little study.[16]

There are a couple of partial exceptions to the areal allocation guide suggested here, the first of which is minerals. The exception is only partial, because many minerals and mineral products have so low a value in relation to weight that they can stand long overland hauls only in settled areas or where the volume of mineral or mineral product to be shipped is big enough not to leave a large quantity of excess transport capacity. This suggests that the location of activity aimed at the search for minerals in unexploited areas should be guided by prior indications that the area is mineralized and by the transport possibilities, such as rivers or rail routes, over which construction

---

[15] In some cases, of course, the boundary between viable and non-viable areas is so sharp—Chile has many examples, e.g., her northern valleys and mountain barriers—that there is no reason to develop certain types of information beyond the barrier.

[16] This is the judgment of Ing. Augusto Eulacio of FAO (Santiago, Chile). See also Inter-American Committee for Agricultural Development, *Inventory of Information Basic to the Planning of Agricultural Development in Latin America, Regional Report* (Washington: Pan American Union, 1963), p. 38.

costs will be low. Where a distant area appears very promising there may be a possibility of developing a mining district which would be able to support transport. Similarly, more valuable products, such as precious or exotic metals, can support air transport of the mineral or its final product. Thus the search for them can be more extensive. With a sufficiently great rate of production and large enough reserves, petroleum and natural gas can move quite long distances by pipeline. Accordingly the search for them may appropriately be more wide-ranging in some circumstances.

What these remarks on minerals seem to add up to is that quite general geologic studies of unsettled areas may be justified if existing information is not discouraging. A step-by-step procedure would also be desirable here if existing information points to some areas as being better prospects than others.

Another possible exception to our areal allocation guideline is hydrologic and meteorologic data. In each case the natural system in some aspect of which we have a current economic interest may extend into areas without economic activity. The weather systems of the west coast of South America are cases in point.

Here, fortunately, there is a good possibility that satellite photos may be able to substitute in part for conventional weather data from the ocean area, which could be developed only at much cost. As for water, the fact that it can be transported downhill, either in a river or a pipe, may mean that hydraulic information from quite remote areas will have a present use. In these cases, however, costs of collecting reliable data in remote areas on a regular basis may be very high. The personnel available may make it difficult to secure reliable management and reading of even simple instruments, and the various possibilities for automatic recording or radio sending equipment bring with them another set of personnel and maintenance problems.

### SOME SUGGESTIONS FOR MANAGING CERTAIN TYPES OF INFORMATION ACTIVITIES

The remarks that follow do not purport to be a systematic account of how to manage information activities of specific types, for they are far too brief and sketchy. Instead, they are in part the incidental product, on a less general level, of my attempt to relate the problems of the several information fields to economic development.

The incompleteness of these remarks is attributable partly to the fact that the problems of economization in each field must be worked out by the experts in that field working in conjunction with those who will use the information. Just as important, however: the problems of individual countries are so varied and the quality of the agencies that produce and use this information is also so varied that any analysis of general applicability ends up being rather platitudinous and empty of specific content. Hence, the following are simply particular points that have impressed me as important or likely to be neglected.

### Aerial Photography

Since photographs are a tool to develop specific types of information, the photography program should depend on these other programs, remembering, of course, that there is a non-governmental demand for the photos themselves, wanted for a wide variety of uses. Would it therefore be desirable to have stereo pairs available for the whole country, just to be sure the photos are available if needed? Much depends on the circumstances.

First of all, if no use is going to be made of the photos in the fairly near future, why spend prematurely when there are urgent needs for capital? Furthermore, costs of photography go down and the quality of images or the variety of images available improves as time goes on. Nor do all uses require photos of the same scale or stereo pairs with the same angle of view.[17] In addition, cultural information deteriorates with age, although the old photo will still be of value where the change from the old to the new photo is itself of interest. This consideration suggests the desirability of trying to anticipate the various cases in which it is desired to measure change over time by use of air photos. The areas involved should be included in the early photography. Perhaps inclusion on a sampling basis would be sufficient.

On the other hand, if information derived from air photos is to form the basis of a land tax of the type that Chile is now using, photos are required for all of the area to be included in the system. The whole country may not have to be covered, however, as was the case with Chile.

### General Purpose Maps

It should be relatively easy to get a feel for the demand for general purpose maps. The cost of making certain types of maps, especially

---

[17] For expert opinion along these lines, see W. Schermerhorn, "Planning of Aerial Surveys for the Over-all Development of the Natural Resources of a Country," in *Proceedings of United Nations Seminar on Aerial Survey Methods and Equipment,* Mineral Resources Development Series No. 12 (Bangkok, 1960), p. 68; and A. P. A. Vink, "Aerial Photographs and the Soil Sciences," paper presented at the 1964 Toulouse Conference (UNESCO/NS/90, Paris, February 28, 1964), p. 21.

planimetric, will be substantially lower once satellite photos are available. There will be little reason not to map a whole country.

Topographic maps, much more expensive, should be developed as demand dictates. This will mean priority for areas in which there is prospective construction activity, including private construction, public works, and highways. Areas of expanding activity will be favored by this criterion. In some cases topographic maps will be wanted as a base for geologic maps. Some of these areas may be distant from presently expanding areas of economic activity, as may be true if the geologic information is wanted for mineral search.

## Geological Data

In our discussion of the guideline suggesting that activities generating information about natural resources should be concentrated in or near areas already being exploited, information useful to the search for minerals was mentioned as a partial exception. We now examine the nature of this exception more closely to see what guidelines can be suggested for geological investigations.

The demand for that part of the activities of a geological organization that is derived from the programs of other governmental agencies presents few problems. There will be demands for help on engineering geology in connection with the many types of structures involved in various government programs—highways, bridges, port facilities, dams, canals, buildings, airports, etc. The water development agencies will want various types of geological studies made as a part of river basin planning work. Groundwater problems will have to be studied as a part of the programs of agencies concerned with water supply for cities and industry or for irrigation.

The satisfaction of these demands from governmental agencies will account for a substantial part of the expenditure of a government for geological information, but there are no especially difficult problems in anticipating the demand or in organizing to satisfy it. So far as the financing of such studies is concerned, it would be desirable that the requesting agency reimburse the geological agency for the work done. A reimbursement procedure will insure that when an agency requests funds for a project the amount will include the cost of geological studies and will not be deceptively low. In addition, the necessity of reimbursement may stimulate the agency demanding the service to compare the price asked by the geological agency with the price asked by a private consulting firm. There may well be circumstances in which it is more economical to buy routine geological service from private firms specializing in it rather than from a governmental unit.

The more difficult problem in providing geological information relates to the search for minerals and petroleum. A full dress analysis of the problem of mineral search is so large and so difficult a problem as to require a separate volume. However, a few general observations may be helpful in preventing useless expenditure.

It is my belief that the general orientation of a geological agency is an important factor in attaining the kind of program that will most benefit a country so far as its mineral resources are concerned. It is assumed in this discussion that a government is interested in the economic return to be had from geological investigations and not in amassing information for its own sake. Geological surveys, like all other activities involving a recognized discipline, are subject to the tendency to orient the agency's activities toward "professional" objectives that may be in conflict with economic objectives. Obviously this does not mean that studies oriented toward the economic objective of providing information which will eventuate in the discovery and exploitation of deposits must be *un*professional. It does mean, however, that the tendency to set too stringent standards of various types must be avoided, and that efforts to attain complete coverage of large areas with maps of certain scales must always be regarded as instrumental rather than goals. That is, complete coverage of an area can be a proper goal only if it is estimated that complete coverage will be productive in economic terms.

At all points in the programming of geological information activities the question must be asked: Will this pay off or not? If the attitude toward commitment of personnel and equipment is not of a persistently questioning nature, distortions in the program may easily become so great that it will be clear to impartial examination that money is being wasted. In particular, the problem of program determination cannot be solved by dwelling upon the "basic" nature of the data being generated. To claim that some one type of data is "basic" is the equivalent of sweeping the problem under the rug and ignoring it. Indeed, if good estimates of the productivity of all types of information could be made, the conclusion would be that they are all equally basic in the sense that another dollar spent on any one of them would produce the same gain—namely, one dollar's worth of gain.

Let us suppose that those who determine the program of the geological agency do in fact possess this questioning attitude, seeking always to eliminate programs that will not contribute to economic product and to expand to proper size those that do. Are there any general guiding considerations to be borne in mind?

In my opinion we must recognize that the problem of devising programs for the early stages of the exploration process, usually determined by and financed by government, is one about which views are far from unanimous. The reasons for this state of affairs are not hard to find, for evaluation of different programs is complicated first of all by the fact that the physical environments of countries are certainly different—unfortunately in ways that are hard to quantify. Thus it may be hard to see that a program suitable for one country may not be at all useful for another. Not only do the physical attributes of countries differ in many subtle ways, but so also do the institutions and organizations available to exploit the information generated. Second, it is difficult to measure the product of activities in these earlier stages. If we think in terms of a sifting process in which techniques that cost little per unit area are used to sift out smaller areas for more intensive study by more costly methods, how many targets are mistakenly rejected by the early siftings? This problem is not completely intractable and can be studied, but there certainly is no good solution as yet. Equally difficult is the probability of estimating the number of targets that eventually will be discovered.

While the quantitative study of the programming of exploration activities is in a rather rudimentary state, the common view of the desirable program involves a succession of siftings, with the more expensive activities reserved for the later stages so that they need be applied only to a smaller area.

Having in mind this sifting idea, the program planner has in front of him not simply a large area about which nothing is known but ordinarily an array of areas, each with a different body of information bearing on minerals and, just as important, with different characteristics that will influence the value of any minerals that are present in the area. Furthermore, he has at his disposal not simply regional geological investigation, geochemical investigation, etc., but each of these coupled with the possibility of using it at different levels of intensity. What are some of the characteristics of the program he should come up with? Is there anything that should be avoided?

First, to reiterate, complete coverage for its own sake by any activity is to be avoided. The aim is, instead, to reject areas as unprofitable prospects for investigation by more expensive techniques—at least until cheaper methods are available.

Second, there are likely to be possibilities for further study in areas in which there has been or is mineral production or in which minerals are known to be present. The nature and level of detail of the additional studies will depend on the information already available. Such areas deserve consideration for further study for two reasons:

(1) Where some targets have already been found, more are likely to be present, unless, of course, the area has already been thoroughly investigated. (2) A deposit found in an already producing area is likely to be more valuable than its physical twin in a non-producing area, for processing and transport capacity may already be available.

What about large areas about which very little is known? Here there is a case for small-scale geological studies to obtain an idea of the gross geologic picture. Satellite photos, supplementing other investigation, may turn out to be particularly useful because of the excellent synoptic view they can give. It may turn out that exploratory magnetic surveys at a considerable altitude are a useful interpretative aid, as may also be geochemical surveys with a low density to hold cost down. The object of such small-scale investigation, using conventional air photos, too, is to develop an understanding of the geology of the area to enable the identification of areas worthy of more intensive investigation, if not of metallogenic provinces.[18]

If a country has a large area that is unknown geologically, should small-scale information be developed for the whole area right away or for only a part of it? Here two guides already discussed come into play. By limiting initial efforts to the more easily accessible parts of the whole area, it will be possible to get deposits to the production stage sooner, thus advancing the time when they begin to yield a return to the country. In view of interest (the productivity of investment), this is an exceedingly important gain. It also enables postponement of the cost of small-scale geologic investigation in areas in which deposits would be developed only later. Of course, if geologic ignorance is not spread uniformly over the whole area, a presently inaccessible area with information suggesting the likelihood of rich deposits may well be worth investigating more intensively.

In general, the decision procedure should emphasize flexibility, in that the status of the different possible areas for investigation should constantly be reassessed in the light of information that has been added to that already available, in the light of new techniques or changes in the cost of using known techniques and changes in prices, or any other factors affecting the value of deposits that may be found.

While the process of search may be thought of as a sifting process, all rejections for further investigation should be regarded as tentative. A change in any one of the circumstances just mentioned may make it

---

[18] See Sherwin F. Kelly, "The Pillars of Our Prosperity and the Impending Drain on Mineral Resources" (reprinted from *Western Miner and Oil Review*, October 1960, by Western Miner Press, Vancouver, B.C., Canada), for a discussion of literature bearing on the identification of metallogenic provinces by using information that can be developed on a small scale.

advisable to resume study of an area. As one of my critics has emphasized so strongly and correctly, regional geology may be studied on
many levels of precision and detail, with strong emphasis on some
aspects of the area's geology and less on others, depending on the
interests toward which the investigation is directed and on the characteristics of the region.[19] Thus, as time goes on and more knowledge
is accumulated about the mineral resources of a country, we should
expect less and less reliance on the extensive survey and more reliance
on intensive studies concentrated on smaller areas.

The preceding discussion is relevant to a country of some size. In the
case of a small country, the same considerations would suggest the
desirability of considering extensive investigations simultaneously for
the small country and a neighboring country (or countries), which
may also be small, of course.

### Hydrologic and Meteorologic Data

As was emphasized elsewhere,* data on a natural flow variable or a
changing state of nature can be gathered only with the passage of
time or by the usually difficult reconstruction of the past. The frequency with which we wish to observe the variable or state will depend
on the rapidity and amplitude of variation in the variable or on the
rate at which the state of nature in question is changing. Thus, geological maps do not have to be redone because of changes in the rocks,
although they have to be for other reasons. The progress of dunes,
changes in vegetation, or the progress of erosion can be studied by
readings taken at intervals of years.

Hydraulic and meteorologic variables, on the other hand, exhibit
great variability over much shorter periods of time. What is more,
we have a strong interest in what may be almost momentary values
of the variables—for example, floods and temperatures below freezing.
To capture them, a continuously operating program must be set up.
Meteorological data are wanted not only for the economically important activity of weather forecasting but also for establishing
climatological characteristics so important for agriculture. The agri-
culturist, especially the innovator, can make good use of the knowledge of some aspect or aspects of the distributions of length of
growing season, date of first frost, date of last frost, diurnal and
monthly temperature distributions, rainfall, snow, and other characteristics.

Hydrologic data are clearly necessary if hydraulic works of any kind

[19] Vincent E. McKelvey of the U.S. Geological Survey, letter of June 22, 1967.
* *Natural Resource Information,* chapter 5.—*Ed.*

are to be erected, although, as we shall see, the data have been most rudimentary or non-existent in many cases.

A group of technical experts in the field of hydro-meteorological networks recently suggested thirty to forty years of data for base gauging stations.[20] Where there is extreme variation in precipitation and runoff, this minimum period might be extended to as much as seventy or eighty years. It is not at all clear what was meant by "minimum requirement." In my estimation, postponement of viable projects for at least thirty to forty years would almost surely be productive of a net loss because of the sacrifice of net rents involved, but perhaps they were not thinking of postponement. Perhaps the suggested minimum number of years represents the number needed before the technicians feel quite certain about the nature of the distribution in question and some of its parameters. The economic goal, however, is the maximization of the present value of the net rents of the resources involved and not the minimization of the discomfort of the hydrologists and meteorologists who are called on to advise on a project. With "insufficient" data, some projects will be designed incorrectly, but the average gain on these may be substantial even though part of the potential gain is lost.

The United Nations *Manual of Standards and Criteria for Planning Water Resource Projects*[21] suggests that records of stream discharge "should be continuous for a period of time which will be typical of the conditions to be anticipated in operating the project." While this suggestion seems at first glance unexceptionable—and probably not very helpful—I believe it to be fundamentally wrong. The primary social object is *not* to discover the "typical conditions" of the streams of the country, but to maximize the present values of the net rents on a *series* of projects. For a country with no historical streamflow data, this may justify or require the construction of projects before data sufficient to represent *typical* conditions have been generated, and this is even more likely in those cases where projects can be constructed and put into operation in smaller pieces.

It is important to understand that the failure of a particular project or number of projects to attain "maximum" return because of insufficient streamflow data at the time of design is not necessarily an indication of poor planning. Rather, a record showing that failure to attain maximum return was never attributable to insufficient streamflow data might well indicate mismanagement. But does it constitute

<hr>

[20] *Nature and Resources*, UNESCO, Vol. I, No. 4 (December 1965). The symposium on design of hydro-meteorological networks was held in June 1965 in Quebec, Canada.

[21] United Nations, New York, 1964, p. 8.

mismanagement not to have enough data available to maximize the present value of the opportunity? The verdict certainly is yes, but the extenuating circumstances may be quite compelling, too.[22]

How far should a country go, then, in trying to anticipate—by many years—the need for these types of data? One possibility is to use the density [23] of gauging stations in developed countries as a guide. A number of such studies have been made, although never with the explicit recommendation that the practice in wealthy countries should guide the others. The practice of the wealthy countries is not the right guide, of course. For one thing, the density of their stations may be wrong even for their circumstances, but, more important, their circumstances are different. The question of payoff from the data can not be avoided, no matter how inexact the answer. And there are areas in some countries where the cost of developing a gauging capability would be very high.

Perhaps some partial guides are possible, reflecting the general view that as the demand for water increases more and more data on streamflow and other water characteristics are needed for proper economizing decisions. The following suggestions are directed to hydrologic data:

1. In areas in which there is potential irrigable land and the possibility of developing water supply, collection of streamflow data should be begun "immediately." Gauging stations are not established overnight, of course, but there is an important difference between a vague intention to institute measurement at some indefinite time in the future and a program that is working systematically to put a network of stations in operation. Needless to say, the designation of such areas must be based on at least a rough judgment that there is a chance of developing economically feasible projects. The location of stations must be related properly to structure sites, relations among streams, and the suitability of the site itself for measurement; and the variables to be measured must be chosen with an eye to the

---

[22] We note in passing that the manual, *Feasibility Studies, Economic and Technical Soundness Analysis, Capital Projects* (Washington: U.S. Department of State, Agency for International Development, Office of Engineering, October 1, 1964) says nothing of the problem under discussion. Although the problem is alluded to in a few places in Ven Te Chow (ed.), *Handbook of Applied Hydrology* (New York: McGraw-Hill, 1964), most of the discussions are based on the presumption, of which the authors are aware, that relevant parameters of the distributions are known. There is no attempt to estimate the value of the marginal product of hydrologic data.

[23] Various measures have been discussed, for example, stations per unit area, stations per capita.

potential projects. Competent technical advice is essential and is easy to obtain if needed.

Similarly, data collection should be begun for potential hydropower sites with possibilities for development.

2. Measurement is needed in flood problem areas. The data are needed not only for the design of storage structures but for the protection of structures susceptible to flood damage and for the design of programs to control flood plain use.

3. In areas where municipal and industrial water supply are beginning to be thought of as problems, stream measurement and groundwater investigation are called for, bearing in mind that the year-to-year solution of such problems does not rest solely on supply adjustment but on demand adjustment as well.

It is likely that the above criteria would result in the establishment of stations on the principal streams of a country and a part of the tributaries, the number depending on the size of the main streams (that is, on their order, in the technical sense) and the characteristics of the terrain through which the streams go. The requirement that the area currently has economic activity or that there be a possibility of viable water projects implies that in some countries uninhabited areas may not have much stream measurement. This is fortunate, for some of these areas present difficult measurement problems, which may even be beyond solution for the countries concerned for some time to come.

Although hydrologic and meteorological data serve purposes that are different in part, the geographic areas of most interest are often the same, and there often will be economies in establishing joint stations. A unified administration of the activities deserves careful consideration.

In Chile and the western United States, there has been no postponement of dam construction to wait for the accumulation of more data.[24] In many cases dams have been constructed before any streamflow data have been available for the stream in question. In other cases a gauge has been established on a stream only years after a dam's construction. The dam itself serves as a gauge, of course, but in the case of Chile the organizations taking possession of a dam sometimes have not reported flow data to the responsible governmental unit; consequently, the date of installation of the first gauge after construction of a dam has some significance for the public records.

---

[24] See tables on streamflow data, appendix B to this chapter. [Not reprinted here.—Ed.]

TABLE 18. *Years of Data Available at Time of Start of Construction of 27 Dams in Western United States*

| Years | Frequency |
|-------|-----------|
| 0– | 6 |
| 10– | 11 |
| 20– | 6 |
| 30–40 | 4 |

Let us consider the case of dams constructed in the western United States and take into account only gauges close to the dam [25] and for which data on the area drained by the dam are available. Taking for each dam the longest record for gauges close to the dam, the information shown in table 18 is obtained.

The simple average for the twenty-seven dams is 17.2 years. (Data for areas of drainage were not available for eight other dams.)[26] If we include the maximum number of years of any station on these streams no matter how far from the dam, the simple average for the whole group of dams rises to 21.9 years.

If similar simple averages are calculated for gauges that are near the dam but not downstream of it, some gauges of long record are eliminated and the averages are lowered to 9.1 years for the twenty-seven dams and to 15.4 for the thirty-five dams.[27]

A similar but not exactly comparable tabulation can be made for Chile (see table 19). Here it was necessary to take the data for the station that was closest to the dam, yielding an average number of years of data of 6.3. In some cases the data available did not indicate this definitely.

If this had been done with the U.S. dams, the average number of years of data available would have been considerably lower—8.1 years as compared with the 17.2 years obtained for the 27 "close" stations above or below the dam. Precipitation data were the basis for design of nine other Chilean dams.

How is it possible to design a dam with little or no flow data? First it may be noted that the need for flow data is less pressing if planned

---

[25] In appendix B to this chapter, table 18 [not reprinted here.—*Ed.*] gauges are classified by the ratio

$$\frac{\text{area drained by gauge}}{\text{area drained by dam}}.$$

Gauges with this ratio between .76 and 1.25 are defined as close. If the ratio is less than one, the gauge is upstream of the dams; if over one, it is downstream.

[26] See appendix B to this chapter, table 19. [Not reprinted here.—*Ed.*]

[27] If a gauge was not installed in the reach above the dam until after construction was started, there was zero years of data available at date of start of construction.

TABLE 19. *Years of Streamflow Data Available at Start of Construction of Dams in Chile for Station Nearest Dam*

| Years | Frequency |
|-------|-----------|
| 0 | 10[a] |
| 1–4 | 3 |
| 5– | 4 |
| 10– | 2 |
| 15– | 0 |
| 20– | 0 |
| 25– | 0 |
| 30– | 1 |
| 35– | 1 |
| 40– | 0 |
| | 21 |

[a] Lago Pullingue and Lago Puyehue have been assigned zero years although the precise dates of start of construction were not available.

withdrawals are rather clearly small relative to the relevant aspect of the stream's flow. However, data are potentially productive even in cases of this type because a structure is involved that is exposed to the forces of high flows and must be designed to withstand them.

Apart from this, precipitation data may be available and can be made use of, especially if they can be related to flow data of adjacent basins or to flow data for a part of the basin in question. People living in the locality may be able to give useful estimates of extreme stages and frequencies. And the period of construction will provide at least one year of data, with modifications of design possible at least during the first part of the period of construction. In Chile's case, these possibilities were not sufficient to prevent some notable cases of overcapacity, especially for a group of dams constructed around the 1920's. These dams, together with costs (in escudos of 1964 value), are listed in table 20.

Lautaro has been empty 90 per cent of the time. Cogotí has had water for only 40 per cent of the planned irrigated acreage. Recoleta

TABLE 20. *Seven Dams in Chile Constructed without Streamflow Data, 1919–35*

| Dam | Cost (million escudos, 1964) | Construction initiated in: |
|-----|------------------------------|----------------------------|
| Lautaro | 7.0 | 1928 |
| Huechún | 9.4 | 1929 |
| Recoleta | 13.0 | 1929 |
| Cogotí | 21.0 | 1935 |
| Casablanca | 5.0 | 1929 |
| Cerrillos | .2 | 1931 |
| Laguna de Planchón | 1.3[a] | 1919 |

[a] 1962 escudos.

had to have a feeder canal to supply water from anther stream. The Casablanca reservoirs are underutilized. At Culimo, the flow has been 30 per cent below that estimated.[28]

In some of the Chilean cases it probably would have paid to postpone construction simply in order to accumulate more data. After all, if the expected present value of net rents with little or no data is zero,[29] the improvement from one more year of data need be only as great as the cost of the station for a year, and that is not very much in most cases, but it would have been better still if collection of flow data had begun earlier. In terms of the present example, even with a discount rate of 10 per cent per year the present value of the net rents need improve only by 2.6 times the cost of another year's data to justify starting the collection ten years before construction rather than nine.[30]

*Soil Surveys and Related Studies*

One way to approach the problem of the rate at which soil surveys and related studies should be pursued is to take a look at an effort to develop such information rapidly and on an extensive scale and see what happened. In the Chilean aerophotogrammetric project,[31] one of the immediate objectives was the institution of a new land tax system, under which the value on which the proportional tax would be based would depend on the land capability class to which the project assigned the parcel in question and on the "price" or unit hectare value assigned to land of this class.[32]

Accordingly, the project first located property boundaries on controlled photomosaics, a task that required extensive field work to locate the property boundaries. It should be noted that this property line identification was only for tax purposes. In addition, plots were classified according to present use, using, for example, a classification with seven categories for lands with extensive cultivation.[33] In addi-

---

[28] See René Villarroel and Heinrich Horn, *Rentabilidad de las obras de regadío en explotación construidas por el estado* (Santiago: Dirección de Planeamiento del Ministerio de Obras Públicas, 1963), p. 16.

[29] I do not assert that it must be zero without formal data. Casual observation may permit the design of a structure and plan with a positive present value.

[30] If $k$ is the cost of the 10th year's data, $(1.10)^{10} k = 2.6 k$, which is the amount by which the present value of the opportunity must increase to justify the expenditure.

[31] Hereinafter called "the project" if the reference is clear from the context.

[32] The unit value also varies according to the province and the distance from market in the case of Chile.

[33] Accuracy of classification prior to field check is said to have been 84 per cent. See Luis Vera, *Agricultural Land Inventory Techniques* (Washington: Pan American Union, 1964), p. 67.

tion, soils were classified (350 soil series were classified) with underlying information on weathering, drainage, texture, density, stoniness, slope, and other characteristics indicated on photomosaics. Finally the plots were assigned to land capability classes.[34]

The property boundaries and land capability assignments coming out of these procedures seem to have functioned satisfactorily so far as land taxation is concerned and the classifications developed have also served to give an excellent portrayal—for fairly large areas—of the various classifications made.

But are the data sufficiently accurate to be relied on in the evaluation of, say, an irrigation project? Are they sufficiently accurate to be useful to the person managing a farm, assuming he would be willing and able to use the data?

The answers to these questions, so far as data coming directly out of the project are concerned (that is, with no reworking or additional field sampling), are probably no. A soil sample was taken, on the average, for every 29 square kilometers, or every 11 square miles. More important, however, is the fact that Chile is undertaking a $2.5 million soils survey project [35] that will work largely in areas already covered by the aerophotogrammetric project. It appears that one of the important tasks of the project is to provide soils data detailed enough for use by the Corporación de la Reforma Agraria (CORA) in the management of the properties it has or will take over. That is to say, the data of the aero project were not adequate for this purpose.[36]

So far as more detailed soil surveys are concerned, the first priority is irrigation and colonization projects if more preliminary investigations have not served to eliminate the project from consideration. Beyond these needs, a soil survey program should not be permitted to get ahead of the capacity to use the data. If the detailed information is going to have an impact on production, it must be put into use by the persons who are making the management decisions for *individual fields,* whether these people are owner-operators, managers of privately owned lands, or bureaucrats managing lands in the hands of the government. It is not difficult to see the overwhelming importance of the system by which technical data on natural resource characteristics and production responses thereto are brought to bear on decisions that affect agricultural productivity.

[34] Ibid., pp. 7, 78.
[35] Financed partly by the UN Special Fund, FAO is the executing agency. See chapter 4, table 12 [of *Natural Resource Information*].
[36] I hasten to add that to my knowledge no official of the Chilean government or of the Organization of American States has ever claimed they were.

If a country is not going to adopt a land tax of the Chilean type, how valuable would be information of the same type? A project could derive information on size of farm, land use, soils characteristics, and land capability estimates, all of a level of precision suitable for "regional" studies.[37]

But are soil survey data essential to progress in productivity? In the case of the United States, it is interesting to observe that after sixty years of effort about a half of the farmland has been covered by soil surveys detailed enough for conservation planning.[38] This, however, does not warrant the conclusion that productivity rises very nicely without information on soils. Apart from the fact that proper use of soil information is but one factor in productivity, a comprehensive extension system was in operation, as well as other ways of disseminating information, which made it possible for farmers to develop a good deal of soil information on their own account even though their ground was not yet included in a soil map. A soil survey does not start from a level of no information.

Certainly data on farm size and current land use [39] can be developed more easily from photomosaics and air photos than by any all-ground method. The same is no doubt true of soil information, subject to the limitations of precision in a large and rapid survey mentioned above.

These types of data would be extremely useful, no matter what type of planning is done for the agricultural sector. Even in a system in which agricultural production decisions are made entirely by private operators responding to market prices, a government could make use of such data, especially for size of farm and land use, since they may be relevant to possible government programs. Perhaps soil information of the regional type would be less valuable to such a government, but the possibility of checking on the progress of erosion would be of value in some countries. In areas of very low income, however, my opinion—and it is only that—is that other opportunities for investment would yield a higher return, having in mind principally education of both young and adults on many fronts.

It should be noted that the types of information just discussed provide a picture of only certain parts of the agricultural system. To understand how it functions, other methods would have to be used to

---

[37] In the case of land use statistics, the experience and difficulties of the United States may contain some valuable lessons for countries that are expanding their land use data programs. The subject is discussed comprehensively in Marion Clawson with Charles L. Stewart, *Land Use Information* (Washington: Resources for the Future, 1965).

[38] Ibid., p. 214.

[39] But there are important limitations on the types and detail of information than can be developed without extensive ground checking.

obtain data on output and yield by crop and location, inputs and outputs in physical and value terms for different types of farms by location, and so on. Although such information is not within the scope of this study, gathering of data by aerial methods is effective in some cases because it is a means by which a comparatively small group of well-trained professionals and subprofessionals can do the whole job without having to rely on an administrative machine and personnel whose principal objectives are in directions quite different from the production of reliable data. If the economic series on inputs and outputs of farm enterprises are gathered by a sampling program rather than by attempts at complete coverage, a similar advantage can be gained, namely, the use of trained and disciplined personnel. Sampling is not the answer to all data needs, but it should be evaluated as a possibility for all types of data.[40]

### SHOULD STUDIES OF NATURAL RESOURCES BE INTEGRATED?

An "integrated study of natural resources" is commonly taken to mean the simultaneous study of all the resources in an area. Such a study necessarily will involve specialists from several disciplines. The advantage is thought to be a better and more useful description and evaluation of the area's resources than if one type of specialist studied all aspects of the resources or if the specialists worked in isolation from each other. "Simultaneous study of resources" can mean different things, however, in that different experts studying a given area at the same time may pursue their work rather independently, with collaboration taking place only at the administrative level, or they may collaborate closely at the substantive level. In the former case, simultaneous work will reduce cost but will have little effect on the products of the study. The Chilean aerophotogrammetric project, although often cited as an integrated project, is not regarded by some experts familiar with its operation as involving a close interdisciplinary cooperation at the substantive level. On the other hand, some of the studies of the Peruvian general resource agency, Oficina Nacional de Evaluación de Recursos Naturales, do exhibit a close collaboration between the specialists, as does also the preliminary study of the Guayas basin prepared by the Organization of American States.[41]

---

[40] Even aerial methods, which in a sense make or seem to make complete coverage possible, are better looked on in many cases as a means of increasing the efficiency of ground sampling, or, what is the same thing, a means of reducing the number of field samples required to attain a given level of precision.

[41] The Peruvian studies are cited and discussed in chapter 7, p. 182; the Guayas basin study is referred to in chapter 3, p. 67 [of *Natural Resource Information*].

The arguments for substantively integrated studies generally seem to stress what might be called the unity of nature. That is, natural phenomena of many different types, although often investigated in separate compartments, frequently are closely interrelated. One may think, for example, of climate, geomorphology, and vegetation; of climatic history and mineral deposition; or of man's simplification of the biologic environment by cultivation practices and the rise of "pests." As the argument goes, in all cases we are dealing with a complex system that is in a moving equilibrium with respect to the natural and man-made forces for change that are acting on it. If we propose to alter the balance of these forces, for example, by developing a natural resource, the whole system must be considered if we are to predict and evaluate the outcome. The following is a good and typical statement of the point:

> Experience acquired in the last twenty years in the evaluation of natural resources demonstrates that different methods must be combined to obtain optimum results.
>
> The first of these is to adopt . . . an ecological point of view. That is, we must constantly remind ourselves of the interactions between living things and their physical and biological environment. With this point of view it is possible to work with nature instead of against it. This point of view is particularly necessary in regions in which the environment is relatively little known, and it can help to avoid failures attributable to the incorrect use of agricultural or industrial methods which might give good results in other ecological conditions. In the most general sense, this ecological focus embraces sociological considerations, which all too frequently are not taken into account.
>
> The second method, which of course is not independent of the first, is the integration of studies of the environment since the various elements are interrelated. . . . The use of aerial methods can facilitate the making of those combined studies a great deal. . . . Moreover, in regions not well known and to which access is difficult, integrated studies offer the additional advantage of being done together, which definitely is less costly than a series of individual studies.
>
> Finally, . . . a "conservation focus" should be adopted, . . . which means to give attention not only to the possible ways of utilizing the resources and mechanisms of nature, but also to the basic disturbances and irreversible processes which human intervention can unchain and leave as the actual net result.[42]

Surely there is much force to these views, a force which should have been evident to educated people in western countries at least since

---

[42] UNESCO, Department of Natural Sciences, Division of Scientific Research on Natural Resources, "Aspectos principales del tema recursos naturales y su utilización" (UNESCO/CASTALA/2.1.1., Paris, September 8, 1965), p. 4. (My translation from the Spanish version.)

Marsh wrote his classic, *Man and Nature,* more than a hundred years ago.[43] Since his time many more cases of unnecessary waste and destruction of natural resources have accumulated, resulting from a failure to perceive or take into account important changes flowing from the exploitation of natural resources.

But the fact that the repercussions flowing from human intervention in natural systems are sometimes hard to perceive soon enough to avoid them does not point to the desirability of doing all studies of natural resources in an integrated fashion. It does point to the desirability of organizing things in such a way that specialized knowledge has the opportunity to point out effects that are likely to go unnoticed without its help, but this does not require simultaneous study. It may be more convenient and more responsive to demand for information if the different specialists study an area at different times. Once again, the idea of a *tabula rasa* seems to be lurking behind the argument for integrated studies, but in reality our knowledge of an area often will be sufficient to enable the conclusion that one of a few specialties is of dominant importance in the study of an area. In such circumstances, a too thoroughgoing insistence on an integrated study will result in a pro forma and sterile participation of the specialists who have little to contribute. There will be a tendency for studies to take on a purely technical orientation to the neglect of economic objectives which in my view should be orienting from the very beginning those natural resource studies that are a part of an economic development program. The specialized personnel required for integrated studies are so scarce that great care must be taken to use them where they are most needed.

In some circumstances partly or wholly integrated studies are desirable, however. That is, there are occasions on which two or more specialties should be united in the simultaneous study of an area.

One of the circumstances in which an integrated study is desirable is the case of areas with only minor or no economic activity which are thought to present some possibilities for development. These might be, for example, "new lands" adjacent to already exploited areas or brought close to them by the possibility of cheap transportation. Here all aspects of the area must be appraised if only to evaluate investment for transportation and other investment of the public utility type which may service a variety of economic activities.

A second situation calling for a more or less integrated study is when comprehensive use of the hydraulic resources of a river basin

---

[43] George Perkins Marsh, *Man and Nature, or, Physical Geography as Modified by Human Action* (Cambridge: Harvard University Press, 1965). This is essentially a republication of the original edition, published by Charles Scribner in 1864.

is being considered. Here a number of resources may be affected, if only by being covered up with water, and all of these must be evaluated both to design and evaluate the final proposal.

Even in these two cases there is a question of which specialists should participate and to what extent. Having in mind the objective of avoiding failures that the specialist's study or knowledge could have helped avoid, it is necessary that they be consulted in what might be called a "touch-base" procedure at two stages. The first is at the stage when the (potentially) integrated study is being designed. Taking into account the knowledge he already possesses of the area in question, the specialist should be able to suggest at this stage how intensive should be the participation of his specialty. Later, when the report of the study is under preparation, those specialists who did not participate very actively in the study should be given the opportunity to criticize the proposals formulated, perhaps when they are at the draft stage. Care is required at this point, for as projects develop in the minds of their designers they tend to acquire a momentum of their own. The intervention or criticism of the specialist must not come so late in the process that his critical remarks have no influence.

The idea here is that the specialist many times will be able to say, on the basis of knowledge that already exists, "this is all very well, but you have failed to take into account a certain factor which will reduce returns by $x$ per cent." Or he may be able to remind the enthusiasts that a similar project was undertaken elsewhere under similar circumstances, with disastrous results.

*We conclude, then, that the reasons usually adduced for integrated studies are cogent so far as the participation of different disciplines is concerned, but that the question of simultaneous study of an area must be decided case by case. In some circumstances it will be advantageous.*

## WHAT ARE SOME OF THE ORGANIZATIONAL PROBLEMS?

The extent to which the basic objectives of natural resource information programs are achieved will depend in part on the organization of the different types of agencies involved and on the relations between them. The fact that the information programs develop physical data on natural resources but that these data are used by agencies whose main concern is of an economic nature gives the problem of organization a special importance. The following discussion is confined largely to governmental questions, having in mind principally the problems faced by a country of substantial size. Those of smaller countries constitute a special and more difficult situation, discussed elsewhere.*

*The basic premise to keep in mind in considering organizational problems is that information activities should provide data and help contribute to the formation of a steady flow of investment projects in the industries concerned, or contribute to a reduction in the cost of managing and using certain natural resources.*

The various governmental functions that impinge on these questions of organization are the following:

1. Economic planning.

2. Determination of the allocation of the governmental budget. Our interest is in the budget allocations to the agencies that produce natural resource information.

3. The making of investment and operating decisions for resources administered in whole or in part by the government. Here are included agencies that "administer" a certain type of resource—e.g., a ministry of agriculture, a department of irrigation, a forest service, or an air pollution control agency.

4. Dissemination of information to be used by private users of resources in investment and operating decisions.

5. Generation of natural resource information. The usual pattern is one of several agencies, some of them independent. This is often true of the cartographic service (frequently named a "Military Geographic Service" or something similar because of the military's interest in maps) and the geological survey organization. But some natural resource information agencies are attached to the executing ministries that use the information. For example, soil survey units may be attached to a ministry of agriculture which also contains the extension service function (not necessarily with that title) by which information is put into the hands of farm managers.

So far as Latin American governments are concerned, the first function, planning, is not performed in a very thoroughgoing manner in some of the governments, because the planning function is somewhat divorced from the agencies that control the government's investment decisions. The budgetary function may nominally be located in a single agency, perhaps a treasury ministry, but the budgetary process is always far more complicated than this, the power of budgetary decision in fact being often dispersed among a number of centers of power.

* See *Natural Resource Information,* chapter 7.—*Ed.*

Although all of the above functions are involved in the problem of organizing the natural resource information agencies, our interest is principally in these agencies themselves. There are two main questions to be discussed:

First, should the natural resource information activities be administered together in a single agency or not?

Second, whether these activities are together in a single agency or not, what should be their relations with agencies performing the other functions listed above?

### A Single Agency Containing
### All Natural Resource Information Agencies

There are several possible variants of the single agency for all types of natural resource information. Each of the variants discussed here has serious weaknesses.

One possibility is a single agency that works exclusively on the basis of integrated surveys. While this might be attractive to someone who can see only the interrelations of resources, the reality is that a strong demand for one type of information in a certain location often arises entirely independently of demands for other types of information for the same place. There is no reason to think that demands for resource information are always to spring into existence simultaneously for the same location. It would be surprising if this were to happen, for at any given moment certain types of information pertaining to a particular geographical area may be further developed than are other types. Why redo the same task just to be working in an integrated manner? And, as noted earlier, at a particular point in time the type of project in view, being quite specialized, may need only one or a few types of information.

Another type of single agency would be what might be labelled a natural resources institute, that is, an institute located at the side of the mainstream of governmental activity and which would possess a substantial degree of autonomy, but which in all probability could not get along without substantial financial support from the government.

Support for the institute type of organization perhaps arises from the idea that since the activities that generate information are technical, or sometimes scientific, they ought to be off at the side where the continuity of their work will not be disrupted by the constant revisions of programs necessary to meet the uncoordinated demands of the public and the various governmental agencies concerned with the administration of natural resources. This argument rests on a mistaken view of the main function of these agencies, which is to supply information to meet the information demands of public and private economic units. While the activities of information agencies may contribute to the development of science, this contribution should be ancillary to the main purpose. Furthermore, the separated institute form of organization makes it difficult to develop needed close working relations between the natural resource information personnel and the users of the information. For example, some of the personnel of the information agencies ought to play a part in the process of project conception and elaboration. Effective channels of communication are needed between the information agencies and those that use the information, both in order to make effective use of the information and also to make the information programs responsive to the demands for information.

A single agency which was not off at the side as a separate institute would avoid its disadvantages, for it now would be easier to develop responsiveness to demands for information and arrangements that would make for more effective use of the information. But if all the organizations that produce natural resource information are contained in this agency, it probably will contain too much. The work of some natural resource information is so closely bound up with executive departments or ministries on the one hand, or with public enterprises on the other, that their work is far more useful if the information organization is a part of the using agency. This seems to be the case with soil units, which are more effectively used if they are in the agency which is concerned with putting the information to use in the management decisions made by farm operators. The same type of argument applies to the activity that develops data on forests. Here a part of the "inventory" capability may well be directed very closely to operational needs (especially preparation of operation plans), or for private operators who may not have effective access to private capabilities of this sort. Another case in point is that of the government petroleum operation. If the exploration function is performed by the government rather than by contract or a concessionaire, an operation of any size would probably wish to develop its own geological capability to take advantage of the specialization that has developed within this field and to secure a better coordination between the exploration work and operations plans.

There is no neat solution to the problem of where to put information organizations requiring close connections with the using agencies. If there are demands for information from multiple sources, economies of large-scale operation probably would indicate the desirability of only one organization, perhaps located in the appropriate executive department. If demands are large enough, multiple information units are feasible so far as economies of scale are concerned, since the higher costs associated with excessively small units can be avoided, but problems of coordinating their work remain.

### A Small General Resource Information Agency

Can resource information be organized in a way that will leave certain units in executive departments where such a course seems to be justified, but will still achieve an effective response to widely differing demands for information? Let us examine the following organization scheme with this question in mind.

Those information units that require a close relation with an operating program would be located in the appropriate executive department. The others would function as separate, specialized units, but their activities would be "coordinated" in various ways by a small general agency for resource information. The information units not in executive departments could exist as independent agencies with the general agency also existing as a separate agency, or, perhaps preferably if tradition and bureaucratic politics permitted, they could be brought into a single resource information unit.

In the latter case, however, the separate information-producing activities should continue to function in a substantially independent manner. There are solid reasons for the specializations of function that have developed. These involve substantial independence of programs, specialization of personnel and equipment, professional esprit de corps, and so on. This independence would not be complete, however, for the general resource information agency would perform certain functions which would impinge on the specialized resource information units.

A general resource agency with the usual specialized information activities organized as separate agencies is now used in Chile and Peru. However, the functions of the general resource information agencies differ one from the other, and in both cases they differ from the functions of such an agency as is envisioned here.

What should be the tasks of the small general resource information agency? Six are suggested here.

1. It would be the appropriate agency to conduct such integrated surveys of natural resources as are made. It would not be necessary that the agency have sufficient personnel of its own to staff such studies completely, for personnel could be borrowed from the specialized information units such as a geological or mapping organization. It would be preferable that these adjust their programs to the temporary loan of

personnel rather than that the general agency be forced to embark on specialized studies to keep a large staff busy. The agency should have some capability in economic analysis on its staff, considerably more than the more specialized agencies. As a part of this task, it might take the lead or at least participate strongly in such assessments of regional economic potential as are made. Such assessments, which presumably are to help potential investors, both governmental and private, often seem to ignore information on the quality and quantity of various resources.

2. Studies of the various natural resources in any one country are numerous, but many of the reports are hard to locate. The general resource information agency would be well advised not only to keep up to date some type of "inventory" record of all this information, but also to summarize or present in useful form the various types of extant information. This stock of information represents the present understanding of the country's resources; consequently it is important that it be available to many people in forms easily understood so that investment plans can be based on the best information available at the time. As a part of this task, the general agency would necessarily be conversant with the current programs of the specialized information units. Even quite general information about natural resources has an important influence on the investment process because it is an important determinant of the allocation of efforts to conceive and develop specific investment opportunities.

In the case of Chile, the Instituto de Investigación de Recursos Naturales (hereinafter called IREN) has compiled a bibliography of studies of the natural resources of Chile, indicating where each publication can be found. In the case of Peru, the Oficina Nacional de Evaluación de Recursos Naturales (hereinafter called ONERN) has published several volumes on different aspects of natural resources which summarize and organize the available information.

3. The need for natural resource agencies to adjust their programs to the demands of the users of the data has received a great deal of emphasis. But how are these agencies to know what the demands are? In those cases where information is sold—as may be the case with maps, photographs, and photomosaics, for example—the volume of sales provides indication of the behavior of demand and can be used to give something of an indication of changes in demand, for example, as between localities. Nor is there any reason why maps, etc., should not be sold rather than given to governmental agencies. In the case of certain types of special projects, it would be entirely reasonable to do such studies for a fee to be paid by the agency requesting the study. Not only is this a salutary way to avoid idle requests for more and more

studies, but it provides for financing of the service agency on a meaningful basis.

Unfortunately, however, such devices cannot be applied on so large a scale that all the finance problems of these service agencies are taken care of. The problem lies in the diffuseness of the benefits that flow from the different types of studies. If we can presume that users understand the value of the information, then we can say that at a minimum they should be charged a price equal to the cost of providing one more copy of the results, but in those cases where there is a problem of getting potential users to acquire and learn to use the information, perhaps a price below even this level would be justified, for a time at least.

Apart from such solid evidences of demand as sales receipts provide, the general resource information agency could well be assembling other information which, while far less definitive than sales receipts or fees, is still useful. For one thing, the agency should be examining the programs of the agencies using resource information to see what is implied for the activities of the agencies that have to provide the information. The task is more complicated than merely examining the work program, because the lead time required for many types of information is considerable. Consequently, a special effort must be made to obtain careful estimates of the nature and location of activities which require resource information for their planning rather far into the future.

The tasks suggested here and under point 2, above, can be as simple or as complex as one cares to make them. Strauss has suggested that the relevant facts might be summarized in a series of tables. This information could provide the basis for further investigation and deliberation to the extent desirable in the context of a particular country.[44]

In Strauss's scheme, information would be presented in a series of five tables, as follows:[45]

*Table I* would indicate the various resource information agencies operating in the country, the size and nature of their programs, and their source of money.

*Table II* would summarize the present state of knowledge of natural resources for each discipline or resource.

*Table III* would summarize the type of information needed for programs or projects needing resource information.

[44] See Estevam Strauss, "Recursos naturales y planificación económica en América Latina, Parte II," mimeo (Santiago: Instituto Latinoamericano de Planificación Económica y Social; November 1965).

[45] Appendix A to this chapter contains the row and column headings of these tables.

*Table IV* would present, for each project or program, the types of information needed at each stage of the project, information available, and additional investigation needed, together with date when needed, cost, and source of funds.

*Table V* would take the information in table IV and classify it by discipline and type of study demanded. The annual cost of making the studies would be estimated. Present capacity would be compared with capacity required to produce the studies demanded.

The tables may seem to suggest that the determination of the demand for resource information and next year's information program is simpler and more mechanistic than it actually can be. While one should not think that a mechanistic determination of the demand for information or next year's program can be made by looking at projects and making a few calculations, a good part of the information in these tables constitutes an indispensable point of departure for making adjustments in information programs so that demands will be met more effectively. Some of the information required for the tables exists either in information-producing units or in user agencies. Its assembly in one place would provide a better basis for budget decisions and for coordination of the programs of different information units, recognizing, at the same time, that most countries would have much difficulty in assembling the data for the whole group of tables and in keeping them up to date.

A study of the demand by governmental agencies for natural resources information has been made for Nicaragua by the Natural Resources Division of the Inter American Geodetic Survey with the assistance of the Oficina de Planificación de Nicaragua, by means of a questionnaire and interviews.[46] The study was made as part of the preparation for the tax improvement and natural resources inventory project, but many aspects of the study are applicable to the continuing problem of determining the size and content of a resource information program and can be adapted to it. The information gathered differs from that asked for in Strauss's tables in several respects, mainly in that the types of information are specified in much greater detail. The Nicaragua report is perhaps less mechanistic. While a good deal of this detail is a breakdown of material customarily contained in, say, a geological or soils study, it is interesting to observe differences in agency response as to their need for each detailed category.

The availability of a completed study of user agency demands for

---

[46] *Survey of Data Needs of User Agencies,* U.S. Army, Inter American Geodetic Survey, Natural Resources Division, Fort Clayton, Canal Zone, April 1966. The study was prepared for the Oficina de Planificación de Nicaragua and the USAID Mission to Nicaragua.

resource data makes quite clear the uncertainty surrounding many of the demands. Nor can one take negative responses ("No, I don't use that type of data and don't want it.") at their face value. Perhaps the data are used elsewhere or perhaps they should be used.

4. The general resource information agency could perform an important function of coordination. Although the programs of the specialized information units can and should be pursued in substantial independence, there are several points at which they are related either to each other or to user agencies. In the first place, the general agency, which will have a rather comprehensive view of the demand for the different types of information, should be consulted by the specialized information agencies in preparing their annual budgets and work programs. Secondly, in many countries there are several agencies collecting similar types of data. In this case, some agency ought to have the authority to harmonize certain aspects of their activity, such as types of data to be collected, location of stations, method of presentation, and standards of precision.

Although the work programs of the specialized information units are independent to a substantial degree, it may be possible to arrange work schedules so as to reap some savings. By consolidating demands for aerial photography, it may be possible to let larger contracts at some saving. An examination of work schedules by location may also reveal opportunities for different information units to work simultaneously in the same areas, not to make an integrated study but to reap the savings that are possible by simultaneous field operations or by consecutive field operations which can keep some capital facilities in more continuous operation. These considerations perhaps are not too important in thickly populated areas where facilities of all types are readily available, but in sparsely settled or remote areas they have a much greater importance.

5. As a result of having compiled information on demands for information and on the work programs of the specialized information units, the general resource information agency would be in a position to give valuable advice to the budget authority on the programs of these agencies and to make suggestions for changes in budget. It would be possible, and perhaps desirable, to make the specialized information units subordinate to the general agency for budget purposes, although such subordination need not involve any change in administrative autonomy within each specialized agency.

The problem dealt with here is a delicate one from the point of view of interagency relationships. The established specialized information agencies are likely to cherish their present autonomy, if they have it. While a new general agency conceivably could establish a satisfactory coordination of information activities by persuasion over a period of years, the task of getting the general agency to function in the manner envisioned here would be facilitated if the general agency had budgetary power. Such power would in fact change the programs of the specialized agencies only in those cases where the agency had been pursuing a program that ignored changing demands or the related activities of other information agencies.

6. The final function suggested for the general agency is to arrange and stimulate the participation of resource information specialists in project formation and evaluation within the government. More generally, the task of the agency is to act as an intermediary between the information specialist and those involved in the investment decision process, outside as well as within the government.

Within the government, the goal certainly should not be the participation of all resource information people in project formulation and evaluation, but a sufficient number should participate so as to work toward twin goals: (*a*) to get economists and engineers in the "planning commission," if there is one, and in the executive departments (where natural resource projects often are formulated) to understand the significance of resource information for their work, and (*b*) to get resource information people better acquainted with the uses to which their product is put and the way in which it is used.

As a part of this task, the general resource agency would administer the "touch-base" system mentioned earlier, whereby a project that has taken form in a preliminary or working document would be subjected to the rapid scrutiny of various resource experts for the purpose of detecting places where important information has not been used.

Clearly, one aspect of this task is to show potential users how to use resource data. The general agency could well supplement the already existing efforts of this type of activity by the specialized information agencies. This work should be directed to private as well as governmental users.[47]

*Implications of Orienting Resource Information*
*to the Investment Decision Process*

The desirability of close relations between natural resource information agencies and user agencies, with an eye to improving investment decisions, has been stressed throughout this study and in this section in particular. There are important advantages to be gained from an eco-

---

[47] For example, ONERN in Peru has given courses in photo interpretation of natural resources to employees of various government agencies. IREN in Chile views education in the use of its materials as an important task.

nomic orientation at all stages of the process of assembling natural resource information. While one can not but agree with Christian's and Stewart's view that premature assessment of economic feasibility may lead to error that may perpetuate itself, the neglect of an economic orientation can result in the collection of data that will never have any economic significance. It should be possible for the units in a decision structure to learn to discriminate between estimates of feasibility based on different quantities of data and to understand that assumptions are not data. If we can't get this far, the outlook for the quality of government investment decisions is rather bleak.[48]

Our emphasis on viewing the management of natural resource information as a part of the process of making investment and operating decisions within government has led inexorably to a consideration of the procedures and the people who will be using the data. In order to promote better use of data as well as to shape data programs to conform to demands, the general resource information agency has been viewed as the vehicle through which these goals can be approached, not immediately, but more closely with the passage of time. On the other hand, it should be noted that there has been no suggestion of centralizing the process by which natural resource investment projects are conceived and evaluated. To do so would be to run the risk that a point of view resting on inappropriate objectives would unduly influence investment decisions. Capture of the process by those who can see only the productivity of the type of investment with which they are familiar —whether that be roads, dams, or whatever—is to be avoided. To avoid this, the necessity for having different types of specialists participate and confront each other has been emphasized, as has also the desirability of buttressing evaluations with relevant data.

The view that development of resource information should be closely related to the process by which investment and operating decisions are made casts doubt on the advisability of large and rapid survey projects designed to produce a great deal of resource data quickly. Rather than develop information far ahead of the capability of using it, which is likely to result in the development of information not well adapted to demands, we should examine the advisability of information projects that continue for longer periods of time. Instead of confining the projects largely to the development of technical information, they

---

[48] The discussion of this point is on p. 128 of the authoritative paper by C. S. Christian and G. A. Stewart, "Methodology of Integrated Surveys," given at 1964 Toulouse Conference on Principles and Methods of Integrating Aerial Survey Studies of Natural Resources for Potential Development (UNESCO/NS/NR/94, Paris, April 17, 1964).

might better put a substantial part of their effort on developing capacity to use resource data. It is perhaps more important to develop economic and engineering personnel who can use technical resource data in project or program design and evaluation than it is to train technicians to develop the technical resource information. Although I am not arguing that a country should not train its own technical resource information personnel, it is true that the international market for some technical services and investigations in the natural resource field is quite well developed. Not only is it possible to write rather definite specifications for many of these jobs, but the country buying the services is protected by a substantial degree of competition. For example, aerial photography certainly can be purchased, as can also the making of topographic maps, and so on down the list. But a country cannot or dare not purchase the making of investment decisions. It really has no choice here but to develop its own nationals. It is not necessary that they be used at all points in the decision process, but nationals with a high level of competence are needed for at least the higher ranks, and it is much better if they clearly dominate all parts of the data using agencies.

### BENEFITS AND COSTS—GOING BEYOND NATURAL RESOURCE INFORMATION

*The final guideline is that a program to improve the quality of natural resource data and its use must develop the economic data required to put resource data to use. Resource data by themselves are useless for investment or operating decisions. The only way to assess the economic potential of an investment opportunity involving a natural resource is to feed the physical data into a calculation of benefits and costs, using relationships between the cost of inputs and the value of outputs derived from actual experience or which are closely related to actual experience.*

This means that the past record of experience is of overwhelming importance, for only by analyzing it can we make plans for the future. Records of inputs and outputs are needed in both physical and value terms, and the inputs from natural resources need to be expressed in quantitative terms of some sort that constitute a description of the quality or qualities of the natural resource. This means that the task of improving census data and of making studies of the operations of industries and separate firms is of great importance. For some types of activity it is possible to use relationships from foreign experience, but the relevance of such experience is always less than complete and in many cases it is positively misleading and not pertinent in any way whatsoever.

Within a government, all types of agencies operating in the natural resources fields, including both information agencies and user agencies, need a strong post-audit program for their activities. The questions are easy to put and hard to answer. How has colonization project X actually turned out? Can we summarize all of its benefits and all of its costs in proper economic terms? Or, why did we decide to develop information on a certain area that has been used by nobody?

Any program of post-audit needs all the help it can get. Consequently, efforts by persons outside the government (even from foreign countries) to evaluate experience should be encouraged and facilitated rather than discouraged, as is so often the case. There is an equally great need for studies of private enterprise in these fields, for in many cases it is the private operator who is managing the natural resource in whose development the government may have had a part.

In situations where our evaluations of past experience are inadequate to provide reliable estimates of the viability of a natural resource project, what can be done? For example, if a project involves the use of resources different from those heretofore used or contemplates the use of new methods of production or new modes of organization, past experience, even though it has been recorded and analyzed, will be to some extent an inadequate basis for estimation. This is likely to be the situation whenever an attempt is made to extend production to unused land, for the very fact that it is idle suggests that it differs from occupied land in important respects. Some of the difficulties may be surmountable, but others perhaps not.

In situations in which the past provides an inadequate basis for evaluation, there is no choice but to accumulate experience, but this need not require an indefinite wait before investment can begin. One possibility is to make extensive use of trial runs or research in the very location in which investment is proposed. With this procedure, at least some of the factors relevant to success or failure will be put to actual test. Usually it will not be possible to put all of them to test, because it will rarely be possible to duplicate completely the situation that will exist after investment is completed. For example, the employees of an agricultural research organization doing a test run on the suitability of an area for colonization will differ in important ways from the colonists who will come later on. There will be significant differences in education, health level, training, work habits, and so on.

It would be easy to assemble an impressive list of authorities who are united in this view. The strong words of John Phillips, writing from an extensive experience in many countries, are typical.

Only by careful study, *in situ,* supported by well-planned and ably conducted pilot projects, would it be possible to offer sound and firmly based guidance about the prospective viability of the numerous propositions which today are advocated by politicians and very senior officials responsible for so-called agricultural and associated development. The highly imaginative and grandiose schemes usually are dismissable because of their not being based on the elements of either agricultural or common sense.[49]

Still another way to accumulate experience before investing large sums is to try to design projects that are divisible, that is, to design them in such a way that a small commitment of funds will provide actual results (not only experimental) before investing the next increment. The example, par excellence, of this strategy is the gradual extension of settlement in small steps. Here there is opportunity for a rather complete test, including some elements of infrastructure. Where divisible projects are possible, and they often are not, they almost become self-evaluating with the consequent elimination of the threat of large-scale failure.

Perhaps the classic illustration of the points we have been making is provided by the post World War II scheme to grow peanuts on huge plantations in East and Central Africa, using ground cleared from uninhabited bush country. This scheme, with a planned capital cost of £24 million, was to be the largest single agricultural development ever undertaken.[50] All possible important mistakes seem to have been made. First, the advice of competent agricultural specialists was ignored. They had forecast failure on the ground that the rainfall regimen (single season rainfall of 25–30 inches) was basically unsuited to agriculture.[51] Second, although extensive research activities were envisaged on all aspects of resources that had anything to do with success, investment was started before research rather than the other way around.[52] Third, large sums ($65 million) were committed when it would have been

---

[49] *The Development of Agriculture and Forestry in the Tropics,* p. 175.

[50] Olive Holmes, *Peoples, Politics, and Peanuts in Eastern Africa,* Foreign Policy Reports (New York: Foreign Policy Association, December 1, 1950), p. 159. See also *A Plan for the Mechanized Production of Groundnuts in East and Central Africa,* presented by the Minister of Food to Parliament by Command of His Majesty, February 1947 (London: HMSO, Cmd. 7030); and *East African Groundnuts Scheme, Review of Progress to the End of November, 1947,* presented by the Minister of Food to Parliament by Command of His Majesty, January 1948 (London: HMSO, Cmd. 7314).

[51] See Leslie H. Brown, "An Assessment of Some Development Schemes in Africa in the Light of Human Needs and the Environment," in *The Ecology of Man in the Tropical Environment* (Morges, Switzerland, 1964), p. 284. This volume contains the proceedings and papers of the Ninth Technical Meeting of the International Union for the Conservation of Nature and Natural Resources, held at Nairobi, Kenya, September 1963.

[52] Edith Tilton Penrose, "A Great African Project," *Scientific Monthly,* Vol. 66, No. 4 (April 1948), p. 325.

possible to proceed in steps small enough to verify that lack of water was a serious problem, that compact and gritty soil caused rapid runoff and rapid wear on implements in one area, that soil nutrients were deficient in another, that in another area monsoon-type rainfall created an erosion problem, and that tsetse fly was a problem as well as other pests and insects.[53] As for cost estimates, ground clearing ran ten times anticipated levels and monthly labor turnover was 10 per cent.[54]

This failure is not attributable to "bad administration," as is sometimes alleged, for no amount of good administration would have brought success. Instead, it is an example of a whole decision process gone wrong. The lessons for such gigantic projects as the Carretera Marginal de la Selva and colonizing the Amazon basin are clear. If these projects are in fact not viable, we should proceed so as to find this out without wasting enormous sums that could have been put to good use elsewhere.

APPENDIX A. ROW AND COLUMN HEADINGS OF TABLES ON THE
STATUS OF RESOURCE INFORMATION IN LATIN AMERICA [55]

Table I. Structure of the System of Investigation for Natural Resources

*Column headings:*
   a) Code
   b) Name of administrative body
   c) Place in administrative hierarchy
   d) Disciplines in which the agency operates
   e) Personnel
        Technical-scientific
        Technical aid
        Administrative
   f) Capital
        Land and buildings
        Equipment
   g) Budget for year
   h) Sources of finance

---

[53] Holmes, *Peoples, Politics, and Peanuts in Eastern Africa*, pp. 159–60.

[54] *Nation*, December 3, 1949, p. 542; and Holmes, ibid.

[55] Taken from Estevam Strauss, "Recursos naturales y planificación económica en América Latina, Parte II," mimeo (Santiago: Latinoamericano de Planificación Económica y Social, November 1965).

**Table II.** Structure of the Present Supply of Knowledge of Natural Resources

*Row headings are disciplines and resources, as follows:*

1) Cartography
2) Aerial photography
3) Integrated photo interpretation and geomorphology
4) Geology
5) Meteorology and hydrology
6) Hydrology
7) Hydrogeology
8) Mineral resources
9) Fossil fuels
10) Seismology
11) Soils
12) Natural pastures
13) Forests
14) Hunting and fishing (non-oceanic)
15) Oceanography and biological resources of the sea
16) General ecology

*Column headings are as follows:*

a) Activities
   Basic data survey
   Laboratory analysis
   Data processing
   Basic research
   Technological research
   Resource administration
   Data distribution
   Distribution of studies

b) Present state of knowledge
   Unit of measure
   Exploratory-scale or precision
   Reconnaissance-scale or precision
   Semi-detailed-scale or precision
   Detailed-scale or precision

c) Present annual capacity
   Reconnaissance-scale or precision
   Semi-detailed-scale or precision
   Detailed-scale or precision

d) Present average unit cost and time required per unit of study with the scale or precision indicated
   Reconnaissance
   Semi-detailed
   Detailed

Table III.  Primary Demand for Natural Resource Information [56]
  a) Programs or projects
  b) Agency responsible
  c) Stages and date of decision at each stage
  d) Natural resources involved in project
  e) Location of project (sheets of national map)
  f) Estimated total cost
  g) Estimated cost of resource investigations
  h) Financial sources

Table IV.  Demand for Natural Resource Studies for the Development of Projects or Programs

*(One for each project or program)*

Project or program
Agency responsible
Location of project

*Column headings:*
  a) Objective
  b) Stages of project
  c) Disciplines involved
  d) Unit of measurement and scale or precision of data
  e) Information necessary (in units)
  f) Information available (in units)
  g) Studies necessary (in units)
  h) Period available for studies—completion date
  i) Agency conducting studies
  j) Cost of studies
  k) Source of funds

[56] In the particular case of Peru, for which the tables were originally prepared, the words are added, "for perfecting and putting into operation the national plan for economic and social development."

Table V. Total Demand for Natural Resource Studies

*Column headings:*
- a)  Discipline
- b)  Studies required
    - i)  within a short period (detailed studies)
        number of projects
        unit of measurement and quantity
        period available
    - ii)  within a period of medium length (semi-detailed studies)
        number of projects
        unit of measurement and quantity
        period available
    - iii)  within a long period (reconnaissance)
        unit of measurement and quantity
        period available
- c)  Average annual expenditure for studies
        detailed
        semi-detailed
        reconnaissance
- d)  Present capacity for studies (measured over the period available) as a percentage of the demand for studies
        detailed
        semi-detailed
        reconnaissance

# THE QUESTION OF
# EXPLORATION STRATEGY

The strategy of using drilling only in the final stages of the sequence of minerals exploration activities, a strategy which seems to me to characterize all commercial operations that enjoy exploration success over a considerable period of time, has been called into question by Griffiths, a geologist, in a way that makes his advice peculiarly applicable to the developing country, for he ends up by strongly suggesting a vast program of drilling on equal spacing [1] to gain geological information and locate mineral deposits. The last paragraph of the article in question is so important that it deserves quotation:

Perhaps the most important question that this approach gives rise to is— what is the expected value of a unit volume of the earth's crust? A suitable precise estimate of this parameter *should* [2] form the basis for national and international planning for industrial development and may be used as a base for evaluating the natural wealth of areas of the earth's crust. Stable geopolitical units could thus be established on a sound fiscal basis.[3]

Reprinted from *Natural Resource Information for Economic Development* (Baltimore: The Johns Hopkins Press for Resources for the Future, Inc., 1969), appendix to chapter 2.

[1] Five-mile spacing is suggested at one point.

[2] Italics are mine.

[3] See John C. Griffiths, "Exploration for Natural Resources," *Operations Research,* Vol. 14, No. 2 (March–April 1966), pp. 189–209. An earlier article which made the

The purpose of this appendix is to consider Griffiths' suggestion in the light of the considerations emphasized so far in this study.

An optimal exploration strategy ought to consist in a sequence of different actions such that with the expenditure of a given sum of money the present value of the deposits found is a maximum. Each of these actions, or activities, produces information about the likelihood of mineral deposits. Although individual firms may specialize in one type of information-producing activity or in one phase of the whole process, we can look at the whole process and ask whether, out of a given sum available for the whole process, the sequence of the actions is correct and whether the allocation of funds to each of the activities is correct. In the case of minerals, including petroleum, one might classify the possible actions into two groups: drilling and all other exploration activities. Then we can ask where drilling activity should come in the sequence of other activities. Should it be all at the beginning, the end, or intermingled? And how should the expenditure be divided between drilling and the other actions? It is easy to see that this problem, which can be posed in a few sentences, is very complex even on a theoretical level. And the application of a theoretical solution would be very hard because of the difficulty of developing quantitative descriptions of both the application of these activities and their results.

Nevertheless, the mineral industries and consultants in the exploration field have worked out an answer to this problem, an answer that by and large schedules drilling in the last stage of the actions taken to verify the presence of a deposit, granted that at times a limited amount of drilling is used to gain geological information at the earlier stages. The strong point of drilling is seen to be highly local verification of presence or absence. In conformity with this view, it is commonly said that drilling is "too expensive" to be used in the earlier stages of exploration activity. What is meant here is not that drilling a hole is

---

same general type of argument is M. Allais, "Method of Appraising Economic Prospects of Mining Exploration over Large Territories," *Management Science*, Vol. 3, No. 4 (July 1957), p. 285. This is a translation of an article appearing in *Revue d'Industrie Minerale*, special issue 1R (January 1956). So far as I can see, my critical remarks about Griffiths' article apply also to Allais' article, although it is important to be aware of a fundamental difference between the two in that Allais does *not* recommend systematic grid drilling. He does recommend a more limited type of effort applied to a large area, such as the Algerian Sahara. Still, the factors I discuss with reference to Griffiths' article are relevant to Allais' article too. A paper given by Griffiths and L. J. Drew at Pennsylvania State University in April 1966, "Grid Spacing and Success Ratios in Exploration for Natural Resources," extends the fitting of binomial and negative binomial distributions to other petroleum basins, and also attempts to determine how the expected success ratio would change as systematic well spacing was changed. Although this paper appears to have been written after the one first cited, the *Operations Research* article is more closely directed to the problems in which we are interested.

more expensive than flying a magnetometer a mile—a comparison that is meaningless—but that, for example, drilling with the spacing of the holes just dense enough to provide the same quantity of information over a large area as would a study of regional geology conducted in the conventional manner, will cost much more.

While Griffiths' study makes some valuable points, important economic problems involved in selecting an exploration strategy are either neglected or are handled incorrectly. Since drilling is expensive, especially in countries with underdeveloped highway systems and overdeveloped topographic relief and/or jungle, the potentialities for misallocation of resources to which the suggestions of this article conceivably might lead are enormous.

Among the valuable contributions or points made in the article are the following—and I do not pretend to an exhaustive coverage:

1. The proper objective for exploratory activity is economic gain, not the finding of a particular type of deposit. As Griffiths points out, this is now the motivation of much private activity.

This objective is the proper one for a country, too, as has been emphasized elsewhere; * outlays to gain information are investment outlays and should be directed toward the same objectives as other investment—maximization of economic gain.

2. The negative binomial fits the locational pattern of known oil wells in Kansas much better than does the Poisson distribution. The important point here is that the Poisson distribution presumes constant probability in all parts of the continuum in which the phenomenon of interest occurs whereas the negative binomial can be used to represent a contagion effect.

Griffiths suggests, no doubt correctly, that oil and mineral deposits are "contagious," i.e., that successes tend to cluster because of the existence of a genetic control. From the point of view of logic, however, even if oil deposits were in fact Poisson distributed it would seem possible for an observed "contagious" distribution to be generated in a situation in which (a) part of the drilling is random and (b) the remainder of the drilling is undertaken on the basis of the mistaken view that deposits are contagiously distributed.[4] I do not suggest that this is in fact the case but merely point it out as an interpretation that may also be consistent with an observed contagious distribution.

The major conclusion of the article—that one should drill on five-

---

* See *Natural Resource Information*, chapter 1.—*Ed.*

[4] This possibility is recognized on p. 2 of the later of the two Griffiths' articles.

mile centers to provide the basis for a natural resource inventory—is based on oil well data for Kansas and Pennsylvania-Ohio. In the case of Kansas, Griffiths estimates that a systematic drilling program with five-mile centers would have had practically certain success since thirteen of the fields were so large or elongate that they could not have been missed. The systematic drilling program would have cost $200.5 million and would have yielded (basing the estimate on production up to only 1959) oil worth $4.2 billion valued at $3 per barrel, "leaving an ample margin for development costs." [5] In the case of Ohio and Pennsylvania a similar result is reached in that wells with six-mile spacing costing a total of $388.5 million would have been more than paid for by the Bradford field alone, worth $2.5 billion with its production valued at $4 per barrel. This is the largest field in the area.

He also notes that in the simulations for Ohio and Pennsylvania the success ratios would have been better than the U.S. average over the period 1944–62 for wells drilled *with* technical advice (p. 196) and almost as good as this for Kansas (p. 198).

He concludes that if we take into account *all* the possible prizes— oil, metallics, non-metallics, water resources—"an exploration program by systematic grid drilling is likely to lead to a *commercial* success with probability approaching unity" (p. 208). Furthermore, we should have a much better understanding of the geology of the first two miles of the earth's crust in the drilled area.

What's wrong with all of this? If there isn't something important that has been missed, then we must conclude that:

1. Exploration programs conducted by private enterprise are missing a good bet and are at present misguided, for private corporations certainly are not doing grid drilling regardless of other information already at hand or that could be developed. Also, that:

2. Government programs designed to develop mineral and water resources are proceeding in the wrong way, for they have persisted up to now in concentrating their efforts on such comparatively cheap methods as studies of regional geology done with the aid of air photos and helicopters instead of a drill.

One of the major faults in this argument is that time, which should have its economic manifestation here as a rate of discount, does not receive explicit attention. Thus the $4.2 billion of Kansas oil, which

---

[5] The derivation of these numbers is not given. Cost of drilling appears to be low, although it would depend strongly on depth and size of hole. The $4.2 billion appears to be too low by 50 per cent.

can't be produced all at once, would look a little different if discounted to the time when the exploratory wells are drilled on five-mile centers. The time when outlays are made and revenues are received is important and can be the decisive difference between the desirability of different economic projects.

What is more, the estimate of $4.2 billion for Kansas oil (at well-head) is based on existing exploration practice and the resulting price. What would happen to the price of copper if, after putting holes all over the world, we found ourselves with twenty times as many copper deposits as we know of now? The procedure for evaluating Griffiths' drilling program ought to deal with this question explicitly. There seems to me to be no basis on which it can be assumed to be of negligible importance.

Clearly, all the wells can't be drilled at once. But if not all at once, what is to determine the rate and locations at which they are to be drilled? What are the relevant considerations? This major problem receives no attention. The impression one gets is that the drilling should take place quickly, for otherwise one would not speak of using the result of the drilling as the basis for "national and international planning for industrial development." But, once again, investment funds have an alternative cost. They could be used to produce capital goods that would yield a real return soon, whereas many of the deposits found under the extensive drilling program would yield their product only in the very distant future.

Let us suppose that the estimates of the results of a systematic drilling program for the three states studied are correct. What is their significance? First, Griffiths is applying his hypothetical program of systematic drilling to areas that are already known to be productive. The results are applicable to other areas only on some strong assumption about their productivity as compared with Kansas, Ohio, and Pennsylvania. This may or may not be true. Griffiths does not give us his position explicitly, but his conclusions seem to imply that other areas do compare favorably with these three states. Certainly the prevailing view is the opposite for most areas.

The all-important question is, how is a Kansas to be found? Part of the historical answer is that it was necessary to drill unsuccessful wildcats which served to lower the success ratio with which Griffiths compares the results of the hypothetical program applied to a known Kansas.

Hovering over the discussion are some important questions about the objective of an exploration strategy. Since they are not considered explicitly, these remarks may not be directed at Griffiths' true position but only at what his position might be. The objective of an exploration program should not be simply to find a program such that costs are covered, as some of his remarks seem to suggest. For private enterprise the goal is to *maximize* profit. Similarly, for a society the goal in the production of natural resource products is to maximize the present value of the year-by-year excesses of consumers' plus producers' surplus over outlays involved in their production. Thus, a program of exploration that just attained *commercial success,* if this means any outcome that covers costs, may be a very inferior program.

The most important result of the systematic drilling program is suggested as being the contribution to determination of the value of a unit volume of the earth's crust, this knowledge to be used for planning industrial development nationally and internationally.

Neither the course of industrial development nor its planning by public and/or private bodies appears to be hampered by inadequacies in estimates of the value of a unit volume of crust. It is not clear why such strong emphasis is placed on the estimate of this quantity, which seems to me to have little significance for private or public investment plans. No one bases his investment decisions on this quantity now, and it probably would not alter decisions even if it were reported that someone's estimate of the present average value had been doubled. The average value of a unit volume of the earth's crust is not, of course, a quantity that will stay the same if there were large changes in exploration strategy such as that proposed by Griffiths. How then are we to know when a correct estimate of average value has been reached?

This question has no answer. But there is an estimate of average value that would be *associated* with the best exploration strategy. The best exploration strategy almost certainly is not the one that will provide the most complete information for an estimate of average value of unit volume of crust or for the planning of industrial development. Our objective is not to maximize information or to minimize the dispersion of outcomes to industrial investments. Insofar as the size of real output sums up our social objectives, the subsidiary objective for exploitation of natural resources is, to repeat, the maximization of their contribution to real product. That is, systematic drilling cannot be justified by showing that the information at our command would be much greater, or that certain planning tasks would be easier, or even that some mistaken investment decisions could be avoided. To justify such a program involves demonstrating that we will be better off in a socially relevant sense. This requires, in turn, consideration of the whole exploration process and explicit attention to the times when outlays are made and products are produced and the values attached thereto.

It is conceivable that a numerical evaluation of Griffiths' program that took account of the factors discussed in this appendix would show it to be the optimum program. In the case of Allais' program, which does not involve grid drilling at the first stage, but less expensive methods, a numerical evaluation conceivably might show it to be optimum. In either case, a basic problem would be the adjustment of the program to prospective demand. The basic economic consideration, systematically dealt with by neither writer, is to avoid making outlays earlier than necessary to produce a given stream of product.

So far as evaluation of the different types of exploration programs is concerned, the correct criterion is the net present value of the deposits found by a given outlay on exploration. This net present value is the result of discounting to a common date all sales of metal produced from the deposits found, all costs of processing ore, and comparing the resulting figure with the discounted outlays on the exploration program. For the purpose of comparing different exploration strategies, one could assume a given discounted outlay on each strategy and compare the resulting product from the two strategies, or one could specify a flow of product and compare the minimum exploration *and* processing outlays required to produce it.

SELECTION 15

# ECONOMIC CONSIDERATIONS IN ASSESSING THE ROLE OF REMOTE SENSING IN COUNTRY DEVELOPMENT

The way in which one views the potential usefulness of remote sensors —and today we presumably are thinking of remote sensors in the context of satellites—depends on the window through which he is looking. Because of professional training and the kinds of problems he is accustomed to working on and thinking about, the scene in front of the economist's window is rather panoramic. It includes the general problem of how a society goes about deciding what things to produce and how to produce them; it includes the economic progress of nations and the study of factors thought to produce it. It also includes remote sensors carried in satellites, but one must use an extremely high-powered telescope to see that part of the panorama. In contrast, I suspect that many specialists are able to see remote sensors in satellites with the naked eye but that it may be necessary for them to put on glasses with some rather fancy lenses in order to see the broader panorama of which remote sensors are but one small part.

Since economic development is our ultimate interest, let us consider

A paper presented at a symposium sponsored by the Agency for International Development on Utility of Remote Sensing as an Aid to Developing Countries, Smithsonian Institution, Washington, D.C., November 19–20, 1970.

briefly the general way in which economists look at this phenomenon. First, over the last couple of decades or so, the explanation of the factors behind economic development has become more eclectic and more complex. For a time after World War II, there was a touchingly naive preoccupation with simplistic explanations, some reducing it all to a matter of increasing the inflow of capital either by increased savings or by imports of capital from abroad. Of course, there were other hobby horses, too. Especially attractive to many economists in underdeveloped countries, as well as in the developed, was industrialization, a slight elaboration on the capital increase theme.

Fortunately, there is not a 100 percent swing in my profession to every passing fashion, and this was true of the study of economic development. Calmer and more erudite voices finally prevailed to the point where there now is widespread appreciation of the fact that the level and rate of economic development are functions of many variables. What a country is at a given time is a result of its whole past history, and not only its own past history but also that of its relations of many different types with other countries. And *whole* past history means exactly that. In tracing the sources of economic development, there can be no facile separation of economic and noneconomic factors, for the simple reason that human beings themselves do not live their lives in separate compartments bearing these two labels, nor do economic institutions and processes function in isolation from their counterparts for other aspects of the society.

At a given time, the results of the history of a country can be summarized in some general state variables. If these are viewed in a static manner, they can be used to explain the level and composition of income. From this more narrow point of view, the level and composition of real output are viewed as the result of:

(1) the quantity and composition of man-made capital goods, both private and public;
(2) human capital (including its quality aspects, such as work attitudes, main motivating forces);
(3) the stock of knowledge and techniques available for use in production;
(4) the quantity and composition of natural capital;
(5) the existence of effective institutions for
    (a) allocating the various kinds of capital (including human) and its services among different uses,
    (b) distributing real product among the individuals in the society,
    (c) transmitting knowledge pertinent to the performance of economic activities.

As soon as we go beyond this static view of things and try to explain in any fundamental way whether and why an economy will grow, we are immediately forced to transfer our thinking from a static to a dynamic, or historical, mold. A country's immediate prospects for progress are limited very strongly by its past history, many of the relevant aspects superficially seeming to have little to do with economics.

To the above list of proximate determinants of the momentary level and composition of real output, we can add another proximate requirement for growth in real output. If economic progress is to take place, the above list of institutional needs must be expanded. The society must have institutions for generating or importing improvements in technique and organization *and* for disseminating knowledge of them and securing their adoption.

The view that economic development is the result of a complex of factors that reach into every corner of a country's culture may seem obvious and hardly worthy of attention, and this is true for those persons who have absorbed this message and for whom this view forms a background against which more detailed and narrower problems related to economic development are considered. The fact is, however, that when you scratch a specialist the reflex response, much more often than not, will reveal the view that his specialty is really the key to economic progress. If you ask him, he will agree with you, all right, that other factors beyond his specialty are important, but it quickly becomes evident that this is an agreement of words rather than substance. If there is to be an adequate assessment of the role of remote sensors in satellites, limitations imposed by specialties and previous experience must be transcended.

While remote sensors can be used to generate information of many different types, as all of us know, so far as economic development is concerned, one of the main areas of application—perhaps the most important—is that of natural resource information. It is appropriate to elaborate our emphasis on the multiplicity of factors involved in economic development by taking a brief look at the role that natural resources play in economic production and in economic progress.

First, on a general level, natural resources are to be regarded as a kind of capital that yields productive services just as does man-made capital. In many cases, of course, they are completely analogous to such unfinished capital goods as a machine tool or building that is under construction. That is to say, investment must be undertaken before the capital instrument can begin yielding productive services. This is most clearly the case with potential mineral-bearing lands, but it is also true of such things as dam sites and frequently of agricultural land itself.

Natural resources are not identical with man-made capital goods. While there are many types of differences, two that are of importance for our purposes are these: (1) the precise location of some natural resources can be determined only by the expenditure of money (mineral lands, fish, and even agricultural lands in the case of "new lands"); and (2) even though the location of a natural resource is known, as with agricultural land in use, it may be possible to increase output by making use of increased knowledge of the characteristics of the resource.

Since natural resources are a kind of capital, it is obviously true that the more natural resources a country has and the better their quality, the better off it will be so far as the size of its economic product is concerned. There is tremendous variation among countries in the value of their natural capital in relation to other forms of capital. This ratio will tend to be equal to the fraction of total national income generated by natural resources themselves, which is something different from that fraction of total national income generated by the natural resources industries.

This ratio—income generated by natural resources to total national income—tends to be very low for developed countries simply because the other forms of capital—human capital and man-made capital instruments—are of dominating importance. In underdeveloped countries where these forms of capital are not present in great abundance, natural resources can have a considerably greater importance in a relative sense. In some cases the form of the natural capital exerts an evident influence on economic activity and colors many aspects of the country's economic and political life.

By and large, however, natural resources do not have the importance in the economic activity of underdeveloped countries that many people attribute to them. However this importance is assessed, it seems to be declining in Latin America, at least. In this region, about 59 percent of the labor force was engaged in agriculture and mining in the period 1935–1940, but by 1965 this percentage had declined to 47 percent, a decline of about one-fifth in the ratio itself.

A similar decline has taken place in the percentage of gross national product originating in agriculture and mining in Latin America. For the period 1935–1940, this was 35 percent as against 27 percent in 1965, the relative decline in this percentage being a little larger than that for labor force participation in agriculture and mining.

While the percentage of national income originating in agriculture and mining would be roughly similar to the percentages for GNP, the percentage of national income going to the owners of natural resources (as distinct from man-made capital) would be much lower. The national income or GNP originating in the natural resources industries includes incomes generated by labor and man-made capital engaged in these industries. These greatly outweigh the income generated by the natural resources themselves.

What lesson can be drawn from these percentages, bearing in mind that the relevant percentage is much lower? The conclusion is that even very sizable increases in the effective quantity of natural resources are not going to have a tremendous effect on the level of a nation's income. This is not the same as saying that investment in natural resources, whether to find them or to find out more about those whose location is already known, is not worthwhile. It may well be, but investment in information on natural resources cannot be expected to provide any royal road to economic progress. It simply is not quantitatively possible.

### OUTLAYS ON INFORMATION AS AN INVESTMENT

The assembly of information on the physical aspects of a country is an investment, that is, it involves outlays of money now that will yield a return only in the future. Therefore, we can say immediately that expenditure on information assembly is to be evaluated as any other investment. The preferred method is to see if the discounted cash flows (or their equivalent) have a positive value. That is to say, the question is whether the present value of the additions to product minus the present value of *all* costs of the project (maintenance, etc., as well as initial capital costs) is positive, using a discount rate that reflects the productivity of investment in other activities of comparable riskiness (which in this country, for example, would be much higher than the rate of interest paid by the government on its securities).

Evaluation of information as an investment poses many difficulties, the major one being that benefits are often rather indirect and diffused, but this is not always the case. In general terms, natural resource and other types of information can be put to the following different types of use:

(1) The evaluation of investment opportunities, both public and private. Obviously these may vary from such well-defined and discrete projects as irrigation to complete programs of mineral exploration from the earliest stages on. The "investment opportunity" may be the provision of background information on a regional basis useful for public and private investment decisions involving regional development as one of the variables (e.g., infrastructure investment).

(2) Improvement of current production operations involving natural resources and other capital.

(3) Satisfaction of direct consumer demands for information (e.g., maps for recreational purposes).

(4) Aid in the discharge of governmental functions not related to investment or improvement of current production (e.g., tax collection).

### PROBLEMS IN EVALUATION

In my opinion, the most important consideration in evaluating any proposed program for gathering more information—whether it be an attempt to estimate numerical values or only a "judgmental" evaluation—is to evaluate the program as a part of the *whole* relevant system. In principle, this is not necessary, of course. If there were available a good estimate of the derived demand for information at the level of one of the components of the whole system, quite a bit could be done with partial evaluations. In reality, however, good estimates of the derived demand for information are not available. The result is that if parts of the system are left out of consideration, some kind of assumption must necessarily be made (and this is often done implicitly) that relates the activities under examination to those parts of the system not under scrutiny. These assumptions are often seriously in error, usually with respect to the (derived) demand for information. If we force ourselves to consider the whole system, errors of this sort are less likely to be made.

There are various ways to describe the components of a system for generating information by use of remote sensors in satellites. Note that many of these components involve intergovernmental considerations or operations: (1) determination of investment and operating program after initial formulation of the system; (2) physical launch and satellite operation; (3) data retrieval, processing, and storage; (4) dissemination of processed data; (5) use of processed data by technical agencies of government or private entities; (6) use of the product of technical agencies by *investment decision* agencies of government or private entities; (7) provision for feedback from entities in (5) and (6) to those in (1).

A complete discussion of the problem of evaluating remote sensors in satellites is not possible here, but perhaps a series of somewhat disconnected comments can serve to give some indication of what is involved in the problem.

### Modes of Operation

While any complete system will involve the components or functions listed above, there are various ways or modes in which the system could be operated. One way to approach the problem of specifying a system is to think of basic modes of operation and of combinations of basic modes. One way to generate a series of possible basic modes is to suppose that the mode of operation will depend on choices made from several dichotomous bases of classification. Thus we might have:

| | |
|---|---|
| multiple objective | vs. single objective |
| multi-country | vs. single country |
| complete areal coverage within a country | vs. limited coverage |
| repetitive | vs. one-time |

Obviously some of these could and should be subdivided, but if we take the classification scheme as it is, there would be twelve different basic modes possible if every dimension must be present in a mode. However, on certain specifications of the classification basis, basic modes could be combined. Thus, it might operate on one group of objectives on a multi-country basis, meaning that the same group of objectives is a target in several countries while the satellite simultaneously operates on single (and different) objectives, each with respect to a particular country.

The point of these remarks is that there are many ways to run a satellite remote sensor program. It is to be expected that the economic viability of these different modes of operation, some basic and some complex, will differ greatly. Therefore, I suspect there is little point in talking about economic viability except in connection with a specification of the particular way in which the system is to operate. In particular, we cannot discuss the economic viability of remote sensors in connection with single objectives unless we are prepared to specify the operation of a whole system involving only that single objective. Of course, many of the components of an evaluation of complete systems must be estimated objective by objective.

## Marginal Productivity

It has already been asserted that evaluation of a complete system is desirable on the ground that omission of some of the components, or functions, is likely to lead to error because of incorrect assumptions relating the components under examination to those excluded.

To see why this is so, let us remind ourselves that the demand for any productive service is a function of the marginal productivity of that service and its price (in our case, information provides the productive service). Without explicit attention to the whole system, the implicit assumptions often seem to be that: (1) marginal productivity does not diminish with more information, implying that there is no limit to the amount of information that can be absorbed at a constant price; and (2) marginal productivity of information is the same in country $X$ (underdeveloped) as in country $Y$ (developed)—what is productive for us will be productive in El Salvador, for example. With respect to the second point, it should be obvious—but it obviously is not—that the lack of, or deficiencies in, information user facilities and institutions in a country has to mean that the current demand for information is zero so far as that country is concerned. There will be no addition to product even though mountains of information are made available.

Marginal productivity of a productive service, such as information, refers to the addition to product brought about by using another unit of the productive service. This additional product will depend on the quantity of this and other productive services already in use. I believe there is a tendency to think that information on natural resources is lacking or doesn't exist unless it is in the form in which it would be expressed by technicians making natural resource surveys. If we stop to think about it, this is not the case, for the lowliest peasant using methods of cultivation and seed varieties that have enabled continuous agriculture for decades or even centuries obviously is in the possession, perhaps implicitly, of some rather useful information. Perhaps this is even clearer if we look at it from another direction, so to speak. Ask a peasant why he doesn't grow corn in a nearby area not now under cultivation. The chances are excellent that he will have what is a rational answer, even by our standards, and even if it isn't, it may be the operationally correct answer, a rational explanation existing of which he is unaware.

But suppose that we are not so naive as to make the gross error of assuming that more information will be very productive because we believe (erroneously) that the present quantity of information is very low. We have already pointed out that additional information may be indigestible, the ability to use it simply not being present, but additional information may be unproductive because it is the wrong kind of information. Some productive services are reasonably homogeneous, such as common labor, for example. An increase in the quantity of common labor will mean an increase in the same kind of productive service already in use. Not so with information. It has so many dimensions and can be expressed in so many different ways that it may or may not represent an effective addition to the stock of information already in use by those making investment and production decisions.

By the same token, the duplication of already existing information does not constitute an addition to the effective stock of information.

Contrast this, again, with the provision of more common labor where duplication *does* constitute an effective addition to productive services. The lesson should be clear.

One specific application of the ideas we have been discussing deserves special mention—information in relation to new lands, or *nuevas tierras,* as the Latinos say. New lands do not obviously constitute a source of demand for large quantities of additional information. Three considerations indicate caution. First, there already exists a great deal of information about these potential lands, and much of it indicates rather conclusively that large areas do not have economic potential with presently usable techniques. Second, the fact that existing boundaries of cultivation are where they are indicates the existence of a very important piece of information: there are (as of this moment) insurmountable obstacles to the extension of cultivation across the line. Third, although there are indeed considerable areas that are potentially usable, the kind of information needed to make them actually usable is, generally speaking, of a rather detailed management type, or at a level of detail that no one seems to contemplate generating by the use of satellites.

### Cost Saving

When a proposed program is evaluated by the cost-saving method, the usual implicit assumption is that a demand for the information exists and is large enough to pay for the total cost under the old method. This implicit assumption is warranted in those instances where the activity or product is subjected to the test of the market, but if this is not the case, as is often true of information, serious error can result.

Suppose that 100 units of product X are being produced each year at a total cost, including return on investment, of $10 each and that they are being sold at a price of $10. If a new method of production will reduce the cost by $1, it will be true that social product will be increased by at least $100. Actually, the increase will be somewhat more because of the larger quantity that people will wish to buy at a price of $9. The total increase in social welfare will be approximately $100 plus 50¢ times one-half the increase in the quantity produced and sold.

Suppose, however, that the article in fact has no value, that there is no demand for it. It still will be true, of course, that social product will rise if the same quantity continues to be produced at a lower cost. In our example, the increase would be $100. So far so good. But suppose some fellow with a little training in economics comes up with this argument: We can't estimate the value of X on the market, but whatever it is, we can be sure that at a lower price its users would like to have more. Therefore, when the cheaper method of production is adopted, let us increase the output at the same time—say by 20 percent. Far from increasing social product, this change would reduce it by $80 ($9 × 120 minus $10 × 100 = $80).

It turns out, however, that all these calculations based on cost saving are of little significance in comparison with the important fact—there is no demand for product X. Social product could be increased by $1,000, not by using a cheaper method of production, but simply by not producing it and using the productive services released by this decision for producing something that is wanted.

*Government Expenditures*

Government expenditures ought to be included in any evaluation. We must recognize, however, the great complications that are introduced into evaluation of these programs by the fact that different governments are involved. Not one, but at least three different evaluations must be made. First is evaluation with all countries involved in the system combined—viewed as one society, in effect. Second is an evaluation from the point of view of the United States. A little headway can be made on this evaluation if it is done strictly on an economic basis, but if noneconomic considerations of aid policy are introduced, the problem is greatly complicated. Cost sharing rears its ugly head in this evaluation. The third evaluation is that of the participating country (the United States being viewed as taking the initiative). This evaluation presumably would be on a strictly economic basis, would have to have the cost-sharing aspects of the proposition spelled out, and would be no different in principle from the economic evaluation done by the United States.

*Personnel*

An expanded information program via satellites may harm participating countries by effects operating through personnel. First, even if decisions on participation were based on careful calculations, there is a possibility that the salaries of government officials used in such calculations would not reflect their true marginal productivity to the economy in question. I am not sure whether this consideration is important or not, but I think I have seen cases where able people continue to work for a government that pays them salaries much lower than they could get in private business in the same country or abroad.

Apart from the factor just mentioned, it cannot be denied that the governmental employee in an underdeveloped country will look with great favor on the opportunity to join a program connected with satellites. Not only may there be a little additional money, but there is an undeniable air of glamour. The question is, can the underdeveloped country afford the diversion of talent from other tasks?

## Outlay and Benefit

Expenditures on information, including those directed to remote sensing systems using satellites, will be made ahead of the time when productive services are realized from them. Since this money (read productive services) could have been used either for immediate consumption or to produce other capital goods, it is essential that outlays and benefits in connection with the program under evaluation be dated and discounted. There is no point in amassing information ahead of the time when it will be used. Indeed, given the demands for information, the object of the game is to postpone actual generation of information as long as possible, recognizing, of course, that undue postponement involves increases in certain kinds of costs.

No doubt my remarks will be interpreted by many as advocating a skeptical attitude toward the possible benefits from remote sensors in satellites. This interpretation certainly is justified, but if the advocacy of skepticism seems to point in the one direction, let me hasten to add that I advocate skepticism in the other direction, too. If someone is offhandedly pessimistic about the possible benefits, he too should be warned, for he simply may not have stretched his thinking far enough to have envisioned them.

An attitude of skepticism toward unsupported claims is merely an instrument, however. Our true goal is to find the truth, insofar as that is possible; the matters involved are important enough to warrant strenuous efforts to avoid errors in either direction.

# THE VALUE OF MINERAL SURVEYS
# TO ECONOMIC DEVELOPMENT

Titles are often inadequate indicators of subject matter, and the present one is no exception. My discussion is limited to underdeveloped economies, in keeping with the nature of the symposium. This still leaves the problem quite open-ended, however, and would seem to require discussion of two questions: (1) Do minerals surveys contribute to mineral production? (2) Does mineral production contribute to economic development?

There has been a long controversy over the second question. The substantial effect of mineral production on the structure of industry and on the structure of the national accounts is obvious in the case of countries like Venezuela, Chile, Zambia, Libya, Near East oil-producing countries, and others. But mineral production possibly may produce these effects without raising the long-term rate of growth—in short, without contributing to the orderly change we think of as economic development. For example, many people, especially in underdeveloped countries that are important mineral producers, hold what might be called the enclave view of mineral production; that is, they believe that it fails to develop real (as opposed to monetary) relations with other parts of the economy, and especially so if it is controlled by

A paper presented at the annual meeting of the American Institute of Mining and Metallurgical Engineers, Washington, D.C., February 17, 1969.

foreign-owned companies. We are beginning to learn something of the limitations of this simplistic view, for the relations between mineral production and the rest of the economy can be affected strongly by the conditions under which search for and production of minerals may be carried out.

This range of problems is not what I wish to discuss, however. We shall take for granted the relation between mineral production and the real operations of other parts of the economy and consider only one aspect of the relation between mineral surveys and economic development: *How can the government of an underdeveloped country make use of mineral surveys to maximize the return to the country from its mineral resources?* My discussion of this question reflects the view that the proper use of mineral surveys is intimately bound up with the concession problem, or, in more general terms, with the problem of setting the terms on which search and mining may take place.

The simple and direct question, "Do mineral surveys lead to mineral production?" is avoided. To ask this question is something like asking, "Does investment pay?" The answer in both cases is yes, if properly done. It should be noted in passing, however, that there is great variation of opinion about the effectiveness of mineral survey and related activity—such as governmental geological and geophysical mapping programs—in promoting mineral production. Most, but not all, of the administrators and promoters of such activities say they are sure of their effectiveness, but this has not yet been demonstrated systematically. Some users of their products do not share their enthusiasm.

One final preliminary matter should be clarified. The term *mineral survey* is used here in a general way to refer to activities that produce information bearing on the presence and quality of mineral deposits. The term is not restricted to the survey of a particular area that takes place over a comparatively short period of time, such as the recent Chile–United Nations survey in the Province of Coquimbo.

### General Methods of Administering Mineral Lands

First, let us consider the problem faced by a country in which there are no privately held mineral rights of any kind on potential mineral-producing lands.[1] What are the options open to this government in

---

[1] The mere fact that mineral resources are the property of the state, our own system being very much of an exception, does not preclude the existence in many countries of privately owned rights of various kinds that are the practical equivalent of owning mineral rights in our country or which have the practical effect of long-term options to mineral rights in our sense of the term.

trying to put this natural capital (potential mineral-producing lands) to work in order to obtain a return on this property that it owns? There are two related problems here. One is how and when someone is going to acquire exclusive rights to explore and produce in limited areas so as to warrant the necessary investment.[2] The second problem is how the country is going to reap the financial return from its property.

So far as the granting of exclusive rights is concerned, one method is to give them away—first come, first served, which is the system we use for certain minerals on the public lands. There will be some expense in qualifying for the gift and deciding where you want the gift located. If new lands are opened or if new information becomes available to indicate that prospects for a certain area are better than they were previously thought to be, parcels will be taken up quickly by new owners until there are no additional parcels available whose estimated value exceeds the cost of selecting and qualifying for the gift. This estimated value will be, approximately, the present value of expected net revenues for parcels of the type in question.

Second, the government may grant exclusive rights to a company by direct negotiations that encompass a complex of conditions determining prospective profits. The negotiations will include at a minimum either royalties, special taxes, or the payment of a sum. They also may include a variety of other matters that represent a departure from or an addition to the laws governing the operations of other corporations, such as the provision of certain services by the government and special rates, favorable or unfavorable, on various types of foreign exchange transactions.

Third, concessions may be granted by auction to qualified bidders. In this case, payment of the bid is itself a financial return to the government and perhaps the principal one. The bid may be supplemented, however, by special taxation or by payment of a royalty, perhaps of general applicability and specified by statute or regulation.

One of the most important factors in deciding which of the above methods to use and how to use any particular one is the quantity of information available at the time the exclusive right is granted. This factor can be controlled by the government, at least in part, for it can increase available information—by mineral surveys, for example.

In the case where the government itself explores, develops, and produces, having decided to retain exclusive rights for itself, the prob-

---

[2] The government may reserve these rights to itself, of course, as happens routinely in socialist countries and not infrequently in others. Chilean petroleum is a case in point.

lem of the quantity of information takes a different and more comprehensive form. Here the task is to find an efficient pattern for the sequence and scales of the different exploration activities, with the last step either development or (provisional) abandonment of the prospect area. Our interest, however, is in the cases in which exclusive rights actually are transferred to private economic units, especially the cases in which concessions are bid for or negotiated.

The question is, how far should survey activities be carried before granting exclusive rights in the form of a concession? The context in which this question is considered is that of a country whose prospective production of the mineral in question is so small that it can have only a negligible influence on the price of the mineral product.

## AUCTION OF CONCESSIONS

*Size of Area of Exclusive Rights and*
*Economies of Scale in Survey Activity*

To get a start on this problem, consider a situation in which the specific locations of deposits are not known but in which the form and the parameters of the multivariate distribution of deposits according to location and various dimensions of quality are known by the government and prospective bidders. Assume also that the citizenry at large understands the general significance of the fact that this distribution is known. The importance of this last proviso will be discussed later in connection with the likelihood of expropriation. Finally, assume there is no capital rationing or that firms are large relative to particular bids.

In this case, the only reasons for the government to conduct any mineral survey activity are because it can perform these activities more cheaply than private firms can, or because private firms cannot recoup outlays on surveys, with this factor outweighing any private efficiency advantage. If neither of these two factors is operative, it will be a matter of indifference so far as financial return to the country is concerned whether bidding for exclusive rights takes place with no survey information or with deposits identified and ready for development. If there is little information, the bid will be, say, $X on a given large tract. If more information is available, the price bid for the whole tract will tend to be higher because of competitive market forces by the cost of the additional information and no more, but if the large tract is split into smaller units, the bids for the sub-tracts will be distributed around the mean price per unit area of the large tract. The net return to the government will be the same for a low as for a high level of information.

The important point is that the physical risk inherent in the search for minerals does *not* result *per se* in a lower return to the government if bids are let when the level of information is low, contrary to a commonly held view. Something more is required.

*Averaging Out*

If firms are not large relative to bids, because it is thought that their capacity to use capital is limited,[3] then the possibility of large loss or of failure may affect the ability of the entrepreneurs to get capital for further operations. They may even cease to be entrepreneurs. If suppliers of capital are prone to interpret failure as indicating a lack of ability rather than as an unlucky draw, the firm may no longer be indifferent to the anticipated dispersion of returns from ventures of a given size and type. If it cannot engage in enough ventures to average out the returns to the satisfaction of those sitting in financial judgment, it will have to lower its bids on prospects where little information is available, or avoid them entirely. In turn, the result will be a lower financial return to government if it persists in putting concessions up for bid in cases where little is known about the area involved and where bidders' access to capital is limited as just described.

The practical significance of this consideration is difficult to access. For one thing, there may be a continual flow of the type of investor who tends to overestimate returns to inherently risky mineral prospects. Separate from this is the undoubted preference of some investors for exposure to situations that are potentially ruinous, given their limited capital, even though they are well able to assess the prospects correctly from the point of view of mathematical expectation.

Apart from persistent error in evaluating mineral prospects and risk aversion or preference, it is clear that modern business organization offers many opportunities to both corporations and individuals for consolidating risks and reducing or eliminating the threat of financial disaster judged to be excessive relative to assets, thanks to limited liability and the simple device of easily transferable shares in small units.

At the corporate level, it is possible to form units large enough to be involved in many ventures. The degree of consolidation of risk in oil exploration achieved in this way by some companies is very high, and there are many mineral corporations that at any one time are involved in numerous ventures before the development stage.

However, there are many corporations, partnerships, and individual

---

[a] This may reflect judgment within the firm or by suppliers of capital or both.

entrepreneurs in both oil and minerals whose capital is too limited to avoid risk by engaging in a number of wholly owned ventures. Various devices are available to them for sharing risk with other companies and thereby securing partial participation in several ventures. These are commonplace in petroleum exploration and are used increasingly in minerals, but they can be used only at a cost, of course. Such cost arises from the duplication of evaluation expenses, and this leads to the conclusion that devices that share risk among independent economic units will tend to be used (1) where costs of evaluation are low, as seems to be the case with much petroleum exploration in the United States, and (2) where the costs of evaluation, although too high to be borne by small corporations interested in consolidating risk, are low for a large corporation and low relative to the size of the ultimate project. Some of the large joint corporate mineral ventures are perhaps cases in point, where even the large corporation does not want to take on the whole venture, because of its size, the lack of certain technical or organizational capability, or a desire to reduce visibility to potential expropriators.

At the level of the stockholder, the inherent physical risks of mineral ventures can easily be completely consolidated by investing in various mineral corporations. If stockholders were in control, in the sense of having their very effective consolidation of risk reflected in the decisions on particular mineral ventures, there would be no reason why each of these corporations should not bid on the basis of mathematical expectational values without regard to risk, even if the corporations are small. If a particular venture or corporation fails, this is no different, from the point of view of society or the individual investor, from the failure of a particular venture of a large company, except for the real cost of organizing new ventures and moving personnel and mobile assets to them in the wake of failure. These costs may be higher (or lower) than when the shifting takes place within one corporation.

Although stockholders can easily consolidate the risks inherent in mineral search and production, it cannot be concluded that corporations will proceed to base their bids for concessions on expectational values without regard to risk. First of all, corporate management itself may prefer to run a corporation that continues. Indeed, outside of mining, failure of the corporation does indicate a failure of management in most instances, although in minerals it may indicate nothing of the kind. Evaluations by prospective employers are far from perfect, however, and the ex-engineer or executive looking for a job after venture or corporate failure faces a real possibility of a substantial period of unemployment and of a permanently lower level of compensation even if rehired. Some stockholders and board members, either not understanding the risks or not believing in acting on the basis of expected values, may even accuse management of imprudent action, when the action is in fact expectationally justified and poses no threat to the continued existence of the firm if the particular venture is unsuccessful. It is not surprising that the continuity of the corporation and avoidance of spectacular, if bearable, losses come to be regarded by corporate management as important objectives.

We should expect differences in the importance accorded the continuity objective, of course, depending on the experience of stockholders and mineral corporate management with failure of both ventures and corporations as the result of the risk inherent in mineral exploration. It might be surmised that Canada differs from the United States in this respect.

In my opinion, the net result of the factors discussed so far is to reduce the number of bids and to reduce the level of bids on prospects about which there is little information. This opens the possibility that government can improve the return on its mineral lands by accumulating more information before putting prospects up for bid.

*Size of Concessions and Discontinuities in Concessions Held*

We turn now to a couple of minor factors that tend to lower the level of bids at lower levels of information—that is, factors that can cause bids at different levels of information to differ by more than the lowest feasible cost of providing the additional information.

Consider the situation in which a number of adjoining plots are put up for auction, with no firm winning on more than one plot. Subsequent survey work will be necessary if the auction takes place at a low level of information. It is obvious that plots can be so small as to raise costs if each firm conducts its own survey work, in which case bids must be lower to allow recoupment of this additional cost.

If separate surveys are made in this situation and it is required that results be made available to others at some specified time (recall that exclusive rights have already been granted), the results of a particular firm's survey will be useful to adjoining concession holders because of the continuity of geology across plot boundaries. However, since all the plots were put up for auction by a single holder, the government, we should expect the value of the external benefits as well as the internal benefits to be reflected in the bids, assuming the receipt of benefits from neighbors' survey activity was anticipated at the time of bidding.

Remedies are readily available for difficulties resulting from plot sizes that are too small, however. One obvious possibility is to enlarge the size of the plots put up for auction, although the government may be reluctant to do this if it would result in excessive dominance of mining activity by one or a few companies. In addition, larger plots may reduce the number of bidders.

Another possibility is to do the survey work jointly, although this may not be feasible because of differences in schedules of activities or because of inability to agree on the technical characteristics the survey should have.

*Expropriation and Similar Actions*

Auction of concession rights at a low level of information increases the likelihood of expropriation with less than full compensation, or similar actions, such as new taxes, increased tax rates, unfavorable change in tax administration, or manipulation of exchange rates, that have the effect of reducing present value of the property below what would be anticipated otherwise. If bidders believe that expropriation will be accompanied by less than full compensation for the value of the property or that governmental actions with adverse effects on the value of the property are likely, bids will be lowered accordingly, even though the government in question actually has no intention of expropriating any properties and does not do so.

Suppose less than fully compensated expropriations or similar actions were anticipated to occur and do occur after auctions at low levels of information. Would the government's return on its mineral lands be lowered as compared with the case in which no expropriations are anticipated and do not occur? Not necessarily. Imagine, for example, a system in which the events in question are very numerous and in which less than fully compensated expropriations take place with a relative frequency that is in accord with expectations. *If* the expropriating government can manage the properties so that the present value of subsequent operations is the same as it would have been under private operation (assume for simplicity of exposition that the same discount rate is appropriate for the government and the private company), auction of concessions with low information available to bidders would leave the government in the same position as auction with more information, even if expropriation is more frequent in the former case. The governmental take from winning bids plus gains on uncompensated expropriation would be equal (in terms of present value as of a given date) to winning bids made, say, on the certain knowledge that expropriation would not take place.

Such a situation is not likely to be approximated in the real world, however. If less than fully compensated expropriations occur in a country, subsequent bids for concessions are likely to be lowered, perhaps even to zero, the situation in which foreign mining capital cannot be induced to expose itself to expropriation. Furthermore, the chances are excellent that a government without a long background of experience in running a mining industry will not be able to operate expropriated properties as efficiently as private operators. Thus we conclude that anything that increases the likelihood of expropriation is likely to decrease the government's take on its mineral lands, whether it does or does not expropriate. If it does not, it is in effect paying bidders for concessions for the privilege of making them nervous about expropriation. If it does expropriate, it will have to enlarge these payments and may incur a real loss in operating expropriated properties simply because of ineptitude.

It has not yet been explained, however, why auction of concessions with a low level of information should lead to the expectation of a higher probability of expropriation than auction with more information. The reason, I hypothesize, is that the greater dispersion of returns on sums paid for rights to plots of a given size when the auction is held with little information operates to increase demands for expropriation.

For example, suppose there are ten plots and that it is known that some one of them contains a deposit such that a bid of $100 would be warranted if all subsequent cash flows are discounted at the market rate of return on investment. If the identity of the plot with the deposit were known, $100 would be bid, and the situation would not appear to be much different from that of investment in a company making breakfast food so far as the likelihood of expropriation is concerned. One hundred dollars is paid for the privilege of mining the deposit and $100 is "made," yielding a net result of zero after accounting for market return to capital invested.

If the identity of the plot with the deposit is *not* known, however, only $(\$100-10K)/10$ will be bid for each of the ten plots if $\$K$ is to be spent for additional search information on each plot. The present value as of the date of the auction of the return on the nine barren plots is

| Return from operation | | Cost of rights | | Cost of more information | | |
|---|---|---|---|---|---|---|
| $[\ 0\ ]$ | $-$ | $\dfrac{9(100-10K)}{10}$ | $-$ | $[9K]$ | | $=-\$90,$ |

while on the tenth plot with the deposit it is

| | | | | | | |
|---|---|---|---|---|---|---|
| $[\$100]$ | $-$ | $\dfrac{100-10K}{10}$ | $-$ | $[K]$ | | $=+\$90,$ |

with a final result on all ten plots of zero *after* covering market return on investment, just as in the former case where the identity of the plot with the deposit was known.

It is all too easy, however, to point to the +$90 as an unconscionable return on capital and as a giveaway of the national patrimony. The successful company can point to the corresponding loss of $90 on the nine barren plots, but this may be a less than convincing argument, even if this company itself lost the money in *this* country. The fact is, however, that the market processes by which "averaging out" is achieved do *not* require that the company that happens to get the tenth and winning plot is also the one that gets the nine losers. Other companies may be the losers. And even if the winning company is large enough to average out its ventures, its losing ventures need not be in the country in question. Furthermore, if the country itself is small, the gain made from deposits found in that country may not be offset by losses realized within it if auctions are held with a low level of information.

Thus a high dispersion of returns, which must necessarily accompany auctions with low levels of information because of the risk inherent in mineral exploration, leaves the eventually successful bidders vulnerable to charges of exploitation, which increases the likelihood of expropriation without full compensation or of actions having similar effects on the value of the prospect.

It is clear that the posited relationship between the level of information and the level of bids need not be the same for all underdeveloped countries and, conceivably, might not be present at all. The task of eliminating or attenuating the relationship is a difficult one, however, for it appears to require a long period without expropriations, a long history of political and social stability, and the firm expectation on the part of investors that stability and a policy of no expropriations (unless fully compensated) will continue into the indefinite future. There are few, if any, underdeveloped countries to which this combination of conditions applies.

Of the several factors affecting the level of bids for concessions differentially according to the level of information available at the time of the auction, the leading two probably are (1) the pressures on the corporation to "average out" without running the risk of high losses or failure and (2) the probability of expropriation without full compensation or of governmental actions having similar effects on the present value of a venture. However, empirical evidence that would give us some quantitative indication of the impact of these factors on governmental earnings from mineral resources is very sparse indeed.

Consider the first factor. The question we would like to answer is whether for a *given* large plot of land capital rationing (a shorthand name for the complex of factors embraced in our discussion of "averaging out") causes the return to the *whole given plot* to be lower with a low than with a high level of information. It should be obvious that a simple-minded comparison of the return per acre on 20,000 acres let out for bid on little information with the return per acre on 1,000 acres carefully selected on the basis of a great deal of amassed information will tell us less than nothing—I say less than nothing because some will be misled by this nonsensical comparison. What is missing from the comparison? First, what area (say, area *A*) was related to the 1,000 acres in a way that corresponded to the 20,000 acres in the other case? How much was spent in amassing the information on the basis of which the 1,000 acres were selected? And were the original *A* acres of the same quality as the 20,000? The problem is one of some subtlety.

As for the relation between expropriation without full compensation and the dispersion of returns, economic history supports the view that extremely profitable ventures present tempting targets. After India became independent in 1947, many mineral rights quickly became valueless because they were taken over by the new government without compensation. In many cases they had been acquired originally by the most outrageous chicanery. I would interpret the history of Middle East oil as another case in point, where profits were steadily and relentlessly pared down after World War II by revision of conditions originally in effect. Other examples could be added.

The examples that can easily be added in evidence are extreme, however, and usually involve cases where rights acquired with little information available were not acquired by auction or anything remotely equivalent to it. Nevertheless, it would seem to be as easy to forget that a property was fairly acquired by auction; as noted earlier, even an auction may not be regarded as a fair procedure by a country not in a position to "average out" on auctions of concessions. The proposition that high dispersion of returns, which necessitates some very high apparent returns, results in lower bids because of greater expectations of expropriation would seem to provide the better basis for policy until definitely refuted by solid evidence.

*Insurance against Expropriation*

The argument that dispersion of returns leads to lower bids for concessions via heightened fears of expropriation is weakened by the fact that an increasing number of governments of developed countries will insure their private investors against uncompensated expropriations and some of the actions having similar effects. The United States,

Germany, and Japan have had such an insurance program for a considerable period of time. Programs are also in effect or in preparation in a number of other countries, including Italy, France, Belgium, Switzerland, Denmark, Sweden, and the Netherlands. There has been a strong surge of interest in such programs recently, in some cases representing an extension of older and more limited insurance guaranties available in connection with the financing of export and import transactions.[4]

The provisions of these different programs vary, but a number of the more general questions that arise perhaps can be illustrated by a brief look at the U.S. program, which has been in existence since the late forties. Under this program, insurance is available for new investment in a large number of countries that have signed the required bilateral agreements.[5] The risks covered include inconvertibility of currency, uncompensated expropriation, and damage resulting from war, revolution, or insurrection.

Insurance against inconvertibility is not insurance against devaluation or against losses resulting from manipulation of rates under a system of multiple exchange rates, however. In addition, inconvertibility coverage is limited in the case of equity investment to 200 percent of the initial investment.

The expropriation coverage extends to regulatory or tax actions only if they are discriminatory against foreigners, are not reasonably related to constitutional objectives, or violate generally acceptable principles of international law. A voluntary agreement between the insured and the foreign government that permits the expropriation, which might be entered into in order to gain future benefits of some type, will void any claim for compensation. Losses resulting from *bona fide* exchange control actions are not regarded as expropriation. Finally, on receiving compensation, title to the property must be transferred to the U.S. government, something the corporation may be reluctant to do, again because this may eliminate the possibility of certain future benefits.

Although coverage under the investment guaranty program was about $6 billion at the end of fiscal 1968, experience with settlement of claims is very limited, since more than $5 billion of the coverage has been written during fiscal 1965–1968. While the importance of the coverage to the investor definitely cannot be brushed aside as negli-

---

[4] I am indebted to Miss Betty Burton of the Agency for International Development for information on the insurance programs of other countries.

[5] Among the countries for which insurance against expropriation is *not* available (as of the end of 1968) are Argentina (agreement not yet ratified), Mexico, Guatemala (limited coverage), Iraq, Egypt, Lebanon, and Syria. All other OAS countries are covered.

gible, it is far from complete coverage against harassment, for many such actions would not be covered. Furthermore, any desire to maintain legal rights in anticipation of a later beneficial change in governmental policy nullifies the value of the insurance. While such a policy change might not restore the expropriated property or change the compensation, it might make other valuable opportunities available. The value of the insurance is clearest in cases where the expropriatory act obviously makes continuation of the enterprise impossible, where compensation obviously is inadequate, and where the corporation is giving up thought of future operations of any kind in the expropriating country.

In view of these considerations, the argument relating the level of information to a lower level of bids on concessions because of fear of uncompensated expropriation still retains much of its force, in spite of the availability of insurance against various risks for investors from a number of developed countries. Their risk is much less than it would be without these programs, however.

## NEGOTIATION OF CONCESSION

The preceding discussion of the relation between the bid received for concession and the amount of information available at the time of auction applies almost without change to cases where exclusive rights are transferred by negotiation rather than by auction. The initial contacting and sifting out of prospects is analogous to an auction, and the final round of negotiations can be looked on as a process to determine whether the company is willing to meet the government's (implicit) upset bid.

One difference from the auction method, however, is the greater susceptibility of a negotiated concession to later accusation that it was unjustly granted. The importance of this consideration obviously depends on the reputation the agency that negotiates the agreement enjoys among the people of its country.

## GIVING AWAY EXCLUSIVE RIGHTS

If exclusive rights are given away without special taxation of later operations, the government of the country clearly has abandoned any thought of collecting the value of its mineral lands for the people at large, for these values are given to first comers, who possibly may be foreigners as well as citizens. If we ignore this distributional problem— if, in effect, we assume that takers of mineral rights and others dip into and take from a common pocketbook—there might be a case for some government survey activity where the level of information is low to reduce duplication of effort and because firms that have acquired rights may not be able to reap all the benefits of their survey activity. That is, one firm's survey activity may benefit adjoining land because, to repeat, geological characteristics continue across property boundaries.

A government can reap at least a partial return on the mineral rights it gives away by the use of taxation, however. Note that a royalty differs from certain types of taxes in name only. It may be observed, somewhat apart from the main line of argument, that special taxes can achieve only a partial retrieval of the value of mineral lands for a government because of either or both of two characteristics. First, they do not achieve 100 percent tax on the surplus remaining over the market return on investment made by the private firms. Second, they often are inefficient in the economic sense and thereby prevent the private firms from maximizing the surplus after covering all costs. For example, it is well known that a fixed royalty per unit of product or a royalty expressed as a percentage of gross receipts will result in cut-offs higher than they should be on grounds of economic efficiency.

There is one tax which would appear to permit recovery of the whole value of mineral lands, namely, taxation of profits at 100 percent after strict cost depletion after allowing full market return on invested capital and if loss offsets are completely effective.[6] While such a tax avoids the adverse effect on cut-offs of a royalty, it poses another obviously insurmountable incentive problem, the only solution to which is a tax on the combined return to invested capital and deposit at *less* than 100 percent, in which case the whole of the true rent on the deposits will not be extracted, except in those instances where the ratio of rent to the sum of rent and return on capital happens to equal the tax rate.

Suppose that a government does try to recover a part, if not all, of the value of its mineral lands by imposing special taxes on mining enterprises (certainly not tax relief). Would it be advantageous for the government to provide higher levels of information in order to temper the effects of capital rationing and fears of expropriation? The assumption that mineral rights are given away is continued.

The capital rationing consideration now would have its effect in a diminished number of entrants (i.e., gift takers) at low levels of information as compared with fewer bidders *and* lower bids with auction of concessions. The question of the relation between the likelihood of expropriation and the level of information does not appear to arise where special taxes are used to get a return on mineral lands instead

---

[6] If loss offsets were less than completely effective, the tax rate would have to be less than 100 percent.

of bids for rights. The better prospects at low levels of information will already have been taken up, even if a country's mineral information program as a whole is aiming at providing high levels of information for active areas. Providing more information will not lower the very high apparent returns and will not thereby decrease the likelihood of expropriation.

One caution is in order, however. Where special taxes are the subject of special negotiation along with negotiation of the concession, the situation is the same as that of a negotiated price for the concession. It was argued earlier that the problem of the level of information to be provided under a system of negotiation is equivalent to that involved in the auction of concessions.

### How Should Higher Levels of Information Be Provided?

It appears advisable to wait to convey exclusive rights by auction or negotiation until the availability of more information on mineral prospects can lower the dispersion of returns and thereby induce higher bids (or terms) by reducing the probabilities of large loss or of expropriation and similar actions. But who is to provide the additional information?

One possibility to be considered is that the private sphere could organize to produce this information and sell it to interested firms, thereby reducing or eliminating duplication in the production of information. In effect, competition would result in the division of the cost among the users (and buyers) of the information. Sale of aerial photographs provides a simple example of this mechanism at work. At a higher level of information, it is possible to purchase ready-made photo-interpretations of certain types for some portions of the United States and, no doubt, of Canada.

In the case of the underdeveloped country, however, the demand for information may be so uncertain, possibly because of ignorance of already existing information on mineral possibilities, that private information-producing firms are not willing to do the work in the hope of later sale. Indeed, the possibility may never have occurred to them if they lack familiarity with a country and do not know how to work in it.

If the underdeveloped country decides to advance the level of information by survey work, it will encounter some serious difficulties, the nature of which can only be hinted at here. First is the necessity of developing the capability of making decisions on the nature and pace of the survey program. This is not a once and for all decision; most programs will continue over a period of years, with the constant need to decide where and in what ways the level of information should be increased. The difficulty and dangers in having these decisions made by outside advice seem clear enough.

Among the considerations to be borne in mind in planning the survey program, which may require some integration with the planning of other economic activity, is the desirability of having mineral development take place near already existing facilities if possible. Minerals are often not cooperative in selecting their locations, however. If minerals cannot be developed so as to use existing facilities, the possibility of developing a mineral district in order to make more intensive use of transport and other common facilities should be borne in mind.

The developing country that decides to raise the level of information by survey should distinguish between the task of making basic decisions on the program and the physical execution of that program. In my opinion, the task of making program decisions is difficult to delegate or purchase. The purchase of physical execution, on the other hand, may turn out to be considerably cheaper than execution by the government itself.

Whatever the level of information at which it is decided to grant exclusive rights, the tasks of assembling, presenting, and disseminating all pertinent available information remain of basic importance. These important tasks are not costly but can result in much higher bids. The body of information must be augmented continually, not only by the incorporation of new studies initially in the public domain but also by the assembly and analysis of pertinent data generated in the activities of exploration and production, including that generated by private corporations, once legitimate proprietary interests have been served.

# PART FIVE

## The Quality of the Natural Environment

# EFFECTS OF RESOURCE DEPLETION AND ECONOMIC GROWTH ON THE QUALITY OF LIFE

The effects of resource depletion and economic growth on the quality of life depend primarily, but not exclusively, on the philosophical situation of the members of the society involved. For people corrupted by money and what it enables them to do, economic growth is a disaster—the quality of their lives deteriorates as growth proceeds. For others, higher income may open the way to a much fuller life.

The quality of life certainly is not to be equated with pleasure, nor even with happiness, unless this is defined in a very special way. Some clarification is perhaps to be had by asking what the role of sorrow is in the quality of life. For some people, at least, not to have had exposure to the fundamental trials of life, such as death of loved ones, serious illness, betrayal, and so on, would have meant a life of lower quality, granted that any one of us would no doubt prefer fewer to more trials as we look forward.

I choose to view the quality of life as depending on whether one can see himself as participating in the expression of the values in his

A paper presented to the Conference on Scarcity and Growth: Toward a National Materials Policy, sponsored by the National Commission on Materials Policy and the School of Public Affairs at the University of Minnesota, June 22-24, 1972.

philosophy or in seeing them "worked out" in the flow of events around him. This definition is general enough to be usable by all of us, whether we are nihilists (destructive or passive), Christians, materialists, existentialists (religious or atheistic), or whatever. Each of us has some standpoint from which he can take the measure of the quality of his life. A part of our experiences (which are the raw material for measurement of the quality of life) is made up of work and consumption activities, which are under the control of the individual to a considerable degree. The idea of freedom of choice in these spheres must not be pushed too far, of course, for even though the individual is free to choose among the options available to him, the range and nature of these options are the product of societal forces outside his control. Earning and using income in the conventional sense receive expression in this category of experience. We choose a certain job with its associated activities and at the same time build up a pattern of consumption activities involving a residence, patterns of movement, amusements, and so on.

It will be useful for our subsequent argument to distinguish the experiences arising from work and consumption from those that quite clearly are *not* under the control of the individual, that is, the stimuli that come to him from the environment, as we have come to say. While these two classes of stimuli, distinguished with respect to their controllability by the individual, could be thought of as the raw material from which the estimate of the quality of life is made, it is useful to view them as first filtering through human nature; that is, through our inherited biological nature, which has both psychological and physical components. The significance of the stimuli for the quality of life may undergo modification by having to pass through this filter.

The quality of life, then, depends on our assessment of experience in relation to the values that are a part of the philosophy we hold. The factors on which the quality of life depend may be schematized into four categories: (1) work and consumption experiences, these being a reflection of earning and using income in the ordinary sense; (2) stimuli coming from the environment; (3) our biological inheritance; and (4) the philosophy held by the person in question. Whether one judges the quality of his life to have gone up or down in response to a change in the level of consumption or to a change in environmental quality will depend on the compatibility of the change with biological inheritance and on the particular philosophy held. There is no assurance that an increase in income will lead to a better quality of life.

Consider the possible role of biological inheritance. Increased opulence provides at least the possibility of engaging in activities that we feel would increase the quality of life. But if the manner in which the increased income is obtained or the activities to which it gives rise are increasingly at odds with the built-in behavior modes derived from some hundreds of thousands of years of hunting in small groups, the effect may be adverse rather than favorable, perhaps with our not having the least idea why increased opulence did not do what we thought it would. For example, a rise in income often seems to bring a decrease in physical activity, but if this is very great, various sorts of ailments may develop and life may be shortened—all of this being grist for the estimate of the quality of life.

Apart from adverse effects that arise through the filter of biological inheritance, it can easily turn out that a person feels he has failed to use an increase in income so as to raise the quality of his life, given his philosophy. And if we judge the behavior of others by reference to our own philosophy, how severe the verdict often is! We frequently think that although Mr. Noveau Riche believes his quality of life is improved because of his higher income, he certainly has some strange ideas on how to spend his money! You yourself may be able to think of some cases in which higher incomes have been misused. They might involve, for example, heroin, aimless destruction of property by mobs, hard rock music, etc.

But even though our intentions are good, our philosophy praiseworthy, and we suffer no lapses in our quest for the good, increased income means increased production and consumption activity of one sort or another, and these may give us some things we didn't bargain for and would even pay to be rid of if that were possible. For example, only the perverse or those with problems at home can look forward to the daily commuting grind and its tensions. Who among us welcomes an increase in air pollution? Who is happy over the dimming of the blue clarity of some western skies, even though he knows that this is for a good cause—including neon signs in Los Angeles, air conditioning in Phoenix, or pumping water to irrigate crops that otherwise would have to be grown on my cousin's land in Iowa, presently idle because it is on deposit in the Soil Bank? Greater affluence may bring with it so large an increase in congestion in certain places that the net effect on the quality of life for some is indeed negative, and this apart from increase in population. One thinks of highways, state parks, and so on.

Considerations of this sort lead to the unsurprising conclusion that even so comprehensive an indicator as the Gross National Product (GNP), which is a measure of the change in total command over economic product as expressed (largely) in market transactions, is an imperfect indicator of welfare change or change in the quality of life, with respect not only to quantity but perhaps also direction.[1] No economist with more than two cents' worth of competence ever thought otherwise, of course. The GNP is simply a record of the amount and composition of what are defined as final purchases made by consumers, government, and nonprofit institutions. The compiler of the GNP doesn't ask whether the consumer made wise purchases with his money, he doesn't make a deduction because John Doe spent too much on liquor and caused his family to be unhappy as a result. He takes the purchases as they are recorded, whether made for good or for ill, and deliberately leaves out all those factors bearing on welfare that are not expressed in market transactions or clearly related thereto. To say this is not to criticize the national income accountants. It is simply to state a fact.

However, it is still true that an increase in economic command over resources has the *potentiality* of permitting one to improve the quality of his life, provided his philosophy leads him to make good use of the extra income and provided the adverse external effects accompanying the increased output are not so great as to offset the gain. Or so we say, at any rate. A person justifies his move to a better paying job in this way, at least in part. He looks ahead to the next raise or a succession of raises because, he says, he will know how to use the extra money wisely. This line of thought provides the justification for our concern with economic growth—it at least makes possible a life of better quality, a possibility that is especially important for those in the lower income groups.

Further reflection should remind us, however, that it is all too easy to push this argument too far. While it may be true that many of us would consume more out of a higher income, it really is impossible to escape asking the question, "How much is enough?" if we are concerned with the quality of life or welfare rather than with explaining what men do in the marketplace.

First, start by introspection and ask yourself, would the quality of life be improved if your income were raised by 25 or 50 percent? The question is not whether you would increase your rate of consumption, for it is only too obvious that any one of us could do this with no difficulty. Rather, it is something like this. If you wake up each morning glad to be alive and look forward to the day's activities, would more money cause you to be even more enthusiastic? Or if the morning

---

[1] For an authoritative discussion, see Edward F. Denison, "Welfare Measurement and the GNP," *Survey of Current Business* (January 1971). Reprinted as Brookings Institution Reprint No. 196, May 1971 (Washington, D.C.).

sees you wishing you could regain the oblivion that three or four double martinis gave you the night before, would more money enable you to get out of that trap? If your answer is no to either of these questions, some doubt has been cast on the view that higher income results in a better quality of life.

Try another tack. Ask yourself whether you can perceive a difference in the quality of life of a half dozen friends in your income bracket as compared with another half dozen friends with incomes half as large, assuming the incomes of your acquaintances are sufficiently diverse to permit the comparison. While there will be differences in either direction when comparing particular pairs of friends, I venture that it is far from obvious to you that, on the average, the quality of life associated with the larger income is higher.

Similar doubts arise if we compare persons living at different periods of time. Compare the quality of your life with that of your grandfather, for example. Or compare persons living in different cultures at the same or at different times. It is far from clear that the verdict always goes with the higher income.

Indeed, some primitive societies, as described by anthropologists, are quite attractive in many ways. While some of us might not be willing to trade places with primitive man, perhaps feeling that we have valuable opportunities for self-expression that the primitive society doesn't have, the answer might well be different for many of our fellow citizens. At any rate, it is easy to imagine that the members of some primitive societies were or are well satisfied with their lives. Infant and child mortality commonly are high, but once past these hurdles a person has greater assurance of continued life. How does one pass his time? Work is necessary, of course, but in a hunting society this may require only a few hours a day at an activity highly regarded in a society that hunts for food, an activity that requires enjoyable movement, provides variety, adventure, thrills—in short, an activity that comes naturally, since this is what our ancestors were doing for so long a time. Personal participation in the arts might well be more extensive than in our own society. Much of the time would be spent in camaraderie. There would be religious activities and ceremonies of various kinds to celebrate natural events or events in the life of the group. Relations with other people would be very close. Pressures to accommodate oneself to the group—at least in certain ways—would be very strong.

An attractive picture? In some ways, although the objective in reminding you of it is not to suggest that we would be better off to eliminate nine-tenths of us and return to a primitive state, but to emphasize that a life of satisfying quality can be lived in circumstances very different from ours, including the level of economic income.

An additional factor thought by many to affect the quality of life is the distribution of income. In the above catalogue of determining factors it can be regarded as involved in the philosophy held by a person and also as one of the things external to him in which he has an interest. The precise role of the distribution of income in the quality of life is puzzling, however. First, when we speak of *the* quality of life, whose lives are in question, those of the well-to-do, of the poor, or of those with a typical level of income? The distribution problem as a whole can be viewed as one of justice, but the content of the concept of justice obviously varies greatly among societies. Our problem is not to examine justice in general, however, but to explain how changes in the level of materials consumption may affect the quality of life acting through effects on feelings *about* justice.

If no additional redistribution was wanted by the society, there would be no problem on this score. Consequently, the first question is: How much redistribution of income is and will be viewed as desirable now and in the years to come? My feeling is that a substantial amount of redistribution will be wanted, especially for the "deserving" poor, that is, for those who work but just aren't very productive and can't earn much and for those who genuinely can't work very much or at all and who are experiencing hardship for reasons they are unable to overcome. The precise content of hardship is not fixed but depends on the affluence and ethos of the society.

Let us suppose that substantial redistribution will be viewed as desirable. The next question is whether changes in the level of material affluence affect the ease with which income can be redistributed. Some economists are very strongly of the opinion that redistribution is greatly facilitated by increasing incomes (money income, that is). This is no doubt the correct direction of the relationship, given the perceived need for redistribution. It is quite possible, however, that a part of the need for redistribution arises from the very process by which income increases. That is, unable persons will have greater difficulty adapting to a situation that is changing, as it must for many of them when changes in the demand for labor result from process change, shifts in industry location, etc. In addition, views about the supposed difficulty of redistribution always presume a certain level of knowledge about the facts of the distribution of income on the part of those whose consent to redistribution is needed. It can only be said that the level of ignorance on this score is high. Much better information is becoming available, however. If it can be absorbed by the more affluent so that the need for certain types of redistribution is more clearly understood, redistribution may become more feasible even if the rate of increase in income should slow down.

## THE PESSIMISTIC VIEW

By and large, our speculation up to now has been that an increase in income has a beneficial effect on the quality of life, though possibly very small, provided the circumstances surrounding the increase are not too incongruent with our natural biological heritage and do not produce undesirable external effects in too great a quantity. There is another and more disturbing possibility, however. Could it be that increase in societal income might have a general *adverse* effect on the quality of life—always supposing that "basic" needs have been met? Apart from the possible ill effects accompanying production, there are various ways in which this possibility might be conceived. One is that the philosophical position of a large number of people is such that increased income leads to a lower quality of life as judged, not by their philosophy, but by "ours." The other possibility is that the philosophy of a large number of people is such that an increase in income is bound to fail to enable them to satisfy their expectations. One can envision conflicts within these persons involving a more or less conscious view of life that gets acted out and a more unconscious level with which these actions come into conflict. Or, alternatively, perhaps their philosophy derives from and reflects fundamental defects in human nature.

Argument along these lines is far from new, but its full formulation and application to society, as distinct from the individual, had to wait for the coming of the industrial revolution, which, together with the spread of popular government, made it possible for the common man to express himself, both politically and economically, in a way never possible before. Wise men have always recognized the possibility that accession to wealth would prove to be the downfall of certain individuals, but with the advent of modern productive power and government, the possibility is now open that a whole society, perhaps all societies, inevitably will fail to realize the dream of a high quality of life.

José Ortega y Gasset, the great Spanish essayist and philosopher, has pursued this line of thought in his famous essay, *The Rebellion of the Masses.* He is concerned with pointing out the distinguishing characteristics of what he calls *mass man* and the possible effects that the rise of mass man may have on society. Ortega y Gasset was writing in 1926, but the clarity of his vision is indicated by the fact that we are troubled by the same problems today and share his worries—

unfortunately in a heightened form.[2] "Present day mass man," he said,

has two main psychological characteristics, the unlimited expansion of his basic desires (and therefore of his personality) and a radical ingratitude to all that has made possible the ease of his existence. The two characteristics taken together constitute the well-known psychology of the spoiled child. And, in effect, one would not err by using this as a cuadricula, or framework, through which to examine the soul of present day masses. Heir of a long and inspired past—genius-like both in its inspirations and labors—the new common man has been spoiled by the world around him. To be spoiled is not to limit one's desires; it is to give the impression of a being to whom everything is permitted and from whom nothing is required. A child submitted to this regimen has no experience of his own limitations. Because of avoiding every surrounding pressure, every collision with other beings, he comes to believe in effect that only *he* exists, and he becomes accustomed to paying no attention to the rest, especially because he does not view anyone as being superior to him. . . .

No human being thanks another for the air he breathes, because the air has not been manufactured by anyone. It belongs to that group of things whose presence is taken for granted, to that about which we say, "It is natural," because it is never lacking. These spoiled masses are sufficiently unintelligent to believe that the material and social organization, placed at their disposition like the air, is of the same origin, since it never is lacking, so it would appear, and is almost as perfect as the natural itself.

My thesis, then, is this: the very perfection which the nineteenth century has given to the organization of certain activities of life has led to the beneficiary masses not considering it as organization but as nature. This is the explanation of the absurd state of mind which the masses reveal: nothing preoccupies them more than their welfare, and at the same time they are indifferent to the sources of this welfare. Since they do not see in the advantages of civilization a prodigious invention and a structure which can be maintained only by great and careful efforts, they think that their role is only that of demanding benefits peremptorily, as if they were natural rights. In the riots which scarcity provokes, the popular masses are accustomed to look for bread, and the means they employ is usually that of destroying the bakeries. This can serve as a symbol of the behavior—in vaster and more subtle proportions—of present-day masses in the face of the civilization which nourishes them.

In writing about mass man, Ortega y Gasset was analyzing a class of people with certain psychological characteristics and *not* a social class

---

[2] The next several paragraphs represent my translation and paraphrase of certain passages from his famous essay, *La rebelión de las masas*. It is widely available in English (e.g., *The Revolt of the Masses* [New York: Norton, 1957], but a convenient (abridged) source in Spanish is *Ortega y Gasset, sus mejores páginas* (Englewood Cliffs, N.J.: Prentice-Hall, 1966), pp. 129–163. The passages here are from pp. 58–60 and 112–113 of the first source; in the second source they are from pp. 145–146 and 161–162.

in the sense in which the word *masses* is usually used. Thus a person of low income or low intelligence might well *not* be a member of the class, mass man. Similarly, many of those who customarily think of themselves as belonging to the upper echelons of the society were members of the masses in his eyes. Once upon a time, he reminds us,

. . . men could be divided simply into the wise and the ignorant, into the more or less wise and the more or less ignorant. But the specialist—which is what we have nowadays—cannot be put under either of these two categories. He is not a wise man, because he is formally ignorant of whatever does not enter into his speciality. But neither is he an ignoramus, because he is "a man of science" and knows very well his little portion of the universe. We have to say that he is a sage-ignoramus, a label of grave portent, because it signifies that he is a gentleman who will conduct himself in all the questions about which he knows nothing, not as an ignoramus, but with all the petulance of one who is knowledgeable in his own special field. . . . In specializing him, civilization has made him impenetrable and satisfied within his limitation; but this same personal sense of domination and worth leads him to want to predominate outside his speciality. From which it results that even in the case of specialization, which represents the maximally qualified man (and, there-fore, the direct opposite of mass man), the result is that he conducts himself completely *like* mass man in almost all spheres of life.

The warning is clear. Whoever wants to can observe the stupidity with which the "men of science," and right behind them doctors, engineers, finan-ciers, professors, etc., think, judge, and act today in politics, in art, in religion, and in the general problems of life and the world. This condition of "not listening," of not submitting to superiors, which I have repeatedly presented as the characteristic of mass man, reaches its limit precisely in these partially qualified men. They symbolize and in large part constitute the present-day dominion of the masses, and its barbarity is the most immediate cause of European demoralization.

On the other hand, they provide the clearest and most precise example of how the civilization of the last century, abandoned to its own inclination, has produced this young shoot of primitivism and barbarity.[3]

Would that we could have the reflections of Ortega y Gasset on all that has happened in recent years. Would he interpret the events that have accompanied growing prosperity in most parts of the world as providing even more evidence for his thesis that mass man, in follow-ing his inclinations, will make a mess of things and produce what would be regarded as a lower quality of life, judged on the basis of an adequate philosophy? We might remind ourselves of a few of the changes that have occurred. There is a drug problem of dimensions that surely has no precedent in the history of the world. Crime rates

---

[3] I quote these passages especially for those specialists and experts who feel they have something of great value to offer the world.

have increased greatly in this and other countries. Of course, there is
the possibility that some of the increase is attributable to factors that
would be regarded as special, in the sense that their effects will dis-
appear with time, but whether this is so or not, there can be no question whatsoever that the sense of personal security, in this country,
at least, has sunk to levels all of us would have thought impossible
only ten or twenty years ago. The traditional goal of the university,
although still the motivation of many faculty members and students,
has been substantially subverted, and this in such a way as to hinder
the pursuit of the truth even by those who are dedicated to doing so.

The possibility of attaining consensus through governmental process seems to have been abandoned by considerable numbers of the population. If the ruling consensus is not to your liking, throw a temper
tantrum. Break some windows on Broadway, sack the Dean's office,
threaten physical violence—in short, confront whatever authority happens to be involved with the threat that you will tear his house down
or worse if he doesn't do things the way you want. If someone has the
temerity to point out that this is mindless behavior, he may be re-
assured by learning that this destruction is highly moral, since it is
designed to change and improve a corrupt society. But even the vision
of the better society and *how* to attain it are absent. Somehow, in some
unexplained way, in a way not even explicated in the ideal terms of a
vision, a good society is supposed to rise out of the rubble of destruction.

Other changes would disquiet an Ortega y Gasset as much. As one
who is convinced that men are not insects, so bound by their genetic
inheritance that they cannot learn anything, I take it for granted that
we are influenced by our experiences, though not in a simple way.
In the past, members of our society acquired their view of the world
through a certain variety of experiences, in part absorbed from their
parents, sometimes explicitly but more often from the implications of
their behavior, in part from schools, and from all of their activities
from day to day. In many respects, the view was at odds with reality,
but at least in some spheres of life there was a substantial contact
with reality, and the views were tested and proved by immediate
experience. Now a striking change is introduced. The child, and many
adults, too, are exposed to a new source of information, television.
Here he encounters a different set of influences. What sort of view of
the world is implied in the ads that he listens to and watches on TV?
How does he form his view on what is normal and what is rare
behavior from the run-of-the-mill TV drama? Is violence really so
commonplace? Has sex always occupied so important a place in life?

Mind you, nobody is really trying to subvert the young or even the adults. The script writers are only pandering to what they regard as the tastes and wants of the viewers, to which Ortega y Gasset would no doubt say, "I told you so." And perhaps he did, for all I know, since he didn't die until 1955. He may have spared himself the opportunity to see TV, however.

In short, the question is whether economic progress together with popular government [4] is viable—with either much or little emphasis on free enterprise—or whether there are just too many who can't stand prosperity, too many who don't take advantage of the opportunities that a high level of income gives for living a life of quality.

Although this view, as suggested by the essay of Ortega y Gasset, does not necessarily envision an inevitable decline in the quality of life as coming mainly through successive blows to the quality of the environment, this possibility could easily be accommodated to the argument.

### A More Optimistic View

Perhaps the view that the very nature of mass man will lead him to misuse increasing affluence, thus lowering the quality of life either with or without an accompanying decline in the quality of the environment, is wrong. There really is no objective way to tell, since we don't yet have a historical record to study in which a number of popularly governed societies have tried to maintain their equilibrium in circumstances of increasing affluence. Many people are sure of the answer or are hopeful, of course. Some say they have faith in democracy, and, allowing for a loose use of words, their faith may turn out to be justified. Still, even if failure does not come because of an inherent tendency to misuse rising incomes, rising materials consumption associated with increasing GNP could lead to a deterioration in the quality of life simply because we do not recognize and handle soon enough the associated environmental deterioration. This possible failure to diagnose symptoms and take appropriate remedial action is likely to be a characteristic of both popular and nonpopular governments, since it has its roots in circumstances shared by both.

There are important differences between the Ortega y Gasset model and the one we are about to examine with respect to diagnosis of the ailment and the remedy, however. With the former, you have your choice between an *a priori* diagnosis, based on judgments about history and the nature of man, or waiting until the evidence begins rolling in

---

[4] In the sense of government that is responsive to the "people."

and it becomes apparent that the quality of life is deteriorating because increasing prosperity is being misused. Although I don't see how
a popularly governed society could ever bring itself to make the
*a priori* diagnosis (assuming the thesis is true), it is worth asking what
kind of preventive action would be appropriate.

The diagnosis points to the prescription. Assuming that the nature
of mass man (the fundamental source of the difficulty) is not to be
changed, the thing to do would seem to be to avoid too much prosperity, whether this takes the form of increasingly higher levels of
consumption in the ordinary sense or increasing leisure. The society
should accordingly take care to avoid too much consumption (in general) or too much technological progress—in short, a thoroughgoing
no-growth policy in order to prevent the worst in human nature from
rising to the top. Perhaps a few specific types of consumption could
be increased without harm (health measures?), but not very many.
It is rather difficult to envision society adopting such a policy in order
to save itself from itself, so to speak.

In contrast, let us suppose that the fundamental difficulties lie on
the environmental side and in our possible inability to cope with these
difficulties soon enough. Now the focus is on specific pollutants and
narrower problems. We might envision a progression of difficulties that
would be associated with rising consumption over time if remedial
action is not taken. Initially, the difficulties might be localized—for
example, water pollution below the town of Brunswick, Maryland—
or connected with specific substances whose emission could be controlled rather easily. The cases would accumulate, with more restrictions of one sort or the other, their precise nature depending on how
good we are at devising and executing policies. As restrictions accumulate, the rate of increase in consumption would be slowed down,
perhaps even reaching zero. This could result, for example, from the
need to restrict use of energy because of highly adverse environmental
effects, although even a rigid ceiling on the use of energy need not
result in a cessation of growth in consumption, since technological
progress would continue to be possible within this restriction. Indeed,
we should say not only that it would be possible, but that it would
be likely, for energy has been so cheap, in our country at least, that
we have given very little thought to how we might get along with less.

Along with the increasing number of conflicts arising from the clash
between the desire for higher levels of production (whether this would
arise from higher per capita levels of consumption or partly from this
and growth of population) and the associated pollutants in the ordinary sense, we very likely would begin to experience two other threats
to the quality of life. One of these is the destruction of natural beauty

caused by the proliferation of man-made things into places valued highly by many persons precisely because of their natural state. This process has been going on a long time in this country, including damming and silting of beautiful streams, construction of speedways in national parks, "facilities" of various sorts, etc. The other is an increasing sense of congestion, a problem that probably is mainly urban, but that appears in many other specific locations and on highways because of the greater amount of movement involved in our pattern of life.

The threat to the quality of life arising from these two sources—destruction of natural beauty and congestion—is of the same nature as the threat involving pollutants in the usual sense. While we may not be incapable by nature of living a high-quality life with high-level consumption, we may be unable to cope soon enough with the problems that increasing levels of consumption and production bring. In part, our difficulties are those of reaching consensus. This seems especially true in the case of natural beauty. There is a diversity of tastes here in a fundamental, not a trivial, sense. "Mere taste" is not what is involved, but taste in the important sense, a distinction made by Frank Knight many years ago. Sometimes the diversity seems at once so constrained and so intense as to justify the word *polarization*. Whatever the appropriate description, we are experiencing great difficulty in agreeing on a course of action that seems obviously desirable— why not try to satisfy the whole spectrum of demands? Why not develop some sites but leave others undeveloped, with the proportion in each category reflecting at least roughly the distribution of preferences (present and future) and their intensities? In the case of ordinary goods this is done rather automatically and satisfactorily by the market. In most industries there are businessmen who are eager and alert to respond to the smallest pocket of specialized demand, and they do so for a very good reason: it is possible to make money in this way. In the case of natural beauty, however, there are many cases where decisions cannot be organized by the market; the difficulties standing in the way of forming one are insurmountable. The unfortunate fact is that our political procedures today are such that they do not yield results that resemble closely those provided by the market system in ordinary commerce.

The various types of problems that can be brought under the rubric of congestion are more complex than those involving destruction of natural beauty, and desirable and even possible solutions are not very apparent. One has but to consider the many ways in which congestion or some facet thereof makes itself evident in urban areas to experience a fear that here may be something beyond our capability to solve.

Aside from destruction of natural beauty and congestion, which are somewhat indirectly connected with the level of material consumption and production, there are a number of pollution problems in the more ordinary sense with which we may have our difficulties. Time does not permit us to say very much about them, but we might indicate what some of them are, limiting the list to those problems which appear to be most difficult. True, many pollution problems really do appear to be "ordinary" pollution problems, in the sense that we probably shall be able to cope with them, although not necessarily in the most efficient manner. Some water and air pollution problems seem to fall into this category. This is not to say that the present situation with respect to them is satisfactory—far from it—but that it seems likely that they will be containable without a regeneration of the human spirit or even without fundamental changes in governmental machinery.

A number of the really tough problems—not now but perhaps at some time in the not too distant future—seem to center on energy consumption in one way or another. In the period in which fossil fuels continue to be used, there are a number of potentially very serious problems. Perhaps the easiest is that of power-plant siting, labeled "easiest" here, not because the current worries are misplaced, but simply because it does not present the same order of difficulty as those which we are about to note. Power-plant siting is very similar to the problem of deteriorating sources of raw materials; it is simply a matter of increasing cost and of adapting ourselves to the changed circumstances. These costs are presently expressed in the market, and we are in the habit of adapting to them, usually without any lasting scars. The problems associated with power-plant siting are by definition rather local or regional in nature. If these difficulties should mount to the point where total consumption of electrical energy levels off, we shall have arrived at this point in the most painless way, to wit, by a gradually increasing economy in the use of energy induced by higher cost to the consumer, be he an industry or an individual householder.

Other aspects of the energy future may be less tractable. The consumption of fossil fuels inevitably involves additions to atmospheric carbon dioxide, and there is a possibility that the result may be a fundamental change in climate. There is not yet evidence that such change is occurring, perhaps because of offsetting factors, but the increase of carbon dioxide emissions and its addition to the composition of the atmosphere are proceeding inexorably.

Once the era of fossil fuel consumption recedes into the background, as it will in the near or distant future, depending on your horizon, widespread production of power by atomic fission will bring very serious problems of handling and disposing of radioactive substances, including plutonium, a dangerously poisonous substance, very difficult to contain, and the essential ingredient for making an atomic bomb. It is easy to envision tremendous difficulties arising from the insistence that breeder reactors be provided for all countries even if their societies are not able to handle safely the dangerous substances that will be involved. Safety in this context has many facets, ranging from the technical problems of controlling emissions and transportation of dangerous substances to keeping plutonium out of the hands of criminals, be they inside or outside governments.

The "ultimate" problem that increasing energy consumption may bring is simply the amount of heat added to the earth. To the extent that we tap heat sources already involved in determining the heat balance of the earth, that is, sunlight and geothermal heat, no change in overall heat balance is produced. However, energy consumption is already large enough to affect local and regional heat balances, and it is quite possible that the total will grow to the point where the heat balance of the whole earth will be affected.

Apart from energy, pollution of the oceans and lakes to the point where their ecosystems are seriously altered is a distinct possibility. These bodies of water become the repositories of a wide variety of substances, some of them, such as petroleum and lube oil, introduced in very large quantities, and others of great significance simply because one molecule in the right place can be very damaging.

These diverse potential problems have several characteristics in common. First, their effects may be cataclysmic. Second, the whole earth may be affected. Third, the sources of emissions are numerous and are located in different countries, which makes agreeing on and administering a control system much more difficult than when pollution problems are regional in nature.

If we could see with clarity how rapidly these problems are going to develop and what state the world will be in when and if they do, rational control very likely would entail that we, meaning all the countries on the earth, formulate the general outlines of a control scheme *now* and probably begin to take certain definite actions—certain lines of research if nothing else—now or in the near future. Therein lies the rub, however. Many will say, why should we begin to take remedial action on the mere speculation that something serious may develop? We have more pressing concerns now.

Right or wrong, this view will carry the day. There will be no general organized restriction of consumption until the need is clear even to the most obtuse. Consumption conceivably would decrease spontaneously if in all parts of the world the human spirit underwent regeneration of a fundamental sort. Indeed, this has been advocated by many distinguished prophets over several thousands of years, but these most earnest remonstrations have resulted in just about nothing. Of course, things may be different this time, in that failure to re-generate our spirits may be the prelude to catastrophe on a scale never even dreamed of before. All the same, regeneration is not likely to take place on any large scale. Consequently, it appears that we shall be reduced to restricting the use of this or that substance as it becomes very clear that the penalties entailed are really greater than we wish to bear. We should remember that it really is possible to change the relation between consumption and pollutants produced.

From one point of view, case by case restriction of pollution emis-sion is a quite sensible way to proceed, provided one condition is met, namely, that we do not overshoot the mark in too many cases. By overshooting the mark I mean continuing to use the harmful sub-stance so long and to such an extent that it has in the meantime pro-duced irreversible ill effects in natural bodies or systems of great value to us, either esthetically or in mundane production activities.

If this is the route we have to follow, it should be followed sensibly. One aspect of sensible regulation is to regulate the troublemaker and not something else. If it is air pollution from power plants that is causing the trouble, don't restrict energy consumption but restrict or penalize emissions of the polluting substances, for it may be possible to reduce them and still continue to produce and use electric power. Of course, the task of cutting down the polluting emissions may be so costly that a drop in power consumption would result, but that would merely reflect a rational balancing of the demand for power against the difficulty of reducing emission of the pollutant.

To proceed step by step as the need appears is to place very heavy reliance on monitoring and measurement, and this brings us back to the question posed initially. To what extent can the effect of changes in materials consumption on the quality of life be measured? Of course, there can be no possibility of doing this in any way even re-motely analogous to our measurement of gross national product. This derives from the very nature of the concept, quality of life. As we saw, even to determine the direction of the effect of a change in "material" prosperity on the quality of life requires that we be able to determine the nature of the philosophy held by the people involved and to specify its relation with materials consumption. While many of us no doubt have quite positive ideas about these matters, the situation always is ambiguous and conducive to different and even contradic-tory diagnoses.

The indirect effects of changes in materials consumption on the quality of the environment and on humans themselves, possible avenues through which the quality of life may be affected, are quite another matter, however. Indeed, we have just observed that careful measurement or monitoring is indispensable. Until now, we have really had no monitoring *system* in this or other countries except for certain aspects of water quality and other cases where systematic records of some relevant variable have been maintained over a period of years, often for reasons that had nothing to do with monitoring. The result is that we are genuinely hard put to say whether certain aspects of the environment have deteriorated or not.

Some things are reasonably clear. Although we lack really systematic records of relevant quantities, various aspects of congestion seem to have worsened in many places over the last few decades. For example, I contrast recent trips with my first trips, made some time ago, to the Rocky Mountains west or to northern Minnesota and feel like weeping at the changes. Change of the same magnitude has occurred in many cities, although here the problem is obviously more complex than mere congestion.

The last report of the Council on Environmental Quality [5] gives a picture of the inadequacies in our monitoring systems and also indicates something about what has happened to certain types of pollutants over the last few years, apart from congestion. There is some indication that urban air quality has improved, although the picture is quite mixed, depending on the city and the pollutant. Air pollution is still very severe in a number of cities, however. In fact, it is appalling. If you should want convincing on this score, go some morning to one of the high office buildings in lower Manhattan and look up the island from, say, the fiftieth floor. One can only wonder what aberration could induce all those people to spend so much time in that noxious blanket, the contents of which insinuate itself into the deepest parts of the body, including the brain itself.

Air pollution in nonurban areas appears to have increased, in some cases in a very serious and dramatic way, as with the increased haze in the Four Corners area resulting from burning coal to produce electricity. The clear blue skies of southern Colorado and northern New Mexico could be destroyed.

On the other hand, our dietary intake of a number of pesticides appears to be declining somewhat.

BOD (biochemical oxygen demand) material discharged to water

---

[5] See *Environmental Quality*, the second annual report of the Council on Environmental Quality, August 1971 (Washington, D.C.: U.S. Government Printing Office).

bodies has remained roughly constant in recent years, according to the Environmental Protection Agency, but other types of water pollutants have increased, including nutrients (leading to accelerated eutrophication), sediment, toxic materials of incredible variety, and dissolved inorganic salts from irrigation.

We need to systematize our monitoring system. We already have the beginnings of adequate technique and practice for measuring air and water pollution. Indeed, measurement of water pollution is quite well advanced for those locations where measurement has been thought to be important. The most serious gap is in systematic measurement and compilation of records on the biologic front, both human and non-human. For amounts of money small compared with what we squander ineffectually on all sorts of worthy and unworthy causes, we could keep track of what is happening to ecosystems in many specific locations and learn much more about the effects of environmental deterioration on humans.

## Summary

We have traveled quite a distance in our examination of the relation between materials consumption and the quality of life, starting out with the grand idea of the quality of life and ending up with the monitoring of worms and lesser critters. The main points made can be recapitulated as follows:

(1) There is no necessary connection between the level of materials consumption and the quality of life once a certain rather low level of consumption has been passed.

(2) In some circumstances an increase in materials consumption (and income) can bring about an increase in the quality of life, but whether it does or not depends on the "philosophy of life" held by the members of the society, the consonance of the pattern of life with the basic inherited nature of its members, and consequent "external" effects not comprised in the consumer's budget.

(3) We examined in some detail two specific routes by which an increase in materials consumption might lead to a decrease in the quality of life. The first is the view that mass man in a setting of modern technology and popular government (that is, government that is responsive to the wishes of the populace) will inevitably foul his own nest. That is to say, he is inherently incapable of appreciating the complexity of modern society and what it could do for him. He is incapable of taking advantage of the opportunities presented to him.

In the second case, even if the above view is wrong, we could get into serious difficulty simply because of inability to cope in time with the problems that accompany rising levels of materials consumption. A particularly dangerous point is deterioration in the quality of the environment.

In contrast, the market system should enable us to adapt in a rational way to increasing difficulty in acquiring materials or producing energy that expresses itself through rising costs and prices.

(4) If we are to succeed in coping with the difficulties that may arise, we shall have to do two things: (a) monitor very carefully what is happening to us and to the quality of the environment; and (b) restrict the use of the substance(s) causing trouble.

(5) While growth in production and consumption will have to, and will, cease at some point, there is little likelihood of obtaining the consensus necessary for the imposition of *general* restrictions on production and consumption. Nor is cessation of growth in production and consumption to be expected through a fundamental reformation of the human spirit.

# CAN INCREASING DEMANDS
# ON RESOURCES BE MET?

Clearly demands on resources are going to be satisfied to some extent, depending on the costs involved. These costs can be controlled to a degree by shifting consumption and production processes toward or away from goods and services that draw heavily on natural resources. Even though such adjustments are desirable, it is by no means clear that they can be made.

One class of costs involved is that reflected in the prices of what we might call resource products, such as metals, energy, and food. As the higher-quality resources from which these products come are used up or deteriorate in quality, costs may rise unless we are so fortunate as to have a practically inexhaustible source of the commodity waiting in the wings at constant cost or to be saved by cost-reducing innovations.

The other class of costs involved in satisfying increasing demands on resources is not now reflected, by and large, in the prices of the products ultimately responsible for them. These costs are those occasioned by the side effects of consumption and production activities on other persons or firms. The originator of the ill effect ordinarily does not have to bear its cost. Such costs are produced by the many types of pollution.

A paper presented at The University of Virginia Earth Week Lectures, Charlottesville, Virginia, April 23, 1970.

The possibility of increases in both these types of costs has been recognized by at least a few persons for a long time. For example, the possibility of a large rise in the cost of producing coal, with the exhaustion of all deposits worth anything at all, was examined as long ago as 1906 by Stanley Jevons, a famous British economist, in a volume called *The Coal Question*.[1] He was premature in his concern by a few hundred years, as it turned out.

The possibility of large increases in unintended ill effects flowing from our demands on the services of natural resources was examined in a very comprehensive and competent manner at least as long ago as 1864, when George Perkins Marsh's book, *Man and Nature*, was first published.[2] This study still merits the attention of persons interested in these matters.

Around the turn of the century, both these strands of thought were brought together in a somewhat confused way by what has come to be known as the Conservation Movement. Associated with this movement are such names as W J McGee,[3] Theodore Roosevelt, and Gifford Pinchot.

In spite of the understanding of man's actual and potential effects on nature exhibited by these and other persons, and in spite of the large and obvious changes man had already brought about—denuding Greece and other areas of the world; extending deserts for hundreds of miles in some countries, for example, in Chile; and hastening the extinction or near-extinction of a number of species, including passenger pigeons, the American buffalo, the blue whale, and the dodo bird—most people have viewed these cases as exceptions. Generally speaking, man's activities have been regarded as having no significant and permanent transforming effects on nature, and his drafts on resources regarded as insignificant relative to the quantities available. In particular, streams, the atmosphere, and the oceans have been looked on as having a practically inexhaustible capacity to absorb whatever substances were put into them.

This view has been in the process of changing over a considerable period of time. We have come to realize that production and consumption activities on their present scale are not part of a steady-state system, if we view the whole of the physical environment as part of the system, and that these activities are not of so little importance relative to the physical environment that changes in the state of

---

[1] *The Coal Question: An Inquiry Concerning the Progress of the Nation and the Probable Exhaustion of Our Coal Mines* (New York: Macmillan, 1906).

[2] Again published in 1965 by the Belknap Press of the Harvard University Press.

[3] He used no periods after the letters; W J *was* the name.

natural resources can be neglected for all practical purposes. The report of the President's Materials Policy Commission in 1952, popularly known as the Paley Report, marked this understanding for mineral resources. For this report the questions were: Are we running out of mineral resources? Are the costs of minerals rising? What can be done about it? That is to say, we finally recognized officially that mining activities may be so large relative to the resources available that rising costs may be incurred as time goes on. Since that time, local concentrations of various effluents have risen in many places to the point where people are both annoyed and concerned. In addition, there is a growing realization that some other by-products of man's activities may be the instruments of large-scale disaster for humanity.

Rising costs for materials appear to be the less pressing problem. The rapidity and impact of possible cost increases will be tempered in several ways. First, as it becomes necessary to mine lower-grade materials, larger quantities are available, at least for a number of materials. Second, as any particular material becomes more costly, the rate of its price rise through time is tempered by the tendency for its consumers increasingly to use substitute materials. In some cases, the substitute materials exist in very large quantities that can be produced without incurring increasing costs. Third, as the price of a material rises, it becomes increasingly profitable to recycle it, thus reducing the draft on primary sources. Fourth, technological progress reduces the costs of producing natural resource materials as well as other products.

In any case, even if the costs of some materials rise substantially relative to other prices, the change will come quite slowly. We have a very efficient instrument that enables us to adapt to such situations with comparative ease, namely, the market system. Our technology has advanced to the point where we can visualize the possibility of living satisfying lives even if some commonly used materials should become very expensive. I do not mean to say that there is no economic problem as we usually think of it, but that advanced countries have the institutions to cope with radical changes in the relative prices of resource products, always on the condition, of course, that population growth does not get out of hand. Our principal problem of policy in this area, apart from the matter of population, is to organize things so that the market system can work out the socially desirable result, something that we understand reasonably well, although accomplishing it obviously offers some difficulties.

The costs to which the above remarks apply are those within the ken of those producing and consuming the materials. In contrast, the substances currently causing apprehension are doing so precisely because once emitted from a production or consumption activity they are no longer the direct concern of the economic unit producing them. Who worries about *his* contribution to atmospheric carbon dioxide when he runs his automobile? Who worries about the possible effect of *his* insect spray on oxygen-forming activities in the ocean? Or the effect of *his* sewage on downstream water users?

It is useful to think of these real effects one economic unit has on others as being of two different kinds as far as so-called environmental problems are concerned. In the first class are the effects of effluents whose *total* quantities may possibly alter or stop important biological processes or have other important destructive effects. Included here are the persistent pesticides that do not break down into harmless constituents very rapidly. They present possible threats to photosynthetic activity in the oceans, to the systems of soil bacteria and other creatures, to wildlife, and possibly to humans. DDT is the best-known example to date. Another member of the group is simply atmospheric dust arising from a variety of activities, but having actual and potential effects on climate and photosynthetic activity. Additions to atmospheric carbon dioxide from the burning of fossil fuels is another member of this group; a sufficient increase might produce possibly disastrous changes in climate.

Since Alamogordo, radioactive substances have been added to the atmosphere. They will continue to be added, at rates not yet determined, as we produce more energy from atomic power plants and process the radioactive wastes from these plants and also from any other large-scale uses of atomic energy, such as excavation. Whatever the precise effects of various quantities of radiation may be for humans and other living organisms, it is certain that disastrous quantities and associated effects are possible.

Finally, it appears that crude oil spills must be added to the list. Some of these are deliberate violations of existing regulations and conventions by unprincipled shipping firms, but tanker wrecks and leaks are occurring with sufficient regularity to suggest that they will continue to be related in a rather stable way to the number of crude oil ton-miles accounted for by tankers. The concern here is with possible effects on the great oceanic systems of life.

In the above cases—and perhaps others should be added to the list—we are concerned with the totals emitted and with the total quantities in existence because there is a dispersion mechanism that operates on a large scale, a scale that may involve large parts of the whole globe. Dispersion may not be complete, but the problem remains one of concentrations over quite large areas. In the case of DDT, the combination of oceanic and atmospheric diffusion processes has resulted in universal distribution, with concentrations of surprising uniformity in view of the high localization of initial applications.

To say that a substance is of concern because of its general concentration is not to say that it is harmless if found locally in high concentration. Each of the things listed is also harmful if locally concentrated, with the exception of carbon dioxide. In addition, however, business and household activities produce a wide variety of substances that are toxic, harmful to health in other ways, or just disagreeable because of local concentrations, although global concentrations are not of significance. The list of possible candidates for this group is a very long one, and would include such things as the conflict between mining activity in certain locations and the preservation of areas valued for their untouched appearance, highways and their undesirable effects, the operations of fossil fuel plants, and noise. In the case of both radiation and other effluents the discharge may be to watercourses, lakes, bays, or the atmosphere. That is to say, put enough of these substances into the water or the air and you will have water or air pollution.

Physically, reduction of undesirable effects associated with an emission will involve one of the following: (1) reduction in the activity producing the emission; (2) capturing the emission—probably in the plant if manufacturing is in question—and processing it to whatever extent is necessary either to use the materials again, to yield harmless emissions, or to permit their transport to a safe place of storage; or (3) use of another process or other materials that will perform the same functions but do not involve the production of noxious emissions. No one of these physical options is superior to the others in all cases. Which should be adopted in a particular case depends on the nature and seriousness of the effects and the costs associated with each. In short, some ways of dealing with effluents are more efficient, in a comprehensive sense, than others. An important but easily neglected element in assessing these efficiencies is the cost of setting up and operating the political and administrative system required.

To get a more concrete idea of the different methods of control available, consider a simple form of pollution that is obnoxious to some people, namely, empty beer cans at the side of the road. The first thing to observe is that the degree of concern over these beer cans, lying around in the millions by now, varies from no concern whatsoever for many, perhaps most, people to intense revulsion for some. But let us assume that some kind of governmental action is to be undertaken, it being obviously impossible to get all beer drinkers to stop tossing their cans out of car windows without some sort of incentive. What can be done? One option is to prohibit the drinking of beer. There is empirical evidence on the viability of this measure. Another is to prohibit the use of cans or bottles for beer, which comes close to prohibition. Or we might tax beer heavily enough to reduce its consumption considerably but not completely.

If we say that there is no harm in drinking beer, however, we will have to deal with the cans at the roadside. Prohibiting the tossing of the beer can might conceivably work if enough policemen were provided, but some will note that we haven't even been willing to provide enough police to reduce murders, robberies, and other crime to what many of us would regard as acceptable levels. Another option would be to put a tax on aluminum beer cans, thereby encouraging a switch to bottles, which are as permanent as aluminum cans. One could impose a large tax on all beer containers that do not decompose rapidly in the roadside environment, thereby stimulating efforts to design containers that will permit avoidance of the tax. Still another scheme, much discussed in connection with both beer cans and automobiles, would be to levy a tax on beer cans and use the proceeds to pay those willing to collect and bring empty beer cans to designated collection stations.

The difficulty with the use of prohibition and detailed direct regulation is that a far more efficient solution may be available but impossible to put into effect because of the rigid course of action dictated by the direct regulation. I think we can say that the most efficient way of handling an emission is likely to be some way of imposing the costs of the emission on the unit producing it. This unit and its customers, provided with a strong incentive to use a substitute product or process in order to reduce or eliminate the tax, will incidentally reduce or eliminate the emission in a way that reflects a proper balancing of all of the costs involved in the problem, including the costs incurred by switching to the substitute product or process. There are circumstances, however, in which it would be very difficult to set up a system of emission charges. In some cases the costs of the alternative courses may be such that outright prohibition or some form of direct regulation is in fact the most efficient way of handling the situation.

The fact that various mechanisms for controlling emissions can be described provides no indication or assurance that adoption of any one of them is likely or even possible. Similarly, the fact that some persons may think that certain emissions must be brought to certain specified levels in the very near future is but one element in the total situation that will determine whether such control is instituted or not. The attainment of control necessarily involves various social and political processes whose operation may raise serious obstacles.

One of the most serious obstacles to control of substances whose

potentially undesirable effects are associated with locally high concentrations is simply our poor understanding of their effects, amount-
ing in many cases to ignorance. Many deleterious effects, both on
"natural" organisms and processes and on man himself, may take a
long time to develop. The researcher faces three unattractive options.
(1) He can use high rates of exposure on animals or on the system
under study. If undesirable effects are observed, he will leave his clients
pretty much in the dark as to the probability of similar effects under
a regime of smaller rates of exposure of humans or of the system
for long periods of time. (2) He can experiment with low rates of
exposure over long periods of time, thus delaying urgently needed
results and increasing the cost of experiment greatly. (3) He can
resort to statistical analysis of past data, if available. This is quite
feasible and useful in some cases, but difficult or useless in others
because of the multiplicity of possible variables affecting outcome and
because of high co-variation among possible causative agents. These
difficulties are multiplied by the fact that the number of potentially
deleterious substances to which we are exposed, both in articles consumed and in emissions, is increasing at such a rapid rate that there
is little hope of detecting a high percentage of the truly dangerous.

In the face of these circumstances we confront the possibility that
some of the substances we consume, voluntarily in products and in-
voluntarily in emissions, in fact are to be viewed as time bombs of a
very special type. Even if discovered, they cannot be removed and
rendered harmless. The periods between first exposure, awareness of
ill effects, and control of the substance vary widely. In the case of
thalidomide, thanks to a fortunate perception of possible danger by
Dr. Frances Kelsey, these two periods together were only about three
years in the United States. Unfortunately about eight years passed
between the first use and withdrawal for use on pregnant women in
all countries, at the cost of about 6,000 cases of congenital malforma-
tions. In the case of cigarettes, all the returns are not yet in, but we
have seen enough already to warrant the conclusion—in my judgment,
at least—that they constitute a terrible scourge not perceived by very
many persons for almost half a century, by which time it was too late
even for those willing to stop smoking.

On a more comprehensive scale, we might ponder the significance
of a reported approximate constancy in life expectancy at age 65 in
the United States over the period from 1960 to 1966. The death rate
for males in the United States aged 55–64 years has remained con-

stant from 1958 to 1967. For those 65–74 years of age it has risen by 3.5 percent.[4]

Suppose, however, that the ill effects of an emission or activity are well demonstrated and that this is widely understood. At this point, a frequent obstacle to control is the tendency by the interested parties to view control as an all-or-none affair. For example, mining activity in or near wild areas is obnoxious to the users of those areas. The prospect of obtaining a viable solution to this problem is considerably diminished if one side opposes mining activity every time it rears its head on the public lands or if the other side claims that mining activity is justified wherever an exploitable deposit is found.

The general difficulty exhibited in this and other disputes is the inability to conceive and understand how somewhat more subtle solutions might work. Some feel, for example, that charges on effluents to streams might turn out to be simply a license to pollute, but if any use is to be made of the assimilative capacity of some streams, and this can hardly be escaped, we need to understand that outright prohibitions or uniform discharge standards are very likely to make far less efficient use of this assimilative capacity than a reasonably good system of effluent charges. Of course, if the alternative to uniform discharge standards is no control at all, the standards certainly would be preferable in some cases.

The obstacles to control of widely dispersed emissions are similar in nature, but more significant because of the vastly more destructive potentialities. For example, although locally concentrated substances may sometimes constitute a time-bomb menace to health, the production of *additional* ill effects ordinarily can be eliminated in a comparatively short time and the situation restored, with the partial exception of genetic effects. The widely dispersed substances also may constitute a time-bomb menace, but it may be impossible to restore the original situation, even with the most rigid control, once the ill effects have been perceived. That is, in the former case individuals are harmed, but they can be replaced. In the case of wide dispersion, some basic functions of a large ecosystem may be impaired. For this reason, it becomes very important not to go beyond the point of no return. When a process is completely understood, it is comparatively easy to avoid doing this. If it is not well understood, even the most careful monitoring of some variables known to be involved in the

---

[4] See, for example, U.S. Department of Health, Education, and Welfare, *Toward a Social Report* (Washington, D.C.: U.S. Government Printing Office, 1969), p. 4, and *Vital Statistics, 1967* (Washington, D.C.: U.S. Government Printing Office, 1969), pp. 1–4.

problem may be of little use in keeping us on this side of no return from disaster. What good does it do to monitor very carefully a highly accurate gauge if the meaning of the gauge reading is not understood? I am afraid that this characterizes some of the problems that beset us; otherwise we should witness a higher degree of consensus among the various technical experts on just where we are.

Let us suppose, however, that the technical experts substantially agree that we face what might be called an "ultimate crunch" situation, in which prompt and highly disruptive remedial action is required on a large scale to avoid disaster. Such a situation could arise, for example, with certain pesticides. It might become necessary to reduce the consumption of fossil fuels, perhaps to zero. It might be necessary to reduce dust-producing activities, including the burning of fossil fuels. Or, if you want to contemplate the truly ultimate crunch, some being more ultimate than others, imagine that it is necessary to reduce the consumption of fuels producing carbon dioxide to zero *and* that atomic power production must be kept at a small percentage of present consumption to keep radioactivity of substances in the atmosphere at an acceptable level because of inability to capture and store safely a large enough fraction of the radioactive wastes.

When one thinks of the difficulty of convincing the population at large of the necessity of control that would disrupt the accustomed way of life on a scale never before seen, the prospect of success is not bright. There would be no experience to point to, no similar necessity having arisen in the past. Of course, the situation perhaps would not be much worse because of this. After all, we have had plenty of experience with the San Andreas fault and with the fact that rivers do in fact flood on known floodplains, all of which has not prevented a great deal of construction practically astride the fault and directly on the floodplains of the country.

It is easy to imagine the clamor that would arise. Opposition experts would spring up. Reassuring voices would label the first group of experts as alarmists. Some unknown fraction of the population would not be concerned enough about the welfare of future generations to see their own lives disrupted, even though they clearly perceived the danger. At best a period of years would be required to develop the consensus necessary to take drastic measures, and it might not be attainable, a situation that calls for speculation in still other directions.

The fact that the people of the world are separated into nations, some of whose cultures have much in common but many of which are very different, adds still another complication. The question would be, who is going to reduce his consumption of energy and by how much? It would be pointed out, correctly, that a handful of countries—called advanced—bear the main responsibility for the situation. If some margin remained, they would be asked to make the more radical adjustment in their consumption of energy. If no margin remained, who would be best able to make the transition to a solar energy economy? Would any nation still have the will to help another?

It is not at all clear, of course, that these terrible situations will ever develop, for the true dimensions of our problem have not yet been traced out. We need to monitor the potentially dangerous situations very carefully and to make great efforts to improve our understanding of their physical and biological aspects.

In addition, appropriate action requires that the best understanding of the problems be widely shared. It may be that many people really don't care very much about reducing pollutants and their undesirable effects and are not inclined to worry about possible dangers to future generations. Certainly the first step, however, is to make sure that such attitudes do not reflect an incorrect understanding of the situation. It therefore does seem appropriate that a day be set aside for considering these problems. I, for one, hope that we shall continue to do this in the years to come.

# SELECTION 19

# "NATURAL" AREAS

### (*with* ALLEN V. KNEESE)

The problems of natural areas, including wilderness, and seashores share certain similarities, chief among which is the fact that in each case private enterprise may not be the best suited to meet the wide variety of demands for the services these areas can provide.

Some of the demands for the services of natural areas can be quite well satisfied by private enterprise, however. Private campgrounds, fishing camps, hunting camps, and resorts have been with us for a long time, and so have private beaches. In addition, many of the demands for the services of natural areas are satisfied by state governments and the federal government through the provision of campgrounds, state parks, and similar areas. The costs of providing these services, incidentally, are covered to a considerable extent by fees levied upon the users, even though the management of the property is in the hands of a governmental unit. Another step in this direction was made early in 1965, with the federal government's sale of $7 automobile stickers, entitling purchasers to enter any federal recreation area during the period of a year. The funds raised by this means will contribute to a Land and Water Conservation Fund set up to preserve and acquire land for recreational use.

Beyond the comparatively simple popular demands on natural

Excerpt reprinted from Orris C. Herfindahl and Allen V. Kneese, "Some Problems Associated with the Use of Rural Areas," *Quality of the Environment: An Economic Approach to Some Problems in Using Land, Water, and Air* (Washington, D.C.: Resources for the Future, Inc., 1965), chapter 6, pp. 74–79.

areas, such as providing a campground or a spot by a stream or lake for a picnic, there is another which presents a different and more difficult problem. This is the demand for large and, to varying degrees, uncrowded pieces of country where a person can "stretch his spirit." In this country, unlike some others, the real or implied "No Trespassing" signs that surround every piece of private property constitute a very real barrier to the wanderer who desires the freedom to walk over and to feel that he is a part of a larger area that extends beyond where he happens to be at the moment. Yet there are some who would be willing to pay substantial sums of money for the privilege of walking over lands that give the impression of being limitless.

Is it possible for the private market to satisfy these demands? Judging by experience in the eastern part of the United States, it is not. In the West the problem has not yet arisen because there are still large tracts in the hands of the federal government to which people with this particular taste can go. If their quality of sheer size should be destroyed—perhaps by the intrusion of highways or other accouterments of civilization—it is not likely that private enterprise would be able to assemble comparably large areas to which nature lovers would have access.

The problem of preserving large wild areas for the enjoyment of the few who demand and use them is a difficult one. It is true that only a small percentage of the population uses such areas in any one year. This use may be, however, a once or a few in a lifetime experience for many people. They may be willing to pay an annual fee for the preservation of these opportunities even if they see them and directly experience them infrequently or perhaps not at all. There is nothing strange about this, for many solicitations for funds use the mails and use them successfully even though the donors of the funds never see directly the things for which the funds are spent. Wild areas are not necessarily in a different category. The destruction of wilderness imposes an external diseconomy on such people whether they ever see the area or not. But it is very difficult to discover how extensive is this demand without the active participation of such individuals in a market.

It is true that, compared with other highly developed countries, the United States has a tremendous total acreage in wild land. On the other hand, if one looks at those areas which were designated as "wilderness tracts" in 1960 by the Outdoor Recreation Resources Review Commission, it is obvious that few are in tracts that could be regarded as large by most standards. Table 21 shows this rather clearly. The first column lists class intervals in terms of acreage; no area of less than 100,000 acres is included. The second column converts each area into an equivalent square. Thus, the first class interval

TABLE 21. *Frequency of Wilderness Areas by Size*

| Thousands of acres | Approximate equivalent square (*miles on a side*) | Frequency |
|---|---|---|
| 100– | 12 | 23 |
| 200– | 18 | 15 |
| 300– | 22 | 7 |
| 400– | 25 | 6 |
| 500– | 28 | 2 |
| 700– | 33 | 5 |
| 1,000– | 40 | 1 |
| 1,500– | 48 | 4 |
| 2,000– | 56 | 1 |
| 2,500– | 62 | 0 |
| | | 64 |

*Source:* Tabulated from Outdoor Recreation Resources Review Commission, *Wilderness and Recreation: A Report on Resources, Values, and Problems,* ORRRC Study Report 3 (Washington, D.C.: U.S. Government Printing Office, 1962).

is made up of those wilderness areas with a total number of acres of 100,000 up to 200,000. An area of 100,000 acres is equal to that of a square with a side of 12.5 miles, a square that would be rather confining to that minority of the population which enjoys extensive hiking.

The areas presently classified as "wilderness" often are of outstanding natural beauty and attractiveness. There is, accordingly, a persistent pressure to develop access to them. Obviously, it is impossible to satisfy this demand for very long—essentially a demand to have the comfort of civilization away from crowds and yet to be on the edge of or in a wild area—for as demand is satisfied, the remaining wild area is steadily reduced. In the United States, "development" and the provision of access have seemed to be almost inexorable up to this point. It seems inevitable, therefore, that the problem of preserving wilderness areas and areas of natural beauty will become more acute as time goes on.

A problem analogous to that of wilderness is presented by shorelines. Less than 2 percent of the total ocean shorelines of the contiguous states is in public ownership for recreation. It is true that access is possible on a considerable part of the privately owned shorelines and that there is a well-developed market for beach activities; but there is a component of demand for undeveloped shoreline similar to that for wilderness, and this is not at all likely to be satisfied by the offerings of private enterprise.

The demand for wilderness areas and for long, untouched shorelines is a demand to be free from the external diseconomies of development. If these demands are to be satisfied under public auspices, an estimate of their strength must be made to set against the sacrifice of revenues the areas could earn if they were used in other ways. If in some manner it was discovered that the devotees of wild areas and untouched shoreline were willing to pay a sum of money at least this large, total real national product would be increased by leaving the areas wild and untouched. But even if ways could be found to organize the payment of such a sum, the further question would arise as to whether the payment should, in fact, be exacted.

It is important to note that there may be not only one but two relevant tests of what a natural area is worth to these people. On the one hand, the question can be posed as it has been above: How much money would these people *be willing to pay* in order to secure the services of this type of area? On the other hand, the question could be asked in this way: How much would these people *have to be paid*, in the event the services of the area were taken from them, in order to make them feel that they were as well off as they were before its loss? If, in such circumstances, the services of the area constituted a large part of their real income, it is quite likely that the amount of money these people would have to be paid would be larger than the sum they would be willing to pay in order to secure the services of the area.

To take an extreme case, consider a person who has only a subsistence income, but who is able to enjoy the services of a wilderness area or a park. If payment for the services were required of such a person, he could pay very little if anything. If, on the other hand, he were to be deprived of the services of the area and be compensated fully—i.e., to the extent that he would regard himself as well off as he was before—the compensation required might well be larger than his actual money income.

The second compensation test frequently seems relevant in condemnation proceedings. When people are ousted from places to which they have become deeply attached, any money compensation that may be made is never commensurate with the distress caused them by the forced move. In such cases an external cost is imposed on these people and real income is simply destroyed.

It is important to realize that these valuation problems may be present with many kinds of external benefits, whether they come from wilderness areas, city parks, birdlife, beaches, national parks, or beautiful urban environments. To some people the psychic satisfaction they derive from these areas forms a significant part of their real incomes. If we hope to move toward optimum environmental quality it is necessary to learn much more about these problems. Needless to say, it would be extremely difficult to obtain honest estimates of the amount of damages involved in our second compensation test. Accordingly, compensation in condemnation proceedings tends to hew pretty much to market value.

As we look over the varied kinds of demands and external effects that have been discussed in connection with the rural environment, one feature stands out as common to all of them: They all involve preferences which are far from uniform among the population, far less than are those for good health, for example. In this respect they are similar to certain aspects of the demand for urban environmental quality.

In thinking about the severity of these problems, about the direction in which they are likely to develop, and about the means we might use to deal with them, it is essential to bear in mind that a wide spectrum of demands is involved. The demand for natural areas runs the gamut from wilderness areas and national parks to spots for picnics or places where one can walk for a few minutes in the evening. The goal of private and public action should be to satisfy all of these demands so as to get the largest excess of benefit over costs. This goal cannot be achieved or even approached if only that type of service is provided which is demanded by most of the customers. This makes no more sense—and as bad sense—as supplying houses in one design regardless of variations in taste. Unfortunately, there seems to be a tendency for governmental agencies to cater to the most numerous group in their particular constituency and to neglect the demands of others. This tendency needs to be resisted, as indeed it is by good administrators.

*Appendixes*

# APPENDIX A

# *ASSIGNMENTS AND ACTIVITIES*

1957    Consultant with the Committee for Economic Development on problems in defining the federal budget.

1960    Visiting professor, summer session, University of Colorado.

1963    At the request of the Planning Commission of the Government of India, spent two months with the Resources and Scientific Research Division of the Commission as consultant in the formulation of a program of studies on the mineral resources of India. Submitted his observations in a report, "Mineral Studies and the Fourth Plan." The report detailed data regarded as essential to long-term analysis and suggestions for analysis of data to be collected.

1965    Member of the President's Task Force on Natural Resources.

1970–72  In Paracas, Peru, in collaboration with the Oficina Nacional de Evaluación de Recursos Naturales, conducted seminar on the development and use of information about Latin American natural resources. Consulted with ONERN officials about Peruvian resource problems and with members of the Instituto de Investigación de Recursos Naturales. Continued to serve as chairman, economics study group, National Academy of Sciences Committee for International Environmental Programs, studying environmental aspects of materials policy at the request of the National Commission on Materials Policy. Served on National Academy of of Sciences panel on geography and human and cultural

291

resources, a part of the Committee on Remote Sensing Programs for Earth Resource Surveys. Served on ad hoc advisory panel of Board on Science and Technology for International Development, Office of Foreign Secretary of National Academy of Sciences. With Allen V. Kneese and Charles Cicchetti, taught seminar on natural resource economics during winter term, University of Michigan School of Natural Resources. Served in advisory capacity at meeting of National Materials Advisory Board to consider status of specialty metals industries.

# APPENDIX B

# *BACKPACKING CHECKLIST*[1]

| X = Indispensable | s = summer |
|---|---|
| V = Luxury or as indicated | w = autumn or spring |
| * = Other option | a = winter |

| Item | Weight (oz.) | 1 day | 2 to 3 days | Long hike |
|---|---|---|---|---|
| *Clothing* | | | | |
| Stocking cap | 3 | Xw | Xw | Xw |
| Gaiters | 3 | Vw | Vw | Vw |
| Dacron pants | 10 | Vw | Vw | Vw |
| Dacron jacket | 18 | Vsa* | Vsa* | Vsa* |
| | | Xw* | Xw* | Xw* |
| Down sweater | 23 | Vsa* | Vsa* | Vsa* |
| | | Xw* | Xw* | Xw* |
| Down parka | 41 | Xw* | Xw* | Xw* |
| Net underwear: | | | | |
| Shirt | 8 | Xaw* | Xaw* | Xaw* |
| Pants | 8 | Xaw* | Xaw* | Xaw* |
| Heavy underwear | | Xw* | Xw* | Xw* |
| Down booties | 6 | | Vw | Vw |
| Down mitts | 4 | Xw* | Xw* | Xw* |
| Choppers | 11 | Xw* | Xw* | Xw* |
| Lined one-finger mitts | 6 | Xw* | Xw* | Xw* |
| Unlined leather gloves | 6 | Xw* | Va | Va |
| Wind parka ⎫ Wind pants ⎭ | 40 | Vw | Vw | Vw |
| Rag socks | 4.5 | Vs* | Vs* | Vs* |
| | | Xaw | Xaw | Xaw |

[1] Intended as a master list including everything one might need or wish to take on a hike or camping trip.

| Item | Weight (oz.) | 1 day | 2 to 3 days | Long hike |
|---|---|---|---|---|
| Thin socks | 1.5 | X | X | X |
| Belt | 3 | X | X | X |
| Sweater | 25 | Vsa* | Vsa* | Vsa* |
| Pants | 13 | X | X | X |
| Cotton-dacron shirt | 12 | X | X | X |
| Undershorts | 4 | X | X | X |
| Rain parka | 7 | V* | V* | V* |
| Rain chaps | 13 | V* | V* | V* |
| Small hiking boots | 44 | X* | X* | X* |
| Large hiking boots | 65 | X* | X* | X* |
| Waterproof boots | 72 | Xw* | Xw* | Xw* |
| Cap or hat (summer) | | Vsa | Vsa | Vsa |
| Skivvy shirt | 4 | Vaw | Va | Va |
| *Shelter and sleeping* | | | | |
| 2-man tent and poles | | | | |
| (5 lbs., 8 oz.) | 88 | | X* | X* |
| 3-man tent and poles | | | | |
| (7 lbs., 10 oz.) | 122 | | X* | X* |
| Ultimate tent and poles | | | | |
| (with liner) | | | | |
| (11 lbs., 8 oz.) | 184 | | Xw | Xw |
| Sleeping bag | 64 | | X | X |
| Stakes (long): | | | X* | X* |
| 10 orange plastic | 12 | | | |
| 10 Sears, Roebuck | | | | |
| aluminum | 7.5 | | | |
| 10 thin long wire | 5 | | | |
| 10 smaller cast | | | | |
| aluminum | 17 | | | |
| 10 larger cast | | | | |
| aluminum | 23 | | | |
| Ensolite: | | | | |
| ½-inch | 25 | | Xw | Xw |
| ¼-inch | 12 | | Xa | Xa |
| Plastic groundcloth | | | | |
| Lean-to (Whelan) | According to specifications | | | |
| *Cooking and fire* | | | | |
| Saw | 12 | | V | V |
| Axe | 49 | | | |
| Sterno (small can) | 5 | VaXw | X | X |
| Match case | 1 | X | X | X |
| Kerosene stove (empty) | 31 | Vaw | V | V |
| Primus stove (empty) | 22 | | | |
| Alcohol stove and stand | 9 | | | |
| Folding oven | 13 | | V | V |
| Stove platform | | | | |
| Flasks (empty): | | | | |
| Pint | 4 | | | |
| Quart | 6 | | | |
| Grate | 5 | Vw | V | V |
| Canteen (empty) | 9 | V | V | V |
| Water (quart) | 33 | V | V | V |
| Plastic water carrier | 4 | | V | V |

| Item | Weight (oz.) | 1 day | 2 to 3 days | Long hike |
|---|---|---|---|---|
| Pots: | | Vaw | X | X |
|   1 pot | 9 | | | |
|   2 pots | 12 | | | |
|   3 pots | 17 | | | |
|   4 pots | 19 | | | |
| Frying pan and sack | 9 | Vaw | X | X |
| Metal plate (Boy Scout) | 2.5 | | X | X |
| Plastic plate | | | | |
| Knife, fork, spoon: | | Vw | X | X |
|   Plastic | 1 | | | |
|   Metal | 3 | | | |
| Can opener | 4 | Vaw | V | V |
| Large spoon | 2 | Vaw | X | X |
| Corkscrew | 2 | V | | |
| Small pancake turner | 2 | | X | X |
| Small pliers | 2 | Vaw | X | X |
| Plastic cup (nesting) | 1 | Vw | X | X |
| Dishwashing stuff | 6 | | X | X |
| Bear rope and pulley | 6 | | V | V |
| Coffee maker and filters | 4 | Vaw | X | X |
| Coffee | | Vaw | X | X |
| Cocoa and tea | | Vaw | X | X |
| Shortening | | Vw | V | X |
| Salt and pepper | | Vw | X | X |
| Sugar | | Vw | X | X |
| Fuel: | | Vaw | V | V |
|   Kerosene (8.1 oz./000 Btu) | | | | |
|     quart | 27 | | | |
|     pint | 14 | | | |
|   Gasoline (7.8 oz./000 Btu) | | | | |
|     quart | 25 | | | |
|     pint | 12 | | | |
|   Alcohol (13.8 oz./000 Btu) | | | | |
|     quart | 26 | | | |
|     pint | 13 | | | |
| | | | | |
| *Miscellaneous* | | | | |
| First aid kit: | | X | X | X |
|   In plastic bag | 18 | | | |
|   In rubberized bag | 21 | | | |
|     lip salve | sunburn preventative | | | |
|     bandages | Off (insect repellent) | | | |
|     bandana | burn ointment | | | |
|     Band-Aids | Desenex | | | |
|     tape | aspirin | | | |
|     scissors | vitamins | | | |
|     Nivea | miti-mites (Lomotil) | | | |
| Candle and lantern | 5 | | V | |
| Flashlight (2-cell) with batteries | 7 | V* | X* | X* |
| Midget flashlight (1-cell) with batteries | 1.5 | V* | X* | X* |
| Extra batteries | | | | |
| Dark glasses | 3 | V | V | V |

| Item | Weight (oz.) | 1 day | 2 to 3 days | Long hike |
|---|---|---|---|---|
| Ordinary glasses | 3 | V | V | V |
| Wristwatch | 2 | V | V | V |
| Notebook and pencil | 1 | V | V | V |
| Toothbrush, dental tape, and small soap | 3 | | X | X |
| Toothpaste | 5 | | X | X |
| Towel (face) | 3 | | Xw | Xw |
| Wash and Dri's | | | | |
| Toilet paper (full roll) | 6 | V | X | X |
| Battery shaver and batteries | 9 | | V* | V* |
| Razor, blades, shaving cream, and container | 9 | | V* | V* |
| Parachute cord | 4 | | X | X |
| Shoe laces | | | V | V |
| Sewing kit | 2 | | X | X |
| Campfire permit | | | V | V |
| Shoe wax | | | | X |
| Swiss army knife | 4 | X | X | X |
| Hunting knife | 4 | V | V | V |
| Thermometer | 2 | V | V | V |
| Pedometer | 2 | V | V | V |
| Whistle | | X | X | X |
| Wind gauge | 1 | V | V | V |
| Compass | 3 | V | V | V |
| Packframe, rain cover, straps | 57 | V | X | X |
| Knapsack | 29 | V | | |
| Mosquito net | | V | V | V |
| Skis and poles | | V | V | V |
| Ski wax | | | | |
| Snowshoes | | | | |
| Snowshoe repair items | | | | |
| Talc (for boots) | | | | |
| *Photographic equipment* | | V | V | V |
| 35mm camera | 41 | | | |
| 8mm movie camera | 74 | | | |
| Lens case, including: | | | | |
| 2 lenses, sunshades, tubes, lens cleaner and tissue | 67 | | | |
| Film: | | | | |
| 35mm | | | | |
| 8mm | | | | |
| Tripod | 57 | | | |
| Flashgun and bracket | 9 | | | |
| Flashbulbs | | | | |
| Exposure meter | 8 | | | |

# APPENDIX C

## ACROSS THE BARRENS BY CANOE

In midafternoon of July 15, 1964, an Otter with two canoes tied to its pontoons circled in to land on Sifton Lake, 260 miles east and a little north of Yellowknife. This marked the beginning of a four-week trip by canoe down the Hanbury and Thelon Rivers ending at Baker Lake Post, about 500 canoe miles further east.

We were a party of four. Each of us will readily confess that he had dreamed for years of making such a trip. Three of us, Irving K. Fox, David B. Brooks and myself are employees of Resources for the Future, Inc., a non-profit organization located in Washington, D.C., which engages in and sponsors research in the social sciences on natural resource problems. The fourth member of the party was my son, Henry, a 13-year-old who, by that time, had already had an extensive experience in wilderness backpacking and river canoeing.

We had a number of reasons for taking this trip. After all, the Barrens are natural and they are a resource, thus providing ample reason for persons interested in the development or preservation of natural resources to take a look at them. We were especially interested in seeing a part of the Thelon game preserve, one of the largest and most interesting in the world, to gain some first-hand feeling for the problems involved in preserving its unusual and beautiful forms of life.

Reprinted by permission of Information Canada from *North/Nord* (September–October 1965).

We began packing food and equipment about two weeks before leaving Washington. The first leg of the trip was a seven-day auto journey of 3,800 miles from Washington, D.C., to Yellowknife. We spent a day in Yellowknife rounding up the last of our food supplies, getting our canoes, which we rented from the Hudson's Bay Company (we did not have to worry about returning the canoes from Baker Lake Post), and getting the last of our various permits.

## THE RIVER

After checking packs and equipment against the checklist, we waved goodbye to our pilot, loaded our canoes, and started down the Hanbury River, beginning about 95 miles above its junction with the Thelon, which comes up to meet it from the south. The elevation at the starting point is about 1,200 feet and at the junction about 530 feet. An average fall of 7 feet per mile is sufficient to produce fairly numerous rapids, so it was on this part of the trip where most of the portaging took place, but some of the rapids can be run even with open (undecked) loaded canoes.

Running an unknown river is an art of some difficulty. First, there are paddling techniques to be mastered, for river canoeing skills are more demanding than those required to push a canoe through a lake. Second, a great deal of experience is required to learn how to negotiate rapids and to learn the ins and outs of how water behaves when flowing over and through rocks. Extensive experience is necessary to develop one's judgment to the point where he can decide reliably whether he and his partner can negotiate a rapid.

If one has the requisite skills and experience, then he is ready to go down the river. The rules for survival are very simple: Never get committed in a rapid (that is, don't go beyond a place where you are able to stop) unless you know what is ahead and know that you can recover boat, gear, and yourself if you dump. On the Hanbury River there are numerous places where violation of this rule will produce a quick death. These are the places where one portages. In places, we paddled part or all of some rapids that earlier parties had portaged. In other places, we portaged where others had paddled. Neither maps nor advice can be trusted—although they are helpful. One must look at things with his own eyes and apply the basic survival rule with great care, for the water is very cold and competent medical help for severe injuries is simply not available.

We had about 7 miles of portaging on the Hanbury. Most of these were short—around a quarter or a half mile—but one, around Dickson Canyon, in which the water falls over 200 feet within a mile or so, was about 2½ miles over big hills, through boggy ground, and finally through some trees and brush.

Although every bend in the river brought a new vista, the daily routine was much the same over the whole trip. When we rose at about 6 A.M., the sun had already been up for hours, since we were just a few degrees below the Arctic Circle. We would light the fire, using driftwood or Arctic willow, and get the coffee going. But once we passed the point on Aberdeen Lake where the Dubawnt River comes in from the south with a load of flotsam driftwood, there is *no wood* available. So for the last half of the trip, we loaded our canoes with so much firewood that toward the end of the trip we left a couple of small wood piles. Their discovery by the Baker Lake Eskimos will probably cause considerable puzzlement.

Those not preparing breakfast would strike the tents (bugproof—a must), pack the equipment, and start loading the canoes.

We would start paddling about one-and-a-half to two hours after arising. In midmorning we would stop for a short rest and get out of the canoes to walk around. This was especially welcome since we all kneel while paddling to increase efficiency and to lower our center of gravity. Our rear ends would rest against the rear seat or, in the case of the bowman, against the front thwart since we had removed the front seats because they are too low for kneeling all day in comfort.

Noon lunch was always served cold to save time. Midafternoon brought another rest. Then along about 6 o'clock, we would start looking for a good campsite. Ten to 11 hours after starting out in the morning we would stop. Then one or two men would start on the dinner—right away! The rest would unload the canoes, erect the tents, and get out the sleeping gear. After paddling hard all day, fatigue and the sudden cessation of work would leave us rather chilled, so much so that on some days we welcomed a down parka.

I believe that each one of us fully expected to encounter black flies and mosquitoes in numbers that would be almost unbearable. Actually, we suffered hardly at all from bites. Perhaps a third of the time the bugs were so bad at mealtime that we would have to eat in the tents. Even so, we probably consumed many of the critters in our stew and potatoes. All in all, though, the bugs were only mildly annoying. Modern insect repellent is quite effective against mosquitoes, and a head net, which we wore a third of the time, is even more effective.

Sometimes we would vary our daily routine. We were wind-bound about three days. And on a couple of occasions we started paddling at 3:30 A.M. to try to get across exposed water before the wind came up. Beverly, Aberdeen, and Schultz Lake are so big that one must be very careful not to be out on them when the wind comes up. It was our practice to skirt the shore. Toward the end of the trip we were running a little short of time, and this with a plane scheduled to leave Baker Lake Post only once a week. On several days we would stop to cook dinner about 4:30 P.M. and then resume paddling until it was almost dark—say until 9 or 10 P.M. A little more time would have been most welcome.

All this no doubt sounds like a great deal of hard work, perhaps rather boring. Hard work it was, but never boring. It is a memorable experience to be in the midst of the Barrens several hundred miles from civilization and to know that your return depends on your own effort rather than on an airplane. But the best memories of all are of what we saw and heard. On the Hanbury are beautiful rapids where the river has cut its way deep into the rock. Eskers stretch across the countryside in defiance of the present drainage pattern, sometimes cut by today's river.

Birds take possession of the Barrens in the summertime. Canada geese are present in very large numbers and leave their calling card on every shore. Around July they are moulting and can fly only a few feet, but their honkers are as good as ever, and there was a great deal of noise and energy spent in trying to entice the two canoes away from the goslings. There are a few whistler swans, also likely to be moulting. Pintails whiz by, quacking their way to new speed records. Herring gulls and Arctic terns are resting at this time and see in us a threat that has to be frightened off by long bombing runs by the gulls (Score: one hit.) and dive bombing attacks by the terns. The most wonderful sounds of all are the screams of the peregrine falcon. They come to meet you upstream of the nest and keep circling with a constant barrage of piercing screams until you are far enough downstream for the nest to be safe once again. Occasionally a ptarmigan and its chicks may be seen, all in summer dress rather than the white of winter.

The number of mammals seen is far smaller. One has occasional glimpses of little critters that appear to be members of the weasel family. The siksik (Arctic gopher or ground squirrel) is plentiful and is not shy at all as he scurries about stripping grass seeds for his food supply.

The real thrills in the Barrens are provided by the large mammals. We were not lucky enough to see any grizzlies or wolves, although there were tracks. But muskox are attracted by the good feeding to be had near the river, especially along that part of the Thelon where the trees are thinning out to nothing. Solitary caribou are a frequent sight and always give a lot of thought to the problem of what to do about *that thing* floating toward them in the water.

One evening as we were returning from portaging our canoes around Dickson Canyon, we looked across the river to see a group of some 70 or 80 caribou wheeling down the side of a large hill that sloped down to the river, first going in one direction and then turning the column in another direction. This group joined another larger group that was feeding on the bottomland along the river. Somebody gave the signal, and away they went, climbing up to the top of the canyon opposite us. In single file, the group of 200 cantered past us at a very rapid pace, with the calves doing very nicely. All the running the caribou do seems to be rather aimless, but the ability to cover large distances quickly perhaps has a great survival value, for it greatly increases their chances of finding good feed. At the end of the trip we were told we had missed a herd estimated at 150,000 by only a week. Perhaps we shall be lucky enough to see this sight on the next trip.

On the last half of the trip there are three large lakes to be traversed —Beverly, Aberdeen (the largest), and Schultz. Aberdeen is bordered by magnificent white beaches stretching for miles. One day when the wind was too strong to paddle against without exhausting ourselves we "tracked" the canoes (that is, pulled them on 100 foot lines, bow and stern) for about 8 miles until the wind went down a little. Incidentally, you can "line down" some rapids which, for one reason or another, cannot be paddled. When you "line down," each of the two men has a line from bow and stern respectively, and you walk along the shore or wade, sometimes with the canoe going well out into the river to avoid rocks. A great deal of work and time is saved if the canoe and the gear do not have to be portaged.

At one point on Aberdeen Lake we were windbound for almost two days. In the morning of the second day we were visited by an Eskimo from a summer camp a few miles away. I had the names of Eskimos we might meet at this camp. I read down the list until we were rewarded by a wide grin when I came to "Oovayoo." He neither spoke nor understood English except for payoff words such as rifle, canoe, Arctic fox, caribou, and the like. He had mastered a very clear "Thank you," however.

Oovayoo tried very hard to tell me something, pointing at my map and sweeping on toward Baker Lake. Since he kept pointing at the various rapids indicated on the map, I concluded he was offering his services as a guide, which was a service we definitely did not want. We invited him to stay for lunch, after which he left.

Late that afternoon the wind went down. We loaded up and began paddling. On coming to the Eskimo camp, all the women and kids came down to see us. We gave the kids some candy and the ladies some tobacco and cigarette papers. Then one of them handed some slips of paper with names to Henry. Obviously they were messages to be taken to Baker Lake—a request Oovayoo had tried to get across without success. I hope that if someone reads this who knows Oovayoo he will tell him how sorry I am that I didn't understand his request.

The last 50 miles of the trip were full of action. First came a vigorous rapid, one which I believe can be run safely. Tyrell's description (see bibliography) of the difficulties here seem to me to be badly mixed up. Perhaps the water was much higher when he came along. Be that as it may, we portaged it, making camp a little way downstream. The next and last day we made about 45 miles, thanks to very fast water, even though we spent a whole hour examining the rather long rapid on a big, left-curving bend near the mouth of the river. Notes from earlier parties indicated there wasn't much to this rapid, but the comparatively low water we had turned it into something very interesting indeed. The waves in the middle of a big river are always three or four times higher than they seem to be from the shore. In this case, the wave lengths were long enough to permit the canoe to ride up and down—all the time moving like an express train—while we struggled to avoid the more violent portions of the river. No—I believe we did not violate the basic rule for survival, for the river was shallow at the bottom of the rapid and provided a good place to recover. A spill would have been bitterly cold, however, for the water was about 44°F. Needless to say, we wore life jackets.

There are a few points about equipment that might be helpful to others who do this or similar trips. First, a 17- or 18-foot aluminum canoe is very serviceable and stays at 75 or 85 pounds respectively: that is, aluminum does not absorb water. Second, we pre-packaged the food for each meal, using a cycle of menus. We relied heavily on frozen dried foods for meat and vegetables. My calculations were based on 4,000 calories a day for a 155-pound man and protein standards were more than met. Caloric intake was boosted by using comparatively large amounts of vegetable shortening in potatoes, stews, etc., and eating lots of nuts. Our food weighed only 1⅔ pounds per man per day (average weight per man was 140 pounds), which is something of a record so far as I know. Yet we all felt the food was delicious. One rat in the party gained four pounds. The youngest gained slightly, and the two oldsters lost only small amounts—to their disappointment.

All food that couldn't stand immersion was packed in large waterproof bags. These bags are heavy, about 12 pounds each, but they do pretty well guarantee that you will be eating, no matter what. On portages we carried these bags and all the other gear on Kelty packframes, which are very rugged and have a belly strap which enables the wearer to transfer 30 to 40 pounds of his load directly to the pelvic girdle, with the shoulders having to bear only the remainder of the load. We used these same packframes to carry the canoes. The middle thwart rested on large hooks (made of $5/16$ inch wire rod) strapped to the frame. This is far superior to the usual yoke if the canoe has to be carried an appreciable distance.

The final point on equipment is to have plenty of warm clothing. Personally, I'm in favour of down parkas even in the summer. Not only do they feel good at the end of a day—open, of course—but in the event of immersion or illness they would be very valuable.

The total weight of the party was about 1,300 pounds, including 150 pounds for canoes, 560 pounds for bodies, 250 pounds of food, and the remaining 440 pounds for containers, canoeing gear, rifle, photographic equipment, clothing, shelter, and a host of other items. By making various compromises with safety, for example, by using less reliable containers for food, weight could have been cut somewhat—perhaps by as much as 50 pounds, but we preferred to have the extra insurance. Our weight was not at the point where a 50-pound saving would have shortened portage time appreciably, nor would it have made any noticeable difference in our paddling speed.

In talking with people about this trip it has been interesting to observe the keen interest in how many times we turned over, how serious the injuries were, or whether we ran out of food—as if such experiences are to be expected on a canoe trip of this sort. This is a dangerous attitude for anyone who goes on a trip like this, for it means that the person does not know how these and other "adventures" can be avoided. We hold with Stefansson, who once said, ". . . an adventure is a sign of incompetence." [1] In his zeal to make the point clearly, it may have been formulated a little too forcefully, but by and large it is certainly correct—for the person who wants to live to take another trip.

Some adventures—meaning by this a situation dangerous to life from which you have extricated yourself only with much difficulty—are truly unavoidable. Certain medical emergencies are of this sort, and there are a few other things that can happen to you from which there is no escape. On some occasions death simply cannot be resisted. Apart from these unusual cases, however, there is no need to have dangerous adventures.

Being interested in wilderness travel by primitive means, I have paid close attention for a number of years to the accounts of parties that have found themselves in serious difficulty. The sources of their

---

[1] *My Life With the Eskimo* (New York: Collier Books, 1962), p. 49.

troubles are many and varied—inability to pace the party so as to prevent fatigue, insufficient physical stamina, inadequacies of equipment, bad judgments made under the pressures of time or weather, and so on. It is especially impressive to observe how inadequacies of preparation tend to be linked to each other in a cumulative fashion. The final cause of disaster often cannot be traced clearly to any specific lack. Instead, a whole series of little inadequacies seem often to exert more and more pressure until, finally, a disastrous decision is made or a rash action taken which could easily have been avoided.

Careful preparation is clearly in order—including scheduling, physical conditioning, and planning of food and equipment. But the best way to insure adequate preparation is not to go too far beyond one's past experience. A step-by-step development of one's capabilities and experience will practically insure that each day is sheer pleasure. With adequate preparation, the Barrens are a friendly place in the summer. We are already looking forward to the next trip.

*Part of the dreaming involves reading, and there is quite a literature that relates more or less closely to the particular route we took. The earliest item is the journal of the remarkable Samuel Hearne, the first white man to go overland from Hudson Bay to the Arctic Ocean at Coppermine. Other items include David T. Hanbury's* Sport and Travel in the Northland of Canada; *the accounts of the Tyrell brothers; accounts about John Hornby who, together with two companions, starved to death in 1927 at a beautifully wooded place on the Thelon River now called Hornby Point; Ernest Thompson Seton's* Arctic Prairies; *some of Vilhjalmur Stefansson's books; and some of Farley Mowatt's writing about the general area and its problems.*

# BIBLIOGRAPHY

## BOOKS

1 *Copper Costs and Prices: 1870–1957*. Baltimore: The Johns Hopkins Press for Resources for the Future, Inc., 1959. Excerpts reprinted in this volume.

2 *Three Studies in Minerals Economics*. Washington, D.C.: Resources for the Future, Inc., 1961. Excerpt reprinted in this volume.

3 (With Allen V. Kneese) *Quality of the Environment: An Economic Approach to Some Problems in Using Land, Water, and Air.* Washington, D.C.: Resources for the Future, Inc., 1965; third printing 1969. Excerpt reprinted in this volume.

4 (With Edward Ackerman and David Bramhall) *Provincia de Magallanes: Recursos naturales y desarrollo industrial* [Province of Magallanes: Natural Resources and Industrial Development]. Santiago, Chile: Fundación Ford, Programa de Asesoria en Desarrollo Urbano y Regional en Chile, 1968.

5 *Natural Resource Information for Economic Development*. Baltimore: The Johns Hopkins Press for Resources for the Future, Inc., 1969. Excerpts reprinted in this volume.

6 *Los recursos naturales en el desarrollo económico*. Santiago, Chile: Textos del Instituto Latinoamericano de Planificación, 1970.

7 (With Allen V. Kneese) *An Introduction to the Economic Theory of Resources and Environment*. Columbus: Charles E. Merrill Publishing Co., 1974. Excerpt reprinted in this volume.

8 *Resource Economics: Selected Works of Orris C. Herfindahl,* ed. David B. Brooks. Washington, D.C.: Resources for the Future, Inc., 1974.

305

### PUBLISHED PAPERS

9    "Some Fundamentals of Mineral Economics." *Land Economics* (May 1955). Reprinted in this volume.

10   "Effects of Stabilization Meaures on Economic Growth." *Atlanta Economic Review* 6 (March 1956).

11   Book Review: *Capital and Output Trends in Mining Industries, 1870–1948,* Occasional Paper 45, by Israel Borenstein (New York: National Bureau of Economic Research, 1954). *American Statistical Association Journal* (March 1957). Reprinted in this volume.

12   "Tax Policy for Stability and Growth." *American Economic Review, Papers and Proceedings* (May 1957).

13   "What Is Conservation?" Lecture delivered at Colorado School of Mines, August 12, 1960. Resources for the Future Reprint 30 (1961). Also published in *Three Studies in Minerals Economics*. Reprinted in this volume.

14   "Why the Conflict: A General View." *Mining Engineering* (July 1961).

15   "Mineral Import and Stabilization Policies." Paper presented at the American Institute of Mining and Metallurgical Engineers Meeting, Society of Mining Engineers Minerals Economics Program, New York, February 19, 1962. Resources for the Future Reprint 36 (1962).

16   "Goals and Standards of Performance for the Conservation of Minerals." *Colorado School of Mines Quarterly,* Vol. 57, No. 4 (1962). Reprinted in *Natural Resources Journal* (May 1963). Excerpt reprinted in this volume.

17   (With Irving Fox) "Attainment of Efficiency in Satisfying Demands for Water Resources." *American Economic Review* (May 1964). Resources for the Future Reprint 46.

18   "Development of the Major Metal Mining Industries in the United States, 1839–1909." In *Output, Employment, and Productivity in the United States after 1800.* Studies in Income and Wealth No. 30. New York: National Bureau of Economic Research, 1966. Reprinted in this volume (without appendixes).

19   "Depletion and Economic Theory." In Mason Gaffney, ed., *Extractive Resources and Taxation.* Madison: The University of Wisconsin Press, 1967. Reprinted in this volume.

20   Book Review: *Investment and the Return to Equity Capital in*

*the South African Gold Mining Industry, 1887–1965,* by S. Herbert Frankel. *American Economic Review* (December 1968).

21  "The Value of Mineral Surveys to Economic Development." In *Proceedings of the Council of Economics,* Annual Meeting, 1969. New York: American Institute of Mining, Metallurgical, and Petroleum Engineers, 1969. Reprinted in this volume.

22  "Is Resource Economics Unorthodox?" *Journal of Soil and Water Conservation* (January–February 1969). Reprinted in this volume.

23  "Problems of Governments in the Provision of Information for Materials Supply." In *An Interamerican Approach for the Seventies: Materials Technology—1.* New York: United Engineering Center of the American Society of Mechanical Engineers for the Southwest Research Institute, 1970.

24  "Algunos problemas en el uso de los inventarios de recursos naturales por países en vías de desarrollo." In N. Bernardes, ed., *Segunda mesa redonda sobre recursos naturales.* Rio de Janeiro: Comisión de Geografía, Instituto Panamericano de Geografía e Historía, 1972.

25  (With Allen V. Kneese) "Measuring Social and Economic Change: Benefits and Costs of Environmental Pollution." In *Proceedings,* Conference on the Measurement of Economic and Social Performance, Princeton, N.J., November 1971. New York: National Bureau of Economic Research, forthcoming.

26  "Some Problems in the Exploitation of Manganese Nodules." In Lewis M. Alexander, ed., *The Law of the Sea: Needs and Interests of Developing Countries.* Proceedings of the Seventh Annual Conference of the Law of the Sea Institute, University of Rhode Island, Kingston, Rhode Island, June 26–29, 1972. University of Rhode Island, February 1973.

UNPUBLISHED PAPERS AND REPORTS

27  "Concentration in the Steel Industry." Ph.D. dissertation, Columbia University, 1950.

28  "The Development of the Copper Industry: A Brief Account." 15th New England Regional Conference of the American Institute of Mining and Metallurgical Engineers on the Basic Metals Industry, Schenectady, New York, May 18, 1961.

29  "Some Ideas on Economic Theory for Natural Resources." George Washington University lectures, 1962.

30  "Mineral Studies and the Fourth Plan." Report prepared for the Planning Commission of the Government of India, May 27, 1963.

31  "Some Notes on the Problem of Providing Information for the Development of Natural Resources." Requested by Programme of Natural Resources, United Nations, Santiago, Chile, September 25, 1965.

32  "La información sobre los recursos naturales y su importancia para el desarrollo económico." Instituto Latinoamericano de Planificación Económica y Social, Santiago, Chile, December 1966.

33  "Priorities in Investment in Natural Resource Information." Presented to the United Nations Science and Technology Committee, May 4, 1967.

34  "Stockpiling and the Defense Materials System." Lecture at the Industrial College of the Armed Forces, November 1968.

35  "The Implications of Alaskan Oil." Prepared for the President's Task Force on Natural Resources, January 1969.

36  "The Long-Term Outlook for Copper and Nickel." Prepared for the annual meeting of the Minnesota section of the American Institute of Mining and Metallurgical Engineers and the 30th University of Minnesota Mining Symposium, Duluth, January 14, 1969.

37  "Problems in the Use of Resource Inventories by Underdeveloped and Small Countries." Mid Atlantic Division of the Association of American Geographers of the National Academy of Sciences annual meeting, January 25, 1969.

38  "Identification and Study of Policy Problems in the Minerals Industries." Presented to the House Republican Task Force on Earth Resources and Population, May 22, 1969. Excerpt printed in this volume.

39  "Some Comments on the Regional Studies of IREN." Prepared for Instituto de Investigación de Recursos Naturales (Santiago) and Oficina National de Evaluation de Recursos Naturales (Lima), 1970.

40  "Can Increasing Demands on Resources Be Met?" University of Virginia Earth Week Lectures, Charlottesville, Virginia, April 23, 1970. Printed in this volume.

41  "Economic Considerations in Assessing the Role of Remote Sensing in Country Development." U.S. Agency of International Development–sponsored symposium on Utility of Remote Sensing

as an Aid to Developing Countries, Smithsonian Institution, Washington, D.C., November 19–20, 1970. Printed in this volume.

42 "Defining the Problem of Environmental Quality." Centennial Conference on Quality of the Environment, Ohio State University, Columbus, Ohio, November 16–18, 1970.

43 "Notes on Transfer of Natural Resource Information among Countries." Prepared for the National Academy of Sciences Panel on Science and Technology Information for Developing Nations, March 30, 1971.

44 "Trade-offs for a Better Environment." Remarks before the Governor's Conference on Economic Development and the Environment, University of Maryland, October 28, 1971.

45 "Expropriation, Confiscation, or Neither?" and "The NEP (New Economic Program) and Trade in Natural Resource Commodities." Memoranda prepared for the State Department Conference on the Impact of Economic Nationalism on Key Mineral Resource Industries (Foreign Service Institute series on Science and Technology in Foreign Affairs), November 1971.

46 "Effects of Resource Depletion and Economic Growth on the Quality of Life." Prepared for Conference on Scarcity and Growth: Toward a National Materials Policy, sponsored by the University of Minnesota and the National Commission on Materials Policy, Minneapolis, June 22–24, 1972. Printed in this volume.

47 "Some Federal Policies Affecting Exploitation of Minerals." Paper prepared for Resources for the Future, Inc., November 25, 1972.

# *INDEX*

Accidental finds, 94–95; effect on copper prices, 128–32

Accumulation of capital. *See* Capital accumulation.

Adirondack State Park, 51

Aerial photography, 183

Agricultural resources: development of tropical rain forests, 179–81; information management, 196–97

Allais, M., 219$n$, 224

Aluminum, 118, 124

American Association of Oilwell Drilling Contractors, 138$n$

American Bureau of Metal Statistics, 115$t$

American Petroleum Institute, 43$n$, 44$n$, 137$n$, 138$n$

Automobile: effect on the environment, 25–26

Barraclough, Solon, 178$n$

Bartlett, Richard A., 165$n$

Beer cans: clean-up proposals, 278–79

Benefit–cost analyses: effect on conservation policy, 53–57; in resource economics, 4–6; use of natural resources information, 211–14

Berryhill, H. L., Jr., 86$n$

Borenstein, Israel, 155$n$; capital and output trends, 133–38

Bowen, Howard, xiii

Bradley, Paul G., xx$in$

Brooks, David B., xv

Brown, Leslie H., 213$n$

Burton, Betty, 247$n$

Capital: and output in mineral industries, xxiii, 133–38

Capital accumulation: in minerals conservation, xx–xxi, 58–61; minerals policy, 12

Capital recovery, 42–43

Chase National Bank, 137$n$

Chile: aerophotogrammetric project, 194–95; Instituto de Investigación de Recursos Naturales, 205, 209$n$; streamflow data for dam construction, 191–94. *See also* Latin American Institute for Economic and Social Planning, Santiago.

Chow, Ven Te, 190$n$

Christian, C. S., 210

Christianity: attitudes toward nature, 25$n$

Christodoulou, D., 178$n$

Christy, F. T., Jr., 83$n$

Ciriacy-Wantrup, S. V., xx, xxviii$in$, 22$n$

Clawson, Marion, 196$n$

Colonization: Chilean aerophotogrammetric project, 194–95; and natural resources information, 178–79

Columbia University, xii

Committee for Economic Development, xiii

Conservation: capital accumulation of minerals, 58–61; conflicting definitions of, xx, 47–52; of energy materials, 61–63; investment, xviii; policy formation, 52–57

Consumption: control of minerals, 59–61; effect on environment, 25–27; effect on quality of life, 255–73; of energy materials, 61–63; future adaptions, 28–30; role in conservation, 48–57

Copper: cumulative supply curve, 125–27; deterioration factors, xxiii, 119–24; long-run stability in price, 128–32

Copper mining, xxiii; compared with manufacturing industries, 114, 117–18; concentration in, 113–18; number of mines and output per mine, 163

311

Corporations: expropriation protection for, 246–48; investment in developing nations' mineral lands, 240–42; minerals policy effect on, 12–13; mineral lands taxation problems, 243–46

Costs: effect on conservation policy, 53–57; effect on exploration activity, 39; effect on natural resources demand, 274, 276, 279; of exploration, 38–42; of natural resources information, xxiv, 173–75. *See also* Benefit–cost analyses; Cumulative supply curve; Depletion economics.

Council on Environmental Quality, 271

Cumulative supply curve, 104–11; for U.S. and world, 125–27

Dams: information management, 191–94

Demand: effects on exploration activity, 39; growth rate of copper, 123–24; for natural resources information, 175n; projections for minerals, 59

Denison, Edward F., 258n

Depletion. *See* Deterioration.

Depletion economics, xix, xxi; basic problem, 66–72; effect on natural resources information, 176; exploitation of different grades of deposit, 72–78; exploration, 78–80; joint production, 82; mineral supply, 82–88; substitution of metals, 80–81

Deterioration, 64; copper resources, xxiii, 119–24; and the cumulative supply curve, 110–11, 125–27; effect of economic growth on, 265–72; effect on employment to output ratio, 158–59; effect on minerals investment, 93–94

Developing countries: administration of mineral lands, 236–51; provision of mineral surveys, 250–51; use of satellite remote sensors, xxv, 225–35

Development. *See* Economic development.

Discount rate: effect on exploration activity, 39

Dispersion: and investment in mineral deposits, 97–98

Distribution of income: effect on quality of life, 260–61

Domike, Arthur L., 178n

Dozier, Craig L., 178n–79n, 180n

Drew, L. J., 219n

Drilling: effect on profit, 43–46; exploration strategy, xxiv–xxv, 218–24

Dubos, René, 26

Duncan, D. C., 86n

Eaton, Lucien, 160

Echo Park, 49

Eckle, E. C., 160n

Ecology ethic, 24

Economic development, xxii–xxiii; administration of mineral lands, 236–51; effect on copper prices, 128–32; effect on environment, 265–72; effect on quality of life, 255–73; metals mining industries, 164–67; minerals exploration strategy, 218–24; natural resources information effects, 171–217; population effects, 21–22; role in conservation, 48–57; use of satellite remote sensors, 225–35

Economic theory, xx; for future problems, xix, 19–24, 32; for minerals industries, xxi–xxii, 35–46; resource economics, 3–6. *See also* Depletion economics.

Economies of scale: in exploration activity, 39

Effluents. *See* Pollution.

Eldridge, Douglas, 135n

Emissions. *See* Pollution.

Employment in metal mining industries (1839–1909), xxiv, 147–52; compared with all employment, 150t, 151–52; compared with all minerals industries, 149–51; distribution of, 148–149

Employment to output ratio, 152–64; behavior of, 156–57; minerals deterioration effects, 158–59; number of mines and output per mine, 162–64; quality of mineral deposits effects, 157–58; rate of change, 156–57; technology effects, 160–62; transportation effects, 158–59

Energy: conservation outlook, 61–63; effect on environment, 266–72; future adaptions, 28–29; preservation of, 282–83

Environment, xxv; economic growth effect on, 265–72; man's effect on, 24–27; preservation of natural areas, 284–88; preservation of natural resources, 277–83; "ultimate crunch" concept, 282–83

Environmental Protection Agency, 271

Equilibrium: in minerals investment, 101–4. *See also* Long-run equilibria.

Eulacio, Ing. Augusto, 181n

Exhaustion. *See* Deterioration.

Exploration, xxii–xxiii, 35; capital recovery, 42–43; constant cost of, 38–40; in depletion economics, 78–80; effect on copper prices, 128–32; effect on profit, 43–46; and minerals investment,

94–95, 96–104; natural resources information management, 186; in the petroleum industries, 43–46; rising costs of, 40–42; role in economic development, 166; role in minerals policy, 14; strategy for minerals information, xxiv–xxv, 218–24. *See also* Accidental finds.
Exploitation. *See* Depletion economics.
Expropriation: problems of investing in mineral lands, 243–46; protection against, 246–48

Foreign countries: minerals policy toward, 11
Fox, Irving, xv
Future development: economic planning, 19–24; man's adaption, 25–30

Gauging stations, 190–94
Geological surveys: exploration strategy, 218–24; natural resources information management, 184. *See also* Mineral surveys; Soil surveys.
Gordon, Richard L., xxi*n*
Government: administration of mineral lands, 237–51; effect on minerals exploration investment, 103–4; foreign minerals policy, 11; giving away mineral rights, 249–50; minerals exploration programs, 221; natural resources information role, 11, 200–11, 230, 234–35; negotiation of mineral lands, 248; policy as minerals owner, 11–12; provision of mineral surveys, 250–51; role in economic efficiency, 10–11; use of minerals surveys, 237–39
Gray, L. C., 35*n*
Griffiths, John C.: minerals exploration strategy, 218–24
Gross national product: effect on quality of life, 257–58; natural resources information effect, 228–29

Haigh, R. W., 136*n*
Hait, A. G., 44*n*
Hays, Samuel P., 50*n*, 51*n*
Herfindahl, Anna Marie Rogers, xii
Herfindahl, Orris Clemens (1918–1972), xi–xvii, xxviii*n*, 15*n*, 116*t*, 129*n*, 155*n*, 162*n*; with Howard Bowen, xiii; at Columbia University, xii; with the Committee for Economic Development, xiii; death, xvii; in India, xiv, xxiv; with Allen Kneese, xv–xvi; with the Latin American Institute for Economic and Social Planning, Santiago,

Chile, xiv; marriage to Anna Marie Rogers, xii; at the National Income Unit, xii; out-of-door interests, xvi–xvii; philosophy, xvi, xxix; with Resources for the Future, Inc., xiii–xvi; at the U.S. Bureau of Mines, xiii; at the University of Colorado, xv; at the University of Illinois, xiii; at the University of Minnesota, xii
Hetch-Hetchy, 51
Holmes, Olive, 213*n*, 214*n*
Horn, Heinrich, 194*n*
Hotelling, Harold, xxi*n*, 35*n*, 40*n*, 65, 130*n*
House of Representatives Republican Task Force on Earth Resources and Population, xix, 7*n*
Humid regions. *See* Tropical rain forests.
Hydrologic surveys, 182, 188–94

Income: and quality of life, 258–61
India, xiv
Information. *See* Natural resources information.
Instituto de Investigación de Recursos Naturales (Chile), 205, 209*n*
Integrated surveys: of natural resources, 197–200
Investment: behavior for copper, xxiii, 128–32; in conservation, xxviii; cumulative supply curve, 104–11; economic efficiency, 10–11; in information-gathering techniques, xxv; in mineral deposits, 96–101; in mineral exploration, xxviii, 96–104; in minerals industries, xii, 93–95; in natural resources information, xviii, xxiv, 171–217, 229–30; natural resources information oriented toward, 209–11; principles, 95–96
Iron ore: number of mines and output per mine, 162–63
Irrigation: Chilean aerophotogrammetric project, 194–95

Jevons, Stanley, 275
Joint production: in depletion economics, 82
Julihn, C. E., 121*n*, 160

Kansas: oil exploration strategy, 220, 221–22
Kelly, Sherwin F., 187*n*
Kelsey, Frances, 280
Kneese, Allen V., xv–xvi, xix, 15*n*

Laitman, Leon, 173n
Land. See Mineral lands.
Landsberg, Hans H., 85
Latin America. See also names of individual countries.
—natural resources information: effect on economic development, 228–29; organization, xxiv, 201; surveys of uninhabited regions, 178–82; tables, 206–7, 214t–17t
Latin American Institute for Economic and Social Planning, Santiago, Chile, xiv
Leong, Y. S., 123t
Lerner, Joseph, 136n
Long-run equilibria: exploration costs, 38–42

McGee, W J, 48, 275
McKelvey, Vincent E., 188n
McLean, J. G., 136n
Manufacturing industries: concentration in, 114, 117–18
Maps: natural resources information management, 183–84
Marginal net returns of (mines), 36–38
Marginal productivity: of natural resources information, 231–33
Market system: economic efficiency, 10–11; effect on conservation policy, 53–57; effect on natural resources demand, xxvi–xxvii, 3–4, 276; ethical values, xxix
Marsh, George Perkins, 199, 275
Martinez, Alberto, 174n
Masing, Ulv, 179n
Mason, Edward S., xxviiin
Mass man: concept, 261–65
Measurement. See Monitoring.
Merrill, Charles White, 124n
Merton, Henry R., 140t
Metal mining industries (1839–1909), xxiii–xxiv, 139–67;
—employment, 147–52; compared with all employment, 150t, 151–52; compared with all minerals industries employment, 149–51; distribution of, 148–49; employment to output ratio, 152–64;
—output, 141–47; growth of value, 145t; indexes of value, 143t; percentage value, 144t; world, 140;
—regional development, 142, 145–47, 164–67
Metals. See Minerals.
Meteorologic surveys, 182, 188–94
Meyer, H. M., 121n

Milliman, Jerome, 139n
Mineral lands: auction of concessions, 239–48; giving away exclusive rights, 248–50; investment, 96–101; negotiated concession, 248; size effect on exploitation, 39
Mineral surveys: defined, 237; in developing nations, 250–51; effect on land value, 239–43; government use of, xxv, 237, 239. See also Natural resources information.
Minerals: cumulative supply curve, 104–11; depletion economics, xxi, 66–88; exploration strategy, 218–24; forecasting demand for, 59; information management, 185; information value, 181–82; investment in exploration, 96–104; investment process, xxii; President's Materials Policy Commission report on, 276; rate of capital accumulation, xx–xxi, 58–61
Minerals industries: capital and output trends, 133–38; conservation policy, 55; economic concepts, xxi–xxii; employment in, 149–51; exploration capital recovery, 42–43; exploration costs, 38–42; investment in property, 96–101; investment principles, 95–96; investment process, 93–95; policy problem identification, 7–11. See also Metal mining industries.
Minerals policy: economic efficiency, 10–12; effect on private interests, 12–13; exploration role, 14; toward foreign countries, 11; government as minerals owner, 11–12; for national security, 12; problem identification, 7–11; problem projections, 8–9; rate of capital accumulation, 12; research and analysis, 13; for technological progress, 12
Mining, 36; concentration in (copper), 113–14, 115t–16t; constant costs of exploration, 38–40; effect on employment to output ratio, 162–64; marginal net returns, 36–38; rising costs of exploration, 40–42. See also Copper mining; Metal mining industries.
Monitoring: resources, xxviii–xxix, 268–72

National Bureau of Economic Research, xxiii, 116t
National income: natural resources information effect, 228–30
National Income Unit, xii

National security: minerals policy for, 12

Natural areas: preservation of, xxvi, 284–88

Natural resources: conservation of, xix; definitions of conservation, 48–52; in economic development, 164; economic theory, 3–6; economic value, xxvii; meeting demand for, xxvi, 274–83; population effects on, 18–19; supply of, xix

Natural resources information: areas to survey, 176–82; benefit-cost analyses, 211–14, 235; gathering activities, 182–97; and government minerals policy, 11; integrated surveys, 197–200; investment, xxviii; for investment in property, 96; organization and administration guidelines, xxiv, 171–217; organization problems, 200–217; quantity, 173–75; tabular organization, 206–7, 214t–17t; use of satellite remote sensors 225–35. *See also* Geological surveys; Hydrological surveys; Mineral surveys; Soil surveys.

Nature preservation: ethics, 24, 25n; role in conservation, 50–52

Netschert, Bruce, 85

Nicaragua, 207

Oficina Nacional de Evaluación de Recursos Naturales (Peru), 205, 209n

Ohio: oil exploration strategy, 221–22

Oil. *See* Petroleum industry.

Oil spills, 277

Ortega y Gasset, José, xxvi; on mass man, 261–65

Outdoor Recreation Resources Review Commission, 285, 286

Output. *See also* Depletion economics; Employment to output ratio.

—(1870–1948): capital-output ratio in mining industries, xxiii, 133–38;

—(1839–1909): growth of value of metals, 145t; indexes of metals, 143t; in the metal mining industries, 141–47; percentage value of metals, 144t

Paddock, Paul, 177n

Paddock, William, 177n

Paley Report. *See* President's Materials Policy Commission.

Pennsylvania: oil exploration strategy, 221–22

Penrose, Edith Tilton, 213n

Perloff, H. S., 150t

Peru: Oficina Nacional de Evaluación de Recursos Naturales, 205, 209n

Pesticides, 277

Petroleum industry: conservation policy, 53–54; exploration activities, 43–46; exploration strategy, 218–24

Pfeifer, Gottfried, 179n

Phillips, John, 179, 180n, 212–13

Pinchot, Gifford, 48, 49, 50, 275

Plaza V., Carlos, 178n

Pollution: abatement, xxvi, 268–72, 277–83; biological hazards, 280

Population: effect on economic development, 21–24; effect on natural resources, 18–19; growth outlook, 30–31

Potter, Neal, 83n, 154t

Powell, John Wesley, 48

Precipitation surveys. *See* Meteorologic surveys.

Preservation. *See* Nature preservation.

President's Materials Policy Commission, 86, 94n, 130n, 276

Prices: effect on minerals exploration investment, 103–4; long-run stability effects (copper), 128–32; in minerals policy projections, 8–10; resources deterioration effects (copper), 122–24; in weighting schemes, 141n–42n. *See also* Depletion economics.

Private interests. *See* Corporations.

Production: control of minerals, 59–61; deterioration effects (copper), 120–24; effect on quality of life, 255–73; future processes, 28–30. *See also* Economic development; Output.

Profit: exploration effect, 43–46

Public policy: conservation policy formation, 52–57; definitions of conservation, 50–52; effect on economic theory, 20–21. *See also* Minerals policy.

Quality of life, xxix–xxx; concepts, xxvi, 255–73

Radioactive wastes, 277

Railroads: growth effect on metal mining industries, 146

Ramsey, Frank, 58n

Rate of discount, 39

Rates of return: in minerals investment, 97–100

Recreation: conservation policy effects, 55

Recycling: future adaptions, 28–30. *See also* Scrap recovery.

Rein, Selma, 139n

Remote sensors. *See* Satellite remote sensors.

Resource economics: compared with other economics, xviii–xix, xxvii, 3–6

Resources for the Future, Inc., xiii–xvi

Rogers, Anna Marie. *See* Herfindahl, Anna Marie Rogers.

Roosevelt, Theodore, 275

Rosenbluth, Gideon, 116$t$

Russell, Clifford S., 17$n$

Sargent: on resource economists, 3–6

Satellite remote sensors: evaluation of, 230–35; for gathering resource information, xxv, 225–29; investment in, 229–30

Schermerhorn, W., 183$n$

Schurr, Sam, 140$n$

Scrap recovery: consumption of recycled copper, 118$n$; effect on copper demand, 124; effect on exploration, 41

Shorelines: preservation of, 287

Skinner, Walter E., 115$t$

Snyder, David E., 179$n$

Social costs: of minerals policy, 14

Social welfare function: for future problems, 19–24, 31

Soil surveys, 194–97

Spofford, Walter O., Jr., 17$n$

Stamp, L. Dudley, 180$n$

Stevens, Horace J., 115$t$

Stewart, Charles L., 196$n$

Stewart, G. A., 210

Stigler, George, xii

Strauss, Estevam, 173$n$, 206, 207, 214$n$

Subcommittee on Antitrust and Monopoly, 117$t$

Substitution: in depletion economics, 80–81

Supply: in depletion economics, 82–99. *See also* Cumulative supply curve.

Taxation: capital recovery in the minerals industries, 42–43; control of minerals production and consumption, 60–61; effects on capital and output statistics, 134–36; on land with free mineral rights, 249–50; problems of investing in mineral lands, 243–46

Technological progress: on conservation of energy materials, 62–63; effect on cumulative supply curve, 111, 125; effect on employment to output ratio, 160–62; effect on exploration rate, 42; effect on materials and energy supply, 22–23; and the environment, 266–72; and minerals investment, 100–1; minerals policy for, 12

Topographic maps, 184

Trade: future adaptions, 31

Transportation: effect on economic development of uninhabited regions, 181–82; effect on mining employment to output ratio, 158–59; and growth of metal mining industries, 146; natural resources information, 177

Tropical rain forests: development problems, 179–81

Tryon, F. G., 160$n$

Underdeveloped countries. *See* Developing countries.

Uninhabited regions: natural resources information, 177–82

United Nations, 189

United States: cumulative supply curve, 125–27; metal mining industry growth (1839–1909), 142, 145–47; minerals role in regional development, 164–67; natural areas, 285–86

U.S. Bureau of Census: metal mining industries data, 141; metal mining industries employment data, 147–48, 154$t$

U.S. Bureau of Labor Statistics, 44$n$, 45$n$

U.S. Bureau of Mines, 115$t$, 117$t$, 123$t$, 124$n$, 126$t$, 131$n$, 140$t$; economic information activities, 11; Herfindahl with, xiii

U.S. Department of Health, Education, and Welfare, 281$n$

U.S. Geological Survey, 131$n$; economic information activities, 11; metal mining industries data, 141

University of Colorado, xv

University of Illinois, xxii

University of Minnesota, xii

Valderrama, Alejandro Medino, 179$n$

Vera, Luis, 194$n$, 195$n$

Villarroel, René, 194$n$

Vink, A. P. A., 183$n$

Vuillquez, Jean, 118$n$

Walsh, Myles A., 177$n$

Water resources surveys. *See* Hydrologic surveys.

Weed, Walter Harvey, 115$t$

White, Lynn, Jr., 24$n$–25$n$

Whitney, J. D., 140$t$, 141$n$

Wilderness: preservation, 285–87

Willingness to pay: role in resource economics, 4

Wrather, W. E., 131$n$

Zapp, A. D., 86